Selections from English Wycliffite Writings

SELECTIONS FROM

ENGLISH WYCLIFFITE WRITINGS

Edited with an Introduction, Notes and Glossary by
ANNE HUDSON

CAMBRIDGE UNIVERSITY PRESS

Cambridge
London · New York · Melbourne

Published by the Syndics of the Cambridge University Press
The Pitt Building, Trumpington Street, Cambridge CB2 1RP
Bentley House, 200 Euston Road, London NW1 2DB
32 East 57th Street, New York, NY 10022, U.S.A.
296 Beaconsfield Parade, Middle Park, Melbourne 3206, Australia

First published 1978

Printed in Great Britain at the
University Press, Cambridge

Library of Congress Cataloguing in Publication Data

Main entry under title:

Selections from English Wycliffite Writings.

Bibliography: p. 233
Includes index.
1. Lollards – Addresses, essays, lectures. I. Hudson, Anne, 1938–
BX4900.S44   270.5   77–1506
ISBN 0 521 21667 2

CONTENTS

PREFACE

I am indebted first to the authorities of the various collections from whose manuscripts extracts are here printed for their permission to include these passages: the British Library, Cambridge University Library, the Bodleian Library Oxford, Durham University Library, Westminster Diocesan Archives, the Governing Body of Christ Church Oxford, the President and Fellows of Corpus Christi College Oxford, the Rector and Fellows of Lincoln College Oxford, Norfolk Museums Service (St Peter Hungate Museum, Norwich), the Master and Fellows of Trinity College Cambridge, the Board of Trinity College Dublin, the Master and Fellows of Trinity Hall Cambridge. To the assistants in these libraries, and to those in other libraries in this country and in Austria, Czechoslovakia and France, whose manuscripts I have used for the notes, I am grateful for help; to Miss Jean Preston of the Huntington Library I owe details about a manuscript used in no. 18 and help in obtaining photocopies of the relevant leaves. The present selection was undertaken as a preliminary to a full edition of the standard Lollard sermon-cycle and of other related writings, and I am glad to acknowledge generous aid from the University of Oxford towards the purchase of photographs for this larger project, and to the University and the British Council for travel grants to visit Brno, Prague and Vienna. I am indebted to Dr J. I. Catto, Dr E. Ruth Harvey and Mr E. P. Wilson for permission to consult their unpublished theses, and to Dr Gerald Morgan, Miss Susan Reynolds, Dr Norman Tanner and Dr Christina von Nolcken for help on details and for informal discussion. For information, assistance and encouragement I should like to thank Professor J. A. W. Bennett, the Hon. Mrs Margaret Buxton, the Dean of Christ Church Dr Henry Chadwick, Dr Ian Doyle, Dr Neil Ker, Professor Angus McIntosh, and especially Professor Norman Davis and Dr Pamela Gradon.

August 1976

LIST OF IMPORTANT DATES

c. 1354 Wyclif came to Oxford.

c. 1361 Wyclif's first writings on logic, extending to 1371/2.

c. 1370 began teaching on theology.

1372 Wyclif's *Principium* as doctor of theology.

1374 went as envoy to Bruges to confer with papal authorities.

1376 summoned to London on instigation of John of Gaunt; preached against bishop Wykeham and Good Parliament.

1377 February, bishop Courtenay of London summoned Wyclif because of his preaching, but case never heard because court dispersed at rising of Londoners; June, death of Edward III, accession of Richard II; autumn, bulls of pope Gregory XI reached London, listing 19 errors of Wyclif.

1378 attempts to procure Wyclif's condemnation in England unsuccessful; composition of *De Veritate Sacre Scripture, De Ecclesia*; outbreak of papal schism.

1379 composition of *De Officio Regis, De Potestate Pape, De Eucharistia*.

1380 Oxford university commission set up to consider Wyclif's Eucharistic teaching.

1381 Peasants' Revolt; May, Wyclif retired to Lutterworth.

1382 Blackfriars' Council condemned 10 propositions of Wyclif's as heretical, 14 as erroneous; recantation of Repingdon; flight abroad of Hereford; composition of *Trialogus*; edicts against writings and followers of Wyclif.

1384 composition of *Opus Evangelicum*; 31 December, death of Wyclif.

1391 recantation of Hereford.

1395 *Twelve Conclusions of Lollards* displayed in London.

1401 enactment of statute *De heretico comburendo*; 23 February, execution of William Sawtry; recantation of Purvey; debate on biblical translation in Oxford.

ABBREVIATIONS

For short titles used in the Notes see the Select Bibliography pp. 231

BIHR *Bulletin of the Institute of Historical Research*

BL British Library

CA *Catena Aurea* (see p. 167)

CCSL *Corpus Christianorum Series Latina*

CSEL *Corpus Scriptorum Ecclesiasticorum Latinorum*

CUL Cambridge University Library

EETS Early English Text Society (volumes in the Original Series cited without prefixed letters, ES prefixed for Extra Series, SS prefixed for Supplementary Series)

EHR *English Historical Review*

EV Early Version (see p. 163)

GO *Glossa Ordinaria* (see p. 162)

JTS *Journal of Theological Studies*

LV Later Version (see p. 163)

MED *Middle English Dictionary* (Ann Arbor, 1952–).

ODCC *The Oxford Dictionary of the Christian Church*, 2nd ed. F. L. Cross and E. A. Livingstone (London, 1974).

OED *Oxford English Dictionary* (Oxford, reissued 1933).

PG *Patrologia Græca*

PL *Patrologia Latina*

STC *A Short-Title Catalogue of Books printed in England,...1475– 1640*, ed. A. W. Pollard and G. R. Redgrave (London, 1926).

V *Biblia Vulgata*

WB Wycliffite Bible

NOTE ON THE TEXTS

The base text has been transcribed in each case from the manuscript, and this text has been collated with all other known manuscripts; details are given in the notes to each passage. Variants in the collated manuscripts have not been recorded, unless they provide the basis for emendation or have some particular interest explained in the notes. In general, since the base text was chosen for its excellence, its readings have been allowed to stand unless they are manifestly impossible. Emendation is indicated by square brackets when letters or words have been added, and by a footnote when more serious alteration is required. Corrections made by the scribe are not noted, nor are obvious dittographies recorded. Modern punctuation and capitalisation have been introduced. In the transcription of the texts abbreviations have been expanded without notice, following the usual conventions but having regard to the normal spelling habits of the scribe in question. A few points should be noted: expansion to *per* or *par* follows the modern spelling of the words in question; the abbreviation *ih̄u(s)* is expanded *Iesu(s)*, the form *Ihesu(s)* in no. 24 being so written out by the scribe; the abbreviation *an̄crist* is expanded *anticrist* (since the sense normally favours *anti-* rather than *ante-*), though where the scribe has written out *antecrist* this form is retained.

Each text is numbered by line except for the biblical passages (nos. 6–8, 11) which are numbered by the biblical verses; in no. 7 the chapter division of the translation corresponds to the Vulgate and not to the Authorised Version division. Biblical references in the footnotes are according to the Authorised Version.

INTRODUCTION

In 1379 or 1380 Adam Stocton, an Austin friar at Cambridge, copied a tendentious passage from Wyclif's *De Potestate Pape* into his notebook, now Trinity College Dublin MS 115, p. 179. Against it in the margin he added 'Hec venerabilis doctor magister Iohannes Wyclyf'. Within a very short time, probably only a year, he erased 'venerabilis doctor' and substituted 'execrabilis seductor'.[1] This familiar anecdote summarises neatly the acclaim and the opprobrium which Wyclif's name has attracted, and points to the period in Wyclif's life when his contemporaries came to realise that his thought was not merely attractively radical but also dangerously heterodox. Since 1380 opinions of Wyclif have hardly been more temperate: both parties in the Reformation period regarded Wyclif as a precursor of Luther, Zwingli and Calvin; only in the twentieth century has there been an attempt to reduce Wyclif to 'a mere schoolman', with the implication of obscurity and ineffectuality that is attached to the term.[2]

The facts of Wyclif's life are frequently obscure, and the order and dates of his many writings have not been fully determined. Many details of his career are not here important; they have been discussed in biographies listed below.[3] The significant points can be briefly summarised. From 1356 to 1381 Wyclif spent most of his time in Oxford, despite his appointment to various ecclesiastical benefices and despite an absence of some months in 1374 in royal service on a mission to Bruges. He was embroiled, apparently innocently, in a dispute concerning the wardenship of Canterbury College Oxford, to which he was appointed by archbishop Islip in 1365; in 1367 as a secular priest

1 See Gwynn 238–9.
2 Aston (1965), 24–51; J. Crompton, 'John Wyclif: a Study in Mythology', *Transactions of the Leicestershire Archæological and Historical Society* xlii (1966–7), 6–34; for Tunstall's view of Wyclif's influence on the reformers see A. G. Dickens, 'Heresy and the Origins of English Protestantism', *Britain and the Netherlands* ii, ed. J. S. Bromley and E. H. Kossmann (Groningen, 1964), 65–6.
3 Bibliography section Ia.

he was expelled by Islip's successor, Simon Langham, when the college was taken over again by the Benedictine house of Christ Church Canterbury. The official attack on Wyclif's teachings began in 1377, but it was not until 1380 that a formal condemnation by an English authority was issued; in 1382 at a council held at Blackfriars in London, often known as the Earthquake Council from the earth tremors that were felt during its proceedings, ten heresies and fourteen errors drawn from Wyclif's writings and embracing many of his most fundamental doctrines were condemned. Slightly earlier, in 1381, Wyclif withdrew from Oxford to the living of Lutterworth, a living that he had held in absence since 1374; he died in Lutterworth on 31 December 1384.

Despite the possibility that Wyclif may have had some influence on John of Gaunt, uncle of Richard II, and despite the allegations made soon after the crisis that he had been implicated in the events of the Peasants' Revolt in 1381, Wyclif's real importance lies in his university teaching. He gained influence first as a philosopher in the period before 1371, a time when Oxford philosophy had declined from its earlier eminence. His renown as a realist philosopher spread rapidly: by 1380 his ideas were the subject of debate in Prague.[4] He began to lecture on theology by 1371, and was in dispute with other masters in the university on questions that later figured in the condemnations. From an early date in this period comes Wyclif's commentary on the Bible, the only complete biblical commentary from the second half of the fourteenth century and one which, by concentrating its author's attention on the primary Christian document, probably gave rise to many of his later theories.[5] Parallel to the series of philosophical tracts which Wyclif had written in his early life appeared twelve works on theology and ecclesiastical polity covering the whole range of medieval speculation. Three dealt with various forms of law: *De Dominio Divino*, *De Mandatis Divinis* and *De Dominio Civili*, for the last of which the *De Statu Innocencie* prepared the ground. The *De Veritate Sacre Scripture* examined the basis of Christian evidence, whilst the *De Ecclesia*, *De Officio Regis* and *De Potestate Pape* scrutinised the structure of Christian society, both ideal and actual. The *De Eucharistia* discussed, with disastrous results for Wyclif himself, the most important sacrament of the medieval church. The *De Simonia*, *De Apostasia* and *De Blasphemia*, some of which may have been put together after Wyclif's retirement to Lutterworth, cover, in increasingly vehement terms, some of the prevalent abuses of

4 See Šmahel 17–18, and E. Stein, 'Mistr Mikuláš Biceps', *Věstník královské české společnosti nauk, Třída Filosoficko Historicko* 1928 (1929), 43–4.
5 See Smalley (1953) and (1964), and Benrath (bibliography section Ib).

the church.[6] Alongside these were written a vast number of shorter works dealing with individual questions, or answering named opponents. The lengthy *Trialogus* provides a summary of Wyclif's final position, bringing together the views which he had reached during his life. Of sermons actually preached by Wyclif only a relatively small number survive as the *Sermones Quadraginta*; the much larger sets of sermons, systematically covering the Sunday gospels and epistles and the gospels for saints' days, were not an anthology of sermons that Wyclif actually used, but were a literary production, composed in the sequence in which they now stand, and were probably intended for the use of other preachers.[7] Wyclif's last work, finished, as an early scribe explains, at the same time as his life, was the *Opus Evangelicum*, a return to the biblical commentary but with a strongly controversial slant.

Of the 132 separate works that can reasonably be assigned to Wyclif, considerably less than half survive at all in English manuscripts, whilst only sixteen are found in more than one English copy; so efficient was ecclesiastical eradication of Wyclif's writings. The confiscation and destruction began with the 1382 condemnation, but the Carmelite Thomas Netter still had access to a large number of works when he wrote his *Doctrinale Fidei Catholicae* against Wyclif and his followers between 1421 and 1427.[8] Interest in Wyclif's ideas obviously survived his condemnation and death, but after 1407 when archbishop Arundel ordered the head of each Oxford college to conduct monthly enquiries into the views of its members, forbade the discussion of certain topics in the schools, and required more zealous hunting out of books, little sympathy or continued overt interest in Wyclif is long traceable.[9] By 1414, when sedition, following the Oldcastle rising, was added to heresy, even Peter Payne, the Lollard principal of St Edmund Hall, thought it wiser to leave for the continent.[10] Payne found his way to Prague, where he was certain of a warm welcome. Following the early reception of Wyclif's philosophical views in Prague, John Hus and his friends had taken up the Englishman's ideas concerning the church. Though Hus never followed Wyclif into heresy on the nature

6 For the dates see Workman, and the editions in the Wyclif Society.

7 See W. Mallard, 'Dating the *Sermones Quadraginta* of John Wyclif', *Medievalia et Humanistica* xvii (1966), 86–105; also the Prefatio to *Sermones* i–iii.

8 For manuscripts of Wyclif's works see Loserth and Thomson (1928), and *Notes and Queries* NS xx (1973), 443–6; Netter had, for instance, manuscripts of the *Trialogus, De Eucharistia, De Ecclesia* and *De Oratione* of which no English copy now survives.

9 For the order see Wilkins iii. 314–19; for some late interest see the note by N. R. Ker, *Bodleian Library Record* iv (1953), 292–3.

10 See A. B. Emden, *An Oxford Hall in Medieval Times* (Oxford, 1927), pp. 133–61, and Emden, *Oxford* iii. 1441–3.

of the Eucharist, the fear of Wycliffism coupled with political conflict led to the condemnation of Hus at the Council of Constance.[11] To Hussite interest in Wyclif's writings, which did not cease with the death of Hus at the stake in 1415, we owe our knowledge of the majority of Wyclif's Latin texts and of a few Lollard Latin tracts. Through Hus also some of Wyclif's ideas came to Luther. Directly, Lollardy prepared the ground for the reformation in England, by establishing groups of men who were accustomed to radical ideas on the church and authority within it, and who regarded the text of the Bible in the vernacular with special reverence. Indirectly, Wyclif's theories, through the medium of Hus's writings and of Hussite copying, reinforced those of the later reformers.[12]

In what then did Wyclif's heresy consist? The ideas taken individually show little that was completely original. The first condemnatory bull from pope Gregory XI in 1377 named Marsilius of Padua and John of Jandun as Wyclif's teachers in his errors; later opponents added amongst others the names of Berengar of Tours, William of St Amour, Richard FitzRalph and William Ockham. This somewhat motley collection points to one crucial factor in Wyclif's heresy: the combination of theological, political and popular radicalism in a single programme of reform, a programme, moreover, that found appeal beyond the confines of the university lecture room. The 1377 bull lists nineteen errors.[13] Amongst these, two strands of Wyclif's thought can be seen to have offended the authorities. The first, in which the influence of Augustine, Marsilius and FitzRalph can be discerned, dealt with dominion: that only a man in a state of righteousness can truly be said to have authority, whether over inanimate objects or over animate nature. Since God alone is in a position to ascertain the righteousness of any individual, this tenet might be thought to have theoretical interest alone. But the claims of the papacy and of the priesthood to spiritual and temporal authority depended upon the descent of their offices from those of Peter and the first apostles, and their jurisdiction was asserted to derive from the office and not from the individuals who filled that office. The attack upon clerical power inherent in this theory was carried further by Wyclif's claim that, since God alone could know the mind of man, God alone could pronounce absolution on the sins of

11 For a recent biography see M. Spinka, *John Hus a Biography* (Princeton, 1968); for the movement Hus gave rise to see H. Kaminsky, *A History of the Hussite Revolution* (Berkeley and Los Angeles, 1967).

12 See Dickens, and Aston (1964), 149–70.

13 *Historia Anglicana* i. 346–56; for more details of the errors, references to Wyclif's works and discussion by modern critics, see the notes to the texts below (esp. nos. 1–3).

the contrite man; true contrition and faith were the only prerequisites of absolution, and the minister of the church could at best only act as God's mouthpiece, whilst, if he acted against God's judgment, his action was invalid and blasphemous. Excommunication, the church's ultimate refusal to grant absolution, was subject to the same proviso. Associated with the stress on God's absolute knowledge, though not mentioned specifically in the 1377 bull, was Wyclif's determinism, that the church on earth was composed of the *predestinati*, those who would be saved, and the *presciti*, those foreknown to damnation. The second aspect traceable in the 1377 bull attacked the church's position from another angle: Christ and the early apostles had taught that Christians should be subject to temporal powers, that the clergy's business was with spiritual matters and that they should neither possess more earthly goods than were necessary for their immediate survival, nor wield power of any kind over secular authorities. The contemporary church, with all its wealth and property and with its claims to exemption from many of the usual laws and taxes imposed by the secular ruler, was consequently corrupted from the evangelical ideal propounded in the gospels. Here the two strands meet: if the contemporary church were thus corrupted, what chance existed of the righteousness of its ministers, and therefore of their true dominion, temporal or spiritual? Here was indeed material not only for reformation but also for revolution.

In 1377, however, Wyclif for a number of reasons escaped final condemnation; he seems to have had friends at court, and to have been supported by the university, partly from sympathy with his ideas and partly from a dislike of papal interference in Oxford's affairs. The turning point came in the next five years, culminating in the Earthquake Council in 1382.[14] The first three articles censured as heresies then point to the cause of Wyclif's loss of support and ultimate downfall: his denial of the miracle of transubstantiation in the Eucharist, the heresy which became the most obvious mark of his followers. Wyclif's views on the Eucharist seem to have been unsettled for some years before he set forth his heretical opinion publicly in 1380. The details of this opinion, and its background, are examined in the notes to nos. 1 and 21 below. By the late fourteenth century the bounds of orthodoxy had been defined too closely to admit of Wyclif's interpretation, especially since it implied, coupled with the denial of the priestly power of absolution, a challenge to sacerdotal authority. Many who

14 *Fasc. Ziz.* 275–91; see also J. H. Dahmus, *The Prosecution of John Wyclyf* (New Haven, 1952), pp. 89–128.

had sympathised with Wyclif's earlier teaching now deserted him, and his opponents rejoiced to find an easy means of effecting his downfall.

In the questions both of jurisdiction and the Eucharist, Wyclif increasingly stressed the importance of a single source of authority in the church, the Bible; this concentration led to his designation as *Doctor Evangelicus*.[15] Coupled with a revulsion from contemporary abuses, Wyclif's regard for the Bible led to other views for which he was censured: a rejection of all forms of 'private religion' (that is religious life involving separation from the ordinary community), of special prayers, of images, pilgrimages and indulgences, of all worldly display in the church. His aim that the Bible should be better known amongst the laity (an aim that was carried further by his followers) and should be regarded as the single valid form of law by every Christian, prepared the way for what his enemies regarded as social anarchy. If the Bible were accessible to all, and every man were to be his own interpreter of its precepts, then secular as well as clerical authority would come under challenge. It is hardly surprising that eventually the Wycliffites were pursued with the same fervour by the lay powers as by the ecclesiastical hierarchy.[16]

Who then were Wyclif's followers? In the early days of his Oxford teaching it seems clear that the original combination of his ideas appealed to a wide variety of men; it has been observed 'for several years, until it became too dangerous to agree with him, probably a majority of that not notably revolutionary body, the University of Oxford, would have gone with him most of the way in most of what he said'.[17] From an early period he antagonised the monks in the university by his criticism of the worldliness of their orders, but not until the full exposition of his Eucharistic theology did he lose the support of the friars.[18] Concerning some of Wyclif's closest followers in Oxford, Repingdon, Hereford and Aston, the writing of Thorpe (below no. 4) provides some information; the first reverted to contemporary respectability almost immediately on Wyclif's condemnation in 1382, though the others persisted rather longer. But, though few university names can be listed as certain followers after 1382, no doubt

15 There is a balanced account of recent arguments over Wyclif's exact position in relation to contemporary thought about the Bible in H. Oberman, *The Harvest of Medieval Theology* (2nd ed., Grand Rapids, 1967), pp. 361–93.
16 For the early stages see H. G. Richardson, 'Heresy and the Lay Power under Richard II', *EHR* li (1936), 1–28.
17 R. W. Southern, *Western Views of Islam in the Middle Ages* (Cambridge, Mass., 1962), p. 77.
18 See Gwynn 211–79.

because of the charge of heresy that detection would have involved, evidence of the activity of a large and well-educated band of disciples can be pieced together. In section II below some of the main points concerning the organisation of the Bible translation are summarised. Between 1384 and 1396 a large compilation known as the *Floretum* (abridged as the *Rosarium*) was produced, a collection of authorities, biblical, patristic, scholastic and canonistic, on a range of moral and ecclesiastical topics; the topics are arranged in alphabetical order, with cross references, for ease of use by a preacher or tract writer. In the *Floretum* are quoted a large number of lengthy passages from Wyclif, and the attitude traceable in quotations from other writers is often his. In both of these projects, the Bible translation and the *Floretum*, scholars with access to books and a wide range of knowledge must have been involved.[19] It is equally clear that money and organisation must have been available for the dissemination of these and other texts. Though few manuscripts of Wyclif's Latin writings now survive in England, there is evidence for widespread knowledge of them (in the writings of opponents such as Netter or Gascoigne in the fifteenth century, and in stories of the bonfires made of them), and for attempts to make them more accessible to teachers. Indexes were made, and summaries provided; the *Floretum* was widely circulated, and was probably not the only such compilation. Amongst the English writings of Wyclif's followers, the long standard sermon-cycle (see below p. 11) was copied with unusual care and corrected meticulously. Where the work was done is unclear, though the household of a Lollard knight such as Sir Thomas Latimer could have provided the safety and the money to support the men involved, and though Latimer was ordered in 1388 to produce his Lollard books and quires for inspection by the authorities, his home village, Braybrook in Northamptonshire, was in 1407 known to two Czech scholars as a place where Wyclif's Latin works could still be found.[20]

Already before Wyclif's death some of his followers preached his ideas outside Oxford. In 1382 Repingdon, Hereford and Aston went around the towns and villages of north Hampshire teaching so openly that a mandate against them was sent by William of Wykeham, bishop of Winchester, to the rector of Odiham. In Leicester by the same date a group of artisans were known as adherents and as copiers of Wycliffite literature. By 1384 the ecclesiastical authorities had issued injunctions against Wyclif's followers over a very wide area of the country. The

19 See Hudson (1972) and *JTS* NS xxv (1974), 129–32.
20 McFarlane (1972), 192–6.

term *Lollard* (originally apparently derived from the Dutch *lollen* 'to mumble' and used for any kind of vagabond or religious eccentric) came to be applied to Wyclif's followers about the time of his death: the first official use so far known is in bishop Wakefield of Worcester's register in 1387.[21] By writers such as Netter, the terms Lollard and Wycliffite were used as synonyms (as they are here). The number and influence of Lollards in the fifteenth century are matters of considerable obscurity. After the failure of the rising against Henry V led by the Lollard Sir John Oldcastle in 1413, Lollardy certainly ceased to be a major political force and lost any effectual intellectual leadership. But the movement persisted, both in towns such as Bristol, Coventry and Leicester, and in country areas, notably Kent, East Anglia and from the Chilterns westward through the villages of the Berkshire downs. In these parts investigation of Lollards recurred throughout the fifteenth century.[22] To judge by the number and detail of the tracts written to refute Wyclif's views in the first half of the fifteenth century, these views must have continued to arouse support in university circles. Similarly, it is probable that there were considerably more enquiries into Lollardy than the preservation of episcopal records allows one now to ascertain: in some cases, as with the Norwich series mentioned below (no. 5), heresy investigations were not entered into the main episcopal register but were kept in a separate and less durable book. The copying of Lollard texts continued until some were printed by supporters of the early reformers; certain catchwords and phrases are found from the late fourteenth century down to the Puritans of the seventeenth century. Even if the late fifteenth-century Lollards were not politically or intellectually influential, it seems clear that their way of thought, fostered in the schools which they held, made easier the acceptance of the ideas of Luther and the other reformers by the ordinary people in the country.

In recent years it has become fashionable amongst historians to sever the Lollard movement from Wyclif, to argue that Lollardy was the product of economic and social forces, lacking any coherent programme or intellectual backbone, becoming increasingly eccentric and dispersed, and that Wyclif himself was a schoolman, neither able nor desirous of contact with men whose lives lay outside the university.[23] That such a view is untenable should appear from the notes to the present selection. The view arises from concentration upon documentary

---

21 Aston (1960), 36 n. 1.
22 See Thomson (1965) *passim*.
23 See especially McFarlane (1952), though some of the views there are modified by the same author's later work (1972).

evidence, particularly that of episcopal registers, where only a bare statement is recorded by the opposing official, sufficient to procure the Lollard's condemnation. Implicitly, the tracts of those who opposed Wyclif's views after his death, Rymington the Cistercian, Woodford the Franciscan, Netter the Carmelite, Gascoigne the secular priest, all assume that by refuting Wyclif they are destroying the basis of Lollard thought. Explicitly, the Lollards' own writings reveal their debt to Wyclif's thought and phraseology, as they also show that their views are by no means without logical, patristic or canonistic backing (however their use of those authorities might be challenged). Certainly, in some respects the Lollards went further than Wyclif, in their rejection of priestly office, for instance, or in their opposition to images and pilgrimages; but the seed of their ideas can always be found in Wyclif. The selection below also reveals a community of ideas and assumptions between texts of very different types. Documentary material provides evidence of links between Lollard groups in different parts of the country: the notes to no. 5 below show this around 1430; the circle at Tenterden in the early sixteenth century included a man whose parents had been Lollards and had moved there from Lincolnshire, and from Maidstone a Lollard woman migrated to the like-minded group in Coventry when she had been condemned in Kent.[24] That Wyclif himself was only the unwitting and unwilling father of the Lollard movement can also be challenged: references within his writings are most reasonably interpreted as indicating his interest in, even if not his initiation of, wandering preachers, 'poor priests' or 'true priests'; hints are also available to suggest that he may himself have begun the popularisation of his own writings.[25] Though Wyclif never became the popular leader that Hus in his lifetime was, and Lollardy unlike the Hussite movement never became involved with a movement towards national identity and independence, Wyclif's view was not bounded by the schoolroom, as both his followers and his opponents recognised. The anonymous Dominican author of the *Pharetra Sacramenti*, writing probably in the early years of the fifteenth century, speaks of the *Lollardorum familia* with its head Wyclif, spread widely through the country.[26] The more illustrious and zealous Thomas Netter opens the *Doctrinale* (i. Prol.) with imprecations against 'so many of this sect of

24 Lambeth register Warham f. 169v of 1512; Lichfield register Blythe f. 100 of 1511.
25 See Cannon, and Wilks (1972).
26 CUL MS Ff.6.44, f. 61; the text also survives in Lambeth MS 392 and Eton College 170. My knowledge of the work derives from the kind information of Dr Neil Ker.

Wyclif, standing in line of battle, provoking the church to war; fear-lessly they preach, they publish their doctrines, they boast themselves in their strength', and continues with an elaborate simile of Wyclif and his followers as Goliath and the Philistines, himself as the inexperienced David. The terms that such authors use (and this was written after the failure of the Oldcastle rising), and the long series of edicts from ecclesiastical and secular authorities, hardly suggest that Lollardy was a negligible, or an intellectually disreputable, force.

One of the primary ways in which a Lollard might be recognised was his possession of English books, quires and pamphlets: from 1382 onwards commissions to enquire about Lollards mention that such things should be examined. Foremost amongst suspicious books was the vernacular translation of the Bible, ownership of which was for-bidden to the laity after 1407 unless prior permission had been obtained from a bishop for possessing a copy in a translation earlier than Wyclif. The circulation of the Bible translation is discussed below in the intro-duction to the note to Part II. Apart from the Bible translation, a con-siderable body of literature that may fairly be described as Lollard survives.[27] None of the English texts can certainly be ascribed to Wyclif himself, despite the desire of modern critics to associate him directly with many of them;[28] assignment of any to named Wycliffites is almost always only hypothetical.[29] With few exceptions (of which *The Lanterne of Liȝt* is one, see below no. 22) identification of the texts as Wycliffite is on the similarity of their contents with the views of Wyclif, as these are expressed in his Latin works, or with the views of Lollards as these are known from heresy proceedings or from tracts by their opponents; for obvious reasons the texts do not proclaim themselves as Lollard. Most of the texts, if not all, probably date from the period between Wyclif's death in 1384 and the failure of the Oldcastle rising in 1414; dating is, by the generalised nature of the criticism of contemporary affairs contained in them, hazardous but there is no positive evidence in favour of an origin after about 1425 for any of the texts printed below. Certainly, copies were made after this date, in some cases down to the sixteenth century (see no. 17), but it would appear that either the movement lacked original writers after

---

27 Not all the texts mentioned in investigations can be identified; for a convenient collection of some texts known in the early sixteenth century as Lollard see C. Cross, *Studies in Church History* xi (1975), 269–79.

28 See *Manual* 360–7, 521–7.

29 See the introduction to the notes to nos. 2, 3, Part II, 24 and 27 below; a sermon in Bodleian MS Douce 53, ff. 1–30, is there ascribed to William Taylor but the contents are commonplaces of Lollard writings.

the first fifty years of its existence, or that the means for the circulation of their writings were no longer available.

The selection of texts below has been made with two main considerations in mind: first, to show the range of Lollard interests and the balance of their preoccupations; second, to illustrate the various types of Lollard tract, sermon and satire. The first of these considerations is amply explained in the titles given to the extracts and in the notes. Of the second more may here be said. The mandates against Lollards mention books, quires and pamphlets. The last two of these were, in varying degrees, ephemeral productions, and it is not surprising that no pamphlet and only one quire (see no. 26) survives in anything like its original form. But the contents of nos. 3 and 27, the *Twelve Conclusions* and the *Disendowment Bill*, were declaredly circulated in pamphlet form; no. 16, with its authorities against images and pilgrimages, may have started as a quire similar to no. 26. At the other end of the scale comes the sermon-cycle from which four are here printed (nos. 10, 13, 21B, 23). Though the individual sermons are brief enough, they are always found in large groups, forming bulky manuscripts. In its most complete form (found in eleven manuscripts) the cycle contains 294 sermons, providing the preacher with two sermons, one on the gospel and one on the epistle, for each Sunday in the church's year, a sermon for a number of specified saints' days (limited in accordance with Lollard disapproval of post-biblical saints), and for a larger group of unspecified commemorations of saints and martyrs, and for over a hundred specified weekdays. The majority of the manuscripts that contain all or part of this programme are handsome in appearance, well written and carefully corrected, rubricated and headed for ease of public use. Like the early Bible translation manuscripts they would seem to be productions of a well-organised and prosperous centre for the dissemination of Lollard texts. Thirty-one manuscripts are known to survive, a large number for a vernacular prose work, and especially large when it is remembered that many must have been destroyed by the ecclesiastical authorities.[30] From the preservation in manuscripts it would seem that no. 15, *Vae Octuplex*, was closely associated with this sermon-cycle. Outside this group and the Bible translation, with its associated commentaries (for which see below in the bibliography section IV, and introduction to the notes to no. 9), the manuscripts are less handsome; for most texts fewer copies survive, and these copies are smaller and less richly decorated. But even in these humbler books evidence of some organisation is found: the

30 See Hudson (1971) for further details of this cycle.

long discourse of which an extract is printed as no. 18 survives in three very similar manuscripts, two written by the same scribe, and is also extant in a variant version. Anthologies of Lollard tracts are common: nos. 16, 17, 19, 20 and 21A derive from various examples of these.

Of obvious literary interest most of these Lollard texts have almost nothing.[31] As with all medieval English religious prose, the didactic purpose is paramount; only rarely here is there any attempt, such as is found in *Ancrene Wisse* or Rolle, to arouse devotion or attract interest by the skilful manipulation of prose style and rhetoric. Perhaps more surprising is the frequent lack of any effort to convert the reader: though texts such as no. 16 endeavour to urge a point of view, many of the sermons preach by allusion to common assumptions shared by the preacher and his congregation. There is, however, some exploitation of differing literary structures. In the case of the Bible translation and commentary, the structure is necessarily imposed by the original; with the confessions the inventory is obviously dominant. But some variety of technique is visible in the texts of Parts III and IV. The sermons, including *Vae Octuplex* (no. 15), are all of the old type, not utilising the sophisticated subdivisions of the new, or university, type of medieval sermon.[32] But the influence of university determinations is seen in the structure of proposition and corollary in nos. 3 and 24. Similarly, the constant citation of lists of authorities, in texts such as nos. 16, 18, 21A, 22, is a technique derived from learned sources, a technique of which the *Floretum* provides the prime Lollard example. The dialogue in no. 26 is a structure used by Wyclif himself, as in the *Dialogus* and *Trialogus*, and in other vernacular Lollard writings;[33] this too has a lineage in scholastic writing, as in FitzRalph's *De Pauperie Salvatoris* and Ockham's *Dialogus*. Elements of satire are found in many of the texts, but no. 17 is written in the familiar medieval satirical form of an *Epistola Sathanae ad Cleros*.

To separate the Lollard writings in English from those in Latin is in many respects misleading. As has been explained, the *Floretum* provides a source book of authorities comparable to that given for individual topics in some of the extracts here. In *The Lanterne of Li3t* the quotations are given in Latin first, followed by an English translation.

---

31 For a recent view see H. Hargreaves, 'Wyclif's Prose', *Essays and Studies* NS xix (1966), 1–17.

32 See W. O. Ross, *Middle English Sermons* (EETS 209 (1940)), pp. xliii–lv.

33 Three other dialogues are certainly of Lollard origin: that between *Reson and Gabbyng* (based on Wyclif's *Dialogus*) in Trinity College Dublin 245, ff. 154v–161, that between a secular priest and a friar in the same library MS 244, ff. 212v–219, and that between *Jon and Richerd* in Trinity College Cambridge B. 14.50, ff. 35–55v.

Parallel to the *Tractatus de Regibus*, an extract of which appears as no. 25, is a Latin Lollard examination of the clauses of the coronation oath of Richard II to show the necessity of secular correction of the clergy; a Latin tract against images provides a comparable series of arguments to no. 16.[34] Many of the Lollard ideas set out in the texts here are found more fully expressed in the *Opus Arduum*, a commentary on the Apocalypse written by a Wycliffite whilst imprisoned by the ecclesiastical authorities between Christmas 1389 and Easter 1390.[35] Since this now survives only in Hussite copies preserved in continental libraries, little use of its evidence has hitherto been made. Recent investigations have brought to light further Wycliffite writings in Latin, thus increasing the amount of material arguing the Lollards' own case.[36] A few of the most important parallels between these and other Latin works and the English writings are cited in the notes. In one respect, however, the English texts are of crucial importance: they used, in a way that had not systematically been attempted since the days of Ælfric, the vernacular for the discussion of theological and political topics. To contemporary opponents, as the discussion of biblical translation between 1390 and 1410 makes clear, this was a major charge against the Lollards:[37] to those interested in the development of English as a medium for literature and education, on the other hand, it is their greatest achievement.

34 The first survives in Prague University Library X.E. 9, ff. 206–207v, Vienna 3928, ff. 189–90 and Vienna 3932, ff. 155v–156; the second in Prague University Library X.E 9, ff. 210v–214.

35 See Hudson (1973), pp. 446–7.

36 An important set of sermons has been found in the Bodleian Library by Dr C. von Nolcken, who is preparing a study of it.

37 See the tracts printed by Deanesly, pp. 401–37, and material in MS Laud misc. 706, ff. 102–3 and in MS Bodley 649, ff. 14–16 (for some notice of these see R. M. Haines, *Studies in Church History* viii (1972), 143–53 and xii (1975), 143–57); for the continuance of the objection to use of the vernacular, including the charges against Reginald Pecock's anti-Lollard use of it, see C. Cross, *Church and People 1450–1660* (Glasgow, 1976), pp. 13–52.

Part 1
The Nature of Wycliffite Belief

I

Wyclif's Confessions on th Eucharist

Prima confessio Wyclyf de sacramento

I knowleche þat þe sacrament of þe auter is verrey Goddus body in fourme of brede, but it is in anoþer maner Godus body þan it is in heuene. For in heuen it is seue fote in fourme and figure of flesshe and blode. But in þe sacrament Goddus body is be myracle of God in fourme of brede, and is he nouþer of seuen fote, ne in mannes figure. But as a man leeues for to þenk þe kynde of an ymage, wheþer it be of oke or of asshe, and settys his þouȝt in him of whom is þe ymage, so myche more schuld a man leue to þenk on þe kynde of brede. But þenk vpon Crist, for his body is þe same brede þat is þe sacrament of þe autere, and wiþ alle clennes, alle deuocioun, and alle charite þat God wolde gif him, worschippe he Crist, and þan he receyues God gostly more medefully þan þe prist þat syngus þe masse in lesse charite. For þe bodely etyng ne profites nouth to soule but in als mykul as þe soule is fedde wiþ charite. Þis sentence is prouyde be Crist þat may nouȝt lye. For as þe gospel says, Crist þat nyght þat he was betrayede of Iudas Scarioth, he tok brede in hise hondes, and blesside it, brak it, and gaf it to hyse disciplus to ete; for he says, and may not lye, 'Þis is my body'.

Secunda confessio Wyclyf

We beleue, as Crist and his apostolus han tauȝt vs, þat þe sacrament of þe autere white and ronde, and lyke tyl oure brede or ost vnsacrede, is verray Goddus body in fourme of brede; and if it be broken in þre parties os þe kirke vses, or elles in a þousande, euerylk one of þese parties is þe same Godus body. And right so as þe persone of Crist is verray God and verray man, verray godhede and verray manhede, ryth so, as holy kirke many hundruth wyntur has trowyde, þe same sacrament is verray Godus body and verraye brede, os it is forme of Goddus body and forme of brede, as techith Crist and his apostolus. And þerfore seynt Poule nemyth it neuer but whan he callus it brede; and he be oure beleue tok his wit of God in þis. And þe argument of

5

10

15

20

25

30

16 Matt. 26. 20-6   29 I Cor. 11. 23-9, I Cor. 10. 16-17

heretykus agayne þis sentens [is] lyth to a cristene man for to assolue. And right as it is heresie for to trowe [þat Crist is a spiryt and no body, so it is heresie to trowe] þat þis sacrament is Goddus body and no brede, for it is bothe togedur.

35   But þe most heresie þat God sufferide come tyl his kirke is to trowe þat þis sacrament is an accident wiþ[outen] a substance, and may on no wyse be Goddus body. For Crist sayde be witnesse of Iohun þat 'Þis brede is my body'. And, if [ȝ]e say þat be þis skylle holy kirke hat bene in heresie many hundred wyntur, sothe it is, specialy sythen þe
40   fende was lousede (þat was, be witnes of angele to Iohun Euangeliste, aftur a þousande wyntur þat Crist was steuede to heuen). But it is to suppose þat many seyntes þat dyede in þe mene tyme before her detȝ were purede of þis erroure. Owe! howe grete diuersite is betwene vs þat trowes þat þis sacrament is verray brede in his kynde, and betuene
45   heretykus þat tellus þat þis [is] an accident wiþouten a subiecte. For before þat þe fende, fader of lesyngus, was lowside, was neuer þis gabbyng contryuede. And howe grete diuersite is betwene vs, þat trowes þat þis sacrament in his kynde is verray brede and sacramentaly Goddus body, and betwe[n] heretykes þat trowes and telles þat þis sacrament
50   may on none wyse be Goddus body. For I dar sewrly say þat, ȝif þis were soth, Crist and his seyntes dyede heretykus, and þe more partye of holy kirke beleuyth nowe heresye. And [h]e[r]fore deuoute men supposene þat þis consayle of freres a[t] London was wiþ þe herþdene; for þei put an heresye vpon Crist and seyntes in heuyne, wherfore þe erthe
55   tremblide, fayland ma[n]nus voys ansueride for God, als it dide in tyme of his passione, whan he was dampnyde to bodely deth.

Crist and his modur, þat in gronde had destroyde alle heresyes, kepe his kyrke in ryght beleue of þis sacrament. And meue þe kyng and his rewme to aske scharpely of his clerkus þis offys: þat alle his
60   possessioneres, on payne of lesyng of alle her temperaltes, telle þe kyng and his rewme wiþ suffycient growndyng what is þis sacrament; and alle þe ordres of freres, on payne of lesyng of her legyauns, telle þe kyng and his rewme wiþ gode groundyng what is þe sacrament. For Y am certayne of þe thridde partye of clergye þat defendus þise doutes, þat
65   is here sayde, þat þei wil defende it on payne of her lyf.

31, 33, *see notes*   37 John 6. 48–58   38 ȝe] þe; holy] þat holy   40 Rev. 20. 2–3
41, steuede] steuenyde   48 in his] þat in his   52 herfore] before   53 at] and
55 mannus] maynus   55 Matt. 27. 51–3, Mark 15. 38, Luke 23. 45

2

Sixteen Points on which the Bishops accuse Lollards

Þes ben þe poyntis wiche ben putte be bischoppis ordinaris vpon men whiche þei clepen Lollardis:

Þe first: þe brede or þe oost in þe auter, sacrid of þe prest, it is very Goddis body, but it is þe same bred in kynde þat it was before.

Þe secunde: þat schrift of mouþe is not nedeful to helþe of soule, but only sorowe of hert doþ awey euery synne.

Þe þred: þat no man is holdoun to tiþe in manere nowe vsed of þe chirche, but suche tiþis and offiri[n]gis be þe lawe of God schuld be deled to þe pore nedi men.

Þe fourte: þat þer is no pope, neþer was any siþ þe tyme of seint Peter þe pope.

Þe fifte: þat neiþer bischoppis neiþer popis curs byndiþ any man not, but him þat is first cursed of God.

Þe sexte: þat neiþer pope neþer bischoppe may graunt any pardoun, but þe lest prest haþ as myche power to graunte suche pardoune as þe pope.

Þe seuent: þat þer schulde be bot oo degre aloone of prestehod in þe chirche of God, and euery good man is a prest and haþ power to preche þe worde of God.

Þe eiȝte: þat neiþer þe pope may make lawes, neiþer bischopis co[n]stitu-ciouns, and þat no man is holden to kepe suche lawes and constituciouns made be bischopis or popis.

Þe nynþe is þat it is aȝens þe lawe of God þat bischopis and oþer prelatis of þe chirche schulden haue temperal possessions, for by Goddis lawe þei schulden go oon fote preching þe worde of God.

Þe tente: þat is þat prestis weren not ordeyned to sey massis or mateynes, but onli to teche and preche þe worde of God.

Þe eleuenþe: þat it is not leful to preye to seint Marie neiþer seientis, seying þe latanye or oþer orisouns, but onli to God men owen to preie.

Þe tuelfþe: þat neiþer crosse ne ymages peynted or grauen in þe worschip of God or any oþer seyntis in þe chirche schuld be worschipid, and, þouȝ a man sauȝe before him þe same crosse wereon Crist sufferred deþ, he schulde not worschipe it, for, as it is seid, al þat worschipen þe crosse or ymages ben cursed and done mawmentri.

Þe þrittenete: it is not medeful neiþer leueful to go on pilgrimage.
35 Þe fourtenete: þat it is not leueful to sustene liȝttis in þe chirche before
þe crucifix, neiþer before any oþer ymages.

Þe fiftenete: þat it is not leueful to sle any man, neiþer in dome neiþer
ouȝt of dome, neiþer Sarsines, neiþer paynemes, be batel as knyttis done
wane þei asailen þe hooli londe, for it is seide in þe gospel þat þou
40 schalt not sle.

Þe sixtenete: þat exorsismes doun in þe chirche, as halowing of þe watur,
brede and salt, and askis and suche oþer, ben pure craft of nigromancie,
wiche is þe worschiping of þe fende.

Whoeuer schal see þes sixtene poyntis, be he wele ware þat in
45 eueriche of hem i[s] hidde trewþe and falsehed, and who þat euer
grantiþ al, grantiþ myche falsehede, and who þat euer denyeþ al, denyeþ
many trewþes. Þerfor witte welle þis þat, wane a coupulatif is madde,
þouȝ þer be many trewþes, if it afferme a falshed, it schal be denyed
al togidur; falsenes is so venemus.

50   Trewe cristen men schulden answere here aviseliche, trewliche
and mekeliche to þe poyntis and articlis þat ben put aȝens hem: aviseliche þat þei speike not vnkonnyngliche, trwliche þat þei speike not
falseliche, and mekeliche þat þei speike not prowdeliche in her answere,
and þan schal[l] be grace in þer speiking or answering be þe helpe of
55 Crist. For cristen men schulden beleue þat þe sacrament on þe auter is
verrely Cristis body sacramentli and spirituali, and mo oþer maneres
þan any erþely man can telle amonge vs. For Crist þat mai not lye seid,
schewyng þe bred þat he helde in his hande, 'Þis is my bodi'. And
þerfore seiþ Ierom in his epistile to Elbedie, 'Here we, þe brede þat Crist
60 brack and ȝaf to his discipulis to ete was his oune bodi, for he seide
"Þis is my body", and so be oure beleue it is boþe Cristis bodi and bred
of lijf.' And so God forbede þat we schulde seie þat þis blessid sacrament were but breed, for þat were an heresye, as to sey þat Crist is man
and not God. But we seyn þat it is boþe brede and Cristis body, riȝt as
65 Crist is boþe God and man, as seint Austin seiþ. And seint Hillari seiþ,
'Þe bodi of Crist þat is taken of þe auter is figure siþ bred and wyne ben
seen wiþouȝtforþe, and it is verri trewþe siþ Cristis body and his blood
is beleued wiþinneforþe.' *Hec ibi.*

2. Also we graunteyn þat schrifte of mouþe is nedeful to al suche þat
70 ben counselid of God for to make it mekeliche. But ȝut very contricioun is more nedeful, forwhi wiþouȝten schrift of mouþe may a syneful
man be saued in many a caas, but wiþouȝten veri contricioun of herte

45 is] it 54 schall] schalt
71 schrift] schirft

mai no syneful man of discrecioun be saued. Þerfore seiþ þe comyn lawe, as autorite witnessiþ, 'Þe wylle of a man is rewarded, not þe werke: wille is in contricioun of hert, and werke is in sc[h]rifte of mouþe. 75 Þerfore it is certeyn, clerer þane liȝt, þat synnes ben forȝeuen be contricioun of hert.' *Hec ibi.* Þerfore very contricioun is þe essencial parte of penance, and confecioun of mouþe is þe accidental parte. But naþeles confessioun of hert done to þe hiȝe prest Crist is as nedeful as contricioun. 80

3. Also we graunten þat men ben holden and boundoun, be þe boonde of manis lawe and counsel not contrarie to Goddis lawe, to paie tiþus and offryngis to curatis in al trewe manere nowe vsed, for þat ende þat curatis do þer office as God haþ comanded hem. And if þei lyuen as curatis schulden, and spenden þe goodis of þe chirche to Goddis wor- 85 schippe in hemself and oþer pore puple, þane ben þe tiþus paied to þe pore men and nedi, for þei hemself ben pore.

4. Also we beleuen þat oure lord Iesu Crist was and is cheffe bischoppe of his chirche, as seint Peter seiþ, and schal be vnto þe dai of dome. And we supposen þat þer han ben many hooli faderris, popis, siþen seint 90 Petrus tyme, þouȝ þis name 'pope' be not seid in Goddis lawe, as seint Clement, seint Clete and oþer many moo. And so we graunten þat þe pope of Rome schulde next folowe Crist and seint Peter in maner of lyuynge, and, if he do so, he is worþily pope, and, if he contrarie hem moost of al oþer, he is most anticrist. 95

5. Also we graunten þat neiþer bischoppis curse ne popis bynden any man anemptis God, but if þat bounde acorde wiþ þe bonde of God. And if a man is vnriȝtfuly cursed of þe pope or of þe bischope for Goddis cause, if he suffer it pacientli, he schal fare myche þe better for þer curse, and þei þat cursen schullen fare myche þe wers, for, as seint 100 Austin seiþ, 'I seie not þis foolehardili, þat if any man is cursed wroung- fulliche, it schal harme hym raþer þat curseþ, þane him þat sufferiþ þis curse, for þe Hooly Goost puttiþ no suche peyne of curse to any man vndeserued.'

6. Also we graunten þat boþe þe pope and bischoppis moun lefully and 105 medefully graunte suche pardouns and indulgence as ben grunded in hooli write, and þat in þre maners. Oon is þat þei moun bi þer office denounce or schewe þe wille of God, houȝ he forȝeueþ synne, and þat trewe denounsi[n]g is forȝiuyng be þer office of presthode. In þe secunde maner þei moun forȝeue and relese penance folily enioyned to men and 110 foly avowes and boondis þat men haue bounden hemself wiþ, and þat

90, 91 seint] seiint

is clepid indulgence or dispensacioun. And in þe þridde maner þei moun
forȝeue trespas þat men han doun aȝens hem in as myche as liþ in hem,
and so it is vndurstanden þat Crist seiþ in þe gospel, 'Forȝeueþ, and it
schal be forȝeuen to ȝow'; and þus whateuer synnes þei schullen forȝiue,
þei ben forȝeuen, and whateuer þei losen vpon þe erþe, it schal be losed
in heuene. Neþerles sale-pardouns þat smacchen symonye makeþ boþe
þe graunter and hym þat bieþ it acursed of God.

7. Also we graunten þat þe state of prestis schulden be oon in very
vnite, and þe order is al oon as anempte þe substance boþe in þe pope
and bischopis and symple prestis, but þe degrees in hem ben diuerse,
boþe heier and lower. And as God haþ grauntted hem þe keies of power
and knouyng of his lawe, so al prestes of office han euene power of
ordere of prestehode. But summe passen oþer in power of iurisdiccioun
and in excellence of þe keies of kunnynge. And þouȝ lewde men ben
good lyueris and wise men, ȝit ben þei not prestes of office, ne þei be
not bounden to preche of office, al be it þat þei be prestes spirituali, as
seiþ Crisostom and Lyncolne, and so þei may teche þer wyfes, þer
childeren and þer seruantis to be of good maners.

8. Also we graunten þat popis mown medefully make lawes and decres,
and bischoppis constituciouns, and kyngs statutis, so þat þilke lawes and
ordinaunce furþer men to kepe þe lawe of God, and þan men ben
holden to kepe hem. And if þei make any lawes contrarie to Cristis
lawe, men ben as grettly boundon to aȝenstande þoo wicked lawes as
þei ben bounden to kepe þer good lawes. And þerfore seiþ God be
Ezechiel þe prophete, 'Nil ȝe go in þe comaundementis of ȝoure
faderis, neiþer kepe ȝe þer doomys, neiþer be ȝe defouled in her mawmentis; but kepiþ my mandementis and my lawes and my domes.'

9. Also we granten þat bischoppis acordyngly wiþ Goddis lawe mown
haue temperal goodis and possessiouns in resunable mesure, so þat þei
spenden hem as Goddis awmyneris, and not holding hem as wordely
lordes. For Crist seiþ in þe gospel, 'Ȝe schullen not haue lordschipis, as
lordes and kyngis of þe puple.' And seint Peter seiþ, 'Be ȝe not hauynge
lordschipe in þe clergye', and so, þouȝ b[i]schoppis ride or go, so þei
do wel þer office, þei ben excused.

10. Also we graunten þat prestes weren ordeyned of Crist to teche and
preche þe puple, and not onli þat but also to preie and to mynyster þe
sacramentis of God, and lyue w[e]lle. And of goode ordinaunce of hooli
chirche þei ben ordeyned be men to sei boþe matynes and messis, in
wiche ben conteyned gospell and pistill and oþer bokis of hooly wriȝte,

114 Matt. 6. 14   127 it] ȝit   136 Ezek. 20. 18   142 Mark 10. 42–3
143 I Pet. 5. 3   144 bischoppis] boschoppis   148 welle] wille

for þat ende þat þei schulden aftur þer redinge declare it to þe puple in
þer modur tounge. For seint Poule seiþ, 'I wole þat alle prestes speike
wiþ langages', as ben orisouns and lessouns in Latyn, 'but more I
wole þat þei preche'.

11. Also we graunten þat it is boþe leueful and medeful to preie to oure
Lady and to alle halowus, so þat þe entent of oure preiour be do
principally to Goddis worschipe. And in oure preiouer we schulden not
þenke þat oure Lady or oþer seyntis mowun graunte any þing of
hemself, but þei knowen Godis wille and preien þat it be fully don, and
so þer preier is herde. And so þe letanye is riȝt good, and it be wel vsed;
but wane prestis or religious singen þe latanye for pride, for ipocrisie or
for couaitise þan þei plesen not God, but þe fende and þe worlde, wiche
ben þe maistris þat þei seruen.

12. Also we beleuen þat neiþer þe crosse þat Crist was don vpon,
neiþer any oþer roode or ymage maad of mannys hand schulde be
worschipid as God, ne as resonabel creaturis, for wosoeuer worschipiþ
hem so doþ mawmentrie and is cursed. But naþeles þe making of
ymages trewly peynted is leueful, and men mowen leuefuliche worschippe hem in sum manere, as signes or tokones; and þat worschipe
men done to hem, if þei louen hem and vsen hem to þat ende þat þei
ben ordeyned fore, as clerkis don her bokis, dispising þe avowes,
preiers and sacrifice and misbeleues vnlawfully don to hem.

13. Also we graunten þat it is leueful and medeful to go on pilgrimage
to heuenwarde, doing werkes of penance, werkis of riȝtfulnes and
werkis of mercy, and to suche pilgrimage alle men ben boundoun
after þer power wile þei lyuen here. For þe prophete seiþ in þe Sawter
booke, 'Lorde be þow not stille, for I am a straunger and a pilgrime as
alle my faderis weren.' Suche pilgrimage mai we wel do wiþout seching
of dede ymages and of schrynes.

14. Also we graunten þat it is leueful in mesure [to haue] liȝttis before
ymages, and holde torchis before þe auter, so þat it be doune principally
for þe worschip of God and not to þe ymages, and oþer werkis of
riȝtwissenes and of mercy to be not left þerfore. For Crisostom seiþ,
'Þei þat honouren chirchis doun a goode werke if þei kepine oþer werkis
of riȝtfulnes.' But men schulden as wel sette suche liȝte in þe chirche
þouȝ þe ymages weren aweye, as þouȝ þei weren þere, or ellis þe loue
þat þei ȝyuen to ymages smacche[þ] mawmentrie.

15. Also we graunten þat it is leueful to sle men in dome and in batellis,
if þo þat doun it han autorite and leue of God. And if þei sleen any man,

152 I Cor. 14.5   156 halowus] halowuus   159 godis] goodis
176 Ps. 39. 12   178 seching] scheching   187 smaccheþ] smacchen

190   cristen or heþen, aȝens þe autorite of God, þei ben acursed and breken
þe comandement of God. And so it is like þat fewe or none ben nowe
slayne be þe autorite of God.

16. Also we graunten þat halowing of holy watur, of brede, salt and
asken ben leueful, for þei ben deuouȝte preiers and blessings, and þer is

195   noon exorsisioun don on holi bred but a preier as good as oure gracis,
and not alle exorsisiouns ben craft of nigramancye and worchinge of
þe fende; for Crist and his apostilis vseden þe office of an exorsiste in
casting ouȝt of fendes to mannys saluacioun. And naþeles, þo þat setten
her bileue þat euery drope of hooli watur doþ awey a synne, and takeþ

200   none heede how hali watur is a token þat we haue euermore nede of
repentance in hooly chirche alle þe wile we lyuen, ben foule bigilid.

3

Twelve Conclusions of the Lollards

We pore men, tresoreris of Cryst and his apostlis, denuncyn to
þe lordis and þe comunys of þe parlement certeyn conclusionis and
treuthis for þe reformaciun of holi chirche of Yngelond, þe qwiche
ha[þ] ben blynde and leprouse many ȝere be meyntenaunce of þe

5   proude prelacye, born up with flatringe of priuat religion, þe qwich is
multiplied to a gret charge and onerous [to] puple her in Yngelonde.

Qwan þe chirche of Yngelond began to dote in temperalte aftir
hir stepmodir þe grete chirche of Rome, and chirchis were slayne be apropriacion to diuerse placys, feyth, hope and charite begunne for to fle out

10   of oure chirche; for pride with his sori genealogie of dedly synnes
chalingith it be title of heritage. Þis conclusiun is general and prouid be
experience, custum and manere, as þu schalt herin aftir.

191 god] good
4 haþ] han

Þe secunde conclusion is þis. Oure usuel presthod, þe qwich began in Rome, feynid of a power heyere þan aungelis, is nout þe presthod þe qwich Cryst ordeynede to his apostlis. Þis conclusion is prouid for þe presthod of Rome is mad with signis, rytis and bisschopis blissingis, and þat is of litil uertu, nowhere ensample[d] in holi scripture, for þe bisschopis ordinalis in þe newe testament ben litil of record. And we can nout se þat þe Holi Gost for oni sich signis ʒeuith oni ʒiftis, for he and his noble ʒiftis may not stonde with dedly synne in no manere persone. Þe correlary of þis conclusion is þat it is ful vncouth to manye þat ben wise to se bisschopis pleye with þe Holi Gost in makyng of here ordris, for þei ʒeuen crownis in caracteris in stede of whyte hartys, and þat is þe leueree of antecryst brout into holy chirche to colour ydilnesse.

Þe thirdde conclusiun sorwful to here is þat þe lawe of continence annexyd to presthod, þat in preiudys of wimmen was first ordeynid, inducith sodomie in al holy chirche; but we excusin us be þe Bible for þe suspecte decre þat seyth we schulde not nemen it. Resun and experience prouit þis conclusiun. For delicious metis and drinkis of men of holi chirche welen han nedful purgaciun or werse. Experience for þe priue asay of syche men is, þat þe[i] like non wymmen; and whan þu prouist sich a man mark him wel for he is on of þo. Þe correlary of þis conclusiun is þat þe priuat religions, begynneris of þis synne, were most worthi to ben anullid. But God for his myth of priue synne sende opyn ueniaunce.

Þe ferthe conclusiun þat most harmith þe innocent puple is þis: þat þe feynid miracle of þe sacrament of bred inducith alle men but a fewe to ydolatrie, for þei wene þat Godis bodi, þat neuere schal out of heuene, be uertu of þe prestis wordis schulde ben closid essenciali in a litil bred þat þei schewe to þe puple. But wolde God þat þei wolde beleue þat þe Doctour Euangelicus seyth in his *Trialoge, quod panis materialis est habitudinaliter corpus Christi.* For we suppose þat on þis wise may euery trewe man and womman in Godis lawe make þe sacrament of þe bred withoutin oni sich miracle. Þe correlari of þis conclusiun is þat if Crystis body be dewid with euerelasting ioye, þe seruise of Corpus Christi imad be frere Thomas is vntrewe and peyntid ful of false miraclis. And þat is no wondir, for frere Thomas þat same time, holding with þe pope, wolde haue mad a miracle of an henne ey, and we knowe wel þat euery lesyng opinli prechid turnith him to velanye þat euere was trewe and withoute defaute.

Þe fyfte conclusiun is þis: þat exorcismis and halwinge made in þe chirche of wyn, bred and wax, water, salt and oyle and encens, þe ston

28 Ezek. 16. 56

of þe auter, upon uestiment, mitre, crose and pilgrimes stauis be þe
uerray practy[s] of nigromancie rathere þanne of þe holi theologie.
Þis conclusiun is prouid þus: for be siche exorcismis creaturis been
chargid to ben of heyȝere uertu þan here owne kynde, and we sen no þing
of chaunge in no sich creature þat is so charmid but be fals beleue, þe
whiche is þe principal of þe deuelis craft. Þe correlary of þis þat, if þe
bok þat charmith hali water spred in holy chirche were al trewe, us thinkis
uerrily þat holy water usid in holi chirche schulde ben þe beste medicine
to alle manere of sykenesse; *cuius contrarium experimur.*

    Þe sexte conclusiun þat mayntenith michil pride is þat a kyng and
a bisschop al in o persone, a prelat and a iustise in temperel cause, a curat
and an officer in wordly seruise, makin euery reme out of god reule. Þis
conclusiun is opinly schewid, for temperelte and spirituelte ben to partys
of holi chirche, and þerfore he þat hath takin him to þe ton schulde
nout medlin him with þe toþir, *quia nemo potest duobus dominis seruire.* Us
thinkith þat hermofodrita or ambidexter were a god name to sich
manere of men of duble astate. Þe correlari is þat we, procuratouris of
God in þis cause, pursue to þis parlement þat alle manere of curatis
boþe heye and lowe ben fulli excusid of temperel office, and occupie
hem with here cure and nout ellis.

    Þe seuenthe conclusiun þat we mythtily afferme is þat special
preyeris for dede men soulis mad in oure chirche preferryng on be name
more þan anothir, þis is þe false ground of almesse dede, on þe qwiche
alle almes houses of Ingelond ben wikkidly igroundid. Þis conclusiun is
prouid be to skillis. On is, for preyere meritorie and of ualue schulde
ben a werk proceding of hey charite, and perfyth charite accepte no
persones, *quia diliges proximum tuum* etc. Qwerfore us thinkis þat þe
giftis of temperel godis to prestis and to almes housis is principal cause
of special preyeris, þe qwiche is nout fer from symonie. Anothir skil:
for special preyere mad for men dampnid to euerelasting peyne is to
God gretli displesing. And, þow it be doute, it is lythli to trewe Crystis
puple þat þe founderes of þe almesse housis for here uenimous dotaciun
ben for þe most part passid þe brode way. Þe correlari is: þe preyere of
ualue springand out of perfyth charite schulde enbrace in general alle
þo þat God wolde haue sauid, and leue þer marchaundise now usid for
special preyeris imade to mendynauns and possessioneris and othere
soulis prestis, þe qwiche ben a puple of gret charge to al þe reme
mayntenid in ydilnesse, for it was prouid in a bok þat þe kyng herde
þat an hundrid of almes housis suffisede to al þe reme, and þerof
schulde falle þe grettest encres possible to temporel part.

54 practys] practyf   67 Matt. 6. 24   69 we] for we   79 Matt. 19. 19

Þe viii conclusiun nedful to telle to þe puple begylid is [þat] þe pilgrimage, preyeris and offringis made to blynde rodys and to deue ymages of tre and of ston, ben ner of kin to ydolatrie and fer fro 95 almesse dede. And þow þis forbodin ymagerie be a bok of errour to þe lewid puple, ȝet þe ymage usuel of Trinite is most abhominable. Þis conclusiun God opinly schewith, comanding to don almesse dede to men þat ben nedy, for þei ben þe ymage of God in a more liknesse þan þe stok or þe ston, for God seyth nout, *Faciamus lignum ad ymaginem et* 100 *similitudinem nostram aut lapidem*, but *faciamus hominem etc.* For þe heye worchipe þat clerkis clepin *latria* longith to þe godhed alone, and þe lowere worchipe þat is clepid *dulia* longith to man and to aungel and to lowere creatures. Þe correlari is þat þe seruise of þe rode, don twyes euery ȝer in oure chirche, is fulfillid of ydolatrie, for if þe rode tre, 105 naylis, and þe spere and þe coroune of God schulde ben so holiche worchipid, þanne were Iudas lippis, qwoso mythte hem gete, a wondir gret relyk. But we preye þe, pilgrym, us to telle qwan þu offrist to seyntis bonis enschrinid in ony place, qweþir releuis þu þe seynt þat is in blisse, or þe pore almes hous þat is so wel enduwid? For men ben 110 canonizid, God wot how, and for to speken more in playn, trewe cristemen supposin þat þet poyntis of þilk noble man þat men clepin seyn Thomas, were no cause of martyrdom.

Þe ix conclusiun þat holdith þe puple lowe is þat þe articlis of confessiun þat is sayd necessari to saluaciun of man, with a feynid 115 power of absoliciun enhaunsith prestis pride, and ȝeuith hem opertunite of priui calling othir þan we wele now say. For lordis and ladys ben arestid for fere of here confessouris þat þei dur nout seyn a treuth, and in time of confessiun is þe beste time of wowing and of priue continuaunce of dedli synne. Þei seyn þat [þ]e[i] ben commissariis of God to 120 deme of euery synne, to foulin and to clensin qwom so þei lyke. Þei seyn þat [þ]e[i] han þe keys of heuene and of helle, þei mown cursyn and blissin, byndin and unbyndin at here owne wil, in so miche þat for a busschel of qwete or xii.ᵈ be ȝere [þ]e[i] welen selle þe blisse of heuene be chartre of clause of warantise, enselid with þe comown sel. 125 Þis conclusiun is so seen in use þat it nedith non othir prof. *Correlarium*: þe pope of Rome þat feynith him hey tresor[er] of holi chirche, hauande þe worthi iewel of Crystis passiun in his keping, with þe dissertis of alle halwen of heuene, be qwiche he ȝeui[þ] þe feynid pardoun *a pena et a culpa* – he is a tresourer most banisschid out [of] charite, seyn he may 130 deliueren þe presoneris þat ben in peyne at his owne wil, and make himself so þat he schal neuere come þere. Here may euery trewe

100 Gen. i. 26 118 for] þat for 120², 122, 124 þei] he 129 ȝeuiþ] ȝeuid

cristene man wel se þat þer is michil priuy falsnesse hid in oure chirche.

135   Þe tende conclusiun is þat manslaute be batayle or pretense lawe of rythwysnesse for temperal cause or spirituel withouten special reuelaciun is expres contrarious to þe newe testament, þe qwiche is a lawe of grace and ful of mercy. Þis conclusiun is opinly prouid be exsample of Cristis preching here in erthe, þe qwiche most taute for to

140   loue and to haue mercy on his enemys, and nout for to slen hem. Þe resun is of þis þat for þe more partye þere men fythte, aftir þe firste strok, charite is ibroke; and qwoso deyth out of charite goth þe heye weye to helle. And ouer þis we knowe wel þat no clerk can fynde be scripture or be resun lawful punschement of deth for on dedly synne and nout for

145   anoþer. But þe lawe of mercy þat is þe newe testament, forbad al mannisslaute: *in euangelio dictum est antiquis, Non occides.* Þe correlary is: it is an holy robbing of þe pore puple qwanne lordis purchase indulgencis *a pena et a culpa* to hem þat helpith to his oste, and gaderith to slen þe cristene men in fer londis for god temperel, as we haue seen. And

150   knythtis þat rennen to hethnesse to geten hem a name in sleinge of men geten miche maugre of þe King of Pes; for be mekenesse and suffraunce oure beleue was multiplied, and fythteres and mansleeris Iesu Cryst hatith and manasit. *Qui gladio percutit, gladio peribit.*

         Þe xi conclusiun is schamful for to speke, þat a uow of conti-

155   nence mad in oure chirche of wommen, þe qwiche ben fekil and vnperfyth in kynde, is cause of br[i]ngging of most horrible synne possible to mankynde. For þou sleyng of childrin or þei ben cristenid, aborcife and stroying of kynde be medicine ben ful sinful, ȝet knowing with hemself or irresonable beste or creature þat beris no lyf passith in worthinesse to

160   ben punschid in peynis of helle. Þe correlary is þat widuis, and qwiche as han takin þe mantil and þe ryng deliciousliche fed, we wolde þei were weddid, for we can nout excusin hem fro priue synnis.

         Þe xii conclusiun is þat þe multitude of craftis nout nedful, usid in oure chirche, norsschith michil synne in wast, curiosite and disgysing.

165   Þis schewith experience and resun prouith, for nature with a fewe craftis sufficith to nede of man. Þe correlari is þat, sitthin seynt Powel seyth, 'We hauende oure bodili fode and hilling, we schulde holde us apayed', vs thinkith þat goldsmethis and armoreris and alle manere craftis nout nedful to man aftir þe apostle schulde ben distroyd for þe

170   encres of uertu. For þou þese to craftis nemlid were michil more nedful in þe elde lawe, þe newe testament hath voydid þese and manie others.

         Þis is oure ambaciat, þat Cryst has comaundid us for to pursue,

---

146 Matt. 5. 21   **153** Matt. 26. 52   **167** I Tim. 6. 8

at þis time most acceptable for manie causis. And þou þese materis ben here schortly knit, þei ben in another book longli declarid, and manie othere mo al in oure langage, þe qwyche we wolde were communid   175 to alle trew cristene men. We preye God of his endeles godnesse reforme oure chirche al out of ioynt to þe perfectiun of þe firste begynni[n]gge. Amen.

4

Thorpe's evidence about Wyclif's university followers, 1407

And I seide þanne þus to him, 'Ser, my fadir and my modir, whoos soulis God asoile if it be his wille, spendiden moche moneye in dyuerse placis aboute my lore, in entent to haue me a preest of God. But whanne I cam into ȝeeris of discressioun I hadde no wille to be preest; and herfore my freendis weren ofte riȝt heuy towardis me. And þanne me   5 þouȝte her grucchynge aȝens me was so disesi to me þat I purposide herfore to haue laft her companye. And whanne þei perseyueden þis in me þei spaken sumtyme ful fair and plesyng wordis to me; but for þi þat þei myȝten not make me to consente of good herte for to be preest þei spaken to me feele tymes ful rowȝ wordis and greuous, þretynge and   10 manassynge me in dyuerse maners, schewynge to me ofte ful heuy cheere. And þus boþe in faire maner and in greete, þei weren longe tyme as me þouȝte ful bisie aboute me or þat I consentid to hem to be preest. But at þe laste whanne in þis mater þei wolden no longer suffre myn excusaciouns, but eiþir I schulde consente to hem eiþir I schulde   15 bere euere her indignacioun, ȝhe, ser, her curse, as þei leten, I þanne, seynge þis praiede hem þat þei wolden fouchesaaf for to ȝeue me lycence for to gon to hem þat weren named wyse preestis and of vertues

17 praiede] praieden

conuersacioun to haue her counseile, and to knowe of hem þe office and
20   þe charge of preesthode. And herto my fadir and my modir consentiden
ful gladli and þei ȝauen to me her blessyng and good leue to go, and þei
token me money to spende in þis iornay.

And so þanne I wente to þo preestis whom I herde to ben losid
or named of moost holi lyuynge, and best tauȝt and moost wyse of
25   heuenly wysdom. And, ser, I comowned wiþ hem to þe tyme þat I
perseyued, bi her vertues and contynuel occupacioun þat her honest
werkis and charitable passid her fame which I hadde herd biforehonde
of hem. Wherefore, ser, bi ensaumple of þe doctryne of þese men and
speciali for þe goodlich and innocent werkis whiche I perseyuede þanne
30   of hem and in hem, after my kunnynge and my power I haue bisied me
þan, and tanne into þis tyme to knowe in partie Goddis lawe, hauynge a
wille and a desyre to lyue þeraftir, willnynge þat alle men and wymmen
bisieden hem feiþfulli heraboute. If þanne, ser, eiþer for plesynge or
displesynge of hem þat ben neiþer so wise ne of so greet vertuous conuer-
35   sacioun in my knowynge, neiþer bi comoun fame in ony oþir mennes
knowynge of þis londe, as þese men weren of which I tooke my counseile and myn enformacioun, I schulde now forsake, þus sodeynli,
schortli and vnwarned, al þe lore þat I haue bisied me fore þis þritti ȝeer
and more, my conscience schulde euer be herwiþ ouer mesure vnquye-
40   tid. And also, ser, I knowe wel þat manye men and wymmen schulden ben
herþoruȝ greetli troublid and sclaundrid; and, as I seide, ser, to ȝou
bifore, [for] myn vntruþe and fals cowardise many oon schulde be putt
into ful greet repreef. Ȝhe, ser, I dreede þat many oon, as þei myȝten
þanne iustli, wolden curse me ful bittirli. And, ser, I drede not þat ne
45   þe curs of God (which I schulde deserue herynne) wolde brynge me
into a ful yuel eende, if I contynuede þus. And if, þoruȝ remorse of
conscience, I repentide me ony tyme, turnynge aȝen into þe wei which
ȝe bisien ȝou now to make me forsake, ȝe, ser, and alle þe bischopis of
þis londe, wiþ oþer ful many preestis, wolden defame me and pursuen
50   me as a relapis. And þei þat now haue, þouȝ I vnworþi be, sum affiaunce
in me heraftir wolden neuer tristen to me, þouȝ I cowde teche and
lyue myche moore vertuousli þan euer I schal conne eiþir do. For, if
aftir ȝoure counseile I lefte vttirli al my loore, I schulde herþoruȝ first
ȝeue occasioun to many men and wymmen of ful sore hurtynge; ȝhe, ser,
55   as it is ful lickli to me, if I consentide þus to ȝoure wille, I schulde
herynne bi myn yuel ensaumple in þat þat in me were sle so manye folkis
goostli þat I schulde neuere deserue to haue grace of God to edefien his
chirche, neiþir mysilf ne ony oþer lyf. And þanne I were moost
wrecchidli ouercomen and vndon boþe bifore God and man.

But, ser, bi ensaumple cheefli of Nycol Herforde, of Ioon 60
Purueye, of Robert Bowland, and also bi þe present doynge of Filip
Repingtoun, þat is now bicome bischop of Lyncolne, I am now lerned,
as many oþer ben and manye mo heraftir þoruȝ Goddis grace schulen be
lerned, to hate and to fleen al sich sclaundre þat þese forseid men
cheefli haue defouliden wiþ principali hemsilf. And in þat þat in hem is 65
þei haue enuenymed al þe chirche of God, for þe sclaundres reuokinge at þe
cros of Poulis, of Hertforde, Purueye and of Bowland. And how Filip
of Repintoun pursueþ now cristen peple, and þe feynynge þat þese
dissimylen now þoruȝ worldli prudence, kepynge so couertli in her
prechinge, and comownynge wiþinne þe boondis and þe teermes whiche 70
wiþouten blame mowen be spoken, and schewid out to þe moost
worldeli louers, wolen not ben vnponyschid of God, for to þe poynt of
truþe þat þese men schewiden out sumtyme, þese wolden not now
strecche forþ her lyues, but bi ensaumple eche of hem of oþer, as her
wordis and her werkis schewen, þei bisien hem þoruȝ her feynyng for to 75
sclaundre and to pursue Crist in his membris raþer þan þei wolde be
pursued.'

And þe Archebischop seide to me, 'Þese men of whom þou
spekist now weren folis and eretikis whanne þat þei weren gessid wise
men of þee and of sich oþir losels. But now þei ben wise men þouȝ þou
and sich oþer demen hem vnwise. Naþeles I wiste neuer noon riȝt sad 80
man þat was ony while enuenymed wiþ ȝoure contagious doctrine.'

And I seide to þe Archebischop, 'Ser, I gesse wel þat þese men
and such oþere ben now wise men as to þis world, but as her wordis
sowneden sumtyme, and her werkis schewiden outward, it was licly to 85
many men þat þei hadden eer[n]is of þe wisdam of God, and þei
schulden haue deserued myche grace of God to haue saued her owne
soulis and manye oþer mennes if þei hadden perse[w]ed feiþfulli in
wilful pouert and in oþir symple and vertues lyuyng, and speciali if wiþ
þese forseid vertues þei hadden contynewid in her bisie and frutuous 90
sowinge of Goddis word, as to many mennes knowynge þei occupieden
þanne alle her wittis ful bisily to knowe þe plesinge wille of God,
traueilynge alle her membris ful besili for to doon þeraftir pureli and
cheeffli to þe preisynge of þe moost holi name of God, and for grace of
edificacioun and saluacioun of alle cristen peple. But wo worþ fals 95
coueitise and yuel counseile and tirauntrie bi whiche þei and manye oþer
men and wymmen ben lad blyndelyngis into an yuel eende!'

And þe Archebischop seide to me, 'Þou and sich oþer losels of
þi sect wolden schaue ȝoure beerdis ful nyȝ for to haue beneficis, for

88 persewed] perseyued   93 besili] blessidli

100 bi Iesu I knowe noon more coueitous schrewis þanne ȝe ben whanne
þat ȝe haue benefices. For lo I ȝaf to him, Ioon Purueye, a benefice no
but a myle out of þis castel, and I herde moore compleynt and wondir
of his coueitise aboute tiþis and oþer dewtees þan I dide of alle þe men
þat weren avaunsid wiþinne my diosyse.'

105   And I seide to þe Archebischop, 'Ser, Purueye is neyþir wiþ
ȝou now here for þe benefice þat ȝe ȝaf to him, neiþir he holdiþ feiþfulli wiþ þe lore þat he tauȝte and wroot biforehonde, and þus he
schewiþ now himsilf to be neiþir hoot ne coold. And herfore he and
hise felowis mowen sore drede but if þei turnen hastili into þe weie þat
110 þei haue forsaken, last þei ben sodeynli vomed out of þe noumbre of
Goddis chosen peple.'

And þe Archebischop seide, 'Þouȝ Purueie be now a fals
harlot, I quitid me to him. But come he more for siche a cause bifore me,
er þat we departen I schal wite wiþ whom he schal holde. But I seie to
115 þee, whiche ben þo holi men and wise of whiche þou hast taken þin
enformacioun?'

And I seide, 'Ser, in his tyme maister Ioon Wiclef was holden of
ful many men þe grettist clerk þat þei knewen lyuynge vpon erþe. And
þerwiþ he was named, as I gesse worþili, a passing reuli man and an
120 innocent in al his lyuynge. And herfore grete men of kunnynge and oþer
also drowen myche to him, and comownede ofte wiþ him. And þei
sauouriden so his loore þat þei wroten it bisili and enforsiden hem to
rulen hem þeraftir; and for þi, ser, þat þis forseid lore of maistir Ioon
Wiclef is ȝit holden of ful manye men and wymmen þe moost acordinge
125 lore to þe lyuynge and to þe techynge of Crist and his apostlis, and
moost opinli schewynge and declarynge how þe chirche of Crist haþ be
and ȝit schal be rulid and gouerned. Herfore manye men and wymmen
accepten þis lore and purposen þoruȝ Goddis help for to conferme
her lyuynge like herto to þis lore of Ioon Wiclef. Maistir Ion Aston
130 tauȝte, and wroot acordingli and ful bisili, where and whanne and to
whom he myȝte, and he vsid it himsilf, I gesse, riȝt perfyȝtli vnto his
lyues eende. Also Filip of Repintoun whilis he was a chanoun of
Leycetre, Nycol Herforde, dane Geffrey of Pikeringe, monke of Biland
and a maistir of dyuynyte, and Ioon Purueye, and manye oþer whiche
135 weren holden riȝtwise men and prudent, tauȝten and wroten bisili þis
forseide lore of Wiclef, and conformeden hem þerto. And wiþ alle þese
men I was ofte homli and I comownede wiþ hem long tyme and fele,
and so bifore alle oþir men I chees wilfulli to be enformed bi hem and of
hem, and speciali of Wiclef himsilf, as of þe moost vertuous and goodlich
140 wise man þat I herde of owhere eiþer knew. And herfore of Wicleef

speciali and of þese men I toke þe lore whiche I haue tauȝte and purpose
to lyue aftir, if God wole, to my lyues ende. For now þouȝ summe of
þese men ben contrarie to þe loore þat þei tauȝten biforehonde, I wot
wel ȝit her loore was trewe whiche þei tauȝten and þerfore wiþ þe help of
God I purpose for to holde and vse þe loore whiche I herde of hem   145
whilis þat þei saten in Moysees chaire and speciali whilis þei saten on þe
chaire of Crist. But aftir her werkis þat þei now schewen I wol not do
wiþ Goddis help, for þei feynen, hiden and contrarien þe truþe which
biforehonde þei tauȝten out pleynli and trewli. For as I knowe wel,
whanne summe of þese men haue ben vndirnommyn for her sclaun-   150
drouus doynge, þei knowelich not þat þei tauȝten errour biforehonde,
but þat þei weren constreyned bi peyne for to ȝeue to telle out þe truþe;
and þus þei chesen now raþer to blasfemen God þan to suffre a while
here bodili persecucioun for þe truþe þat Crist schedde out for his
herte blood.'   155

 And þe Archebischop seide to me, 'Þat loore þat þou clepist
truþe is opin sclaundre in holi chirche, as it is proued of holi chirche.
For al be it þat Wiclef ȝoure maistir and auctour was a greet clerk, and
þouȝ many men helden him a perfit lyuer, ȝit his doctryne is not
apreued of holi chirche but many sentencis of his lore ben dampned as   160
þei wel worþi ben. But, as touchinge Filip of R[e]pintoun, þat was first
chanoun and aftirwarde abbot of Leycetre, whiche is now bischop of
Lyncolne, I telle to þee þat þe dai is comen for þe which he fastide þe
euen, for he neiþir holdiþ now, neiþir wole holde, þe loore, þat he
tauȝte whanne he was no but chanoun of Leycetre, for noo bischop of   165
þis londe pursueþ now scharplier hem þat holden þat wei þan he doiþ.'

 And I seide, 'Ser, herfor ful many men and wymmen also
wondren vpon him, and speken him myche schame and holden him
Cristis enemye.'

 And þe Archebischop seide to me, 'Wherto tariest þou me wiþ   170
sich fablis? Wolt þou not schortli, as I haue seid to þee, submytte þee
to me, or nay?'

 And I seide, 'Ser, I telle ȝou at oo word, I dar not for þe
drede of God submitte me to ȝou aftir þe tenour of þe sentence þat ȝe
haue aboue rehersid to me.'   175

146 Matt. 23. 2

5

Confession of Hawisia Moone of Loddon, 1430

In þe name of God tofore you, þe worshipful fadir in Crist, William be þe grace of God bisshop of Norwich, Y Hawise Moone, þe wyfe of Thomas Moone of Lodne of your diocese, your subiect, knowyng, felyng and vndirstandyng þat before þis tyme Y haue be right hoomly and 5 priue with many heretikes, knowyng [þaym] for heretikes. And þaym Y haue receyved and herberwed in our hous, and þaym Y haue conceled, conforted, supported, may[n]tened and fauored with al my poar. Whiche heretikes names be þese: Sir William Whyte, Sir William Caleys, Sir Huwe Pye, Sir Thomas Pert prestes, John Waddon, John Fowlyn, 10 John Gray, William Euerden, William Bate of Sethyng, Bartholomew Cornmonger, Thomas Borell and Baty hys wyf, William Wardon, John Pert, Edmond Archer of Lodne, Richard Belward, Niclas Belward, Bertholomeu Monk, William Wright and many oþer. Whiche haue ofte tymes kept, holde, and continued scoles of heresie yn priue chambres 15 and priue places of oures, yn þe whyche scoles Y haue herd, conceyved, lerned and reported þe errours and heresies which be writen and contened in þese indenturis. Þat is to say:

Fyrst þat þe sacrament of baptem doon in watir in forme cus-tomed in þe churche is but a trufle and not to be pondred, for alle 20 Cristis puple is sufficiently baptized in þe blood of Crist. And so Cristis puple nedeth noon oþer baptem. Also þat þe sacrament of confirmacion doon be a bisshop is of noon availe ne necessarie to be had, for as muche as whan a child hath discrecion, and can and wile vndirstande þe word of God, it is sufficiently confermed be þe Holy Gost and nedeth noon oþer 25 confirmacion. Also þat confession shuld be maad oonly to God and to noon oþer prest, for no prest hath poar to remitte synne ne to assoile a man of ony synne. Also þat no man is bounde to do no penance whiche ony prest enjoyneth [him] to do for here synnes whyche þei haue confessed vnto þe pr[est], for sufficient penance for all maner of synne 30 is euery persone to abstyne hym fro lyyng, bakbytyng and yuel doyng, and no man is bounde to do noon oþer penance. Also þat no prest hath poar to make Cristis veri body at messe in forme of bred, but þat, aftir

þe sacramental wordis said at messe of þe prest, þer remayneth oonly
material bred. Also þat þe pope of Roome is fadir antecrist, and fals in all
hys werkyng, and hath no poar of God more þan ony oþer lewed man, but   35
if he be more holy in lyvyng; ne þe pope hath no poar to make bisshops,
prestes ne non oþer ordres. And he þat þe puple callen pope of Roome is
no pope, but a fals extorsioner and a deseyuer of þe puple. Also þat he
oonly þat is moost holy and moost perfit in lyvyng in erthe is verry pope.
And þese singemesses þat be cleped prestes ben no prestes, but þay be   40
lecherous and couetouse men, and fals deceyvours of þe puple; and with
þar sotel techyng and prechyng, syngyng and redyng, piteously þay pile
þe puple of þar good, and þarwith þay susteyne here pride, here lechery,
here slowthe and alle oþer vices; and alway þay makyn newe lawes and
newe ordinances to curse and kille cruelly all oþer persones þat holden   45
ageyn þar vicious levyng. Also þat oonly consent of love betuxe man
and woman, withoute contract of wordis and withoute solennizacion in
churche and withoute symbred askyng is sufficient for þe sacrament of
matrymoyn. Also it is but a trufle to enoynt a seke man with material
oyle consecrat be a bisshop, for it sufficeth euery man at hys last ende   50
oonly to haue mende of God. Also þat euery man may lefully withdrawe
and withholde tythes and offringis from prestis and curatis and yeve hem
to þe pore puple; and þat is moore plesyng to God. Also þat þe temperal
lordis and temperel men may lefully take alle possessions and temperal
godys from alle men of holy churche, and from alle bysshops and pre-   55
latis, boþe hors and harneys, and gyve þar good to pore puple; and
þerto þe temperel men be bounde in payne of dedly synne. Also þat it
is no synne ony persone to do þe contrarie of þe preceptis [of] holy
churche. Also þat euery man and euery woman beyng in good lyf oute
of synne is as good prest and hath [as] muche poar of God in al thyng as   60
ony prest ordred, be he pope or bisshop. Also þat censures of holy
churche, sentences and cursynges ne of suspendyng yeven be prelates
or ordinaries be not to be dred ne to be fered, for God blesseth þe
cursyngis [of] bisshops and ordinaries. Also þat it is not leful to swere in
ony caas, ne it is not leful to pletyn for ony thyng. Also þat it is not leful   65
to slee a man for ony cause, ne be processe of lawe to dampne ony
traytour or ony man for ony treson or felonie to deth, ne to putte ony
man to deth for ony cause, but euery man shuld remitte all vengeance
oonly to þe sentence of God. Also þat no man is bounde to faste in
Lenton, ymbren days, Fridays ne vigiles of seyntes, but all suche days   70
and tymes it is leful to alle Cristis puple to ete flessh and [all] maner metis
indifferently at here owne lust as ofte as þay haue appetite as wel as ony

64 of] þe cursyngis þe

oþer days whiche be not commanded to be fasted. Also þat no pilgrimage oweth to be do ne be made, for all pilgrimage goyng seruyth of
75   nothyng but oonly to yeve prestes good þat be to riche, and to make
gay tap[s]ters and proude ostelers. Also þat no worship ne reuerence
oweth be do to ony ymages of þe crucifix, of our Lady ne of noon oþer
seyntes, for all suche ymages be but ydols, and maade be werkyng of
mannys hand; but worship and reuerence shuld be do to þe ymage of
80   God, whiche oonly is man. Also þat al prayer oweth be maad oonly to
God and to noon oþer seyntes, for it is doute if þar be ony suche seyntes
in heuene as þese singemesse[s] aproven and commaunden to be
worsheped and prayed to here in erthe.

Because of whiche and many oþer errours and heresies Y am
85   called tofore you, worshipful fadir, whiche haue cure of my soule, and be
you fully informed þat þe said myn affermyng, belevyng, and holdyng
be opin errours and heresies, and contrarious to þe determinacion of þe
churche of Roome. Wherfor Y, willyng folwe and sue þe doctrine of
holy churche and departe from al maner of errour and heresie, and
90   turne with good wil and herte to þe oonhed of þe churche, considerand
þat holy churche spereth not hyr bosom to hym þat wil turne agayn, ne
God wil not þe deth of a synner but rather þat he be turned and lyve,
with a pure herte Y confesse, deteste and despise my sayd errours and
heresies, and þese said opinions Y confesse hereticous and erroneous,
95   and to þe feith of þe churche of Rome and all vniuersall holy churche
repugnant. And, for as muche as be þe said þinges þat Y so held,
beleved and affermed, Y shewed meself corrupt and vnfaithful, þat from
hensforth Y shewe me vncorrupt and faithful, þe feith and doctrine of
holy churche truly to kepe Y promitte, and all maner of errour and
100   heresie, doctrine and opinion ageyn þe feith of holy churche and
determinacion of þe churche of Roome, and namely þe opinions before
rehersed, Y abiure and forswere, and swere be þese holy gospels be me
bodely touched þat from hensforth Y shal never holde errour ne
heresie, ne fals doctrine ageyn þe feith of holy churche and determina-
105   cion of þe churche of Roome, ne no suche þingis Y shal obstinatly
defende. Ne ony persone holdyng or techyng suche maner of thynges Y
shal obstinatly defende, be me or ony oþer persone, opinly or priuely. Y
shal neuer aftir þis time be no recettour, fautour, consellour or defensour
of heretikes or of ony persone suspect of heresie, ne Y shal neuer trowe
110   to þaym, ner wittyngly Y shal felaship with þaym ne be hoomly wiþ þam,
ne gyve þaym consell, sokour, fauour ne confort. Yf Y knowe ony
heretikis, or of heresie ony persones suspect, or of þaym fautours,

91 Ezek. 33. 11

confortours, consellours or defensours or of ony persone makyng
priue conuenticules or assembles, or holdyng ony diuers or singuler
opinions from þe commune doctrine of þe churche, Y shal late you,   115
worshipful fadir, or your vicar general in your absence, or þe diocesans
of suche persones haue sone and redy knowyng, so help me God atte
holy doom and þese holy gospels! In wittenesse of which þing Y sub-
scribe here with myn owen hand a crosse + and to þis partie indented to
remayne in your registre Y sette my signet; and þat oþer partie indented   120
Y receyve vndir your seel to abide with me vnto my lyves ende. Yoven
at Norwich in þe chapell of your palays þe iiij day of þe moneth
of August, the yer of our Lord a thousand four hundred and thretty.

Part II
The Lollards and the Bible

6

Wycliffite Bible: Isaiah 53

A. Early Version

1 Lord who leeuede to oure heering? and þe arm of þe Lord to
2 whom is it shewid? And it shall steȝen vp as a quik heg biforn hym,
and as a roote fro þe þrestende erþe; þer is not shap to hym ne fairnesse,
3 and wee seȝen hym and he was not of siȝte. And wee desireden hym
dispisid and þe la[s]t of men; man of sorewis and witende infirmyte.
And as hid is his chere and dispisid; wherfore ne wee setten bi hym.
4 Verreli oure syknesses he toc, and oure sorewis he bar; and wee heelden
5 hym as leprous and smyten of God and meekyd. He forsoþe woundid is
for oure wickidnesses, defoulid is for oure hidous giltus, þe discipline
6 of oure pes on hym and wiþ his wannesse wee ben helyd. Alle wee as
shep erreden, eche into his weie bowede doun, and þe Lord putte in
7 hym þe wickidnesse of vs alle. He is offrid for he wolde, and he openede
not his mouþ; as a shep to sleyng he shal be lad, and as a lomb biforn þe
clippere itself he shal bicome doumb, and he openede not his mouþ.
8 Fro anguish and fro dom he is taken awey; þe ieneracioun of hym who
shal tellen out? for kut awei he is fro þe lond of lyueres, for þe hidous gilte
9 of my puple Y smot hym; and ȝyuen he shal vnpitouse men for biriyng,
and riche men for his deþ, for þi þat wickidnesse he dide not, ne
10 treccherie was in his mouþ. And þe Lord wolde totreden hym in
infirmyte. If he shul poten hys soule for synne, he shal seen þe sed of
11 long age, and þe wil of þe Lord in his hond shal ben riȝt reulid; for þi
þat he trauailede, his soule shal seen and ben fulfild. In his kunnyng
he my riȝtwys seruaunt shal iustefye manye, and þe wickidnesse of hem
12 he shal bern. Þerfore Y shal delen to hym manye, and of stronge men
he shal deuiden spoilis, for þi þat he toc into deþ his lyf, and wiþ hidous
gilteres is holden. And he þe synne of manye toc, and for trespaseres
preȝede.

3 last] laft

B. Later Version

Who bileuyde to oure heryng? and to whom is þe arm of þe   1
Lord schewid? And he schal stie as a ȝerde bifor him, and as a roote   2
fro þirsti lond; and neþer schap neþer fairnesse was to him, and we sien
him and no biholding was. And we desiriden him, dispisid and þe laste   3
of men; a man of sorewis and knowinge sikenesse. And his cheer was
hid and dispisid; wherfor and we arettiden not him. Verily he suffride   4
oure sikenesses, and he bar oure sorewis; and we arettiden him as a
mysel and smytun of God and maad low. Forsoþe he was woundid for   5
oure wickidnessis, he was defoulid for oure grete trespassis, þe lernyng
of oure pees was on him and we ben maad hool bi his wannesse. Alle we   6
erriden as scheep, ech man bowide into his owne weie, and þe Lord
puttide in him þe wickidnesse of us alle. He was offrid for he wolde, and   7
he openyde not his mouþ; as a scheep he schal be led to sleing, and he
schal be doumb as a lomb bifor him þat clippiþ it, and he schal not opene
his mouþ. He is takun away fro anguysch and fro doom; who schal telle   8
out þe generacioun of him? for he was kit doun fro þe lond of lyueris,
Y smoot him for þe grete trespas of my puple; and he schal ȝiue   9
vnfeiþful men for biriyng, and riche men for his deþ, for he dide not
wickidnesse, neþer gile was in his mouþ. And þe Lord wold defoule   10
him in sikenesse. If he puttiþ his liyf for synne, he schal se seed long
duringe, and þe wille of þe Lord schal be dressid in his hond; for þat   11
þat his soule trauelide, he schal se and schal be fillid. Þilke my iust
seruaunt schal iustifie many men in his kunnyng, and he schal bere þe
wickidnessis of hem. Þerfor Y schal ȝelde (eþer dele) to him ful many   12
men and he schal departe þe spuylis of þe stronge fendis, for þat þat he
ȝaf his liyf into deþ, and was arettid wiþ felenouse men. And he dide
awei þe synne of many men, and he preiede for trespassouris.

7

Wycliffite Bible: the book of Jonah

Ch. 1.

1   And þe wrd of þe Lord is maad to Ionas, sone of Amathi,
2   seiende 'Rys þou, and go into Nynyue, þe grete cite, and preche þou
3   þerin, for þe malice þerof steȝeþ vp biforn me'. And Ionas ros to fleen
    into Tharsis fro þe face of þe Lord. And he cam doun to Ioppe and
    fond a ship goende into Tharsis, and he ȝaf shiphijre to hem. And he
    wente doun into it to gon wiþ hem into Tarsis fro þe face of þe Lord.
4   Forsoþe þe Lord sente a gret wind in þe se, and a gret tempest is maad in þe
5   se, and þe ship was in perile to be broken; and shipmen dredden, and
    men crieden to her god and senten vesselis þat weren in þe ship into þe
    se þat it were maad liȝtere of hem. And Ionas wente doun to þe ynnere
6   thingus of þe ship and slepte in a greuous slep. And þe gouernour cam
    to hym and seide to hym, 'What art þou cast doun in slep? Rys þou and
    inclep þi God, if parauenture God aȝeenthenke on vs, and wee pershe
7   not.' And a man seide to his felawe, 'Come ȝee, and sende we lott, and
    wite wee whi þis euel is to vs.' And þei senten lotis and lot fel on Ionas.
8   And þei seiden to hym, 'Shew þou to vs for cause of what thing þis euel
    is to vs. What is þi werc? whiche þi lond? And whiþer gost þou? or of
9   what puple art þou?' And he seyde to hem, 'I am an Ebru, and I drede
10 þe lord God of heuene, þat made heuene and erþe.' And þe men dredden
    wiþ gret dreed, and seiden to hym 'What didest þou þis thing?' Forsoþe
    þe men knewen for he fleiȝ fro þe face of þe Lord, for Ionas hadde
11 shewid to þem. And þei seiden to hym, 'What shul wee do to þee, and
12 þe se shal cesen fro vs?' for þe se wente and wex gret on hem. And he
    seide to hem, 'Take ȝee me and sendeþ into þe se, and þe se shal cesen fro
13 ȝou. Forsoþe I wot forwhi for me þis grete tempest is on ȝou.' And men
    roweden to turnen aȝeen to þe drie lond, and þei miȝten not for þe se

---

1 is] was; seiende] and seide   4 is] was; broken] al tobrokun   5 doun to]
doun into; in a] bi a   6 what] whi; and inclep] clepe; God] God to help;
on] of   7 sende] caste; lott] lottis; senten] kesten   8 þi lond] is þi lond
9 heuene and erþe] þe see and þe drie lond   10 what] whi; forsoþe] for;
for] þat   12 sendeþ] þrowe; forsoþe] for; forwhi] þat

wente and wex gret on hem. And þei crieden to þe Lord and seiden, 14
'Lord, wee besechen þat wee pershe not in þe soule of þis man, and
þat þou ȝiue not on vs ynnocent blod, for þou Lord didist as þou
woldist.' And þei token Ionas and senten into þe se; and þe se stod of 15
his boiling. And þe men dredden þe Lord wiþ gret dreed, and offreden 16
ostis to þe Lord and vouweden vouwis.

Ch. 2

And þe Lord made redi a gret fish þat he shulde swolewe Ionas; 1
and Ionas was in wombe of þe fish þre daȝes and þre niȝtis. And Ionas 2
preȝede to þe lord his God of þe fishis wombe, and seide, 'I criede to 3
God of my tribulacioun and he herde me; of þe wombe of helle I criede
and þou herdyst my vois. Þou castedest me doun into depnesse in þe 4
herte of þe se, and þe flod abouteȝaf me; alle þi swolewis and wawes
passeden on me. And I seide, 'Y am cast awey fro þe siȝt of þin eȝen; 5
neþeles eftsoone I shal see þin holy temple. Watris enuirounden me 6
vnto my soule; depnesse enclosede me; þe se hilede myn hed. To þe 7
vtmost places of hilles I wente doun; þe herres of erþe closeden me
togidere into wiþouten ende. And þou shalt reisen vp my lyf of
corupcioun, Lord my God. Whan my soule was anguishid in me I 8
bethoȝte of þe Lord, þat my preȝeere come to þee to þin holi temple.
Þey þat kepen vanytees idilly shul forsaken þer mercy; I forsoþe in vois 9, 10
of preising shal offre to þee whateuere thingus Y vouwede. I shal ȝelde
to þe Lord for helþe.' And þe Lord seide to þe fish, and it caste out 11
Ionas into þe lond.

Ch. 3

And þe wrd of þe Lord is maad þe secounde tyme to Ionas, 1
seiende 'Rys þou and go into Nynyue, þe grete cite, and preche þou 2
þere þe preching whiche Y speke to þee.' And Ionas ros and wente into 3
Nyniue vp þe wrd of þe Lord. And Nynyue was a gret cyte in iourne of
þre daȝis. And Ionas began to entre into þe cite in iorne of o day, and 4
criede and seide 'Ȝitt fourty daȝes and Nynyue shal ben vndirturned.'

---

14 soule] lijf   15 senten] þrewen   16 vouwis] avowis
Ch. 2: 1 in] in þe   2 of] fro   3 of þe] fro þe   4 abouteȝaf]
cumpasside; wawes] þi wawis; þe siȝt] siȝt   6 enuirounden] cumpassiden;
vnto] til to; enclosede] enuyrownede   7 to...doun] Y wente doun to þe
vtmeste places of hillis; herres] barris; shalt...God] my lord God schalt
reise vp my lijf fro corrupcioun   8 of] on   9 idilly ... mercy] forsaken his
merci idili   10 I forsoþe] but Y; preising] heriyng; helpe] myn helþe
11 lond] drie lond   Ch. 3: 1 is] was; seiende] and seide   2 þere] in it
3 vp] bi; in] of þe   4 in] bi þe; vndirturned] turned vpsodoun

5 And men of Nynyue beleeueden to þe Lord, and precheden fasting and
6 weren clad wiþ sackis, fro þe more vnto þe lasse. And þe wrd cam to þe
king of Nynyue, and he ros of his sete and caste awei his cloþing fro
7 hym, and is clad wiþ sac and sat in asshe. And he criede and seide in
Nynyue, of þe mouþ of þe king and of his princes, seiende 'Men and
werk bestis and oxen and sheep, taste not eny thing, neiþer be fed neiþer
8 drinke watir, and be men hilid wiþ sackis, and werc bestis crie to þe
Lord in strengþe; and be a man conuertid fro his euele weie and fro
9 wickidnesse þat is in þe hondis of hem. Who wot if God be conuertid
and forȝiue, and be turned aȝeen fro wodnesse of his wraþe, and wee
10 shul not pershen?' And God saȝ þe werkis of hem, for þei ben conuertid
fro her euel weie; and God hadde merci on þe malice þat he spac þat
he shulde don to hem and dide not.

Ch. 4

1,2 And Ionas was tormentid wiþ gret torment and was wroþ, and
he preȝede to þe Lord, and seide 'Lord I beseche wheþer þis is not my
wrd whan I was ȝit in my lond? for þis thing I beforn ocupiede to flee
into Tarsis. Forsoþe I wot for þou God art meke and merciful, pacient
3 and of myche mercy doyng, and forȝiuende on malice. And now, Lord,
4 I preȝe, tac my soule fro me for deþ is betere to me þan lyf.' And þe
5 Lord seyde 'Gessist þou for þou art wel wroþ?' And Ionas wente out
of þe cite and sat aȝen þe est, and made to hym a shadewing place þere,
6 and sat vnder it in shadewe til he seȝe what bifelle to þe cite. And þe
lord God made redi an yuy, and it steȝede vpon þe hed of Ionas, þat
shadewe were on his hed and couerede hym – forsoþe he hadde
7 trauailid. And Ionas gladede on þe yuy wiþ gret gladnesse. And God made
redi a werm in steȝing vp of grey dai into morn, and smot þe yuy plaunte
8 and it driede vp. And whan þe sunne was sprungen þe Lord comaundede
to þe hote wind and brennende, and þe sunne smot on þe hed of Ionas,
and he swelide. And he axede to his soule þat he shulde dien and seide
9 'It is betere to me to die þan to liuen'. And þe Lord seide to Ionas
'Gessist þou wheþer þou art wel wroþ on þe yuy?' And he seide 'I am
10 wel wroþ vnto þe deþ.' And þe Lord seide 'Þou art sori on þe yuy in
whiche þou trauailedist not, neiþer þou madist þat it wexe, þe whiche

5 vnto] til to   6 to] til to; is] was; sac] a sak   7 seiende] and seide
10 for] þat; ben] weren; þat¹] which   Ch. 4: 1 to þe] þe   2 beforn
ocupiede] purposide; forsoþe] for; for] þat; myche mercy] merciful
5 for] wheþer; est] eest of þe citee   6 shadewe] schade; forsoþe] for
7 gladede] was glad; into morn] on þe morewe; smot] it smoot;
plaunte] om.   8 sprungen] risun   9 vnto] til to   10 þou madist] madist;
þe whiche] which; born] growun; in...pershede] perischide in o nyȝt

was born vnder o niȝt and in o niȝt pershede. And shal I not spare to þe 11
grete cyte Nynyue, in whiche ben more þan an hundrid and twenti
thousend men, whiche witen not what is bitwen her riȝt half and lift,
and many werc bestis?'

11 to] *om.*; an...men] sixe score þousynde of men; werc] *om.*

8

Wycliffite Bible: Luke 15. 11-32

A. Early Version

11, 12   Forsoþe, he seiþ, sum man hadde two sonus, and þe ȝungere seide to þe fader, 'Fader,'ȝif to me þe porcioun of substaunce þat bifalleþ
13   me.' And he departede to hem þe substaunce. And not aftir many daȝis, alle thingus gadered togidere, þe ȝunger sone wente ferr on pilgrimage into a ferr kuntre, and þere wastede his substaunce in liuynge leccherously.
14   And aftir þat he hadde endid alle thingus, a strong hungir is mad in þat
15   kuntree, and he bigan to han nede. And he wente and cleuede to oen of þe burgeisis of þat kuntre; and he sente hym into his toun þat he shulde
16   feden hoggis. And he coueitede to fulfillen his wombe of þe coddes þat
17   þe hoggis eeten, and no man ȝaf to hym. Soþli he, turned aȝeen into hymself, seide 'Hou manye hirid men in my fader hous abounden wiþ
18   loues; forsoþe [I] pershe heer in hungir. I shall risen vp and gon to my fader, and I shal sey to hym "Fader, I haue synned into heuene and
19   biforn þee; now I am not wrþi to be clepid þi sone; mac me as oen of
20   þin hirid men".' And he risende cam to his fader. Soþli whan he was ȝit ferr, his fadir saȝ hym and is stirid bi mercy and he, rennende to, fel
21   on his necke and kiste hym. And þe sone seide to hym 'Fadir, I haue synned into heuene and biforn þee; and now I am not wrþi to be clepid
22   þi sone.' Forsoþe þe fader seide to his seruauntis 'Soone bringe ȝee forþ þe firste stole and cloþiþ hym, and ȝiue ȝee a ring in his hond and shoon
23   into feet; and bringeþ to a calf mad fat and sle ȝee, and ete wee and glade
24   wee in plenteuous eting, for þis my sone was dead and haþ liued aȝeen, he pershede and is founde.' And alle men bigunnen to eten gladly.
25   Forsoþe his eldere sone was in þe feeld, and whan he cam and neȝhede
26   to þe hous, he herde a sinfon and carol or croude. And he clepede oen of
27   þe seruauntis and axede what þese thingus weren. And he seide to hym 'Þi broþer is comen, and þi fader slooȝ a fattid calf, for he resceyuede
28   hym saf.' Forsoþe he was wroþ and wolde not entren. Þerfore his fader
29   gon out bigan to preȝen hym. And he answerende to his fader, seide 'Lo, so manye ȝeres I serue to þee, and I neuere passede ouer þi

B. Later Version

And, he seide, a man hadde tweie sonis, and þe ȝongere of hem 11, 12
seide to þe fadir, 'Fadir, ȝeue me þe porcioun of catel þat falliþ to me.'
And he departide to hem þe catel. And not aftir manye daies, whanne alle 13
þingis weren gaderid togidere, þe ȝongere sone wente forþ in pilgrimage into a fer cuntree, and þere he wastide hise goodis in lyuynge
lecherously. And aftir þat þat he hadde endid alle þingis, a strong 14
hungur was maad in þat cuntre, and he bigan to haue nede. And he 15
wente and drouȝ him to oon of þe citeseyns of þat cuntree; and he sente
him into his toun to feede swyn. And he coueitide to fille his wombe of 16
þe coddis þat þe hoggis eeten, and no man ȝaf to him. And he turnyde 17
aȝen into hymsilf, and seide 'Hou manye hirid men in my fadris hous
han plentee of loouis, and I perisshe here þoruȝ hungur. I shal rise vp 18
and go to my fadir, and I shal seie to him "Fadir, I haue synned into
heuene and bifore þee; and now I am not worþi to be clepid þi sone; 19
make me as oon of þin hirid men".' And he roos vp and cam to his 20
fadir. And whan he was ȝit afeer, his fadir siȝ him and was stirid bi mercy,
and he ran and fel on his necke and kisside him. And þe sone seide to 21
him 'Fadir, I haue synnyd into heuene and bifore þee; and now I am
not worþi to be clepid þi sone.' And þe fadir seide to hise seruauntis 22
'Swiþe brynge ȝe forþ þe firste stole and cloþe ȝe him, and ȝeue ȝe a ryng
in his hond and shoon on hise feet; and brynge ȝe a fat calf and slee ȝee, 23
and eete we and make we feeste, for þis my sone was deed and haþ lyuid 24
aȝen, he perisshide and is foundun.' And alle men bigunnen to eete.
But his eeldere sone was in þe feeld, and whanne he cam and neiȝide to 25
þe hous, he herde a symfonye and a croude. And he clepide oon of þe ser- 26
uauntis and axide what þese þingis weren. And he seide to him 'Þi broþer 27
is comen, and þi fadir slouȝ a fat calf for he resseyuide him saaf.' And he 28
was wrooþ, and wolde not come yn. Þerfore his fadir ȝede out and
bigan to preye him. And he answeride to his fadir, and seide 'Lo, so 29
manye ȝeeris I serue þee, and I neuere brak þi comaundement, and þou

comaundement, and þou neuere hast ȝoue to me a kide þat Y shulde wiþ
30   my frendus be fulfild. But aftir þat þis þi sone þat haþ deuourid his
31   substaunce wiþ hores cam, þou hast slayn to hym a fattid calf.' And he
seide to hym 'Sone þou art euermor wiþ me, and alle my thingus ben
32   þine. Forsoþe it bihofte to eten plenteuously and to ioȝen, for þis þi
broþer was dead and liuede aȝeen; he pershede and is founden.'

neuere ȝaue to me a kyde þat I wiþ my frendis shulde haue eeten. But   30
aftir þat þis þi sone þat haþ deuourid his substaunce wiþ hooris cam, þou
hast slayn to him a fat calf.' And he seide to him 'Sone þou art eueremore   31
wiþ me, and alle my þingis ben þine. But it bihofte to make feest and to   32
haue ioie, for þis þi broþer was deed and lyuide aȝen, he perisshide and
is foundun.'

9

Glossed Gospel commentary on Luke 15. 22–4

A. Shorter Version

Forsoþe þe fadir seide to his seruauntis 'Soone brynge ȝe forþ
þe firste stoole and cloþe ȝe hym, and ȝiue ȝe a ryng in his hond
and shoon into þe feet; and brynge ȝe a calf maad fat, and sle
ȝe and ete we, and plenteuously ete we, for þis my sone was
deed and haþ lyued aȝen, he perishide and is founden.' And   5
alle bigunnen to ete plenteuously.

his seruauntis Þe fadir spekiþ not to þe sone but to þe seruauntis, for
he þat doiþ penaunce preieþ, but he takiþ not answere bi word, but he
seeþ mercy spedeli in worchyng. *Crisostom.* Þes seruauntis ben good
aungels, eþer prestis, whiche in baptim and word of prechyng cloþen   10
þe soule wiþ Crist. *Teofile.* Þes seruauntis ben prechours of recounselyng.
Bede here and *Austyn* in *Questiouns of þe Gospels.* **firste 'stoole:** þat is
innocence and glorie which Adam loste. Þei bryngen forþ þe firste stoole
whanne þei affermen þat dedly and erþli men shulen be citeseyns of
aungels and eiris of God, and euene eiris of Crist. *Bede* here and *Austyn*   15
þere. Eþer þe firste stoole is cloþing of wisdom; þerfor men taken þis
stoole to cloþe þe sikenesse and nakidnesse of bodi bi þe uertu of goostly
wisdom. *Ambrose* here. **a ryng in þe hond** A ryng is a signet of uerry
feiþ, bi whiche alle biheestis ben prentid in þe hertis of men bileuynge,

19 bileuynge] bileuynynge

20   eþer ernes of þe weddyngis bi whiche holy chirche is spousid to Crist.
Bede here and *Austyn* þere, and *Ambrose* here in sentence. Wel a ryng is
ʒouun in þe hond þat feiþ be knowun bi werkis, and werkis be maad sad
bi feiþ. *Bede* here. **shoon:** þat is makyng redi of þe gospel, þat þe cours
of oure soule goynge to heuenli þingis be kept clene fro erþli þingis.
25   *Bede* here and *Austyn* þere and *Ambrose* here in sentence. Wel þe hond
and feet, þat is werkis and goyng, ben ourned þat we lyue riʒtli and
haste to euerlastynge ioyes. *Bede* here. **a calf:** þat is þe Lord Iesu Crist,
whom he clepiþ a calf for þe sacrifice of his bodi wiþout wem. *Crisostom*,
Bede here and *Austyn* þere. **Fat,** for his flesh is so ful of goostli uertu þat
30   it suffice for þe helþe of al þe world. *Crisostom* and *Bede* here. **sle ʒe:**
to bringe þe calf and sle is to preche Crist and to shewe his deeþ, for
þanne he is slayn as freshe to ech man whanne he bileueþ hym slayn.
Bede here and *Austyn* þere. Þanne his flesh is etun whanne þe sacrament
of his passioun is resseyued bi mouþ to clensyng, and is biþouʒt in herte
35   to suyng. *Bede* here. **ete we:** not oneli þe sone þat lyuede aʒen, but also
þe fadir and his seruauntis eten þe fleishe of þe holi calf, for þe mete of
þe fadir is oure helþe and þe ioye of þe fadir is remyssioun of oure
synnes, and not oonli of þe Fadir but also of þe Sone and of þe Holi
Goost. For as oo wille and worchyng is in þe godhed, so o loue is of þe
40   holi and vnseperable Trinite. *Bede* here and *Ambrose* here in sentence.
was deed: þis may be vndurstondun of him þat doiþ penaunce for
noon dieþ no but he þat lyuede sum tyme. He þat bileueþ not in Crist
is euere deed, and whanne heþen men bileuen, þei ben quykenyd bi
grace. He þat slood lyueþ aʒen bi penaunce. *Ambrose* here. **perishide:**
45   he perishiþ which was, for he þat was not may not perishe. Heþen men
ben not, a cristen man is; as it is writun 'God chees þo þingis þat ben
not, þat he shulde distrie þo þingis þat ben,' þat is he chees þe puple of
heþen men whiche was not, þat he shulde distrie þe puple of Iewis.
Mankynde was in Adam, and alle we perishiden in him. Þerfore man is
50   refourmed in þat man þat perishide, and þilke man maad to þe ymage
and lickenesse of God is repareld bi þe pacience and large ʒifte of God.
Ambrose here. As to condiciouns of vices, þe deed sone was dispeirid as
to mankynde, which is chaungeable and may be conuertid fro vice to
uertu. He is seid lost for it is lesse to be lost þan to be deed. Eche man
55   clensid of synne and maad pertener of þe fat calf is maad cause of
gladnesse to þe fadir and his seruauntis, þat is to aungels and prestis.
Teofile. **ete plenteuously** Holi chirche alargid þorou þe world halewiþ
now þese metis and feestis, for þilk calf is offrid to þe Fadir in þe Lordis
bodi and blood, and fediþ al þe hous. *Bede* here and *Austyn* þere.

46 I Cor. 1. 28

B. Longer Version

a ryng in his hond A ring is a signet of very feiþ, bi which alle biheestis
ben markid bi certeyn preentyng in þe hertis of men bileuynge; eþer a
ring is ernes of þo weddyngis bi whiche holy chirche is spousid. And
wel a ryng is ȝouun in þe hond þat þe feiþ be shewid bi werkis, and þat
þe werkis be made stidfast bi feiþ. *Bede* here and *Ambrose* in sentense.   5
shoon Shoon shewen þe office of prechyng, þat þe going of soule
strecchynge to heuenely þingis be kept clene and vndefoulid fro þe
filþe of erþely þingis, and þat it, kept bi ensaumplis of formere men, go
sikir on serpentis and scorpiouns. Þerfore þe hondis and feet ben
ourned, þat is werkis and goyng: þe werk is ourned þat we lyue riȝtly,   10
þe goyng is ourned þat we haaste to euerelastyng ioies, for we han not
here a cite dwellyng but we seken þe cite to comyng. *Bede* here and
Ambrose in sentense. Eþer a ryng in þe hond is ernes of þe Holy Gost for
takyng part of grace, which is wel signyfied [bi] þe fyngir. *Austyn* þere.
A ryng is a signet of clene feiþ and expressyng of treuþe; a shoo is   15
prechyng of þe gospel, and þerfore þis sone took first wisdom. Anoþere
mysterie is which no man knowiþ, no but he þat takiþ: he took a signet
of his fyngris and dedis, and sum kepyng of good entent and goyng,
lest he hirte in ony place his foot at a stoon, and lest he, disseyued of þe
deuel, forsake þe office of prechyng of þe Lord. Þis is þe makyng redy of   20
þe gospel, dressing hem þat ben redy to heuenely goyng þat we go not in
fleysch but in spirit. *Ambrose* here. Shoon in þe feet ben making redy
of þe gospel, to touche not erþely þingis. *Austyn* þere. Eþer þe lord
comaundiþ a ryng to be ȝouun to hym þat is a signet of þe sauyour,
eþer more a noble tokene of Cristis incarnacioun, and ernes of weddyn-   25
gis bi whiche Crist spousiþ holy chirche, whanne a soule risyng vp fro
synne is ioyned to Crist bi þe ring of feiþ. Þe Lord comaundiþ þat
shoon be sett on þe feet, eþer to kepe þe steppis þat he go saddly bi þe
slipir weie of þis world, eþer for þe sleyng of menbris, þat is synnes don
bi þe menbris; for þe cours of oure lif is clepid a foot in holy scripture,   30
and þe lickenesse of mortifiyng is sett in shoon, for þei ben made of
skynnes of deed beestis. *Crisostom*. **A calf made fat:** þat is þe lord
Iesu Crist, whom he clepiþ a calf for þe sacrifice of his body vnwemmed.
He seide hym made fatt, for he was so fatt and plenteuouse þat he
suffice for þe helpe of al þe world. Forsoþe þe fadir offeride not þe calf,   35
but ȝaf to oþere men hym to be offerid, for while þe Fadir sufferide, þe
Sone consentyng was crucified of men. *Crisostom*. A fatt calf is þe lord
Iesu, bi fleysch fillid bi shenschipis. *Austyn* þere. Crist is wel seide fatt,

9 Luke 10. 19   **12** Heb. 13. 14   **19** Ps. 91. 12; Matt. 4. 6

for his fleysch was so ful of gostly vertu þat it suffice for þe helþe of al þe
40 world into odour of swetnesse, þat is, to sende þe odour of offeryng in
þe cros to God, and to preie for alle. To brynge þe calf and to sle is to
preche Crist and to shewe his deeþ, for þanne as fleysch he is slayn to
eche of vs, whanne he is bileued slayn. Þanne his fleysch is etun gostly
whan þe sacrament of his passioun is resseyued bi mouþ to clensyng and
45 is biþouȝt in herte to folowing. *Bede* here. Þat þe fadir comaundiþ to
brynge þis calf is þat þei preche hym, and in prechyng hym to come into
þe entrailes of þe hungry sone. Also þe fadir comaundiþ þat þei sle þis
calf, þat is, þat þei telle his deeþ, for þanne he is slayn to eche man whanne
he bileueþ hym slayn. *Austyn* þere.

10

Sermon on Luke 15. 11-32

Homo quidam habuit duos filios. Luce xv

Þis gospel telliþ a parable as þe nexte gospel bifore. Luyk seiþ
þat Crist tolde how *a man hadde two sones, and þe ȝonger of hem seide to
his fadir 'Fadir, ȝyue me a porcioun of [þe] substaunce þat falliþ to me.' Þe fadir
departi[d] him hise goodis. And soone aftir, þis ȝong sone gadride al þat fel to him*
5 *and wente forþ in pilgrymage into a fer cuntre; and þere he waastide hise goodis
lyuynge in lecherie. And after þat he hadde endid alle hise goodis, þer fel a greet
hungir in þat lond, and he bigan to be nedi. And he wente out and cleuede to
oon of þe citeseyns of þat cuntree; and þis citeseyn sente him into his toun to kepe
swyn. And þis sone couetide to fille his bely wiþ pese-holis þat þe hoggis eten, and*
10 *no man ȝaf him. And he, turnynge aȝen, seide 'Hou manye hynen in my fadris
hous ben ful of looues, and I perische here for hungir? I schal rise and go to my
fadir, and seie to him "Fadir I haue synned in heuene and bifore þee; now I am
not worþi to be clepid þi sone; make me as oon of þin hynen".' And he roos and
cam to his fadir. And ȝit whanne he was fer, his fadir saie him and was moued*
15 *bi mercy and, rennynge aȝens his sone, fel on his nek and kiste him. And þe sone*

4 departid] departiþ

seide to him 'Fadir, I haue synned in heuene and bifore þee; now I am not worþi
to be clepid þi sone.' And þe fadir seide to hise seruauntis 'Anoon bringe ȝe forþ þe
first stoole and cloþe ȝe him, and ȝyue ȝe a ryng in his hond and schoon on hise
feet; and bringe ȝe a fatt calf and sle him, and ete we and fede vs; for þis sone
of myn was deed and was quykened aȝen, he was perisschid and is foundun.' And   20
þei bigunnen to feede hem. And his eldir sone was in þe feeld, and whanne he cam
and was nyȝ þe hous, he herde a symphonye and oþir noise of mynstralsie. And þis
eldir sone clepide oon of þe seruauntis and axe[de] what weren þese þingis. And
he seide to him 'Þi broþir is come, and þi fadir haþ sleyn a fatt calf, for he haþ
resceyued him saaf.' But þis eldir sone hadde dedein and wolde not come yn.   25
Þerfore his fadir wente out and bigan to preie him. And he answeringe seide to his
fadir 'Lo, so many ȝeeris I serue to þee; I passide neuere þi maundement, and
þou ȝauest me neuere a kide for to feede wiþ my freendis. But aftir þat he, þis þi
sone þat murþirde hise goodis wiþ hooris is come, þou hast killid to him a fatt
calf.' And þe fadir seide to him 'Sone þou art eueremor wiþ me, and alle my   30
goodis ben þyne. But it was nede to ete and to make myri, for he, þis þi broþir,
was deed and lyuede aȝen; he was perishid and is foundun.'

      It is comunli seid þat þis man is Iesu Crist, þat boþe is God and
man; and bi his godhed haþ two sones, þe eldir sone is þe folc of Iewis,
and þe ȝonger heþen folc. Þese two sones weren for a tyme wiþ God bi   35
grace and kyndeli witt. But þis ȝonger sone of þese two seide priueli to
his fadir þat he wolde haue bi himsilf goodis þat schulde falle to him,
whanne heþen men wolde haue propre boþe lawe and oþir ȝiftis of God,
and so þei wolden be rulid bi her owne witt and not fulli bi God. And so
richessis of þis sone ben goodes of kynde and goodis of grace. And God   40
suffride þis sone to be rulid apart bi his owne witt, but God ȝaf him
goodis of kynde and goodis of grace in al þis tyme, for ellis þese heþen
men myȝten not be but if þei hadden goodis of kynde of God. And
manye partis of þis sone, as Iob and Ietro and oþir, hadden goodis of
grace of God, for ellis þis sone hadde al be lost. Soone after þis ȝonger   45
sone wente awey fro God bi synne; but ȝit þese heþene men for a tyme
loueden God and serueden him wel. And so þis fer cuntre is þe lijf of
man in synne, and wasting of þese goodis is slouþe of Goddis seruyce
bi hem, and lecherous lijf is yuel loue of þe world and þe fleisch, byneþe
mannes spouse. Siþ God is spouse of mannes kynde, he þat loueþ to   50
moche þe world and his fleisch, lyueþ lecherously wiþ hooris vndir his
spouse. And so þes folc hadde eendid alle þeir goodis whanne hem wantide
ȝiftis of grace, and alle her ȝiftis of kynde þei wastiden in yuel vss. Þis
hungir þat fel in þis cuntre is wanting of knowing of truþe wiþ kyndely
desijr to knowe truþe. Oon of þe citeseyns is þe feend, as al þis world is   55

27 maundement] comaundementis

Goddis cuntre and diuerse feendis of helle han will to tempte to dyuers
synnes; and he sendiþ man to his toun whanne he lediþ man to his
felowis, for þere þei han dyuers restingis. But al þis schewiþ greet nede
of man. Þat man kepiþ hoggis þat norischiþ fleschli synnes, boþe in him
60 and oþir men, as many cuntrees doen now. And so man coueitiþ to be
fild wiþ pees-holis, whan he desiriþ for to kunne mannes science oþir
þan Goddis science; for science of God fediþ men wel and oþir science
is mete for hoggis, and it makiþ men fatt here but not aftir domesday.
Sum men seien þat pees-holis ben vanytees of kyndli sciencis, for
65 pesis ben dyuers fro whete, as creaturis dyuersen fro God; draf is
science of goodis, as worldli lawe and þe popis lawe, for alle þese lawis
seken good but noon as doiþ Goddis lawe, for Goddis lawe holdiþ þe
best good, and oþir lawis good of þe world. And so þei dyuersen fro
Goddis lawe, as draf dyuersiþ fro clene drynk. Many [men] trauelen to
70 kunne þese lawis, and ȝit þei failen toolis þerto, for man moot haue
worldli spencis þat wolen craftily lerne þese sciencis. But man is turned
in himsilf whanne his conscience bitiþ him; þat mannes soule fariþ
moche beter þat serueþ God bi hise lawis.

So þat hous of þis fadir is hooly chirche þat holdiþ trewe men.
75 [L]oues ben dyuers articlis of bileeue þat cristen men han, and seruauntis of þis hous ben men þat ben now riȝtwise. But þe sone is þat man to
whom God haþ ordeyned blis, and is now riȝtwijs and profitiþ to
Goddis chirche. And so þenking and rysyng of men to come to þis
fadir ben dyuers gracis of God, bi whiche he moueþ men to loue hym.
80 Whanne a synful man knowiþ þe soþ þat God is his fadir in kynde,
([for] boþe his soule and his bodi God made of nouȝt, as Moyses seiþ),
þanne man makiþ his confessioun 'Fadir I haue synned in heuene and
bifore þee.' Soþ it is man may not synne, but if he synne aȝen God and
aȝens al þe world. And so þis man synneþ in heuene but, for he woot
85 þat God seeþ alle synnes, and he hopiþ forȝifnesse of him, þerfore he
seiþ þat he haþ synned bifore God þat is his fadir. And, for þe greet
synne þat he haþ don to God, he is not worþi of hymsilf to be clepid his
sone. God makiþ man as oon of hise hynen whanne he ȝyueþ him grace
for a tyme, and makiþ him to do wel hise werkis. And ȝit if man be Goddis
90 sone he coueitiþ to haue þis grace, for þe moost peyne þat man haþ is
peyne þat he takiþ of synne. And if a man schal be dampned, and be
Goddis hyne for a tyme, ȝit he haþ lesse peyne in helle for þat tyme þat
he is Goddis hyne. God oure fadir seeþ vs afer, long bifore þat we
comen to him, for bi mercy þat he haþ he moueþ [vs] to do þus. God
95 renneþ aȝens vs whanne he helpiþ vs to [do] good. God falliþ vpon

75 loues] sones   81 Gen. 1. 27

oure necke whanne he stiriþ vs to be meke; [God] kissiþ þanne his man
whanne he ȝyueþ him grace of sone, and makiþ him oon wiþ Crist his
sone and partener of Cristis meryt, and þanne þis sone makiþ eft þis
schrift. God seiþ þanne to hise seruauntis to bring forþ soone þe first
stole whanne þei schewen mannes innocence; and þat man is ordeyned 100
of hym to blisse, for þis stoole is long and narwȝ, and makiþ alle be
prestis þat schal be saued. And þis lastiþ round wiþ man, for it schal
euere be wiþ him in blis. Þis stoole is derkid for a tyme bi wickid lijf
þat man haþ, but it is clerid bi goode aungels and goode men þat seruen
God. Man is cloþid þus wiþ vertues; and þanne men seen afer þis 105
stoole for men gessen he schal be saaf, for goode þat comeþ of hise
vertues. Þis ryng þat is vpon þe fyngirs is bileeue in sutil werkis, to
make man to deserue heuene, for schort werkis þat he doiþ here. And
if þis hope turne to bileeue þat þis man schal be saaf, þanne boþe þis
stole and þis ryng ben brouȝt forþ to mannes siȝt, how man is weddid 110
wiþ Crist þe which is spouse of hooly chirche. And þis man synneþ not
aftir as Adam dide not, ne apostlis, but if it be liȝt venyal synne þat
lettiþ not þis stoole or wedding. Þat mannes feet ben hilid wiþ schoon
þat haþ mynde of deede seyntis, and is boþe hardi and redi to renne
after Crist in his cause. 115

  Þis fatt calf þat men schulden ete is Cristis bodi þat men offren,
and so it is þe sacrid oost þat is in figure Cristis bodi. Crist was deed in
his tyme and ordeynede for to feede men goostli bi his bodi, for it is
fatt breed herto. And þus God wiþ hise aungels is glad of þis ȝonger
sone. But þis eldir sone, whanne þe fadir and þe ȝonger sone eeten þus, 120
was in þe feeld of literal witt þat þei ȝyuen to Goddis lawe: and Iewis
han ȝit dedeyn of cristen men as Poul seiþ. Þese melodies þat weren
maad ben steringis of þe Hooli Goost, as vpon Witsondai þe apostlis
knewen alle langagis. And symfonye and croud weren herd whanne
apostlis knewen alle wittis, and þer was maad a greet sound whanne þe 125
Hooly Goost tauȝte hem. Þis eldir sone clepide oon þat seruede to
[h]is ȝonger broþir whanne men of þe oold lawe herden Petir þat was of
boþe telle hou þis comyng of þe Goost was profecied bi oolde profetis.
But ȝit þe fadris of þe oolde lawe hadden dedeyn of þis comyng and
seiden þat þei hadden serued God many ȝeer ful stably, and ȝit he vouch- 130
ide neuer saaf to feede hem þus wiþ a kide, for manna and pask lomb
weren but figuris to þis calf. But bifore þe dai of doom schal Iewis be
recouncilid to Crist, whanne he schal telle hem of his witt hou he haþ
ordeyned hem to blis. And letting of antecrist schal bi grace be putt

---

96 God] and   122 I Cor. 1. 23   123–6 Acts 2. 2–4   127 his] þis
127 Acts 2. 14–21   131 neuer] neuerer

135 awey for couetise of þe pope lettiþ þe Iewis to turne to Crist. And so þis
    elder sone is euere wiþ God bi sum part siþ Crist took his manhed of
    kynde of þis elder sone. And it helpiþ moche here for to knowe a greet
    persoone, and now bi oo part and now bi anoþir, verifie wordis of þis
    gospel, as þe kynde of þe Iewis now is clepid eldir and now ȝonger, for
140 þer ben dyuerse resouns of bigynnyng and eending of hem. And so for
    Crist and oþir apostlis was þis soþ þat alle myne ben þyne. And for
    oþir partis of þis greet persoone was þis soþ þat he grucchide. And so
    þis ȝonger broþer was deed bi synne and quykened bi grace, and so ech
    word of þis gospel is soþ to witt of þis parable.

    141 John 17. 10

11

Wycliffite Bible: John 10. 11-18

A. Early Version

11   I am a good shepherde. A good shepherde ȝyueþ his soule for
12   his shep. Forsoþe a marchaunt, and þat is not shepherde, whos þe shep
ben not his owne, seeþ a wlf comende, and he lefeþ þe shep and fleeþ,
13   and þe wlf raueshiþ and disparpliþ þe shep. Forsoþe þe marchaunt
14   fleeþ for he is a marchaunt, and it perteneþ not to hym of þe shep. I am
15   a good shepherde and I knowe my shep and my shep knowen me. As þe
fader haþ knowen me and Y kn[owe] þe fader, and I poote my lyf for
16   my shep. And I haue oþere sheep þat ben not of þis folde, and it bihoueþ
me to leden hem to; and þei shuln heren my vois, and it shal be maad o
17   folde and o shepherde. Þerfore þe fader looueþ me, for Y pote my soule
18   þat eftsoone I take it. No man takeþ it fro me, but I pote it fro myself;
I haue power to poten it, and I haue power to taken it aȝeen. Þis maundement I haue taken of my fader.

      15 knowe] kneȝ

B. Later Version

    I am a good shepperde. A good shepperde ȝeueþ his lyf for his   11
sheep. But an hyrid hyne, and þat is not þe shepperde, whos ben not þe   12
sheep his owne, seeþ a wolf comynge, and he leeuiþ þe sheep and fleeþ,
and þe wolf rauissheþ and disparpliþ þe sheep. And þe hirid hyne fleeþ   13
for he is an hiryd hyne, and it perteyniþ not to him of þe sheep. I am a   14
good shepperde and I knowe my sheep and my sheep knowen me. As þe   15
fadir haþ knowen me and I knowe þe fadir, and I putte my lyf for my
sheep. I haue oþere sheep þat ben not of þis foolde; and it bihoueþ   16
me to brynge hem togidere; and þei shulen heere my vois, and it shal
be maad oo foolde and oo shepperde. Þerfore þe fadir louiþ me, for I   17
putte my lyf þat eftsoone I take it. No man takiþ it fro me, but I putte it   18
of mysilf; I haue powere to putte it, and I haue power to take it aȝen.
Þis maundement I haue taken of my fadir.

12

Glossed Gospel commentary on John 10. 11-16

Y am a good schepparde. A good schepparde ȝyueþ his soule
(þat is his liyf) for his scheep.

good schepparde Crist wolde not adde good, no but yuele scheppardis
weren. Þo yuele scheppardis ben nyȝt þeues and day þeues, or hirid
hynes. Crist is þe dore, schepparde, ischer, scheep, lioun and stoon by
summe licnessis, not bi propirtes: for bi propirte he is God, and sone
of God wiþout bigynnyng, and in tyme man, sone of man and sone of
God togidere. *Austyn.* Crist is dore bi himsilf and entriþ bi himsilf; and
we entren bi him for we prechen him. Petre and oþere postlis and alle
goode bischopis ben scheppardis and membris of o schepparde, but
noon is þe dore, no but Crist. *Austyn.* **His liyf** Crist ȝaf his liyf for his
scheep, and in oure sacrament turneþ his body and blood, and bi fode
of his fleisch filliþ his scheep þat he aȝenbouȝte. Scheppardis owen to
ȝyue first her catel for Cristis scheep and, if it is nede, her liyf for þe
same scheep. He þat ȝyueþ not his catel for þe scheep whanne schal he
ȝyue his liyf for hem? *Greger.* Goode scheppardis schedden her blood
for þe scheep, not þorou pride but charite; þerfor þey weren goode
scheppardis. Eretikis þat suffriden ony disese for her wickidnessis and
errours boosten of name of martirdom; þey diden not for þe scheep but
raþere aȝenus þe scheep, for to stele liȝtliere bi þis colour, for þey ben
wolues. Poul seiþ, 'Þouȝ Y schal ȝyue my body so þat Y brenne wiþout
charite, it profitiþ noþing to me.' *Austyn.* But hou haiþ he charite
which also conuyct loueþ not vnyte þat Crist comendiþ? *Austyn.*

Forsoþe a marchaunt or hirid hyne, and þat is not schepparde,
whos ben not þe scheep his owne, seeþ a wolf comynge and he
leeueþ (or forsakiþ) þe scheep and fleeþ, and þe wolf rauyschiþ
and disparpiliþ (or scateriþ) þe scheep. Forsoþe þe marchaunt
fleeþ for he is a marchaunt and it perteyneþ not to him of þe
scheep.

Marchaunt Skilefuly þey lesen þe name of schepparde while þei louen
more erþely substaunce þan þe scheep. He is a marchaunt þat holdiþ þe

21 I Cor. 13. 3

place of schepparde, but sekiþ not wynnyngis of soule, þat coueytiþ
erþely profitis and ioyeþ bi onour of prelacie. He is not schepparde but
marchaunt which fediþ not þe lordis scheep for most entere loue but
to temperal meedis. *Greger.* Whateuer prelat loueþ not Crist frely or for 35
himsilf sekiþ not God for himsilf, but serueþ God for temperal þingis,
and desiriþ onour of men. He is a marchaunt not sone, and haþ resseyued
his meede. *Austyn.* Whoeuer sekiþ of God ony þing outtakun God,
sekiþ not God chastly. *Austyn.* **Wolf**: þe deuel is þe wolf. *Austyn.* Wolf
is vniust man and rauenour þat oppressiþ feiþful and meke men. He þat 40
semeþ schepparde and is not forsakiþ þe scheep and fleeþ, for while he
drediþ perel of him he presumeþ not to wiþstonde his vnriȝtfulnesse;
he fleeþ not in chaunginge place but in wiþdrawinge counfort; he
fledde for he say vnriȝtfulnesse and was stille. *Greger.* He fleeþ þat seeþ
men synnynge greuously and reproueþ not but is stille. *Austyn.* Þe deuel 45
is þe wolf |þat sekiþ þe deþis of soulis, þe wickid spirit torendiþ soulis
of cristen men in temptacioun, and he þat holdiþ þe place of schepparde
haþ not cure of bisynesse; soulis perischen and he is glad of erþely
profitis. *Greger.* **Marchaunt** Þe deuel sleeþ cristen peple bi temptaciouns
but þe marchaunt is stirid bi no feruour of loue aȝenus synnes for he 50
sekiþ onely outmere profitis; he suffriþ recchelesly ynnere harmes of
þe floc. *Greger.* No man harmeþ more in þe chirche þan he þat doiþ
weywardly and haþ þe name of ordre or of holynesse, for no man presumeþ
to reproue him, and þe synne is strecchid forþ gretly into ensaumple.
Whanne a synnere is onourid for reuerence of ordre, it were betere to 55
hym, which set in ordre of holynesse distrieþ oþere men bi word or
ensaumple, þat he were deed in seculer abite and trauel, þan he in holy
office were ensaumple of synne to oþere men, for if he aloone felde
doun he schulde haue lesse turment in helle. *Greger.* Whanne prestis
synnen al þe peple is turnyd to do synne; þerfor prestis schulen ȝelde 60
resoun for synnes of al þe peple. *Crisostom.* Prelatis ben worþi so many
deþis hou manye ensaumplis of perdicioun þey senden to her sugetis.
Greger. Þe profete Aggey seiþ, 'Axe þou prestis þe lawe'; þe glos þere
seiþ, 'A prest owiþ to kunne þe lawe of God, ellis he proueþ himsilf no
prest of God.' He þat studieþ to resseyue holy ordre bi ȝuyyng of priss, 65
is no prest but coueytiþ in veyn to be seid. A prest þat getiþ a chirche by
money schal not onely be pryued of þe chirche but also degradid fro
onour of presthod. Ech cristen man knowiþ þat it is eresie of symonye
to bie or sille auteris, tiþis and þe Holy Goost. Þey þat bien or sillen holy
ordris mown not be prestis, for curs to þe ȝyuer and curs to þe taker: þis 70
is eresie of symonye. *Greger.* Prelatis office stondiþ in word of liyf, þat

63 Hag. 2. 11

is preching of holy writ, in ensaumple of holy lyuyng and in swetnesse of ynnere charite. *Grosted.* If curatis prechen not þe word of God þei schule be dampned. *Grosted* and *Greger.* If ony curat kan not preche, þe propir remedi is to resigne his benefice. He may recorde þe text of þe gospel and of þe pistle in þe wouke and so preche þe same to his sugetis, and þus he schal profite myche, for Crist and þe postlis precheden þus. *Grosted.* A curat wiþdrawinge ensaumple of holy liyf wiþdrawiþ þe moste part of his office; and sich wiþdrawer is þe worste manquellere þou3 þe sugetis dien not. *Grosted.* Whanne a schepparde or curat wole not blame synneris, in beynge stille he sleeþ hem. *Greger* and *Grosted.* A curat 3yuynge yuel ensaumple to his sugetis is gilti of þe deþ of hem, þou3 þei lyuen þorou Goddis grace. *Austyn* and *Grosted.* Þei þat 3yuen cure of soulis to man vnmy3ti, vnkunnynge or not willinge to fede hem duly ben gilty of alle þe soulis þou3 þei ben saued þorou Goddis grace. To make vnable prelatis or curatis in þe chirche is þe hi3este degre of greet trespas. *Grosted.* A reccheles schepparde and by yuel ensaumple sleynge his sugetis is worse þan vnwise beestis and þe crucifieris of Crist. *Grosted.* Coueytouse men ben foolis; to be led by councel of hem is to dispose of capouns bi councel of foxis and to dispose of scheep bi councel of wolues. *Grosted.* Crist seiþ in þe gospel, 'If þe blynde lediþ þe blynde þei fallen boþe in þe dich.' Al kynde of men haþ sum trauel and sum liking, but clerkis taken of ech staat þat þat likiþ and fleen þe trauel. Þerfor in þe dom alle statis schulen forsake hem and blowe hem awey, and þerfor þes clerkis schulen be in helle, where is noon ordre but euerlastinge hidousnesse. *Bernard.* He is vnworþi to haue mylk and wolle which fediþ not þe scheep; if he wakiþ not in keping of þe floc he etiþ and drinkiþ dampnacioun to hymsilf. Clerkis schulen come bifore þe trone of Crist, a greuouse playnt of peplis schal be herd by whose hiris þey lyueden and diden not awey þe synnes to whiche þey ben maad blynde lederis and treccherouse mediatours. *Bernard.* A clerk trauelinge bisily and fruytefuly lyue of þe auter. To 3yue not to pore men þe gooddis of pore men is sacrilegie. Þe goodis of þe chirche ben patrymonyes of pore men, and by cursid cruelte it is takun fro hem whateuere þing þe mynystris and dispenderis (treuly not lordis or welderis) taken ouer liflode and cloþing. *Bernard.* For yuele prelatis ben cause of corupcioun of feiþ and cristen religion; nedely þey ben cause of vnbileue or vnfeiþ-fulnesse, of dissencioun, of eresie and of viciouse liyf þorou al þe world. And for þei tellen not Cristis gospel bi word and holy lyuyng and for feruent loue of soulis, þey ben ded in hemsilf and sleeris of soulis bitakun to her cure; and þou3 þey diden none oþere malices þey ben

91 Matt. 15. 14

antecristis and satanas transfigurid into an aungel of liȝt, nyȝt þeuys and
day þeuys, sleeris and distrieris of scheep, makinge þe hows of preier a
denne of þeuys. And siþen þe liyf of prelatis is bok and lernyng of þe
floc, and þey ben maistris of alle yuels, þei ben eretikis. And siþen þey   115
mysusen þe seed of Goddis word bi which þey schulden gendre soulis
into euerlastinge liyf, þey ben worse þan bodily sodomytis, siþen þe
mysusi[n]g of þe betre vertu is more yuel and more abhomynable. Yuele
prelatis ben most opynly leseris of al þe world. Þe cause, welle and bigynnyng of so greet yuel is þe court of þe pope for it distrieþ not þes yuels, siþen   120
it may best and is most holdun and for it makiþ vnable prelatis and curatis.
Grosted. Y gesse þat God suffriþ no more preiudise or harm þan of yuele
prestis. *Greger.* Chosun men of God, clensid bi hondis of prestis, entren
into heuenly cuntre; and schrewid prestis and vnpytouse þorou reprouable
liyf hasten to þe turmentis of helle. Yuele prestis ben lik to þe watir of   125
baptim which, waishinge awey þe synnes of men cristenyd, sendiþ hem
to heuenly kingdom and itsilf goiþ doun into swolewis. *Greger.*

> Y am a good schepparde and Y knowe my scheep, and my scheep
> knowen me. As my fadir haþ knowe me and Y knowe þe fadir, and
> Y putte my liyf for my scheep. And Y haue oþere scheep þat ben not   130
> of þis foolde and it bihoueþ me for to lede hem to and þei schulen
> here my voys and it schal be maad o foolde and o schepparde.

Schepparde Crist is a good schepparde; he is dore, he entriþ by himsilf
to his scheep and ȝyueþ his voys to hem þat þey sue him and fynde
lesewis, þat is euerlastinge liyf. He haþ put his liyf for his scheep and if   135
þo men þat puttiden her lyues for scheep ben his membris he þe same
oon dide þis. Crist seide to Petre 'Fede my scheep', þat is putte þou þi
liyf for my scheep. *Austyn.* **Knowe my scheep**: þat is Y loue hem.
Greger. An hirid hyne knowiþ not þe scheep for he visitiþ hem seeldene,
but þe schepparde knowiþ his owne scheep as bisi aboute hem. *Teofile.*   140
Knowen me: þat is þey louynge obeyen. Se ȝe if ȝe knowen Crist and þe
treuþe – not knowe bi feiþ but bi loue and worching. He þat loueþ not
þe treuþe ȝit knowiþ not; he þat seiþ þat he knowiþ God and kepiþ not
his heestis is a liere as Ioon seiþ in his pistle. *Greger.* **Knowe þe fadir**
Crist bi himsilf knowiþ þe fadir, and we bi him. *Austyn.* Þe knowing of   145
Crist and of þe scheep is not euene: 'As þe fadir knowiþ me and Y knowe
þe fadir', þat is: so most certenly 'Y knowe him as he knowiþ me' –
here is euene knowing. *Crisostom.* **For my scheep**: þat is bi þat charite
bi which Y die for my scheep, Y schewe hou myche Y loue þe fadir.
Greger. Crist seiþ þis, schewinge þat he is not a disseyuere. Þe postle to   150

112 II Cor. 11. 14   **113** Matt. 21. 13   **137** John 21. 17   **144** I John 2. 4
150 II Cor. 11. 23–8

schewe him a very maystre aȝenus false apostlis brouȝte yn resoun of perels and depis. *Crisostom.* **Opere scheep**: þat is heþen men. *Greger* and *Austyn.* **of þis foolde**: þat is, of peple of Iewis. *Austyn.* **Lede to**: he and not anoþer lediþ to bi his seruauntis. *Austyn.* **My voys** Lo Crist spekiþ

155 by his seruauntis and his voys is herd bi hem þat he sendiþ. *Austyn.* **O foolde** Crist is maad cornerstoon to þes twey folkis, as to twey wallis. Crist is stoon and dore and cornerstoon, lomb, schepparde and lioun and many oþere þingis whiche he is not bi propirte. *Austyn.* As of twey flockis o foolde is maad, for Crist knyttiþ togidre in his feiþ

160 Iewis and heþen men, while he chesiþ symple men of euer eiþer nacioun to euerlastinge liyf, he lediþ scheep to her owne foolde. *Greger.*

13

Sermon on John 10. 11-18

Ego sum pastor bonus.   Johannis X

Crist telliþ in þis gospel þe maners of a good heerd, so þat herbi we mai wite hou oure heerdis failen now. And defaute of suche heerdis is moost peril in þe chirche for, as riȝt offis of hem schulde moost brynge men to heuene, so [de]faute [in] þis office drawiþ men moost to

5 helle. Crist telliþ of himsilf hou *he is a good heerde.* For he is þe beste heerde þat mankynde may haue, for he is good bi himsilf and mai no wey faile, for he is boþe God and man, and God mai no weie synne. And þus we han þe mesure to knowe a good heerde and [an] yuel, for þe moor þat an heerde is liche to Crist he is þe beter, and þe more þat he straungiþ fro

10 him he is þe worse in þis office.

And eft, whanne Crist haþ ȝouun þe mesure for to knowe good heerdis, he telliþ þe hiȝest propirte þat falliþ to a good heerde: *a good heerde*, as Crist seiþ, *puttiþ his lijf for hise scheep*, for more charite mai noon haue þan to putt his lijf for his freendis, and, if he worchiþ wijsli, for to

15 brynge þese scheepe to heuene, for þus þe heerde haþ moost peyne and

þe scheep moost profit. Þus mai we se who is a good heerde and who
failiþ in þis office. For [as] Crist puttiþ wijsly his owne lijf for hise scheep,
so anticrist puttiþ proudli many lyues for his foule lijf; as, if þe feend
ledde þe pope to kille many þousynd men to holde his worldli staat, he
suede antecristis maners. And, siþ þis proprete of heerde groundiþ   20
charite in men, ech man schulde haue herof algatis more – or lesse, as he
is ferþer fro þis maner þat wole not ȝyue hise worldli goodis to hise
scheep or hise briþeren, whanne þei han greet nede þerto, for suche
ben worse þan mannes lijf. And þus seemen oure religious to be exempt
fro charite, for, nede a man neuere so moche to haue help of suche goodis, 25
ȝhe if þei han stoones or oþir iewels þat harmen hem, þei wole not
ȝyue suche goodis ne value of hem to helpe her briþeren, ne cesse to anoie
hemsilf in bildinge of hiȝe housis, ne to gadere suche veyne goodis if it
do harm to her briþeren. Suche auarous men ben fer fro maners of a good
heerd. And so þese newe religious þat þe feend haþ tollid yn, bi colour to 30
helpe þe former heerdis, harmen hem manye gatis, and letten þis
office in þe chirche, for trewe preching and worldli goodis ben spoilid
bi suche religious. And herfore techiþ Crist to fle hem, for þei ben
raueschinge wolues: summe wolen as breris tere wolle of sheep and make
hem coold in charite, and summe wolen sturdely as þornes slee þe sheep 35
of hooli chirche. And þus is oure modir shend for defaute of mannes
help. And more mede myȝte no man haue þan to helpe þis sory widewe,
for princis of prestis and pharisees þat calliden Crist a gilour han crochid
to hem þe chesyng of manye heerdis in þe chirche, and þei ben tauȝt
bi antecrist to chese hise heerdis and not Cristis. And þus failiþ Cristis 40
chirche. Lord, siþ heerdis schulden passe her scheep as men passen
bletynge scheep, hou schulde Cristis chirche fare if þese heerdis weren
turned to wolues? But Crist seiþ þus it fariþ among þe herdis of þe
chirche, þat many of hem *ben hirid hynes and not heerdis ouer þe scheep, for þe*
scheepe ben not her owne, and so þei louen to litil þe scheep. For, if þei han 45
her temperal hire, þei recken not hou her floc fare. And þus doen alle
þese curatis þat tellen more bi worldli wynnyng þan bi vertues of her
sugetis or soule hele to come to heuene. Suche ben not herdis of scheep
but of dunge and wolle of hem, and þese schal not haue in heuene ioye
of þe scheepe þat þei kepen. *Suche hynes seen wolues comynge to flockis* þat 50
þei schulden kepe, *and þei fleen* for dreed of nouȝt. *And þese wolues*
raueschen þese scheepe and scateren hem for þis eende þat þanne þei mai
sunner perische. And þis mouede Poul to founde noon ordre, for Cristis
ordir is ynow, and þanne schulden alle cristen men be more surely in oo
floc. Lord, if cowardise of suche hynen be þus dampned of Crist, hou   5

38 Matt. 27. 63   53 I. Cor. 3. 4–15

moche moor schulden wolues be dampned þat ben putt to kepe Cristis
scheep? But Crist seiþ a clene cause whi *þis hirid hyne fleeþ* þus: *for he is*
an hirid hyne and þe scheep perteinen not to him, but þe dunge of suche scheepe
and þis dunge sufficiþ to him, houeuer þe scheepe faren. Summe ben
60   wolues wiþoutforþ, and summe ben wolues wiþyn and þes ben more
perilous, for homely enmyes ben þe worste. Yuel wolues ben religious
þat Crist seiþ in Matheu book ben wolues raueschinge, al if þei comen
in shepe cloþis, for bi þis ypocrisie þei disseyuen sunner þe scheepe.
And, al if þeir dwelling be wiþoute parischis of þese scheep, and þei
65   ben straunge and newe brouȝt yn bi þe feend, ȝit þei forȝeten not to
come and visite þese scheepe; but comunli whanne þei comen þei comen
moost for to spoile. And þus doen generali boþe freris, mounkis and
chanouns. But þei ben wolues wiþyn þat seien þat þei han cure of soulis,
and raueschen goodis of þese scheepe and feden hem not goostli, but
70   raþer mouen hem to synne, and waken not in heerdis office.

        But *Crist seiþ he is a good heerd and knowiþ hise scheep and þei him*,
for þe office þat falliþ to heerdis makiþ him knowun among hem. *As my*
fadir knowiþ me and I aȝen knowe my fadir, so, seiþ Crist, *I putte my lijf to*
kepe my scheepe aȝen wolues. And as þis knowing myȝte not quenche
75   bitwix Crist and his fadir, so schulden þese heerdis waken vpon her
scheepe, and þei schulden knowe him, not bi bodili feestis ne oþir signes
þat he doiþ, but bi þre office of heerde þat Crist haþ lymytid to him. It
falliþ to a good heerd to lede hise scheepe in hool pasturis, and whanne
hise scheepe ben hirt or scabbid to hele hem and to grese hem, and
80   whanne oþir yuel beestis assailen hem þanne helpe hem. And herto
schulde he putt his lijf to saue hise scheepe fro suche beestis. Þe pasture
is Goddis lawe þat euermor is grene in truþe, and rotun pasture ben oþir
lawis and oþir fablis wiþoute ground. And cowardise of suche heerdis
þat dar not defende Goddis lawe witnessiþ þat þei failen in two officis
85   suynge after: for he þat dar not for worldis dreed defende þe lawe of
his God, hou schulde [he] defende hise scheepe for loue þat he haþ to
hem? And if þei bryngen yn newe lawes contrarie to Goddis lawe, hou
schulde þei not faile after in oþir officis þat þei schulden haue?

        But Crist þat is heed of heerdis seiþ þat *he haþ oþir scheepe þat ben*
90   *not ȝit of þis floc, and hem moot he brynge togidir and teche hem to knowe his*
vois. And so schal þere be oo floc and oon heerd ouer hem alle. Þese scheepe ben
heþen men or Iewis þat Crist wole conuerte, for alle þese schal make oo
floc, þe which flok is hooli chirche – but fer fro þis vndirstonding þat
alle men schulen be conuertid.

        62 Matt. 7. 15

14
Prologue to Wycliffite Bible, chapter 15

For as myche as Crist seiþ þat þe gospel shal be prechid in al þe world, and Dauiþ seiþ of þe apostlis and here preching, 'Þe soun of hem ȝede out into ech lond, and þe wordis of hem ȝeden out into þe endis of þe world'; and eft Dauiþ seiþ 'Þe Lord shal telle in þe scripturis of puplis, and of þese princis þat weren in it' (þat is, in holi chirche); and as Ierom   5
seiþ on þat vers 'Holi writ is þe scripture of puplis for it is maad þat alle puplis shulden knowe it', and þe princis of þe chirche þat weren þer-inne ben þe postlis, þat hadden autorite to writen holi writ, for bi þat same þat þe apostlis writiden here scripturis bi autorite, and confermyng of þe Holi Gost, it is holi scripture and feiþ of cristene men, and þis dignite   10
haþ no man aftir hem, be he neuere so holi, neuere so kunnyng, as Ierom witnessiþ on þat vers. Also Crist seiþ of þe Iewis þat crieden Osanna to him in þe temple þat, þouȝ þei weren stille, stoonis shulden crie, and bi stoonis he vndurstondiþ heþene men þat worshipiden stoonis for here goddis. And we English men ben comen of heþen men, þerfore we ben   15
vndurstonden bi þese stoonis þat shulden crie holi writ. And, as Iewis, interpretide knouleching, signifien clerkis þat shulden knouleche to God bi repentaunce of synnes and bi vois of Goddis heriyng, so oure lewid men, suynge þe cornerstoon Crist, moun be signified bi stoonis þat ben harde and abidinge in þe foundement. For, þouȝ couetouse clerkis ben   20
wode bi symonie, eresie and manie oþere synnes, and dispisen and stoppen holi writ as myche as þei moun, ȝit þe lewid puple crieþ aftir holi writ to kunne it and kepe it wiþ greet cost and peril of here lif.

For þese resons and oþere, wiþ comune charite to saue alle men in oure rewme whiche God wole haue sauid, a symple creature haþ   25
translatid þe Bible out of Latyn into English. First þis symple creature hadde myche trauaile wiþ diuerse felawis and helperis to gedere manie elde biblis, and oþere doctouris and comune glosis, and to make oo Latyn bible sumdel trewe; and þanne to studie it of þe newe, þe text wiþ þe glose, and oþere doctouris as he miȝte gete, and speciali Lire on þe   30
elde testament þat helpide ful myche in þis werk. Þe þridde tyme to

1 Matt. 24. 14   2 Ps. 19. 4   4 Ps. 87. 6 (Vulgate reading)   12 Luke 19. 40

counseile wiþ elde gramariens and elde dyuynis of harde wordis and
harde sentencis, hou þo miȝten best be vndurstonden and translatid. Þe
fourþe tyme to translate as cleerli as he coude to þe sentence, and to haue
35 manie gode felawis and kunnynge at þe correcting of þe translacioun.

First it is to knowe þat þe beste translating is, out of Latyn into
English, to translate aftir þe sentence and not oneli aftir þe wordis, so
þat þe sentence be as opin eiþer openere in English as in Latyn, and go
not fer fro þe lettre; and if þe lettre mai not be suid in þe translating, let
40 þe sentence euere be hool and open, for þe wordis owen to serue to þe
entent and sentence, and ellis þe wordis ben superflu eiþer false. In
translating into English, manie resolucions moun make þe sentence
open, as an ablatif case absolute may be resoluid into þese þre wordis,
wiþ couenable verbe, *þe while, for, if,* as gramariens seyn; as þus *þe maistir*
45 *redinge, I stonde* mai be resoluid þus *while þe maistir rediþ, I stonde,* eiþer *if*
þe maistir rediþ etc., eiþer *for þe maistir* etc. And sumtyme it wolde acorde
wel wiþ þe sentence to be resoluid into *whanne* eiþer into *aftirward,* þus
whanne þe maistir red, I stood, eiþer *aftir þe maistir red, I stood.* And sumtyme
it mai wel be resoluid into a verbe of þe same tens as oþere ben in þe
50 same resoun, and into þis word *et,* þat is *and* in English, as þus *arescenti-*
bus hominibus pre timore, þat is *and men shulen wexe drie for drede.* Also a
participle of a present tens eiþer pretert, of actif vois eiþir passif, mai
be resoluid into a verbe of þe same tens and a coniunccioun copulatif, as
þus *dicens,* þat is *seiynge,* mai be resoluid þus *and seiþ* eiþir *þat seiþ.* And
55 þis wole in manie placis make þe sentence open, where to englisshe it
aftir þe word wolde be derk and douteful. Also a relatif which mai be
resoluid into his antecedent wiþ a coniunccioun copulatif, as þus *which*
renneþ, and he renneþ. Also whanne oo word is oonis set in a reesoun, it
mai be set forþ as ofte as it is vndurstonden, eiþer as ofte as reesoun and
60 nede axen. And þis word *autem* eiþer *vero* mai stonde for *forsoþe,* eiþer for
but, and þus I vse comounli; and sumtyme it mai stonde for *and,* as elde
gramariens seyn. Also whanne riȝtful construccioun is lettid bi relacion,
I resolue openli þus: where þis reesoun *Dominum formidabunt aduersarii*
eius shulde be englisshid þus bi þe lettre *þe Lord hise aduersaries shulen drede,*
65 I englishe it þus bi resolucioun *þe aduersaries of þe Lord shulen drede him,*
and so of oþere resons þat ben like.

At þe bigynnyng I purposide wiþ Goddis helpe to make þe sentence as trewe and open in English as it is in Latyn, eiþer more trewe and
more open þan it is in Latyn. And I preie for charite and for comoun
70 profyt of cristene soulis þat if ony wiys man fynde ony defaute of þe
truþe of translacioun, let him sette in þe trewe sentence and opin of holi

63 I Sam. 2. 10

writ. But loke þat he examyne truli his Latyn bible, for no doute he shal
fynde ful manye biblis in Latyn ful false, if he loke manie, nameli newe.
And þe comune Latyn biblis han more nede to be correctid, as manie as
I haue seen in my lif, þan haþ þe English bible late translatid. And where   75
þe Ebru bi witnesse of Ierom, of Lire and oþere expositouris discordiþ fro
oure Latyn biblis, I haue set in þe margyn bi maner of a glose what þe
Ebru haþ, and hou it is vndurstondun in sum place. And I dide þis most
in þe Sauter, þat of alle oure bokis discordiþ most fro Ebru; for þe
chirche rediþ not þe Sauter bi þe laste translacioun of Ierom out of   80
Ebru into Latyn, but anoþer translacioun of oþere man þat hadden
myche lasse kunnyng and holynesse þan Ierom hadde. And in ful fewe
bokis þe chirche rediþ þe translacioun of Ierom, as it mai be preuid bi
þe propre origynals of Ierom whiche he gloside. And where I haue
translatid as opinli or opinliere in English as in Latyn, late wise   85
men deme þat knowen wel boþe langagis, and knowen wel þe sentence
of holi scripture. And wher I haue do þus or nay, n[o] doute þei, þat
kunne wel þe sentence of holi writ and English togidere and wolen
trauaile wiþ Goddis grace þeraboute, moun make þe Bible as trewe and
as opin, ȝea and opinliere, in English þan it is in Latyn. And no doute,   90
to a symple man wiþ Goddis grace and greet trauail, men miȝten expoune
myche openliere and shortliere þe Bible in English þan þe elde greete
doctouris han expounid it in Latyn, and myche sharpliere and groundliere
þan manie late postillatouris eiþir expositouris han don. But God of his
grete merci ȝeue to vs grace to lyue wel and to seie þe truþe in couenable   95
manere and acceptable to God and his puple, and to spille not oure
tyme, be it short, be it long, at Goddis ordynaunce.

But summe þat semen wise and holi seyn þus: if men now weren
as holi as Ierom was, þei miȝten translate out of Latyn into English as
he dide out of Ebru, and out of Greek into Latyn, and ellis þei shulden   100
not translate now, as hem þinkiþ, for defaute of holynesse and of
kunnyng. Þouȝ þis replicacioun seme colourable, it haþ no good
ground, neiþer resoun neiþir charite. Forwhi þis replicacioun is more
aȝens seynt Ierom and aȝens þe firste seuenti translatouris, and aȝens
holi chirche þan aȝens symple men þat translaten now into English. For   105
seynt Ierom was not so holi as þe apostlis and euangelistis whos bokis
he translatide into Latyn, neiþer he hadde so hiȝe ȝiftis of þe Holi Gost
as þei hadden. And myche more þe seuenti translatouris weren not so
holi as Moises and þe profetis, and speciali Dauiþ, neiþer þei hadden so
greete ȝiftis of God as Moises and þe prophetis hadden. Ferþermore,   110
holi chirche appreueþ not oneli þe trewe translacioun of meene cristene

87 no] ne

men stidefast in cristene feiþ, but also of open eretikis þat diden awei
manie mysteries of Iesu Crist bi gileful translacioun, as Ierom witnessiþ
in oo prolog on Iob and in þe prolog of Daniel. Myche more late þe
chirche of Engelond appreue þe trewe and hool translacioun of symple
men þat wolden for no good in erþe, bi here witing and power, putte
awei þe leste truþe, ȝea þe leste lettre, eiþer title, of holi writ þat beriþ
substaunce eiþer charge. And dispute þei not of þe holynesse of men now
lyuynge in þis deadli lif, for þei kunnen not þeron, and it is reseruid
oneli to Goddis doom. If þei knowen ony notable defaute bi þe translatouris eiþer helpis of hem, lete hem blame þe defaute bi charite and
merci; and lete hem neuere dampne a þing þat mai be don lefulli bi
Goddis lawe, as weeryng of a good cloþ for a tyme, eiþer riding on an
hors for a greet iourney, whanne þei witen not wherfore it is don; for
suche þingis moun be don of symple men, wiþ as greet charite and uertu
as summe, þat holden hem greete and wise, kunnen ride in a gilt sadil,
eiþer vse cuyssyns and beddis and cloþis of gold and of silk wiþ oþere
vanitees of þe world. God graunte pite, merci and charite and loue of
comoun profyt, and putte awei suche foli domis þat ben aȝens resoun
and charite.

  Ȝit worldli clerkis axen gretli what spiryt makiþ idiotis hardi to
translate now þe Bible into English, siþen þe foure greete doctouris
dursten neuere do þis. Þis replicacioun is so lewid þat it nediþ noon
answer, no but stilnesse eiþir curteys scorn. For þese greete doctouris
weren noone English men, neiþer þei weren conuersaunt among
English men neiþir in caas þei kouden þe langage of English. But þei
ceessiden neuere til þei hadden holi writ in here modir tunge of here
owne puple. For Ierom, þat was a Latyn man of birþe, translatide þe
Bible boþe out of Ebru and out of Greek into Latyn, and expounide ful
myche þerto. And Austyn and manie mo Latyns expouniden þe Bible
for manie partis in Latyn, to Latyn men among whiche þei dwelliden.
And Latyn was a comoun langage to here puple aboute Rome and
biȝondis and on þis half, as Englishe is comoun langage to oure puple.
And ȝit þis dai þe comoun puple in Italie spekiþ Latyn corript, as
trewe men seyn þat han ben in Italie. And þe noumbre of translatouris
out of Greek into Latyn passiþ mannis knowing, as Austyn witnessiþ in
þe secounde book of *Cristene Teching*, and seiþ þus 'Þe translatouris out
of Ebru into Greek moun be noumbrid, but Latyn translatouris, eiþer
þei þat translatiden into Latyn moun not be noumbrid in ony manere.
For in þe firste tymes of feiþ ech man, as a Greek book came to him and
he semyde to himsilf to haue sum kunnyng of Greek and of Latyn, was

  141 in] into

hardi to translate. And þis þing helpide more þan lettide vndurstonding,
if rederis ben not necligent. Forwhi þe biholding of manie bokis haþ
shewid ofte, eiþir declarid, summe derkere sentencis.' Þis seiþ Austyn
þere. Þerfore Grosted seiþ þat it was Goddis wille þat diuerse men   155
translatiden, and þat diuerse translacions be in þe chirche, for where oon
seide derkli, oon eiþer mo seiden openli. Lord God, siþen at þe bigynnyng of feiþ so manie men translatiden into Latyn and to greet profyt
of Latyn men, lat oo symple creature of God translate into English for
profyt of English men! For if worldli clerkis loken wel here croniclis   160
and bookis, þei shulden fynde þat Bede translatide þe Bible and expounide myche in Saxon, þat was English eiþer comoun langage of þis
lond in his tyme. And not oneli Bede but also king Alured, þat foundide
Oxenford, translatide in hise laste daies þe bigynnyng of þe Sauter into
Saxon, and wolde more if he hadde lyued lengere. Also Frenshe men,   165
Beemers and Britons han þe Bible and oþere bokis of deuocioun and of
exposicioun translatid in here modir langage. Whi shulden not English
men haue þe same in here modir langage? I can not wite, no but for
falsnesse and necligence of clerkis, eiþer for oure puple is not worþi to
haue so greet grace and 3ifte of God, in peyne of here olde synnes. God 170
for his merci amende þese euele causis, and make oure puple to haue
and kunne and kepe truli holi writ to lijf and deþ!

But in translating of wordis equiuok, þat is þat haþ manie significacions vndur oo lettre, mai li3tli be pereil. For Austyn seiþ in þe
secounde book of *Cristene Teching* þat, if equiuok wordis be not translatid 175
into þe sense eiþer vndurstonding of þe autour, it is errour. As in þat
place of þe Salme *þe feet of hem ben swifte to shede out blood*, þe Greek word
is equiuok to *sharp* and *swift*; and he þat translatide *sharpe feet* erride,
and a book þat haþ *sharpe feet* is fals and mut be amendid. As þat sentence *vnkynde 3onge trees shulen not 3eue depe rootis* owiþ to be þus *plaum-* 180
tingis of auoutrie shulen not 3eue depe rootis. Austyn seiþ þere. Þerfore a
translatour haþ greet nede to studie wel þe sentence boþe bifore and
aftir, and loke þat suche equiuok wordis acorde wiþ þe sentence. And
he haþ nede to lyue a clene lif and be ful deuout in preiers and haue not
his wit ocupied aboute worldli þingis, þat þe Holi Spiryt, autour of   185
wisdom and kunnyng and truþe, dresse him in his werk and suffre him
not for to erre. Also þis word *ex* signifieþ sumtyme *of*, and sumtyme it
signifieþ *bi*, as Ierom seiþ. And þis word *enim* signifieþ comynli *forsoþe*,
and, as Ierom seiþ, it signifieþ cause *þus*, *forwhi*. And þis word *secundum*
is taken for *aftir*, as manie men seyn, and comynli; but it signifieþ wel   190
bi eiþer *vp*: þus *bi 3oure word* eiþer *vp 3oure word*. Manie suche aduerbis,

176 Rom. 3. 15 (from Prov. 1. 16)   **180** Wisd. 4. 3

coniunccions and preposicions ben set ofte oon for anoþer and at fre
chois of autouris sumtyme; and now þo shulen be taken as it acordiþ
best to þe sentence. Bi þis maner wiþ good lyuyng and greet trauel,
195 men moun come to truþe and cleer translating and trewe vndurstonding
of holi writ, seme it neuere so hard at þe bigynnyng. God graunte to
us alle to kunne wel and kepe wel holi writ, and suffre ioiefulli sum
peyne for it at þe laste! Amen.

Part III
Lollard Polemic

15

The Ecclesiastical Hierarchy

Ve vobis scribe et pharisei ipocrite. Mathei xxiii

Crist biddiþ vs be war wiþ þes false profetis þat comen in
cloþing of scheepe and ben wolues of raueyne. And þese ben speciali
men of þese newe ordris, and moost þese freris þat last comen yn,
for þe feend sutiliþ euer a3ens hooli chirche. Crist telliþ ei3te woos to
þese pharisees, and not oonli wis[ch]iþ hem, but ordeyneþ hem to come   5
to þese ypocritis for þei disseyuen his peple. Þe first woo þat Crist seiþ
is teeld on þis maner: *Woo be to 3ou, scribis and pharisees, ypocritis, þat
closen þe kyngdom of heuenes bifore oþir men, for neþer 3e entren ne suffre oþir
to entre.* Þis may be vndirstondun vpon many maners. First bi þe
lettre, þat þe kyngdom of heuene is þat hooli chirche þat now is in   10
heuene; and so þese pharisees entren not into heuene for bi her loue
þei goen into helle, siþ þei louen erþe and erþli þingis, and litil or nou3t
goodis of grace, and þei drawen wiþ hem moche erþeli peple. Þe secunde
maner of vndirstonding is of hooli writt, þat þei entren not to vndirstonding þerof, ne þei suffren oþir men to vndirstonde it wel. Summe prechen   15
fablis and summe veyne stories; summe docken hooli writt and summe
feynen lesyngis; and so loore of Goddis lawe is al putt abac. And þus
þe laddre þat men schulden come to heuene bi eþer wantiþ rongis, or
ellis is not rerid. Þe þridde vndirstonding of [þese wordis of] Crist mai
be applied to lyuyng of þese pharisees: þei lyuen ypocritis lijf þat hem-   20
silf han foundun, and þei maken oþir men confoorme hem þerto, for
þei seien þat þis lijf is þe best of alle; and so lijf þat Crist ordeynede is
alle putt abac. And þis newe foundun lijf drawiþ men dounward, siþ
freris ben confessours and leden moche peple. And þese scribis helpen
þes pharisees, for prelatis and parsouns and oþir possessioners seien   25
in her lijf þat Crist lyuede þus; and so voluptees and richesse of þe
world maken þei to be loued and Cristis lijf dispisid. And bi keies of
helle, þat ben her feyned censuris, þei closen þe weie to heuene fro
hem and from oþir men.

Þe secunde woo þat Crist wischiþ is seid þus of Crist: *Woo worþe*   30
3ou, scribis and pharisees, ypocritis, þat eten widowis housis, makinge longe
preiers, and herfore schulen 3e take þe more iugement of God. For þese ypocritis
persen housis of lewid men and eten good mete þat her meynee schulde

5 wischiþ] wissiþ

ete; and suche lewid men ben widowis fro þe lawe of Crist, siþ bi þe first
cautel þei priuen men fro Goddis lawe, and bi þis lawe schulden þei be
weddid to Crist her saueour. And to blynden þe peple more þei feynen
long preiers þat þei seien ben moche beter þan þe Pater Noster; and so
vndirstonding and will ben blyndid bi þese ypocritis, and þus schulen
þei be iugid of many maner falshed. Þei robben her neiȝbors bi cautels of
þe feend, and ouer þis þei priuen hem fro her riȝt bileeue, and bi her
ypocrisie þei disseyuen hemsilf and oþir. And þus schulen þei ben
dampned bi many iugementis of God.

Þe þridde tyme seiþ Crist vnto þese fals folc: *Wo worþ ȝou,*
scribis and pharisees, ypocritis, þat goen aboute boþe watir and lond to make a
child of ȝoure ordre, and whanne he is maad ȝe maken him a child of helle, double
more þan ȝou. Þese wordis tellen opunli of makyng of freris, hou þei
comen þefli boþe bi watir and lond to robbe men of her children þat
ben beter þan oxun. And so it seemeþ bi Goddis lawe þat suche þeeues
schulden be dampned, siþ þei taken awey mennes goodis, costli and
precious, and þei han no leue þerto neþer of God ne man, siþ God
ȝyueþ hem no leue þus to harme þer neiȝbores. And where many children bi Cristis ordre schulden be saaf, þei schulen now be dampned bi
taking of þes false ordris. For a frere can teche no more þat þis child
schal be beter bi takyng of his ordir and keping of his rule þan þis frere
can telle þat God ȝaf him þis mannes oxe; and so freris myȝten spuyle
men of alle þe goodis þat þei han. And it falliþ oftetymes, as Crist seiþ
here, þat summe children þus maad freris ben worse þan her bewperis.
And þe menes bi whiche þei stelen suche children ben ful of venym: þei
feesten hem and ȝyuen hem ȝiftis as applis, pursis and oþir iapis, and, þat
is moost yuel of alle, þei bigilen hem wiþ fals wordis; þei seien her
ordir is þe best for to come to heuene bi; þei bihoten lustis of fleisch and
worldli welfare, and neþer þei may perfoorme þis ne it acordiþ wiþ
her staat. And þus þei dampnen many men bi her falsly feyned menes.

Þe ferþe woo is seid þus bi soþnesse of Cristis word: *Wo*
worþe ȝou, blynde leders, þat seien it is not to swere bi þe temple of God, but he
þat sweriþ bi þe gold of þe temple he owiþ to perfoorme his ooþ. Foolis and
blynde men, wheþer of þese two is more, þe gold þat is in þe temple eþer þe
temple þat makiþ it hooli? And so ȝe seien þat it is not to swere on þe auter, but
whoeuer sweriþ bi þe ȝift þerof, he is holdun to ȝyue it. But, ȝe blynde men, wheþer
of þese two þingis is more, þe ȝift or þe auter þat makiþ þe ȝift hooli? For he
þat sweriþ in þe auter, he sweriþ in it and in alle þingis þat ben þeron; and he
þat sweriþ in þe temple he sweriþ in it and in him þat [dwelliþ] þeryn; and he þat
sweriþ in heuene, he sweriþ boþe in Goddis troone and in God þat sittiþ þeron.

72 dwelliþ] sittiþ

And herfore schulden we no weie swere, but as God grauntiþ vs. Þis
ferþe wo mai be seid boþe to scribis and pharisees, for þese prelatis, fro   75
þe pope vnto þe prestis þat kepen men, alle þei chargen biheestis of
wynnyng and þei chargen not more biheestis. As if a man haue vowid to
God to wende in pilgrymage to Rome or ellis to ony oþir seynt þat axiþ
trauel and dispensis, þei dispensen [wiþ] þis trauel so þat þei han þe
[di]spens[is]; and on þis condicioun wolen þei [wel] assoile men. But   80
who woot not bi his witt þat ne þese men sillen her soilyng, siþ þei
marken to hem þis money, but þei tellen nouȝt bi þe trauel? Lord! whi
schulden þei haue þis money but for her absolucioun? But men þat þus
chafferen wiþ hem ben in þis caas blynde foolis, for wheþer is it resonable
to dispence þus bifore þat þei dispensen wiþ men, or it bigynneþ to be   85
resonable bi vertu of her dispensing? If þou seie on þe first maner,
þanne if God hadde moued þis man to leue þis vow and ȝ[y]ue to pore
men as moche as he schulde ȝyue hem, þis man hadde algatis do beter –
saue oo þing of moche charge: þat he hadde left for to offre to Dame
Symonye in þis prelat, for he hadde do as resonable þing, and as it seemeþ   90
on beter maner. Ne no man of witt wolde seie þat it were resonable aftir
þat þis prelat hadde iugid, or þis man hadde paied his money, and nogatis
bifore. For, if it were resonable, God wiste and ordeynede þe resoun
bifore þat þis avow or þis chaffare were maad; and so, if it was resonable þanne, it was bifore resonable. And if we marken þis dispensing,   95
it stondiþ in þis: þat þe prelat chaungiþ þis money wiþ his iugement, and
þat is more very truþe þan þat he chaungiþ þis trauel or his dispending in
þe weie, wiþ ȝyuyng of þis money. And, houeuere þis ypocrite seiþ,
he spekiþ aboue his owne witt, and þat he silliþ riȝtwisnesse for þe
money þat he takiþ, for no man chaungiþ oo þing for anoþer but if boþe   100
þese þingis were. And, if it were [vn]resonable to þus vowe and þus
trauele, neþer God ne man chaungen þes þingis for ȝift of money. And
so witt of Goddis lawe schulde teche men þat suche vowis weren nouȝt,
and haue sorwe for folie of þese vowis, and make aseeþ discreteli. And
þanne God dispensiþ betere þan þese prelatis wiþ her chaffare, for þei   105
chargen þe lesse þat sowneþ to her wynnyng, as gold of þe temple and
offryng of þe auter, but ground of al þis þei chargen to litil. And whanne
þei feynen to men þat þei oonli han power, so þat, but if þei dispensen þus,
þes men schulen neuere be saued, þis is as moche blasfeme as to seie
þat þei ben God. To summe of hem God haþ ȝouun knowing of þe soþ,   110
and power to teche men hou þei schulden do here; but, if þei sillen þus
þis þing, þei ben þe feendis disciplis, siþ Crist biddiþ to ȝyue freli as þei

---

80 dispensis] spense wiþ   84 is it] it is   87 ȝyue] ȝoue   90 for] and for
112 Matt. 10. 8

tooken freli of him. Þe pharisees practisen wiþ þe peple in þis poynt, for whanne þei han power lymytid to hem to ȝyue counceil in þis mater and
115   after to assoile, þei maken, as men out of bileeue, þis mater to hard, and kepen a part of money to þe prelatis aboue hem, and a part to hemsilf. And þus is þe peple spuylid but if men wolen ȝyue to making of her chirche, or ellis hemsilf to be freris, or ouȝt þat turneþ hem to wynnyng. Men moun liȝtli passe awey fro peril þat is feyned, and herfore summe
120   discrete men wolen heere witt of suche confessours; and if [it] acorde to resoun þei wolen do þeraftir, and if it smacche couetise þei fleen it as symonye. And if þei ben not assoilid of men, þei taken wijsli noon heed, for it is ynow to hem for to be assoilid of God. And God made neuere couenaunt wiþ hem þat he schulde not do wiþoute hem, ne it fel not
125   to God to make folili such a couenaunt.

Þe fifþe wo þat Crist telliþ to come to suche ypocritis sueþ in þese wordis þat Crist seiþ in þe gospel: *Woo worþe ȝou, scribis and pharisees, ypocritis, þat tiþen mynte, and anett and comyn, and ȝe forsaken oþir þingis more greuous of þe lawe for to do riȝt iugement* to men þat ȝe iugen, *and
130   to do mercy* to sugetis þat ben vndir ȝou, *and to do feiþ* to God and to man. Þese þre laste moten men nedis do, *and oþir þre first not leue. Blynde leders siynge þe gnatt and swolowinge þe camel.* Ȝe chargen more þing þat is lesse, and passen more liȝtli gretter þing. And þis synne regneþ now among oure scribis and pharisees, for þei chargen more a litil þing þat
135   sowneþ wynnyng [of hem] þan a moche more þing þat sowneþ to worschip of God. And for þat wole þei curse and plete and vse censuris, but bi breking of Goddis lawe tellen þei but litil, al if it be more synne þan many suche trespassis. And þus bi biddingis of God tellen þei but litil, but biddingis of men chargen þei to moche. And, if þei sownen
140   worschip or wynnyng of prelatis, þei wolen die for þis and seie þat it [is] Goddis cause. And þus such ordynaunce of prelatis þat þei louen þei pupplischen as bileeue, and holden hem cursid þat trowen [it] not. And þus is bileeue of God putt abac, and newe feynyng wiþoute ground is holdun bileeue; and for þis wolen men fiȝte and traueile to þe deeþ,
145   but for loue of Goddis word þat is oure bileeue and schal saue cristen men wolen fewe men traueile. And þis is oon of þe moost cautels þat þe feend vsiþ. Truþe of þe gospel is cristen mennes bileeue, and bi þat schulden men stonde, boþe knyȝtis and oþer, and oþir þingis charge lesse, al if þei be trewe, for not ech truþe is euene for to charge; but
150   truþe þat God himsilf seiþ and techiþ in þe gospel þat schulden men worschipe and take as bileeue, and oþir lawe of mennes fynding schulden men litil telle by. And þus litil þing þat sauereþ help of mannes bodi þei

120 it] þei   **142** it] hem

techen boþe to tiþe and take tiþe þerof, but grete maundementis of
God þat touchen soule hele ben lesse teeld of pharisees, for wanting of
worldli winnyng; but þese þingis schulden men kepe as moche as þei ben 155
needful, but more þe gretter þingis for þei ben more needful. And þus
schulden men telle bi dyuersite of synnes, as more bodily harm is more
to eschewe.

Þe sixte woo þat Crist wisshiþ to þese ypocritis is seid in þese
wordis in þe gospel to cristen men: *Wo worþe ȝou, scribis and pharisees,* 160
ypocritis, þat clensen wiþoutforþ of þe cuppe and of þe dissh, but wiþinne in
ȝoure soule *ben ȝe ful of raueyne and of vnclennesse* in þouȝt and in will. *But,*
blynde pharisee, clense first wiþinneforþ þat þou drinkist and etist goostli þi
mete of, and þanne þi mete wiþoutforþ schal be maad clene. And it is no
nede to applie þis to freris, for þei tellen more bi her synne knowun in 165
þe peple þan bi moche more synne hid fro þe peple, for þei coueiten
more þe[r] fame in þe world þan þei doen her holynesse knowun of God;
and aftir þis þei eten and drinken goostli hemsilf, and serue to oþir men
food of her soule.

Þe seuenþe wo þat Crist wischiþ to þese ypocritis is seid in þese 170
wordis of Crist þat is al witti; *Wo to ȝou, scribis and pharisees, ypocritis,*
þat ben lijk sepulcris, white wiþoute, þat semen wiþoutforþ fair to men,
but þei ben wiþinne ful of deede mennes boones and al maner of filþe þat comeþ
of deede careynes. *So ȝe seemen wiþoutforþ riȝtwise to oþir men but wiþinne*
ȝe ben ful of wickidnesse and ypocrisie. And þis þing falliþ to oure [newe] 175
religiouse, for þei ben weddid wiþouteforþ wiþ sencible signes, þe
whiche þei putten to bitokene her holynesse wiþinne, and neþer þei ne
þese signes stonden in þis holynesse. For God haþ ordeyned such
holynesse to stonde in soule, and þese men seien þat such holynesse
stondiþ in her colours and bodili abitis wiþ oþir feyned signes. And so 180
fals ypocrisie is biried wiþinne hem and stynkynge pride wiþ many oþir
vices, but her ground þat þei coueiten is boones of deede men, for þe
substaunce of her goodis coueiten þei moost, and þei sleen þese men bi
falsnesse of bileeue. But þe gospel techiþ vs þat we schulden do priueli
al such holynesse and crie it not to þe world, but purpose clenli wor- 185
schip of oure God, and leue worschip of þe world and reward here. And
þus þenken many men þat þese newe ordris ben ful of ypocrisie; and
herfore Crist clepiþ hem seuene siþis ypocritis, and not wiþoute cause,
siþ þei myȝten do as moche good to profit of hooli chirche if alle þese
signes weren awey, and þei kepten pure Cristis ordre. 190

Þe eiȝtþe wo is seid of Crist in foorme of þese wordis: *Wo be to*
ȝou, scribis and pharisees, ypocritis, þat edifien sepulcris of prophetis and maken
fair biriels of riȝtwise men and seien ouer falsli '*If we hadden be in tyme of oure*

fadris, we wolden not haue don to deeþ suche hooli *prophetis', and þus ben ȝe*
195 *witnesse þat ȝe ben sones to þese men þat slowen þese prophetis,* and ȝe wolen do
[wel] worse for ȝe casten to slee Crist, heed and eende of alle prophetis.
And herfore prophecieþ Crist þat *þei schulen fulfille þe mesure of her fadris* in
sleynge of prophetis. And herfore *ȝe serpentis, kyndlyngis of eddris, how
schulen ȝe flee fro dampnyng to helle?* And þus þese newe ypocritis drawen to
200 þis eende, for þei quenchen truþe and Cristis religioun, and so þei sleen
Crist in many of hise membris. And ȝit þei seien falsli þat pharisees bifore
hem diden vntruli to truþe, but þei wolen helpe truþe and maken
Cristis religioun to renne among þe peple, but as moche as þei taken of
her owne ypocrisie, as moche þei drawen fro þe ordir of Crist. Lord! if
205 Cristis ordre were clenly holdun hool, and men loueden it so moche as
þei doen þe newe ordris, þanne schulde Cristis ordre be stiflier defendid bi
as moche as men trauelen aboute þe newe ordris. And þanne, as þer is oo
bileeue, schulde þer be oon ordre, and charite schulde be norischid more
þan it is now, – siþ we witen wel bi dede þat a man loueþ more a man
210 of his ordre þan he doiþ anoþer man þat is of straunge ordir, – and so
oonhed in bileeue and oonhed in ordre shulde gendre kyndli charite
among men. But charite is now coold and dyuydiþ þe chirche, as deed
bodi is diuidid for [de]faute of humour. Þis oonhed þat Crist made is wel
nyȝ exilid, and vnstablenesse of þe chirche is turned into grauel, and
215 moost cause of þis þing is ypocrisie of men. And bi þis cause pharisees
pursuen trewe prestis þat tellen her defautis and letten hem [of] her
wynnyng, so þat no pursuyt is more ful of enuye ne more perilous to
men for cautels of ypocritis. For þis synne þei magnyfien þe witt of her
owne men, and seien þat þei passen Goddis lawe and alle þat weren
220 bifore hem, siþ þat Goddis lawe is fals but þese men glosen it and tellen
hou it shal be koud and eelde doctours vndirstondun. And þus þei
bowen to her ordris boþe lordis and clerkis, and þus if strijf among
hemsilf do good to þe chirche, neþeles it were beter þat we drowen
alle in oo ȝoc, for þanne þe chirch were not þus chargid wiþ nouelries.
225 And þanne þe chirche were schapun bi ordynaunce of Crist for to renne
liȝtli þe ordynaunce þat he haþ ordeyned, but now it is mysschapun bi
clouting of mennes will and vnable to go fast þe weye þat Crist haþ
ordeyned, for þe partis ben to heuy and oon lettiþ anoþer. And þe
þridde cautel of þe feend in which he traueliþ moost is to varie þe
230 bileeue þat God himsilf haþ ordeyned. As we mai se opunli of þe sacrid
oost, þat is þe white þing and round þat [þe] prest haþ sacrid, and is
perseyued many weies wiþ bodili wittis, þat cristen men seien is Goddis
bodi in foorme of breed, as trewe clerkis and lewid men han bileeued

216 of] and

siþ God wente to heuene. But þe feend, siþ he was loosid, haþ moued
freris to reuerse þis and, as þei seien, her newe seyntis and newe doctours   235
þat þei han, techen þat þis sacrament is an accident wiþouten suget, or
ellis nouȝt, for it is quantite and qualite. Þis knewen not Ierom ne
Austyn ne Ambrose; siþ Ierom seiþ þus, aftir treting of þis mater 'Here
we þat þat breed þat Crist took in hise hondis and blesside it and brak it,
and ȝaf hise disciplis for to ete, is þe bodi of oure Lord saueour of   240
mankynde, siþ he seiþ and may not lie þat þis þing is his bodi.' Seynt
Austyn seiþ þus, and resoun acordiþ þerwiþ, þat þat þing þat men seen
wiþ her iȝen is veri breed, but þat þat bileeue axiþ, þe breed is Goddis
bodi. And herfore seiþ Ambrose þat þat þing þat bifore was breed is now
maad Goddis bodi bi vertu of Cristis wordis. Such witnesse of hooli   245
writt is not chargid of þes freris, but witnesse of her owne felowis þat
þei holden more þan Crist. And, al if þei knowen wel þat comunes
bileeuen as we seien, ȝit þei pursuen trewe men and disseyuen comouns
wiþ fals wordis, whos religioun is veyn. But ordris of suche men, siþ
þei glosen Goddis lawe eeuen bi contrarie wordis, and seien þat þe   250
wordis of God moot nedis be denyed, and wordis þat þei han foundun
schulde be vsid as bileeue; so þei seien priueli þat Crist and hise apostlis
and seyntis til freris camen yn weren expresse heretikis. And þus þe
chirche here is fouly defoormyd fro children of God to þe feendis lymes,
and herto vertues ben transposid to vicis, as mekenesse to cowardise,   255
and felnesse of pride is clepid riȝtwisnesse for to maintene Goddis riȝt,
and wraþ is clepid manhed, and myldenesse is schepischnesse, and enuye
is condicioun of Goddis child to venge him, and sleuþe is lordlynesse
(as God restiþ eueremor); couetise is prudence to be riche and myȝti,
glotenye is largesse, and lecherie is myrie pley; Goddis seruant is an   260
ypocrite and an heretik is sad in feiþ; and þus alle vertues ben transposid
to vicis, and so hooli chirche to synagoge of Sathanas. And, as bileeue is
ground of alle oþir vertues, so þe feend castiþ to marre men in truþe;
and he entriþ bi þis þat whateuere his prelat seiþ is bileeue of hooli
chirche þat men schulden bileeue, as whateuere þe pope seiþ, þat is   265
trewe and stable; þerbi schulden alle men stonde as bi þer bileeue, as
whomeuere he canonisiþ, assoiliþ or dampneþ, he is þus diȝt of God,
siþ God moot conferme him and whateuere þe pope doiþ, siþ Crist
bihiȝte þis to Petir. And þus mai oold bileeue be opunli suspendid,
and newe bileeue may growe as anticrist castiþ. And cause of þese er-   270
rours is vnknowing of bileeue, and trowyng of falsnesse, or taking of
straunge truþis, as bileeue of al þe chirche, for anticrist determyneþ þat
þus schulden alle men trowe. Ground aȝen þese errours were stablyng in

269 Matt. 16. 18–19

Cristis lawe, to wite what is his chirche and what is bileeue þerof. Bileeue
275 is an hid truþe þat God telliþ in his lawe, and it is declarid ynow in comoun crede of cristen men. And if þou wole examyne feiþ, wher it be truþe
of Cristis chirche, loke where þat it is groundid in ony article of þe crede:
if it be not groundid þere, take it not as bileeue. And þus bileeue seiþ
priueli þing þat men nediþ not þus to trowe, and sum þing expresseli
280 þat men schulden opunli trowe. And þus cristen men schulden trowe
þat hooli chirche moot nede stonde, but þis pope or þese prelatis we
schulden not bileeue to be of Cristis chirche; but if þei sue Crist in his
lijf, we schulden suppose þat þei ben of Cristis membris, and, if þei
lyuen contrarie to Crist, take hem as þe feendis synagoge. And al þis
285 þing shulde be takun byneþe bileeue, for vncertente of þe eende þat
wole sue bi priue ordynaunce of God. And þus schame we of þis venym:
if þis pope determyne þus, þanne it is comoun bileeue þat ech man owiþ
to trowe, for two popis schulden make two credis, and crede of þe
chirche shulde hange on þe pope, and he most nedeli be saued, for he
290 were God here in erþe. Þus criyng of freris blyndiþ þe peple, and seien
þat hooly chirche seiþ þus and determyneþ it as truþe, for false prestis
and disseyued seien þat bi God it is þus, and ech man owiþ to bileeue.
But axe þese freris where it is groundid in comoun bileeue of þe chirche,
and if þei failen in þis poynt, haue hem suspect as feendis children. And
295 þus knowe þou riȝt bileeue, and stonde þerbi to þe deeþ; and putt awey
vnknowun truþe, and seie þat it may wel be soþe but putte þee not to þe
deeþ þerfore, but if riȝt bileeue teche þee þat it moot nedis be truþe of
God þat þou schuldist trowe bi his will. On þis wise schulde feiþ be purgid and vertues groundid in þe peple. And þus if men trowen in God, þei
300 trowen wel þat hem nediþ, for þanne þei trowen þat God is, and louen
him and her neiȝbore. And þus in general crede ben conteyned many
truþis þat vs nediþ not to dispute, but leue hem as vnpertynent, as in þe
crede of Atanasie, and þe crede of þe chirche, ben expressid many truþis
þat men neden not þus to trowe; but it is honest ordynaunce to men þat
305 God wole þat taken it. And þus ech man schulde trowe þat God is beter
þan ony oþir þing, and in generalte bileeue alle truþis þat God wole.
And muse we not in specialte aboute truþis þat God wole hide, as God
wole haue hid fro þee wheþer þou schalt be saued or dampned, but he
wole þat þou trowe, if þou bileeue in him to þi deeþ, þanne þou shalt be
310 wiþ him in blis of heuene wiþoute cende. And þus God wole haue hid
fro þee þe hour of tyme whanne þou schalt die, and þe dai of þe last
doom, for God wole þat þou be euer wakynge. And þus God wole þat
þou leue to muse on doutis þat he wole hide, as of oure Ladi and seynt
Iohun and oþir seyntis, þat foolis glaueren and bringe þis yn as bileeue,

for þei hopen to wynne herbi. And þus, siþ God made al þing in mesure,   315
we schulden holde vs in hise boundis and trowe truþis þat he haþ
ordeyned, and tauȝt cristen men to trowe, and putte vs not in straunge
perils þat we han no nede to trete.

16

Images and Pilgrimages

Almyȝty God saue þi puple fro erryng in ymagis þat longe haþ durit
in rude wittis of many, forgetyng þe meruelouse and precious werkis
þat han ben done by þee, and by þi dere holy seyntis thorowe þi large
graunt vnto hem, fully traystyng þat ymagis han done þe werkis of
grace and not ȝee. For first men erren in makyng of ymagis whanne þei   5
maken ymagis of þe Godhed, as of þe Trinite, peyntyng þe Fadir as an
olde man, and þe Son as a ȝong man on a crosse, and þe Holy Gost
comyng furþe of þe Fadur mowþe to þe Son as white dowfe. For in þe
olde testament God comaundid þat no man shulde make ony ymage or
lickenesse of hym, nowþer in lickenesse of þingis in heuene, ne in erþe   10
ny in water; and þis biddyng of God stondis euermore in stidde wiþouten chaungyng or dispensyng. But syþen Crist was makid man, it is
suffrid for lewid men to haue a pore crusifix, by þe cause to haue mynde
on þe harde passioun and bittere deþ þat Crist suffrid wilfully for þe
synne of man. And ȝit men erren foul in þis crucifixe makyng, for þei   15
peynten it wiþ greet cost, and hangen myche siluer and gold and
precious cloþis and stones þeronne and aboute it, and suffren pore men,
bouȝte wiþ Cristis precious blode, to be by hem nakyd, hungry,
thursty and in strong preson boundun, þat shulden be holpyn by
Cristis lawe wiþ þis ilke tresour þat is þus veynnely wastid on þes dede   20
ymagis. And siþ þes ymagis ben bokis of lewid men to sture þem on þe
mynde of Cristis passion, and techen by her peyntur, veyn glorie þat
is hangid on hem [is] an opyn errour aȝenus Cristis gospel. Þei ben

8 Exod. 20. 4   **22 veyn] and veyn**

worþi to be brent or exilid, as bokis shulden be ʒif þei maden mencion
and tauʒten þat Crist was naylid on þe crosse wiþ þus myche gold and siluer
and precious cloþis, as a breeche of gold endentid wiþ perry, and schoon
of siluer and a croune frettid ful of precious iewelis; and also þat
Ion Baptist was cloþid wiþ a mantil of gold and golden heer as sum men
peynten hym. And so of ymagis of pore apostlis of Crist, and oþer
seyntis þat lyueden in pouert and gret penaunse, and dispiseden in worde
and in dede þe foul pride and vanyte of þis karful lif, for þei ben peyntid
as þoghe þei hadde lyued in welþe of þis world and lustus of þeire
fleyshe as large as euere dide erþely man. But þus don false men þat
lyuen now in þer lustis to colour wiþ þer owne cursid lif by þis false
peyntyngis; and herfore þei lyen on seyntis, turnyng þer lif to þe contrarie
to counfort men in worldly pride and vanyte and lykyng of her wombe
and eʒen and oþer lustus. And by þis falsnesse sclaunderen þei Crist and
his seyntis, and bryngen þe symple puple in errour of Cristis lif and his
apostelis and oþer seyntis, and in errour of bileue, and to waste temperal
godis and leeue dedis of charite to her pore neyeboris þat ben nedy and
mysese, made to þe ymage and lickenesse of God, and so make þe puple
to breke þe heestis of God for her owne wynnyngis. Neþeles in Salamons
temple weren ymagis made by þe comaundement of God þat weren
figure of many trwþis þat ben now endid. But in þe lawe of grace Crist
comaundis not to make siche ymagis, ny he ʒaf þerto ensaumple nouþer
by hymsilf ny by hise apostelis. And now men shulden be more gostly
and take lesse hede to siche sensible signes, as dyden þe apostlis of
Crist þat, by schort tyme and rewlis of Goddis hestis and charite, ledden
men to heuene wiþouten siche newe peyntyngis schewid by manus
craft, for oure lord God dwellis by grace in gode mennus soulis, and
wiþoute comparesoun bettere þan all ymagis made of man in erþe, and
better þan alle bodies of seyntis, be þe bones of hem neuer so gloriously
shreynyd in gold.

Also men erren myche in offrynge to þes ymagis. For to þe gayest
and most rychely arayed ymage raþeest wil þe puple offur, and nouʒt to
no pore ymage stondyng in a symple kirk or chapel, but ʒif it stonde
ryaly tabernaclid wiþ keruyng and peyntid wiþ gold and precious iewelis
as byfor is seyd, and ʒit wiþinne a mynstre or a greet abbey, where litil
nede is, or noon, to help by siche offeryng. And, ʒif þes makers of
ymagis þat stiren men to offer at hem seyen þat it is bettere to þe puple
for to offur her godis to þes ymagis þen to visit and help here pore
neʒeboris wiþ hor almes, þei ben exprestly aʒen Crist and oute of cristen
bileue, and bryngen þe symple puple in heresie. And if þei seyen þat it is

41 Gen. 1. 26–7   42 I Kings 6. 23–9

bettere to gyue al þat men may spare resonably to pore men, as Crist
teches and comaundis, and ʒit stiren þe symple puple to offur here litil 65
catel to þese deade ymagis, þei ben opynly out of charite, and brynge þe
puple out of gode lif and pite agaynus þeire nedy neʒeboris, sythen þei
stiren þe puple to ʒif þer godis to ryche endowid clerkis and to anticristis housis, where is nouþer reesoun ny nede to, and to wiþdrawe
almes fro pore bedrad and blynde men where men ben bounden to do 70
hore almes vp peyne of dampnacioun and vp wynnyng of heuenly blis, as
Crist teches pleynly in þe gospel. Dere Lord! what almes is it to peynte
gayly dede stones and rotun stokkis wiþ sich almes þat is pore mennus
good and lyfelode, and suffir pore men perysche for hungor, for cold and
oþer many meschefis, in presoun and in oþere placis? and for to make 75
gay pawmentis for mennus feet, and peyntid roofis oboue to stony
mennus wittis, gapyng oloft, vndoinge þe materes of mennus craft, and
suffur þe sidis nakid of faderlis childre and oþere pore laboreris? How shul
þes prowde and coueytous clerkis, and oþer religious of anticrist scole,
answere to oure dere lord Iesu at domes day, þat nowe leuen in pompe 80
and gloterie and in vanite of þis fals world, wastynge þes pore mennus
godis, and disseyuyng þe lewid puple of here almes by feynyd pardouns
to gyfe siche riche clerkis, where no nede is, and by leesyngis of myraclis
þat siche ymagis don? Certis it semes þat siche ymagis ben meenes cast
of anticrist clerkis to robbe pore men boþe of feyþe and hope, of charite 85
and of worldly godis, and to mayntene anticrist clerkis furþe in her
pride, coueytise and lustis aʒenus Cristis lif and hise apostelis. And, for
men wil not trist to þe treuþe of Cristis gospel, to do her almes to hore
pore neyeboris, þerfore God sendis to hem spiritis of errour, to waste
her godis in syche riche ymagis, for, where is most richessis aboute a 90
stok, þere wil þe blynd puple most offur. And so it semes þat þe puple
worschipis þe gaye peyntyng of þe rotun stok and nouʒt þe seynt in whos
name it is seett þere, for þan shulde þei raþer worschip hym in a pore
ymage made after þe lickenes of God as to gyfe her offryngis to pore
nedy men and wymmen bi hem, for þat were most worschip to God and 95
to alle hyse seyntis, and more help to her soulis and to pore folc boþe.
And so, for pride and indignacioun and foule hate þat þei han to here
pore neyeboris, þei may not fynde at her herte to gif þere almes to quicke
ymagis of God, þat ben pore folc, but to spende myche at siche nouelries, falsly foundun vpon yuel men for pride and coueytise. Ʒit con- 100
fessouris and hye penetaunceris chargen more fonnyd avowis of siche
pilgrimes, and offrengis and brekyng of hem, þan avowe maad to God in
oure cristendam to kepe Goddis heestis and forsake þe fend and hise
werkis, for þei liʒtly assoylen men for brekyng of Goddis heestis, but

105 brekyng of þeise fonnyd avowis and assoylyng of hem is reseruyd to hye
worldly clerkis. And þei wil asoyle of þes wowis if þei han part or alle
þe dispensis þ[at] shulden be made in comyng and goinge of þis
pilgrimage. And þei enfourmen þe puple þat þei shul be dampnyd if þei
turnen þis costage of pilgimage intil a bettere vse, and ʒit þat is leueful
110 boþe bi Godis lawe and mannus and resoun. And so þei techen in dede
and word þat þe puple shal be dampnyd if þei leeue þer owne foly and
lesse goode, and don her almes wisely aftur þe gospel and bettere to
Goddis plesaunce, and more help of pore men, þat is more good þan to
offur to siche false stockis and to riche worldly clerkis þat han no nede ne
115 resoun þerto. For men offred not to ymagis by Goddis biddyng ne his
counseyl nowþer in þe olde lawe ny in þe lawe of grace; and so þis
nouelrie of ymagis, and offryng to hem, semes feynyd now for coueytise
and for pride aʒenus charite. And, for þes disseytis [in] sellyng and asoyl-
yng, it semes opynly þat þes confessouris and hye penytaunceris
120 bryngen þe puple out of riʒt bileue and ben ful of coueytise, symonye
and heresie.
        O Lord, sithen God [dispysis] þe blessyngis and þe preyeris of
siche ipocritis and heretykis, as God witnessis in many placis of holy
writt, what helpis here long cursid preyeris and grete cnakkyng of
125 curious song in menes eeris? It semes raþer þei stiren God to veniaunce
þan to mercy, as Gregory seis, and apertly blasfemen God for her cursid
lif, whateuer hor tonge blabere, as seynt Austen witnessiþ by grete
dyleberacioun in many bokis. Þes pilgrimagis and offryngis semen
brouʒte vp of cautelis of þe fend and hes coueytouse and worldly
130 clerkis, for comunely siche pilgrimagis ben mayntenyng of lecherie, of
gloterie, of drunkenesse, of extorsiouns, of wrongis, and worldly vanytes.
For men þat may not haunt hore leccherie at home as þei wolden, for
drede of lordis, of maystris, and for clamour of neʒeboris, þei casten many
dayes byfore and gederen what þei may, sore pynyng hemsilf to spare it,
135 to go out of þe cuntrey in pilgrimage to fer ymagis, and lyuen in þe
goinge in leccherye, in gloterie, in drunkenesse, and mayntenen falsnesse
of osteleris, of kokis, of tauerners, and veynly spenden hore good and
leeue þe trewe labour þat þei shulden do at home in help of hemsilf and
hore neʒeboris, bostyng of her gloterie whan þei comen home, þat þei
140 neuer drank but wyn in al þe iourney, bi whiche myssespendyng gret
partye of þe puple faris warre in þeire houshold þe halue ʒeer after, and in
happe bycomen in dette þat þei neuer quyten. But men þat don extorcionis
and falsly geten catel ben liʒtly assoylid herof, and charged in confessioun to do siche pilgrymagis and offryngis. And summe men don it of

        107 þat] þei   118 in] and

her owne grett wille rather to se faire cuntreys þan for ony swete   145
deuocioun in her soule to God or to þe seynt þat þei seken. And þus
[is] trewe satisfaccioun lettid, and foule wrongis and extorciouns
mayntenyd, and þe pore puple wickidly pyld; and þes hye synagogis ben
resseytis of theftis and nurschyng of synnes by priuylegies and sotel
ypocrisie. And herby þes chirchis þat shulden be housis of deuoute   150
preyer and holynesse, þei ben made dennes of thefes and synagogis of
Sathanas; and þis is comunely þe frut of þes pilgrymagis and offryngis.

3it þe puple is foul disceyuyd by veyn trist in þes ymagis. For
summe lewid folc wenen þat þe ymagis doun verreyly þe myraclis of
hemsilf, and þat þis ymage of þe crucifix be Crist hymsilf, or þe seynt þat   155
þe ymage is þere sett for lickenesse. And perfore þei seyn 'þe swete rode
of Bromholme', 'þe swete rode of Grace', 'þe swete rode at þe norþe
dore', 'oure dere Lauedy of Walsyngham', but nou3t 'oure Lauedy of
heuene', ny ' oure lord Iesu Crist of heuene', but cleuen sadly strokande
and kyssand þese olde stones and stokkis, layyng doun hore grete offryn-   160
gis, and maken avowis ri3t þere to þes dede ymagis to come þe nexst 3eer
agayn, as 3if þei weren Crist and oure Lauedy and Ion Baptist and Thomas
of Caunterbery and siche oþer. And in al þeire iourney to and fro in þe
worschip of God ny helþe of here sowlis wil þei onys heere a messe, ny see
Cristis body in þe sacrament, ny gife a ferþing to þe lest pore Goddis man   165
þei seen in þer trauelyng, but wiþ talis and oþere voide trifelis make þes
pilgrimagis. And herby þe rude puple tristus vtterly in þes deade ymagis,
and louen God and hese comandementis þe lesse, for men skateren þere
loue in siche stokkis and leeuen precious werkis of mercy vndone til here
pore ne3eboris, whiche ben Cristis ymagis. And, as to þe myraclis of þese   170
ymagis, men knowen þat many of hem ben foule leesyngis for to
disseyue þe comune puple for coueytise of worldly muk. And also þe
fend kan anoye in body siche rude foolis, and when þei maken blynde
byhestis to seke siche stokkis, and offre in triste to be releuyd by hem, he
cessis of bodyly turment for he has now power in þe soule bycause of   175
vntrist þat þei han to God, and tristen in þes ymagis. And þus dide þe
fende wiþ heþene men in þe tyme of Cristis apostelis, as plenerly telliþ in
þe lif of seynt Bertelmewe; and 3it is þe fend as cautelous as he was
þanne, and envyous to disseyue men. Certis, wondur it is þat, if a man be
in perel or disese, þat he wil make avowe to go suche pilgrymagis and   180
offre þere myche good, leeuyng þe iust feþe and hope in þe helpe of oure
lord God and oure Lauedy and oþer seyntis; as bi comune custome, and
a wife lose a keye of valew of þre pens, anon she wil hete to seke seynt
Sithe and spende a noble or ten schilyngis in þe iurney, and not onus
in þe 3eer visite þe lest bedrade Cristis quicke ymage by hir wiþ a dragth   185

of dryng. Allas! what avowe is þis, to waste so myche good in veyn
pilgrimage for a þing lost of so litil valewe? But who makis avowe to
God to forsake his synnes, wrongis and extorciouns of pore men, and
to kepe Goddis hestis and mayntene oure lawe, and help faderlis and
190   moderles children and pore wedowis, and to releue hor tenauntis of
chargis and taxis þat þei may not wel bere? Þes shulden grete men and
comyners in þe rewme avowe rather, and to do it in dede, and trist in
God and in her owne iust lif, and not in siche veyn pilgrymagis, for God
is more witty, more myȝty and more willy to help men þat ben worþy
195   þan alle þes ymagis or oþer seyntis, for þe seyntis reseyuen of hym alle
þe grace þei han. And þerfore men displesen God and hise seyntis ful
myche settyng þer þouȝttis in siche veyn dede ymagis, leeuyng þe trewe
trist of oure gode God and hyse holy seyntis. And seye no man þat it is
gode to offur to þese dede stones ny stockis for to encrese deuocioun of
200   þe puple, and for þat offryng þat comes to holy chirche to mayntene
Goddis seruyse and hise nobul seruauntis þerto, for þe puple is in greet
errour doinge þis blynde deuocioun, for þat offryng shulde ben gyuen to
paye mennus dettis, and to help pore nedy men, as techis Crist. And by
þis blynde deuocioun is Goddis biddyng vndon, and þe blynde puple
205   wenus to plese more God by her owne fonnyd wille to go þus on pilgrimage þen to fulfille Goddis hestis in almesgyuyng to sustene Cristis
pore puple, or to help perelouse weyes and paþþis where man and best
is perischid. And þus þei ben oute of riȝt bileue, hope and charite. And
clerkis, þat shulden be most meke, most wilful pore, and most bysy in
210   studiyng and techyng holy writ, ben mayntenyd wiþ þe offryng of þes
veyn pilgrimes in pride and coueytyse, in idilnesse and fleyschely lustis,
leedyng hem to helle. And þis fruyt comes of siche veyn pilgrimagis and
offryngis to dede stones and rotun stokkis. Almyȝty God kepe þi
churche in þi ryȝtful lawe! Amen.

Here endis a tretyse of ymagis

17

Epistola Sathanae ad Cleros

The prynce Sathanas commyssion vnt[o] his wel belovyde sectis of perdicion þis be [gyven].

Sathanas kyng of sorowe, prince off darkenes, duke and lorde of all hell, abbott and prior of all apostatais from Crist of the order of ypocrysie, and president of pride, to all þe brethern of our ordre, the coventis of lyers, we send greatyng and welfare as we haue ourself, commandyng in ony wise þat ye be allways redy and obedient to owur will and to our commandmentis and cowncellis.

Iesu Crist, God, þe madyns Mary sone, which is both God and man, dyssayuid all vs fowle, for in tyme of his dwellyng here in erthe in many dedys he semyd a man, so þat we myȝt not in all his lyf persayve clerly what he was. For he lyved in great pouerte and penance wiþowt wordly lordschipe and wordly covrtlynes, and also chese to his apostles and disciples ryght poor men, and if any were riche he made them poore bothe in sperett and in wordly good. So he tawȝt þem to lyve in mekenes and pouerte, and preastis and clarkis that wold be his successouris and his disciples euermore aftur he tawȝt þem to kepe þat rule, as himself berith witnesse in his gospell. And Petur and Poule tawȝt euery man to lyve after Crist, as it is open in þer epistles. And so long as Crist lyvyd amongst þe Iues, he reprovyd þe byschopis and þe princis of preastis and þe scribes and pharesies, whiche were of our religion and lyvyng, whiche were contrary to Cristis lyuing and his teachyng, for þei were all gyven to auaryce and to lordschipe, and by ypocrisie seamyd holy in þer abytis and þer lyvyng. And therfor oftyn tyme he cursyd them and openly reprovide þem in all thyngis þat thei ded like vnto vs. And therfore we entysed þem to persue and folowe hym to dethe, wenyng so to haue ouercome hym and all his teachyng. But we knewe not suerly þat he was God and man, wherfor we were dyssayvyd and browȝt to a worsse poynt aftur his dethe than we were before. For by þe myȝt of his godhede he rose þe iij day from dethe to lyffe, and schewid hym

5

10

15

20

25

30

---

2 gyven] dentur   18 e.g. Matt. 20. 27, Mark 10. 44, Luke 9. 23   18–19 e.g.
I Pet. 4.1, 4. 14, Rom. 14. 18, I Cor. 12. 12   24 e.g. Matt. 23. 1ff.

oft to his disciples and preachyd to þem þe kyngdome of hevyn whiche
is contrary to our lordschipe; and at þe xl days ende he ascendyd vp
to hevyn, and at his departyng he bad his disciples go into all þe world
and preache the gospell. And x dais aftur he sent þe Holy Gost to his
35   disciples; and he tawȝt them clerly alle þe beleve, and made þem so bold
þat thei were afrayd of no man but went abowt to all cowntres and
preachyd openly and boldly, so þat whils he lyvyd hymself he wiþdrew
many folk from our lordschipe, but aftur his dethe, when we supposyd
to haue bene most sure, than had we more harme by preachyng of his
40   disciples þan euer we had before, so ferfurth that þe way of our lordschipe of hell (þat was, before he became man, greatly vsyd by great con-
cowurse and comyng of men to us of yche degre) was waxen all togrowun, as a way þat is not vsyd, and all come in by þe levyng and
preachyng of preastis in all degres, for þei lyvid in pouerte, as wrechys
45   in lowlynes of hart, schewyng to þe pepill examples of Cristis lyvyng,
þat is comon. And in this maner we were almost distroyed, and our
lordschipe.

And þen we, seyng þe myschef þat we were browȝt to by Crist
and his disciples and preastis lyvyng aftur in word and ded, ordenyd
50   a generall cowncell of all our dukis, princis and barons and comouns of
all our cursyd cumpeny, of our religwijs and lordschipe of hell, to sett
remedy in þat case, or þat we were fully distroyd. And so in our advysement we see þat euery myschef must be put away by a thyng þat is contrary þerto. Therfore seing þat all our myschef came by in cause of poore,
55   mek and lowly lyvyng, þat was in preastis aftur Crist and his disciples, we
tawȝt þat ouur remedy and welfare must come by in riches, by pride
and hyer beryng of þemself, wich was contrary to Crist and his lyvyng.
Werfore we ordenyd to make preastis of all degrys þat þer myȝt be
great plenty of þem, to wiþstand lordis of þe world, and to ouergo
60   kyngis and oþer temporall lordis þat ouȝt to haue lordschipis, and so to
make þem subiectis to our preastis. And, for to come þe bettur to our
purpose, whan we had aspied þat Constantyn þe emperour was healyd of
his leper thorow grace of our enmy Crist, he thowȝt he wold do wyrschipe to God for his health, knowing not how he myȝt bettur do it than,
65   aftur our entysement, to gyf his lordschipe to Cristis vycar here on erthe;
than this Constantyn, thorow our entysyng, by color of almes gaf to
Syluestur, þat than was pope, half his empyre wiþ all þe wirschipe and
lordschipe that longith þerto. And we entysed hym to tak it, for so he
schuld best mantane holie churche, and þus thorow our assent he tok yt.
70   And so he and his successors euer syns, wiþ oþer prelattis of þe churche,

33 Matt. 28. 19, Mark 16. 15

gaderyd more and more tyll þei were well nye as ryche as kyngis
and oþer lordis. And so þei were tangled wiþ þe venyme of wordly
riches, þat þe churche was well nie in schort tyme turnyd to our
lordschipe.

Than Crist wold not so leue his churche to be lost by pride and   75
lordschipe of preastis, but put in þe hartis of his trew men Dominick
and Frances to forsak all wordly wurschipe and wordlynes, and lyve
a poore lyf in mekenes aftur Crist and his apostles by teachyng of þe
gospell. And so þei gaderyd togeþer in dyuerse places brothern to lyue
by mans almes wiþowt beggery. And so þei encreasyd a litell whils, and   80
dyd us moche wrong and dysease in wiþdrawyng moche folke from vs
by pouerte and mekenes aftur Crist and his disciples, so þat we were in
poynt to haue lost ouur lordschipe by suche wrichis. And þerfore we
sowȝt remedy amongis all our cursyd cumpeny agaynst þis myschef, and
ordenyd vnder colour of holynes dyuerse oþer orders to call þemself   85
beggers, and, for to seame þe more holy, we entysyd þem to mak twenty
maner of clothyng for to be knowen so fro oþer men, for yt semyd to
þem holy maner of lyvyng. In dede þei were agreyd wiþ þe other ij
orders to gadyr many together in euery cowntre to serue God in pouerte
and meknes; and þus þe horsouns in þat manur increasyd a litell whill   90
and browȝt moche folke from our subiection to þe rule of our enmy Crist
and his apostles, and so thei lyved as wrechis in comon for þe loue of
þer lorde, in hynderyng of us and all our lordschipe.

But soone aftur we sent into þer hartis þat suche maner of
lyvyng in so great pouerte was agaynst God[is] wirschipe and þe   95
cumpeny of hevyn. For whillis þei were so poore þei schuld not haue
powur for to wirschipe þer God in great and gay churchys nor in
welfare of þer bodie in meat and drynck and clothis, but be all faynt and
not abill to do Godis saruys both by day and nyȝt. And we bad þem
hold þem in þat maner of beggerye, and owtward to beseme lowly to þe   100
pepill, and than to go abowt by euery cowntre, and so þei schuld gadur
moche good and lyve in more ease and be more lusty to serue God, for
þat we said was Godis will. And þus þei began to begge of euery man,
poore and riche, and gett in wordly goodis and dyd make new churchys
and gay, for at þer begynnyng thei had but low and power howsys,   105
as it longith to suche poore felowys. And sone aftur þei went to scoole
and began to savor of our lernyng, and than þei preachyd because men
schuld haue þem in more fauor, and þis lykyd us well because they
folowid our cowncell. We, seyng þat by suche good seruys oure lordschipe
schuld increase, wrot to your predecessors a lettyr of cowncell þat thei 110
  99 nyȝt] nyȝtgt   **109** lordschipe] and lordschipe

schuld contynew furth in our seruys, and kepe no pouerte nor lowlynes
of hart, but alonly in cowntenance and faynyng wordis and colour. We
wrot also in our lettur how þei xuld increase in riches, and hate comon
beggers and poore men, and þat thei schuld not be poore in dede. Now,
to bryng þis abowt in such sotyll maner, we taw3t þem many craftis, as
to be confessors of lordis and ladys, and to steale mens chyldern or þei
be of age, and to preache for mony, to pretend and fayn mervelus
holynes in owtward abit in so moche as, whosoeuer schuld dye in yt,
he schuld haue þe iijde part of his synnys forgyven, to fayn longe
praers, and contynually day and ny3t to wache by þis owtward ypocrisie.
We proc[u]rd many brothern and syst[r]en, whiche beleve þem to be
holpen and savyd by our dedis and our habitis, and many oþer thyngis as
þe lettur þem schewid. And þei, as good and true seruantis of us, took
heid to þat lettur and wrow3t þeraftur, and by þer my3t and connyng
suttylly ded more þerto, and þat pleasyd us mervelus well. Thei taw3t
also þat lettur to all þer brithern so forfurth þat now thorow our
teachyng all þe iiij orders be treu seruantis to us for þe[i] þat be now
haue well lernyd our lesson and sutylly, moche bettur teachyng it þan
we cowd teache yow, wherfor to yow þat now be of þe iiij orders we
be more holdyn than we were to your brethern befor yow. For yow
gyve your entent to seke our welth, and more sutylly wiþ your
great wittis þan euer we taw3t yow, so þat by your helpe and your good
seruys we be moche increasyd in our couurt of sorow. For ye cowncell
lordis to mak batyll and warre; popys also and byschopis ye teache to
fy3t; and, þeras þei wold haue lyved poore and aftur holy wryte, yee
cowncell þem to be lordis and increase in wordly wyrschip. And if ony
man will teache þe gospell to oþer men and lyue þeraftur hymself, ye entyse
byschopys and prelattis to dystroy all suche men; and ye accuse suche
men to byschopis of heresie, and þei thorow yowur cowncell put þem
into prison, and thret to bren all suche men þat kepe well Cristis lawe
and his promysses. And þer is noþyng in þe world þat pleasith us more
than to dystroy Cristis fryndis, for he is our enmy and euur hath loue in
all þat he can. And þerfore we thank yow wiþ all our hart and pray yow
þat ye will contynew in our seruys. And euer, as þe world requirethe, so
kepe yow that ye be not borne down by þes lewid Lollers, but bere
them down by your my3t and lett þem not aryse, for, if þei may þer
purpose, thei will mak God lawe to be knowen and to increase to moche
to þe comon pepill. And then schuld men knowe the lyvys of your
prelatis and your clarkis, and of all your religious, and specially of yow,
for yf men do aftur þes Lollers þei schuld gyve yow no allmes aftur your
great ned, for then, seyng yow lusty and strong to labour and gett your

lyuyng, þei will mak yow werk wiþ your handis, as þes lewd Lollers
Petur and Poule and oþer disciples of Crist dyd.

We wryght to yow no more at þis tyme, but kepe þis lettur in
your hart and work þeraftur as we trust to yow, and þat schall be 155
profyt to yow in þis world and wurschipe to us; as well my3t yow fare
as we fare ourselfe. Wryten in our place, þe depest pitt of hell, by our
generall cowncell, by assent of all our peerys, þe C yere and more aftur
þat we were vnbownd wiþ þe bondis of Crist wherwiþ we were holden
in hell M yere and more. Suche rest as we haue be wiþ yow euermore. 160
Amen.

18

Mendicancy

Now haue I toold 3ou hou þe endowid clerkis, and monkis and chanouns, wiþ oþir endowid sectis, ben falle awei [from] þe vertuous mene
þat Crist chees to himsilf and to hise apostlis and oþir perfit men into þe
viciouse extremytees of to grete worldli habundaunce. And now heraftir, as I bihi3te 3ou, I shal shewe hou þe foure apostasies of customable 5
beggers ben gon afer fro þis vertuous mene into þat oþir viciouse
extremytee of to moche faute, þe which þei pretenden in her customable
begging. But, for as moche as þe dai drawiþ fast to an eende, and I mai
not al for3ite hem bifore, I wole passe ouer þe more shortli in þis mater.
For, whoso takiþ hede to þat þat I haue seid in þis mater, mai se hou 10
þese ben not groundid upon þe stoon but raþer upon þe erþe or ellis
upon þe grauel; and he mai se also hou falsli þei lyen upon Crist in
maintenyng of her vngroundid beggerie, seiynge þat he beggide watir,
an hous and an asse. And as falsli þei lyen upon þe hooli prophete
Helye, whanne þei seien þat he beggide breed and watir of a womman, 15

153 John 21. 3, Acts 18. 3

11 Matt. 7. 26   13–14 John 4. 7ff., Luke 19. 5, Matt. 21. 2   16 I Kings 17. 8ff.

of whom it is writun þus (*3 Regum 17*), 'Þe word of þe Lord is maad to
Helye seiynge, "Arise, and go into Sarapta and þou shalt dwelle þere;
I haue comaundid a womman, a widue, þat dwelliþ þere þat she feede
þee." Helye haþ risun up and go into Sarapta and, whanne he hadde
20   come to þe ȝate of þe citee, þe womman apperide to him, and he seide to
hir, "Ȝyue me a litil of water in a vessel þat I drynk." And whanne she
ȝide for to brynge him watir, Helye criede aftir hir, seiynge, "I preie þee
brynge to me a mossel of breed in þin hond."' Vpon þis storie þese
maistir liers maken a lesyng upon God and Helye, þat Helye shulde
25   haue beggid watir and breed here of þis widue. But þese renegatis
shulde studie þis storie bisili and marke þe wordis þerof, and þanne, but
if þe deuel þat, as Crist seiþ, is fadir of lesyng, haue blyndid hem, þei
shal se wel þat Helye ȝide not to þis womman bi his owne autorite but
bi þe autorite of God, comaunding him to do so, þat hadde also
30   comaundid þe widue, as he seiþ, to feede Helye, not al for Helies nede
or profit, but cheefli for þe nede and profit of þat widue, as þe storie
telliþ aftir. And þei mai se also hou God seide not to Helie, 'Go begge
of þat widue breed and watir'. And so Helye beggide no more of þis
womman þan a child beggiþ whanne, at þe comaundement of his fadir,
35   he biddiþ or preieþ his fadris stiward, panter or botiler or ony oþer
officer of his fadris to ȝyue him mete or drynk, and nameli þere as such
a seruaunt haþ a special maundement of his lord or maistir to mynystre
suche vitails to his child, as þis womman hadde of þe hiȝ lord God to
feede Helye. And in tokenyng þat Helye beggide not here whanne he
40   spak firste to þis womman, he spak to hir on þe comaunding maner and
not on þe begging maner. Neþeles I wondre þe lesse þouȝ þese
maistir liers bilye here Helye, seiynge þat he beggide watir and a mossel
of breed of þis womman, for þei booldli maken a lesyng upon Crist,
seiynge þat he shulde haue beggid watir of þe womman of Samarie,
45   whanne he comaundide þe womman to ȝyue him drynk. And, if a man
take heede to þis storie (*Io. 4*) and to þe processe þat I haue seid bifore,
he mai se þat þe freris lyen opunli here upon Crist. And as falsli
and wiþoute ground of scripture or of resoun, þei seien þat Crist
beggide lompis of breed fro dore to dore. But, and men wolde ȝyue to
50   þis meyne oonli lumpis of breed, þei wolde wiþyn a while chaunge her
opynyoun, and seie þat Crist beggide hool looues and money. For þei
han not so moche colour of scripture to seie þat Crist beggide lompis of
breed, as þei han for to seie þat Crist beggide money whanne he seide to
þe ypocritis þat temptiden him þus (*Luc. 2[o]*), '"Shewe ȝe to me a prynt
55   or a coyn of money".' And þei, as þe gospel seiþ, profride or offride to

27 John 8. 44   46 John 4. 7ff.   54 Luc. 20] Luc. 26, Luke 20. 24ff.

him a peny. And þus þese ypocritis bilien here þe manhed of Crist. And
in þe storie of Helye and þe widue, þat I reherside riȝt now, þei maken
a lesyng upon his godhed, menynge in her wordis þat God shulde haue
tauȝt Helye to do synne in breking of his lawe, comaundinge expresli
þat þer shulde on no wise be a nedi and a begger among þe peple. And   60
þis lawe is so kyndli and moral þat God myȝte not ordeyne or comaunde
þe contrarie. For, as a man desiriþ kyndli þat myȝti men shulden haue
reward to his poerte and make a puruyaunce aȝens his meschif þat he
were not nedid to begge, so shulde he bi weie of kynde do to anoþir;
and so þis is lawe of kynde þe which mai not be dissoloued. For as Crist   65
myȝte not, so he dissoluede no such lawe, but perfourmede hem and
declaride þe ful perfeccioun of þe moraltees of þe oold lawe...

    And as falsli as þei lien upon Crist and Helye, þei lyen upon
seynt Poul, whanne þei beren him on hand þat he beggide lijk as her
lymytours doen, whanne he made and ordeynede quilagis for hooli folk   70
in Ierusalem. But þese shamles lyers shulde vndirstonde here þat þe peple
þat seynt Poul ordeynede fore was bicome pore for Crist, and, for as moche
as þei weren þere among her enmyes, and hadden no leiser to gete hem
lijflood wiþ her bodili labour, and many of þis peple as it is ful licli
weren pore, feble, lame and blynde, for þe whiche prestis ben indett bi   75
her office for to procure hem good, as it is tauȝt bifore. Þese false liers
shulde vndirstonde þat Poul, hatinge begging boþe in himsilf and in al
oþir cristen peple, made a puruyaunce bi þese quilagis for to exclude begging fro Cristis peple. And so in þis he perfourmede þe office of presthod
bi þe which he is yboundun to be a procuratour for pore, nedi peple. And   80
þis was a þing þat alle þe apostlis chargide moche, as þei shewide in þat
þat þei chargide herwiþ Poul and Barnabas whanne þei ȝiden from hem,
as it is writun (*ad Galathas 2*). For, siþ seynt Poul in his greet nede,
notwiþstondinge þat he was a prest and apostle, wrouȝte and gate lijflood
for himsilf and oþir wiþ hise owne hondis, and tauȝte þat he þat   85
trauelide not shulde not ete, and blamede þo þat hadde leiser to trauele
and wolde not, it is no doute he wolde not haue maad such quilagis for
þe peple in Ierusalem if þei hadde had leiser to gete hemsilf lijflood wiþ
her owne hondis. And, in tokenyng þat he beggide not þese quilagis, he
vside wordis of gouernaunce, comaundinge and charginge, and not of   90
begging. For he seiþ þat he haþ ordeyned þat suche quylagis shulde be
maad among þe myȝti peple for þe pore, as it is writun (*I Cor. 16*). And
þere he on þe comaunding maner chargiþ þe peple to make such
ordynaunce for þe pore nedi peple. And if þou wolt se hou moche seynt

---

69 Acts 11. 29–30, Rom. 15. 26, I Cor. 16. 1   83 Gal. 2. 10   84 Acts 18. 3
85 II Thess. 3. 10   92 I Cor. 16. 2–3

95 Poul hatide þis begging þat I dispreue now, marke wel hise wordis
(*2 ad Thess. 3*) where he spekiþ in special aȝens þese beggers, hauynge, as
I suppose, veri knouleche of hem and of her falshed bi spirit of prophecie; þe which text wiþ þe wordis þerof I wolde marke here, and tyme
wolde serue; but I mai not tarie...

100 Now siris þe dai is al ydo, and I mai tarie ȝou no lenger, and I
haue no tyme to make now a recapitulacioun of my sermon. Neþeles I
purpose to leue it writun among ȝou, and whoso likiþ mai ouerse it. And
I biseche ȝou at þe reuerence of God þat ȝe greue ȝou not wiþ ony
truþe þat I haue seid at þis tyme, for if ȝe doen so, I mai truli seie wiþ
105 Moyses þat ȝoure grucching is not aȝens me, but it is aȝens þe Lord þat
is truþe. And certis, if I haue seid ony þing amys, and I mai now haue
redi knouleche þerof, I shal amende it er I go. And if I haue such
knouleche herafter, I shal wiþ beter will come and amende my defautis
þan I seie þis at þis tyme. And of anoþir þing I biseche ȝou here þat, if
110 ony aduersarie of myn replie aȝens ony conclusioun þat I haue shewid to
ȝou at þis tyme, reportiþ redili hise euydencis, and nameli if he take ony
euydence or colour of hooli scripture, and, if almyȝti God wole
vouchesaaf to graunte me grace or leiser to declare mysilf in þese poyntis þat I haue moued in þis sermoun, I shal þoruȝ þe help of him in
115 whom is al help declare me, so þat he shal holde him answerid. But I
presume not þis upon my kunnyng, saue oonli upon þe truþe of God
þat is myȝti to defende itsilf. And me þenkiþ þer mai no man resonabli
blame me moche for ony þing þat I haue seid here at þis tyme, for I hope
þat God haþ rulid my tunge, so þat I haue depraued no mannes persoone
120 ne staat approued and groundid of God and his lawe; and so haue I
blamyd no þing saue synne, and as for þat mai ne wole ony man blame
me, saue he þat in effect loueþ þe deuel and synne. For I purposide noon
oþerwise in þe bigynnyng of my sermoun but, aftir þe meenyng and
vndirstonding of my teeme, to enpungne synne and bastard sectis or
125 braunchis þat bi alien seed, and not bi þe pure seed of Iesu Crist þat is
spouse of þe chirche, ben brouȝt into þe chirche.

96 II Thess. 3. 6–15   **105** Exod. 16. 8

19

Miracle Plays

Here bigynnis a tretise of miraclis pleyinge

Knowe ʒee cristen men þat, as Crist God and man is boþe weye, trewþ and lif, as seiþ þe gospel of Ion, – weye to þe errynge, trewþe to þe vnknowyng and doutyng, lif to þe styynge to heuene and weryinge, – so Crist dude no þinge to vs but efectuely in weye of mercy, in treuþe of ritwesnes and in lif of ʒildyng euerlastynge ioye for oure contunuely 5 mornyng and sorwynge in þis valey of teeres. Myraclis þerfore þat Crist dude heere in erþe, ouþer in hymsilf ouþer in hise seyntis, weren so efectuel and in ernest done þat to synful men þat erren þei brouʒten forʒyuenesse of synne, settynge hem in þe weye of riʒt bileue; to doutouse men not stedefast þei brouʒten in kunnyng to betere plesen 10 God, and verry hope in God to been stedefast in hym; and to þe wery of þe weye of God, for þe grette penaunce and suffraunce of þe trybulacioun þat men moten haue þerinne, þei brouʒten in loue of brynnynge charite to þe whiche alle þing is liʒt, ʒhe to suffere deþe, þe whiche men most dreden, for þe euerlastynge lyf and ioye þat men most louen and 15 disiren, of þe whiche þing verry hope puttiþ awey all werinesse heere in þe weye of God. Þanne, syþen myraclis of Crist and of hyse seyntis weren þus ef[f]ectuel (as by oure bileue we ben in certeyn), no man shulde vsen in bourde and pleye þe myraclis and werkis þat Crist so ernystfully wrouʒte to oure helþe; for whoeuere so doþ, he erriþ in þe byleue, 20 reuersiþ Crist and scornyþ God. He erriþ in þe bileue, for in þat he takiþ þe most precious werkis of God in pley and bourde, and so takiþ his name in idil, and so mysvsiþ oure byleue. A Lord! syþen an erþely seruaunt dar not takun in pley and in bourde þat þat h[is] erþely lord takiþ in ernest, myche more we shulden not maken oure pleye and 25 bourde of þo myraclis and werkis þat God so ernestfully wrouʒt to vs. For soþely, whan we so doun, drede to synne is takun awey, as a seruaunt whan he bourdiþ wiþ his mayster, leesiþ his drede to offendyn hym, namely whanne he bourdiþ wiþ his mayster in þat þat his mayster takiþ

2 John 14. 6 6 myraclis] in myraclis 18 effectuel] eflectuel 24 his] her

30   in ernest. And riȝt as a nayl smyten in holdiþ two þingis togidere, so
drede smyten to Godward holdiþ and susteyneþ oure bileue to hym.
Þerfore, riȝt as pleyinge and bourdynge of þe most ernestful werkis of
God takiþ aweye þe drede of God þat men shulden han in þe same, so it
takiþ awey oure bileue, and so oure most helpe of oure sauacioun. And,

35   siþ takyng awey of oure bileue is more veniaunce takyng þan sodeyn
takyng awey of oure bodily lif, and whanne we takun in bourde and pley
þe most ernestful werkis of God as ben hyse myraclis, God takiþ awey
fro vs his grace of mekenesse, drede, reuerence and of oure bileue,
þanne, whanne we pleyin his myraclis as men don nowe on dayes, God

40   takiþ more veniaunce on vs þan a lord, þat sodaynly sleeþ his seruaunt
for he pleyide to homely wiþ hym. And, riȝt as þat lord þanne in dede
seiþ to his seruaunt, 'Pley not wiþ me but pley wiþ þi pere', so whanne
we takun in pley and in bourde þe myraclis of God, he, fro vs takynge
his grace, seiþ more ernestfully to vs þan þe forseid lord, 'Pley not wiþ

45   me but pley wiþ þi pere'.

Þerfore siche myraclis pleyinge reuersiþ Crist. Firste in takyng
to pley þat þat he toke into most ernest. Þe second in takyng to myraclis
of oure fleyss, of oure lustis and of oure fyue wittis, þat þat God tooc to
þe bryngyng in of his bitter deþ, and to techyng of penaunse doynge, and

50   to fleyinge of fedyng of oure wittis and to mortifiyng of hem. And
þerfore it is þat seyntis myche noten: þat of Cristis lawyyng we reden
neuer in holy writt, but of his myche penaunse, teris and schedyng of
blod, doying vs to witen þerby þat alle oure doyng heere shulde ben in
penaunce, in disciplynyng of oure fleyssh and in penaunce of aduersite.

55   And þerfore alle þe werkis þat we don [þat] ben out of alle þes þre,
vtturly reuersen Cristis werkis. And þerfore seiþ seynt Poul [þ]at, 'Ȝif
ȝee been out of disciplyne of þe whiche alle gode men ben maad
perceneris, þanne auoutreris ȝee ben and not sones of God'. And
siþ myraclis pleynge reuersen penaunce doying, as þei in greet likyng

60   ben don and to grete likyng ben cast biforn, þere as penaunce is in gret
mournyng of hert and to greet mournyng is ordeynyd biforne, it also
reuersiþ dissipline, for in verry discipline þe verry voys of oure mayster
Crist is herd, as a scoler heriþ þe vois of his mayster, and þe ȝerd of God
in þe hond of Crist is seyn, in þe whiche siȝt alle oure oþere þre wittis for

65   drede tremblyn and quaken as a childe trembliþ seyng þe ȝerde of his
mayster. And þo þridde in verry dissipline is verry turnyng awey and
forȝetyng of alle þo þingis þat Crist hatiþ and turnyde hymsilf awey
heere, as a childe vndir dissipline of his mayster turniþ hym awey fro
alle þingis þat his mayster haþ forbedun hym, and forȝetiþ hem for þe

55 þat] and   56 þat] ȝat   56 Heb. 12. 8

greet mynde þat he haþ to doun his maystris wille. . . And syþen no man   70
may seruen two lordis togydere, as seiþ Crist in his gospel, no man may
heren at onys efectuely þe voyce of oure mayster Crist and of his owne
lustis. And syþen myraclis pleyinge is of þe lustis of þe fleyssh and
myrþe of þe body, no man may efectuely heeren hem and þe voyce of
Crist at onys, as þe voyce of Crist and þe voyce of þe fleysh ben of two   75
contrarious lordis. And so myraclis pleying reuersiþ discipline, for as
seiþ seynt Poul 'Eche forsoþe discipline in þe tyme þat is now is not a
ioye but a mournynge'.

Also, siþen it makiþ to se veyne siȝtis of degyse, aray of men and
wymmen by yuil continaunse, eyþer stiryng oþere to leccherie and   80
debatis as aftir most bodily myrþe comen moste debatis, as siche
myrþe more vndisposiþ a man to paciencie and abliþ to glotonye and to
oþere vicis, wherfore it suffriþ not a man to beholden enterly þe ȝerde of
God ouer his heued, but makiþ to þenken on alle siche þingis þat Crist
by þe dedis of his passion badde vs to forȝeten. Wherfore siche myraclis   85
pleyinge, boþe in penaunce doyng, in verry discipline and in pacience
reuersyn Cristis hestis and his dedis. Also siche myraclis pleying is
scornyng of God, for riȝt as ernestful leuyng of þat þat God biddiþ is
dispisyng of God, as dide Pharao so bourdfully takyng Goddis biddyngis
or wordis or werkis in scornyng of hym, as dyden þe Iewis þat bobbiden   90
Crist, þanne, syþen þes myraclis pleyeris taken in bourde þe ernestful
werkis of God, no doute þat þei scornen God as diden þe Iewis þat bobbiden Crist, for þei lowen at his passioun as þese lowyn and iapen of þe
myraclis of God. Þerfore, as þei scorneden Crist, so þeese scorne God.
And riȝt as Pharao, wrooþ to do þat þat God bad hym, dispiside God,   95
so þese myraclis pleyeris and mayntenours leeuynge plesingly to do þat
God biddiþ hem scornen God. He, forsoþe, haþ beden vs alle to halowyn his name, ȝyuyng drede and reuerence in alle mynde of his werkis
wiþoute ony pleying or iapynge, as al holynesse is in ful ernest. Men
þanne pleyinge þe name of Goddis miraclis as plesyngly, þei leeue to do   100
þat God biddiþ hem, so þei scornen his name and so scornyn hym.

But here aȝenus þei seyen þat þei pleyen þese myraclis in þe
worschip of God and so dyden not þes Iewis þat bobbiden Crist. Also
ofte siþis by siche myraclis pleyinge ben men conuertid to gode
lyuynge, as men and wymmen seyng in myraclis pleyinge þat þe deuul   105
by þer aray, by þe whiche þei mouen eche on oþere to leccherie and to
pride, makiþ hem his seruauntis to bryngen hemsilf and many oþere to
helle, and to han fer more vylenye herafter by þer proude aray heere þan

71 Matt. 6. 24, Luke 16. 13   77 Heb. 12. 11   81 debatis¹] of debatis
89 Exod. chs. 5–12   92 þei] ne þei

þei han worschipe heere; and seeynge ferþermore þat al þis worldly
beyng heere is but vanite, for a while as is myraclis pleying, wherþoru
þei leeuen þer pride and taken to hem afterward þe meke conuersacioun
of Crist and of hise seyntis. And so myraclis pleying turneþ men to þe
bileue and not peruertiþ. Also ofte syþis by siche myraclis pleyinge men
and wymmen, seynge þe passioun of Crist and of hise seyntis, ben
mouyd to compassion and deuocion, wepynge bitere teris, þanne þei ben
not scornynge of God but worschipyng. Also prophitable to men and
to þe worschipe of God it is to fulfillun and sechen alle þe menes by þe
whiche men mowen leeue synne and drawen hem to uertues and syþen,
as þer ben men þat only by ernestful doynge wylen be conuertid to God,
so þer been oþere men þat wylen not be conuertid to God but by gamen
and pley. And now on dayes men ben not conuertid by þe ernestful
doyng of God ne of men. Þanne now it is tyme and skilful to assayen
to conuertyn þe puple by pley and gamen as by myraclis pleynge and
oþer maner myrþis. Also summe recreacioun men moten han and bettere
it is, or lesse yuele, þat þei han þeyre recreacioun by pleyinge of myraclis
þan by pleyinge of oþer iapis. Also siþen it is leueful to han þe myraclis
of God peyntid, why is not as wel leueful to han þe myraclis of God
pleyed? syþen men mowen bettere reden þe wille of God and his
meruelous werkis in þe pleyinge of hem þan in þe peyntynge, and
betere þei ben holden in mennus mynde and oftere rehersid by þe
pleyinge of hem þan by þe peyntynge, for þis is a deed bok, þe toþer
a qu[i]ck.

          To þe first resoun we answeryn seying þat siche myraclis
pleyinge is not to þe worschipe of God for þei ben don more to ben seen
of þe worlde and to plesyn to þe world þanne to ben seen of God or to
plesyn to hym as Crist neuer ensaumplide hem, but onely heþene men
þat euere more dishonouren God, seyinge þat to þe worschipe of God,
þat is to þe most veleynye of hym. Þerfore, as þe wickidnesse of þe mysbileue of heþene men lyiþ to þemsilf, whanne þei seyn þat þe worshipyng
of þeire maumetrie is to þe worschipe of God, so mennus lecherye now
on dayes to han þer owne lustus lieþ to hemself whanne þei seyn þat
suche miracles pleiyng is to þe worschip of God. For Crist seiþ þat
folc of auoutrie sechen siche syngnys as a lecchour sechiþ signes of
verrey loue but no dedis of verrey loue. So siþen þise myraclis pleyinge
ben onely syngnis, loue wiþoute dedis, þei ben not onely contrarious to
þe worschipe of God, þat is boþe in signe and in dede, but also þei ben
gynnys of þe deuuel to cacchen men to byleue of anticrist, as wordis of
loue wiþoute verrey dede ben gynnys of þe lecchour to cacchen felawchipe

to fulfillynge of his leccherie. Boþe for þese myraclis pleyinge been
verrey leesyng as þei ben sygnis wiþoute dede and for þei been verrey   150
idilnesse, as þei taken þe myraclis of God in idil aftur þeire owne lust.
And certis idilnesse and leesyng been þe most gynnys of þe dyuul to
drawen men to þe byleue of anticrist. And þerfore to pristis it is vttirly
forbedyn not onely to been myracle pleyere but also to heren or to seen
myraclis pleyinge, lest he þat shulde been þe gynne of God to cacchen   155
men and to holden men in þe bileue of Crist, be maad aȝenward by
ypocrisie þe gyn of þe deuel to cacchen men to þe bileue of anticrist.
Þerfore, riȝt as a man swerynge in ydil by þe names of God and seyinge
þat in þat he worschipiþ God and dispisiþ þe deuyl, verryly lyinge doþ
þe reuerse, so myraclis pleyers, as þei ben doers of ydilnesse, seyinge   160
þat þei don it to þe worschip of God, verreyly lyyn. For, as seiþ þe
gospel, 'Not he þat seiþ "Lord, Lord" schal come to blisse of heuene,
but he þat doþ þe wille of þe fadir of heuene schal come to his kyndam'.
So myche more not he þat pleyiþ þe wille of God worschipiþ hym, but
onely he þat doiþ his wille in deede worschipiþ hym. Riȝt þerfore as   165
men by feynyd tokenes bygilen and in dede dispisen þer neyȝboris, so
by siche feynyd myraclis men bygylen hemsilf and dispisen God, as þe
tormentours þat bobbiden Crist.

And as anentis þe secound reson, we seyen þat riȝt as a uertous
deede is oþere while occasioun of yuel, as was þe passioun of Crist to þe 170
Iewis, but not occasioun ȝyuen but taken of hem, so yuele dedis ben
occasioun of gode dedis oþere while, as was þe synne of Adam occasioun
of þe comyng of Crist, but not occasion ȝyuen of þe synne but occasion
takun of þe grete mercy of God. Þe same wise myraclis pleyinge, al be it
þat it be synne, is oþere while occasion of conuertyng of men, but, as it 175
is synne, it is fer more occasion of peruertyng of men, not onely of oon
synguler persone, but of al an hool comynte, as it makiþ al a puple to
ben ocupied in veyn aȝenus þis heeste of þe Psauter book þat seiþ to alle
men, and namely to pristis þat eche day reden it in þer seruyse, 'Turne
awey myn eyen þat þei se not vanytees', and efte, 'Lord þou hatidest   180
alle waytynge vanytees'. How þanne may a prist pleyn in entirlodies or
ȝyue hymsilf to þe siȝt of hem, syþen it is forbeden hym so expresse by
þe forseyde heste of God, namely syþen he cursiþ eche day in his seruice
alle þo þat bowen awey fro þe hestis of God. But alas more harme is,
pristis now on dayes most shrewyn hemsilf al day, as a iay þat al day   185
crieþ 'Watte shrewe!' shrewynge hymsilf. Þerfore myraclis pleyinge,
syþen it is aȝenus þe heest of God þat biddiþ þat þou shalt not take

---

156 be] þei ben   **162** Matt. 7. 21   **179** Ps. 119. 37   **180** Ps. 31. 6,
hatidest] hatistde   **183** Ps. 119. 21   **185** al] and al

Goddis name in ydil. It is aʒenus oure bileue and so it may not ʒyuen
occacioun of turnynge men to þe bileue, but of peruertyng. And þer-
190 fore many men wenen þat þer is no helle of euerelastynge peyne, but þat
God doþ but pretiþ vs, not to do it in dede, as ben pleyinge of miraclis
in sygne and not in dede. Þerfore siche myraclis pleying not onely
peruertiþ oure bileue but oure verry hope in God, by þe whiche seyntis
hopiden þat þat þe more þei absteneden hem fro siche pleyes, þe more
195 mede þei shulden haue of God... And so þes myraclis pleyinge not
onely reuersiþ feiþ and hope but verry charite by þe whiche a man shulde
weylen for his owne synne and for his neyeburs, and namely pristis for
it wiþdrawiþ not onely oon persone but alle þe puple fro dedis of
charite and of penaunce into dedis of lustis and likyngis and of fedyng of
200 hore wittis.

So þanne þes men þat seyen 'Pley we a pley of anticrist and of
þe day of dome þat sum man may be conuertid þerby' fallen into þe
herisie of hem þat, reuersyng þe aposteyl, seyden 'Do we yuel þingis
þat þer comyn gode þingis', of whom, as seiþ þe aposteyl, 'dampnyng
205 is riʒtwise'. By þis we answeren to þe þridde resoun seyinge þat siche
myraclis pleyinge ʒyueþ noon occasioun of werrey wepynge and medeful, but þe wepyng þat falliþ to men and wymmen by þe siʒte of siche
myraclis pleyinge, as þei ben not principaly for þeire oune synnes, ne of
þeire gode feiþ wiþinneforþe, but more of þeire siʒt wiþouteforþ is not
210 alowable byfore God but more reprowable. For, syþen Crist hymsilf
reprouyde þe wymmen þat wepten vpon hym in his passioun, myche
more þei ben reprouable þat wepen for þe pley of Cristis passioun,
leeuynge to wepen for þe synnes of hemsilf and of þeire chyldren, as
Crist bad þe wymmen þat wepten on hym. And by þis we answeren to
215 þe furþe resoun, seyinge þat no man may be conuertid to God but
onely by þe ernestful doyinge of God and by noon veyn pleying, for þat
þat þe word of God worchiþ not ne his sacramentis, how shulde
pleyinge worchen þat is of no vertue but ful of defaute? Þerfore riʒt as
þe wepyng þat men wepen ofte in siche pley comunely is fals wittnessenge,
220 þat þei louyn more þe lykyng of þeire body and of prosperite of þe
world þan lykynge in God and prosperite of vertu in þe soule, and
þerfore, hauyng more compassion of peyne þan of synne, þei falsly
wepyn for lakkynge of bodily prosperite more þan for lakkyng of
gostly, as don dampnyd men in helle. Riʒt so, ofte syþis þe conuertynge
225 þat men semen to ben conuertid by siche pleyinge is but feynyd holynesse, worse þan is oþere synne biforehande. For, ʒif he were werryly
conuertid, he shulde haten to seen alle siche vanyte, as biddiþ þe hestis

200 hore] houre   203 Rom. 3. 8   210 Luke 23. 28

of God, al be it þat of siche pley he take occasion by þe grace of God to
fle synne and to folowe vertu. And ȝif men seyn heere þat ȝif þis
pleyinge of myraclis were synne, whi wile God conuerten men by þe   230
occasion of siche pleyinge, heereto we seyen þat God doiþ so for to
comenden his mersy to vs, þat we þenken enterly hou good God is to vs,
þat whil we ben þenkynge aȝenus hym, doynge idilnesse and wiþseyinge
hym, he þenkiþ vpon vs good, sendynge vs his grace to fleen alle siche
vanyte. And for þer shulde no þinge be more swete to vs þan siche maner 235
merci of God, þe Psauter book clepiþ þat mercy 'blessynge of swetnesse',
where he seiþ 'Þou cam bifore hym in blessynges of swetnesse', þe
whiche swetnesse, al be it þat it be likynge to þe spirit, it is while we ben
here ful trauelous to þe body, whan it is verry as þe flesche and þe spirit ben
contrarious, þerfore þis swetnesse in God wil not been verely had while   240
a man is ocuped in seynge of pleyis. Þerfore þe pristis þat seyn hemsilf
holy, and bysien hem aboute siche pleyis, ben verry ypocritis and
lyeris.

And herby we answeren to þe fifte resoun seyinge þat verry
recreacion is leeueful, ocupiynge in lasse werkis, to more ardently   245
worschen grettere werkis. And þerfore siche myraclis pleyinge ne þe
siȝte of hem is no verrey recreasion but fals and worldly, as prouyn þe
dedis of þe fautours of siche pleyis þat ȝit neuere tastiden verely swetnesse in God, traueylynge so myche þerinne þat þeir body wolde not
sofisen to beren siche a traueyle of þe spirite, but as man goiþ fro vertue 250
into vertue, so þei gon fro lust into lust þat þei more stedefastly dwellen
in hem. And þerfore as þis feynyd recreacioun of pleyinge of myraclis
is fals equite, so it is double shrewidnesse, worse þan þouy þei pleyiden
pure vaniteis. For now þe puple ȝyueþ credence to many mengid
leesyngis for oþere mengid trewþis and maken wenen to been gode   255
þat is ful yuel. And so ofte siþis lasse yuele it were to pleyin rebaudye þan
to pleyin siche myriclis. And ȝif men axen what recreacioun men
shulden haue on þe haliday after þeire holy contemplacioun in þe chirche,
we seyen to hem two þingis: oon, þat, ȝif he hadde veryly ocupiede
hym in contemplacioun byforn, neyþer he wolde aske þat question ne   260
han wille to se vanyte; anoþer we seyn, þat his recreacioun shulde ben in
þe werkis of mercy to his neyebore, and in dilityng hym in alle good
comunicacion wiþ his neybore, as biforn he dilitid hym in God, and in
alle oþere nedeful werkis þat reson and kynde axen.

And to þe laste reson we seyn þat peinture, ȝif it be verry   265
wiþoute mengyng of lesyngis, and not to curious, to myche fedynge
mennus wittis, and not occasion of maumetrie to þe puple, þei ben but as

230 wile] while   **234** sendynge] and sendynge   **236** Ps. 21. 3

nakyd lettris to a clerk to riden þe treuþe. But so ben not myraclis pleyinge
þat ben made more to deliten men bodily þan to ben bokis to lewid men.
270 And þerfore, ȝif þei ben quike bookis, þei ben quike bookis to schrewide-
nesse more þan to godenesse. Gode men þerfore seinge þer tyme to
schort to ocupyen hem in gode ernest werkis, and seinge þe day of þer
rekenynge neyȝen faste, and vnknowyng whan þei schal go hennys,
fleen alle siche ydilnessis, hyinge þat þei weren wiþ her spouse Crist in
275 þe blisse of heuene.

Part IV
Lollard Doctrine

20

Biblical Translation

Þis trett[yse] þat folewþ proueþ þat eche nacioun may lefully haue holy writ in here moder tunge.

Siþen þat þe trouþe of God stondiþ not in oo langage more þan in anoþer, but who so lyueþ best and techiþ best plesiþ moost God, of what langage þat euere it be, þerfore þe lawe of God writen and tauȝt in Englisch may edifie þe commen pepel, as it doiþ clerkis in Latyn, siþen it is þe sustynance to soulis þat schulden be saued. And Crist comaundid þe gospel to be prechid, for þe pepel schulde lerne it, kunne it and worche þerafter. Whi may we not þanne writ in Englische þe gospel and al holy scripture to edificacioun of cristen soulis, as þe prechour schewiþ it truly to þe pepel? For, if it schulde not be writen, it schulde not be prechid. Þis eresye and blasfemye schulden cristen men putt fro þeire hert, for it is sprongon bi þe fend, fader of lesyngis (Ion in þe viij capitle). And so þe kynrede of pharesces is cursed of God for þei louen not Iesu Crist, as seynte Poul seiþ, but letten þe gospel to be lernyd of þe pepel. For, if a master of skole knoweþ a sotilte to make his children clerkis, and to spede hem in here lernynge, he, hidynge þis lore from hem þat ben able þerto, is cause of here vnkunnynge. So, if writynge of þe gospel in Englische and of good doctrine þerto, be a sotiltee and a mene to þe comoun pepel to knowe þe riȝt and redi weye to þe blisse of heuene, who loueþ lasse Crist, who is more cursed of God þan he þat lettiþ þis oon knowynge? for he is a satanas contrarius to Crist. But þe kynrede of Caym, of Daton and Abiron wolden þat þe gospel slepe safe, for þei ben clepid cristyne of manye: þei prechen sumwhat of þe gospel, and gloson it as hem likeþ. And þus diden Makamete and Surgeus þe monk: þei maden a lawe after þer owne malice and token sumwhat of þe gospel to a fleschly vnderstondynge, so þat þorow þe lore of hem heþen pepel vnto þis day ben out of here bileeue. And þus oure antecristis now, suynge þe farisees, tellen not verilich þe truþe of þe gospel, for þei lyuen contrariously þerto; and Crist biddiþ his children deeme after þe wirkis.

1 trettyse] trettþ   14 John 8. 44   15 Rom. 16. 17–18   19 doctrine] doctringe
31 biddiþ] bididiþ; Matt. 7. 16 etc.

O! siþ a craft of gret sotilte is myche preised of worldely men, myche more schulde þe glorius lawe of God be loued and preised of Cristis children, for alle þing þat man nediþ, boþe bodily and gostly,
35 is conteyned in þis blissed lawe, and specialy in þe gospel. And herfore Crist in þe houre of his assencioun comaundid to hise diciplis to preche it to alle pepelis – but, we be siker, neiþer only in Frensch ne in Latyn, but in þat langage þat þe pepel vsed to speke, for þus he tauȝt hymself. And here is a rule to cristyne folke of what langage so euere þei be:
40 it is an hiȝe sacrifi[c]e to God to knowe holy writ and to do þeraftur, wher it be tauȝt or writen to hem in Latyn or in Englisch, in Frensche or in Duche, or in ony oþer langage after þe pepel haþ vnderstondynge. And þus clerkis schulden be glad þat þe pepel knewen Goddis lawe, and þei hemself bisily bi alle þe good meenys þat þei myȝte, schulden ocupie
45 hem to make þe pepel knowe þe truþe of Goddis lawe. For þis was þe cause þat Iesu bicam man and suffrid deed on þe tree, so þat bi kepynge of his lor þe pepel myȝte rise fro goostli deed and come to þe blisse þat neuere schal haue eende. And ȝif ony clerke contrarieþ þis and so endiþ, who schal be dampned but suche a quyk fende? And herfore seid
50 Crist to þe fader of suche clerkis 'Not only in bodili breed lyueþ man but in eche word þat comeþ out of Goddis mouþ', þe whiche word is sustynaunce of cristyn menis soulis. For riȝt as bred strengþiþ mannys bodi to traueile, so þe word of God makiþ sad mannis soule in þe Holy Gost, and stronge to worche þerafter. And þis bred is more needful þan
55 is þe firste breed, as þe soule of mann is worþier þan his body. For whanne þe body schal lye stynkynge in þe graue, þan þe soule þat louede þis brede and lyued þerafter schal be in eendeles blysse wiþ Iesu here spouse. And þus ȝif, þorouȝ necligence of oure bischopis and pre- latis and oþer fals techerrs þat ben in þe chirch, þe truþe of Goddis word
60 be not sowen to þe pepel, praie we Iesu Crist bischop of oure soules þat he ordeyn[e] prechouris to warne us to leue oure synnes bi prechynge of his lawe, and þat, as he enspirede þe prophites wiþ wysdom and kunnynge and tauȝt þe appostlis þe weie of al truþe, so lyȝtne he oure hertis wiþ vnderstondynge of his lore and graunte vs gras to lyue þerafter boþe in
65 word and werk. For þoo þat contrarion þe gospel and þe pistil and wolden lette it to be prechid and pursuen þe trewe techeris and lerneris þerof, louen not Crist; wherfore, but if þei amende hem whilis þei haue tyme, þei schullen dye in here synnes. Wel we witen þat scribis and farisees and princis of prestis in Crist tyme weren more contrarius to
70 his techynge þan þe comoun pepel, for þorouȝ entysynge of hem þe pepel criden 'do him on þe cros'. Þe scribis weren wyse men of þe

32 siþ] seiþ   36 Matt. 28. 19   53 mannis] in mannis   61 ordeyne] ordeynt

lawe, and so þei weren þe cl[e]rgie of þe Iwis; þe farisees weren men of religion þat maden to hem custommys and kepten hem as for lawe, and þus þei setten more bi þe laweis þat þei hadden made þan þei diden bi þe lawe þat God ȝaf to hem and þe pepel, þe whiche was sufficiant to bi rulid bi. Þese ypocritis weren eueremore contrarie to Crist, and þe comoun pepel wrouȝte myche after þer counseil. And so Crist eiȝte tymes, as þe gospel telliþ, seid sorowe to h[e]m. And onys þei repreueden Crist for his disciplis wischen not here hondis whanne þei schulden ete, as here custum was; and Crist axide of hem whi þei braken Goddis heestis for here feyned lawes. Beholde now wel þese condiciouns, and loke wheþer oure clerkis don now as yuel or worse, and namely oure religious þat ben fayners of holines, þe whiche pursuen Crist in hise membris, as þe farisees diden his owne person. And ȝut þese feyners seyne þat God is her fader, and his lawe þei kepen and here owne reule boþe; and þis is open falsehed, as here werkis shewen. We knowen þat farisees braken þe lawe þat God ȝaf to hem and to þe pepel for here fayned reule þat þei hemself maden aȝens þe ordeinaunce of God. And þus, ȝif oure ypocritis seyne now þat þei kepen here owne reule and Goddis lawe boþe, biholde to here werkis and ȝe schal fynde þe contrarie. For þe Iwis seiden to Crist þat God was here fader, but Crist seid to hem aȝene ȝif God hadde be here fader þei schulden haue iloued h[i]m. So now in þese daies þei shewen hem faynet loueres and vntrwe children of Crist þat pursuen symple pepel for þei wolde[n] lerne, rede and teche þe lawe of God in here moder tonge. And þerfore beddiþ Crist to trowe to þe werkis boþe of men and wymmen, whatsoeuere here toungis blaberyne. Moreouer, þer ben many boþe of men and wymmen þat ben open enemyes to trouþe and fiȝteris aȝens þe Holy Gost, for þei slaundren þe louers of God and of his word, seiynge þat þei haue eten fleiȝes þat ȝiueþ hem wysdom and vnderstondynge of al Goddis lawe. Þis is a cursid speche and a gret blasfemye stiȝynge vp bifore þe Trinyte to be greuously vengid, but ȝif it be hastily amendid. Preie we þerfore hertily to þe fader of wisdom þat he delyuere us from þis yuel þat is synne aȝenes þe Holy Goost, and ȝeue vs grace to loue his lawe hertily and to lyue þerafter to oure departynge of body and soule. For Crist seiþ in þe gospel, he þat contynueþ to þe eende in loue of him and his lawe wiþ goode and fruytful werkis schal haue þe blisse; he us graunte þat suffrid skornys, betyngis, spettyngis and at þe laste most schameful deeþ for techynge of þe gospel and lyuynge þeraftur, merciful God. Amen.

75

80

85

90

95

100

105

110

77 Matt. 23. 13–33   78 hem] him   79 Matt. 15. 2–3
91 John 8. 41–2   92 him] hem   94 wolden] woldem

21 A

The Eucharist I

Cristen mennes bileeue tau3t of Iesu Crist, God and man, and hise
apostles and seynt Austyn, seynt Ierome and seynt Ambrose, and of
þe court of Rome and alle treue men is þis: þat þe sacrament of þe auter,
þe which men seen betwene þe prestis handis, is verre Cristis body and
5 his blode, þe whiche Crist tok of þe virgyn Mary, and þe which body
di3ed vpon þe crosse and laye in þe sepulcre, and steie into heuen and
shal come at þe daye of dome for to deme alle men aftur her werkis. Þe
ground of þis beleeue is Cristis owne worde in þe gospel of seynt
Matthew, where he seiþ þus, 'Þe whiles Cristis disciples soupeden,
10 Crist toke bred and blessid it and 3aue it vnto his disciples and seyd þus,
"Take 3e and eteþ, þis is my body"; and Crist, takyng þe coppe, did
þankyngis and 3aue it vnto hem and seyde, "Drynkeþ 3e alle herof,
þis is my blood of þe new testament þat shal ben ishedd out into remys-
sion of synnes."' And þe gospel of seynt Marke techiþ þe same wordis
15 also, and þe gospel of seynt Luk techiþ þe same wordis. But þis sacrament is boþe brede and Cristis body togedre, as Crist is verre God and
verre man; and, as Cristes manhed suffrid peyne and deþe and 3itt þe
godhed my3t suffre no peyne, so, þou3 þis sacrament be corupted,
neuerþele[s] þe body of Crist may suffre no corrupcioun, for seynt
20 Poul þat was rauyshed into þe þridde heuen bi autorite of God writeþ
þus in hooly writt, and þree tymes he calleþ þe sacrament bred [a]ftur þe
fourme of consecracion. And also Poule calleþ þe sacrament 'bred þat we
breken'. Also seynt Austyn in þe popis lawe seiþ þus, 'Þat þing þat is
seene is brede, and þe chalis or þe copp þat þei shewen, but vnto þat þe
25 feiþ askiþ to be tau3t þe bred is Cristis body and þe chalis, þat is þe wyne
in þe chalis, is Cristis blood'. And þe oold prest seynt Ierom seiþ in a
pistle þat he made vnto a womman Elbediam, 'Here we þat þe brede
þat Crist brake and gaue it hise disciples to ete is þe body of our Lord
sauyour, for as he seiþ, "Þis is my body"'. Also seynt Ambrose askeþ
30 hou þat þing þat is bred may be Cristis body, and seiþ þat his consecracioun
is made not oonly bi wordis of þe prest but bi wordis and vertu of God

9 Matt. 26. 26–8   14–15 Mark 14. 22–4, Luke 22. 19–20   20 I Cor. 10. 16–17,
I Cor. 11. 23–9, II Cor. 12. 2–5   21 after] oftur   22 I Cor. 10. 16

almyȝti; and so þe þing þat was bred before þe consecracioun is now
Cristis body aftur þe consecracioun, for Cristis word chaungeþ þe
creature. And so of þe bredde is made Cristis body, and þe wyn
mengide wiþ watur in þe chalise is mad Cristis blod bi consecracioun   35
of heuenly wordis. And þe determynacioun of þe court of Rome wiþ
a hundrid bishops and þrittene, sende into many londes, is þis: 'I
knowleche wiþ herte and mouþe þat þat brede and wyn, þat ben put in
þe auter, ben aftur þe consecracioun not oonly þe sacrament, but also
verrey Cristis body and his blood'.   40

    Þenne þe men þat seyn þat þis sacrament is nouþur bred nor
Cristis body, but an axidens or nouȝt, ben fonned heritikis if þei may[n]-
tenen þis errour aȝeyne Iesu Crist and aȝeyne seynt Poule, and aȝeyne
seynt Austyn, seynt Ierom and seynt Ambrose and many moo hooly
seyntis, ageyne þe court of Rome and aȝeyne alle treue cristen men of true   45
beleeue of Iesu Crist. And also þe gospel of Luk seiþ þat þe disciples
knewen Crist in brekyng of bred. And seynt Austyn seiþ in a sermoun
þat he made þat þis bred was þe sacrament of þe auter. And þerfor seynt
Poule calliþ it 'bred þat we breken'. Also seynt Austyn seiþ þat þat þing,
þe whiche is gedryngis of frutis of þe erþe and is halewid bi priuey praier,   50
is Cristis body. Also seynt Yllarie seiþ þat Cristis body þat is taken of þe
auter is boþe figure and truþe: hit is figur þe while bred and wyn ben
sene wiþouteforþe, and it is truþe þe while it is beleeued wiþinneforþe
to be Cristis body in truþe. Also seynt Austyn seiþ þat þe sacrament or þe
sacrifice of þe churche is made of two þingis: þat is of visible liknes of   55
elementis þat ben bred and wyn, and of inuisible flesche and bloode of
oure lord Iesu Crist, as Crist is boþe God and man. Also a grete clerke,
autor of dyuyne office, seiþ 'As oure bishop Iesu Crist is of two kyndes
boþe togidre, verre God and verre man, so þis sacrament is of two
kyndes, of kynde of bred and of kynde of Cristis body', and telleþ many   60
feire treuþes in þis mater.

    A Lord! siþ Crist seiþ þat þis sacrament of þe auter is his own
body, and seiþ also bi seynt Poule þat þis is brede þat we breken, wheþer
cristen men shulun bileeue? For ȝisturdaye [h]eritikis [seiden] þat þis
sacrament is no wise or no maner Cristis body, but accident wiþouten   65
subiecte or nouȝt; [but] þis is nouȝt tauȝt expresly in wordes in eny
party of hooly writt ne be resoun ne bodily witt. But seynt Austyn techeþ
in þre volumes or moo wiþ grete studie and diliberacioun þat þer may
no accident be wiþou[te] subicte, ȝe where he treteþ of þe sacrament of
þe auter. And þe same techeþ seynt Ion wiþ þe gilden mouþe, and þe same   70
techen alle witty philosophurs, and al resoun and witt shewen opy[n]ly

46 Luke 24. 30–5   **49** I Cor. 10. 16   **64** heritikis] keritikis   **66** but] siþen þe same. And þerfor cristen men shulde knowleche and mayntene þe wordis of hooly writte and vndurstonde hem algates in g[e]neraltee, as þe Hooly Goost vndurstondeþ hem, þouȝ oure bodily witt or naked reson

75 may not comprehende hit. A Lord! what wurship don þise new heretikes vnto þis sacrament, whenne þei seie þat [it] is not brede, but accident wiþoute subiecte or nowȝte? And if þer be any accident wiþout subiecte as þei seyne, it is wars in kynde þenne is any lumpe of cleye, as clerkis knowen wele. And whanne þei seie þis sacrament is in no maner Cristis body,

80 but þervndur Cristis body is hidde, for þat is neuer seid of Crist ne hise apostles in alle þe gospeles þat euer God made. A Lord! wheþur þise ȝisturdaies heritikes han fonden a bettir bileue and more trewe in þe tyme þat Sathanas was vnbunden, þenne Iesu Crist vnto hise apostles or eny oþer clerke by a þousand ȝer and more. For in al þis tyme Crist

85 tauȝt neuer þat þe sacrament of þe auter was an accident wiþoute subiecte and in no maner Cristis body, as þis newe ypocrites seyne. But bi him and hise apostlis and seynt Austyn specialy and oþer hooliest seyntis is seid þat þis sacrament is bred and his own body, and þat þer may be noon accident wiþout subiecte. Lord! wheþer men shul forsake

90 Cristis owne wordis and take straunge wordis vnknowen in hooly writt and aȝens resoun [of] þe moost witti and þe best seyntis, for, as men seyne, many ypocritis han hyred by many hundred poundes bishops vnkunny[n]ge in hooli writt for to dampne cristen mennes bileeue and Cristis owne wordis, for enemyte to oon singuler persone þat tauȝt þe gospel of

95 Crist and his pouert, and dampned couetise and worldly pride of clerkis. Lord! wheþer þis be grete deynte þat many capped monkes or oþer pharisees shulde profer hem redy to þe fyre for to mayntene þis heresie, þat þe sacrament of þe auter is an accident wiþout subiecte, and in no maner Cristis body, aȝeyne Cristis owne techyng and hise apostlis and

100 þe best seyntis and þe wisest in Goddis lawe and resoun, and traueilen not spedily to distruyȝe heresie of symonye þat regneþ opynly and is fully dampned in Goddis lawe and mannes also, and to distruyȝe wordly pride and coueitise of prestis aȝeynes Cristis mekenesse and wilful pouert? Hit semeþ wele bi here dedis þat þei conspiren aȝeynes

105 Cristis gospel and his pore lyuyng for to maynten here owne pride, coueitise and worldlynesse and wombe-ioye and ydulnesse and many moo grete synnes. Almyȝty God kepe his churche fro such false prophetis and here sotile ypocrisiȝe and fals heresye! Amen.

74 þouȝ] þorouȝ

21B

The Eucharist II

Vidit Iohannes Iesum venientem ad se. Iohannis 1

Þis gospel telliþ a witnesse, hou Baptist witnesside of Crist boþe of his godhed and eke of his manhed. Þe storie seiþ þus þat *Iohun saie Iesu comynge to him*, and seide þus of oure Lord , '*Lo, þe lombe of God; lo, him þat takiþ awey þe synne of þis world*', for he is boþe God and man. Crist is clepid Goddis lomb for many resouns of þe lawe. In þe oold lawe weren 5
þei wont to offre a lomb wiþoute wem, þe which schulde be of oo ʒeer, for þe synne of þe peple; þus Crist, þat was wiþouten wem and of oo ʒeer in mannes eeld was offrid in þe cros for þe synne of al þis world. And where suche lambren þat weren offrid felde sumtyme to þe prest, þis lomb þat made eende of oþir fel fulli to Goddis hond. And oþir 10
la[m]bren in a maner fordiden þe synne of oo cuntre, but þis lombe propirly for[dide] þe synne of al þis world. And þus he was eende and figure of la[m]bren of þe oold lawe. And þus schewiþ Baptist bi his double speking þe manhed of Crist and his godhed; for oonli God myʒte þus fordo synne, siþ alle oþir lambren hadden wemmes þat þei myʒten 15
not hemsilf fordo. And so, al if prestis han power to relese synne as Cristis vikers, neþeles þei han þis power in as moche as þei acorden wiþ Crist; so þat, if þeir keies and Cristis will be discordinge atwynne, þei feynen hem falsli to assoile and þanne þei neþer loosen ne bynden, so þat [in] ech such worching þe godhed of Crist moot first worche. And 20
herfore seiþ Baptist of Crist, '*Þis is he þat I seide of, aftir me is come a man þe which is maad bifore me, for he was* anoon *my priour.*' For, riʒt as Crist was a man þe firste tyme þat he was conseyued, so God made him þanne priour of al his religioun, and he was abbot, as Poul seiþ, of þe beste ordir þat mai be. '*And first I knewe him not*; I wiste in soule þat he was borun, 25
but I koude not wiþ bodili iʒe knowe hym from anoþir man, and þis falliþ comunli. But, *for to schewe him in Israel, þerfore I baptiʒe þus in watir.*' *And Iohun bar witnes, and seide þat he saie a spirit come doun as a culuer fro heuene* and lefte oþir *and dwelte on him.* '*But God þat sente me to waische in watir, he tauʒte me* and seide þus, "*On whom þou seest þe spirit come doun* 30

4 synne] synnes   24 Col. 1. 18

and dwellynge vpon him, þat is he þat baptisiþ men in þe Hooli Goost." And I
saie, and bar witnesse þat þis is Goddis kyndli sone.'

We schal wite þat þis dowue was a very foule as oþir ben, and so
it was not þe þridde persoone in Trinite, takun in oonhed of þis persoone,

35   as Goddis sone took his manhed. But, for mekenesse of þis dowue, and
mo goode propertees þat sche haþ, sche bitokeneþ þe þridde persoone.
And þis persoone is seid of h[e]r[e], for Iohun seiþ þe spirit cam doun
and dwelte long vpon Crist; and þis spirit was þis dowue, and so it
seemeþ þat þis dowue was God. And so, al if þe two persoones mai be

40   moued in creaturis, neþeles þe Trinite mai not be moued in his kynde;
but it seemeþ þat we mai graunte þat þis dowue was þe Hooli Goost, as
we graunten þat þis persoone was comynge doun in þis dowue. And þus,
as God seiþ in his lawe þat seuene oxen ben seuene ȝeer, and þat þe
sacrid breed is verili Goddis bodi, so it semeþ þat he seiþ þat þis dowue

45   is þe Hooli Goost. But clerkis witen þat þer ben two maners of seyng:
þat ben personel seyng and habitudynel seyng. Þis dowue myȝte not be
God in his kynde, but bi sum habitude it signyfieþ God; and þus, bi
autorite of God, it is God. And if þou seie þat ech þing bi þis schulde be
God, as ech good creature signyfieþ his maker, (as smoke kyndli signy-

50   fieþ fier), and þus seemeþ Poul to speke whanne he seiþ þat Crist schal
be alle þingis in alle þingis to men þat vndirstonden him, for aftir þe dai
of doom al þis world schal be a book and in ech part þerof schal be God
writun, as God schal be in his kynde in ech part of þe world; and þus,
siþ God is bitokened first and moost in ech þing, whi mai men not

55   graunte þat God is ech þing?

In þis moten men vndirstonde dyuersite in wordis and to what
entent þese wordis ben vndirstondun. And þus bi autorite of þe lawe
of God schal men speke her wordis as Goddis lawe spekiþ, and straunge
not in speche fro vndirstonding of þe peple, and algatis be war þat þe

60   puple vndirstonde wel, and so vse comoun speche in þeir owne persoone;
and, if þei speken in Cristis persoone wordis of his lawe, loke þat þei
declare hem for dreed of pryue errour. And scorne we þe argumentis
þat foolis maken here þat bi þe same skile schulden we speke þus, for
God spekiþ þus in wordis of his lawe; suche apis licnessis passen beestis

65   foly, for þei wolden bringe bi þis þat ech man were God. And so [ȝ]i[ue]
we God leue to speke as him likiþ, al if we speken not ay so bi þis same
autorite. Þ[e]s[e] word[is] þat God spekiþ schulde we algatis graunte,
and declare hem to trewe vndirstonding. And recke we not of argu-

37 here] hir   43 Gen. 41. 26   44 Matt. 26. 26, Luke 22. 19, I Cor. 11. 24
50 I Cor. 15. 28, Col. 3. 11   56 in¹] and in   65 ȝiue] if   67 þese wordis]
þis word

mentis þat sophistris maken, þat we ben redargued grauntinge þat we
denyen; for we graunten þe sentence and not oonli þe wordis, for þe   70
wordis passen awey anoon whanne we han spokun hem. And, as
Aristotle seiþ, contradiccioun is not oonli in wordis, but boþe in
wordis and sentence of wordis; and bi þis we seien þat Crist in speche
is not contrarie to himsilf, ne oo part of his lawe contrarie to anoþir.
And þus, if we graunten þat Crist is alle þingis, it sueþ not herof þat   75
Crist is an asse, ne þat Crist is ech þing, or what þing we wolen nempne,
for God seiþ þe toon and he seiþ not þe toþir. But we graunten þat
Crist is boþe lombe and scheep, for Goddis lawe grauntiþ boþe þese two
of him; and so Crist is a lioun and a worme, and þus of many þingis
þat hooli writt telliþ. And it is ynow to seie for dyuersite þat God haþ   80
special sentence of oon and not so of anoþer. And þus þe comoun
vndirstonding schulde we algates holde, but if Goddis wordis tauȝten vs
his propre sence. And such strijf in wordis is of no profit, ne proueþ not
þat Goddis word is ony weie fals. In þis mater we han ynow stryuen in
Latyn wiþ aduersaries of Goddis lawe, þat seien þat it is falsest of alle   85
lawis in þis world þat euer God suffride.

22

The Nature of the Church

What is þe chirche oonli proprid to God, wiþ hir names, licknessis
and condiciouns.
To speke of holi chirche: firste we taken ground of þe gospel where
Crist seiþ (*Mat. xvi*) 'ȝatis of helle schullen not mow haue miȝt aȝen holi
chirche'; vpon þis tixte seiþ Lire þus, 'Þe chirche is not in men bi   5
weye of powere or dignite, spiritual or temperal, for manye princis and

78 Isa. 53. 7, Acts 8. 32   79 Rev. 5. 5, Ps. 22. 6
4 Matt. 16. 18

hiȝe bischopis and oþer of lowere degree, state or dignite are founden to
be apostataas, or haue gon abak from þe bileue; wherfore þe chirch
stondiþ in þoo persoones in whom is knowyng and verri confessioun of
feiþ and trouþe.' But, for þe more cleere declaring of þis mater and
avoiding of obiecciouns þat mai be putt forþe, we schullen vndirstonde
þat þer ben þre chirchis, of þe whiche Goddis lawe often makiþ mencioun,
and miche þei diuersen iche from oþer to hem þat taken good hede; but
witles foolis ben marrid here þat wil not lerne to knowe iche atwynne.
Þe firste is clepid a litil flok, as Crist seiþ (in *Luc. xii*) 'Nile ȝe drede my
litil flok, it plesiþ ȝoure fadir to ȝyue ȝou a kyngdom.' And þis chirche
is clepid þe chosun noumbre of hem þat schullen be saued as it is writen
(*Ecci. iii*) 'Þe sones of wisdam ben þe chirche of riȝtwise men, and þe
nacioun of hem is buxumnesse to God and loue to her euenecristen'. . .

But, howeuere we speken in diuerse names or licknessis of þis
holi chirche, þei techen nouȝt ellis but þis oo name, þat is to seie 'Þe
congregacioun, or gedering-togidir of feiþful soulis þat lastingli kepen
feiþ and trouþe, in word and in dede, to God and to man, and reisen her
lijf in siker hope of mercy and grace and blisse at her ende, and ouercoueren, or hillen, þis bilding in perfite charite þat schal not faile in wele
ne in woo'. . .

What is þe material chirche wiþ hir honourmentis.

The secounde chirche, dyuerse from þis, is comyng togiddir of
good and yuel in a place þat is halowid, fer from worldi occupacioun,
for þere sacramentis schullen be tretid and Goddis lawe boþe radde and
prechid. Of þis chirche spekiþ þe prophet Dauiþ and seiþ (*Ps. lxvii*) 'In
chirchis blesse ȝe to þe Lord God.' In þis place oure graciouse God
heeriþ oure preiers in special manere, and bowiþ his eere to hise seruauntis in forme as he grauntid Salamon (*III Re. ix*) '"Myn iȝen," seiþ God,
"schullen be open, and myn eeris schullen be lefte vp to þe preiour of
him þat haþ iustli preid in þis place."' And þis is clepid a material place
for it is made bi mannes crafte, of lyme, of tymbre and of stoon, wiþ
oþer necessarijs þat longen þerto. For mannes profite þis place is made,
but not so man for þe place, as Crist markiþ in his gospel, for man
schulde not be bigilid (*Mat. xii, Mar. ii, Luk. vi*), 'Þe sabot is made for
þe man, and not þe man for þe sabot.' Man bi vertu of Goddis word
halowiþ þis place, but þis place mai not halowe man, but if man be
firste in cause; as Ierom seiþ 'Þe place halowiþ not þe man, but þe man

---

15 Luke 12. 32   18 Ecclus. 3. 1 (Vulgate)   23 kepen] kempen
32 Ps. 68. 26   35 I Kings 9. 3   41 Matt. 12. 8, Mark 2. 27, Luke 6. 5

halowiþ þe place.' Alas, what woodnes is þis to boost of hooli placis, 45
and we ouresilf to be suche viciouse foolis! Lucifer was in heuene, and
þat is moost hooli place, but for his synne he fel to helle; þe place myȝt
not holde him. Adam was in paradise, þe moost miriest place, and for
his synne he was dryuen out; þe place miȝt not defende him. Þou þat
art neiþir in heuene ne in paradise but in þis wrecchid world, where 50
wenest þou to fynde a place to halowe þee þat leuest not þi synne? Be
þou siker, as God is in heuene, þat it wole not be; for God is in no place
faire serued but þereas his lawe is faire kept of þe peple. Seint Ambrose
seiþ 'Adam þat was þe more worþi was made wiþouten paradise in þe
vnworþier place; Eve þat was lesse worþi was made wiþynne paradise 55
in þe worþier place.'

Miche peple demen it a medeful werke to iape mennes iȝen wiþ
curiouse bilding and manye veyn staring siȝtis in her chirchis. But Ierom
forbediþ þis þing to be don, and dampneþ it vttirli for greete synne now
in þis tyme of Cristis gospel (*Ierom xii. quest. ii*) 'Manye bilden wowis 60
and pilars of þe chirche; þei vndirputten schynyng marbel stoones; þe
beemes glistiren al in gold; þe auters ben dyuerseli araied wiþ preciouse
stoones. But of þe mynystris of God þer is no choise, no riche man leie
to me þe temple in Iurie, boordis, lanterns, sencers, pannes, cuppis,
mortars and suche oþer, made of gold. For þanne þise þingis weren 65
proued of þe Lord whanne prestis offriden oostis, and blood of beestis
was remyssioun of synnes; þouȝ alle þise þingis wenten aforne in figure,
neþeles þei ben writen for vs into whom þe endis of þe worldis be
comen. Now forsoþe Crist, oure pore Lord, haþ halowid þe hous, or þe
chirche, of oure pouerte: bere we þe cros of Crist, and richesse acounte 70
we as cley.' Vpon þis seiþ William de Seint Amor, 'Suche men semen to
turne þe breed of pore men into stoones, and in þis þei ben more
cruelar þan þe deuel þat axid stoones to be turned into bred.' To þis
acordiþ seint Bernard and seiþ, 'O vanite among alle vanites, and no
more vanite þan as miche wodendrem! Þe chirche schynneþ in wowis, 75
and sche nediþ in þe pore; sche wlappiþ hir stoones in gold, and hir
owene sones sche forsakiþ nakid; of þe spensis of nedi is mad a veyn
seruise to riche mennes iȝen.'

But oure newe feyned sectis in þis ben moost to blame, þat
maken greet bildingis þere leest nede were, as mounkis, chanouns and 80
freris, [nonnis, sistris and spitleris], for peple schulde drawe to parische
chirchis and here her seruice þere, as Goddis lawe haþ lymytid, and
ellis þei ben to blame. Lord! what meneþ þise waast placis of þise hidde
ypocritis, but to telle men bi her synagogis where Satanas seet is? Þere

81 from Harley 6613 and [1530?] print

85   lurken togiddir manye raueisching wolues þat spoilen þe peple wiþ
     many fals signes...
         Prechars þat ben in Cristis chirche comen freeli among þe peple,
     as Crist cam fro þe toour of heuene and ȝaue þis charge to hise disciplis
     (*Mat. x*), 'Freeli ȝe han taken ȝoure wisdam, freeli ȝyueþ it ȝe aȝen.'
90   Poule chase raþer to be deed þan ony man schulde avoide his glorie, for
     mede þat myȝt be ȝouun or taken aȝen þe gospel of Iesu Crist ([*I*] *Cor.*
     ix). And þise prechours prechen treweli to edifie þe peple in vertu, as
     Crist comaundid on hooli Þursdai to hise disciplis aforn his stiȝyng
     (*Mar. vltimo*), 'ȝe, goyng forþe into al þe world, preche ȝe þe gospel to
95   iche creature', þat is to iche man þat cheueli is iche creature. And þei
     lyuen vertuousli hemsilf aftir her preching, for to strengþe her hooli
     wordis wiþ þe spirit of lijf whanne þei ȝyuen a trewe ensaumple in dede
     aftir her seiyng. And þis is þe teching of Iesu Crist in þe gospel of seint
     Mathew (*Mat. v*), 'Looke ȝoure liȝt schyne so aforn men of þis world
100 þat þei may se ȝoure good werkis and gloriefie' – not ȝou – but 'ȝoure
     fadir þat is in heuene', of whom comeþ al ȝoure grace.
         But prechours in þe fendis chirche prechen vndir colour for to
     take ȝiftis. But Gregor reproueþ hem (*Gregor om.xviii*), 'Whoeuere
     preche', Gregor seiþ, 'for goodis of þis world, or to make a gadiryng for
105 suche an heuenli office, wiþouten ony doute þei priuen hemsilf of þe
     mede þat is to come, of euerlasting rewarde.' And þei prechen cronyclis
     wiþ poyses and dremyngis and manye oþir helples talis þat riȝt nouȝt
     availen. Þei clouten falsehed to þe trouþe wiþ miche vngroundid mater,
     tariyng þe peple from trewe bileue þat þei may not knowe it. And þise
110 prechours waveren aboute in many fleischeli lustis, as Iude seiþ (*Iude i*),
     'Þise ben spottis in her metis, feestyng and feeding hemsilf wiþouten
     ony drede, worschiping þe persones of men for þei wolde haue wynyng.'
         Redars in Cristis chirche reeden hooli lessouns and tenten to
     her reding wiþ myndeful deuocioun, as Ierom seiþ, 'So reede þou hooli
115 writ þat euere þou haue mynde þat þoo wordis þat þou redist ben God-
     dis blessid lawe, þat comaundid it not oonli to be radde but also þat þe
     reedars schulde kepe it in her werkis. What profit is it to rede þingis to
     be don and not fulfille hem in dede? As a clene mirour of lijf þe lessoun
     of hooli writ is to be had, þat al þat is good mai be mad betir, and þat
120 þat is yeuel may be amendid.' And þise redars reden diligentli þat þat is
     tretable and opunli in scripture, wiþouten interrupcioun or ony fonned
     intermyssioun, wiþouten corrupting or ouerehipping of lettir, word or
     sillable; and þei schal coorde in charite and do alle þingis in ordre.

89 Matt. 10. 8   **91–92** I Cor. 9. 15   **94** Mark 16. 15   **99** Mat. v]
Mat. vi; Matt. 5. 16   **110** Iude i] Iude ii; Jude 1. 12, 16

But redars in þe fendis chirche ianglen her lessouns as iaies
chatiren in þe cage, and wot not what þei menen, striueyng feel siþis for 125
nouȝt iche aȝens oþir, for rulis of her ordinal and manye veyne questiouns.
And if þei vndirstande þe lessoun whanne þat it is radde, or ony part of
Goddis lawe whanne it is declarid, soone þei treden it vndir foot and
haaten it in her werkis. As Ierom seiþ, þe prophete, in witnessing aȝen
alle suche (*Iere. viij*), 'How may ȝe seie, forsoþe we ben wijse; and þe 130
lawe of þe Lord is among vs? Certis þe fals poyntel of þe scribis haþ
wrouȝt open lesyng and ȝoure wijse men ben confoundid, afeerde and
cauȝt in her owene snare. Þei han þrowen abak þe worde of þe Lord;
þer is no wisdam lefte among hem.'

23

The Duty of the Priesthood

Designauit Dominus Iesus. Luce 10

This gospel telliþ hou Crist sente lesse disciplis to preche to þe
peple and ordeyne for þe apostlis. And þese wordis helpen moche for prechyng of symple prestis, for greet apostlis figuren bischops and lesse
disciplis lesse prestis. But þese *disciplis weren two and seuenti* in noumbre,
and so many, as men seien, weren langagis aftir makyng of Babiloyne. 5
And alle Cristis disciplis traueliden to brynge to oon men of þe chirche,
so þat þer schulde be oon heerd and oo floc. Þis noumbre of Cristis disciplis *sente he two and two bifore his face into ech place þat he was to come [to]* for
to preche and to teche, as weren citees and comoun placis. And here mai
cristene men se þe falshed of þese freris, hou þei letten symple prestis to 10
preche þe gospel to þe folc, for, as þei feynen falsly, noon of Cristis
disciplis hadde leue for to preche til þat Petir hadde ȝouen him leue; and

130 Jer. 8. 8–9
9 and³...lawe (39)] *om.* Z

bi þe same skile no prest schulde preche to þe peple but if he hadde leue
of þe bischop or leue of þe pope. Þis gospel telliþ þe falsnesse of þis
freris lesyng, siþ Crist sente þese disciplis to preche comunli to þe peple
wiþoute letter o[r] axyng of leue of seynt Petir. And as Petir schulde not
graunte þis leue in Cristis presence, so prestis in Cristis presence han
leue of Crist whanne þei ben prestis to preche truli þe gospel. And, if þei
prechen þus truli þe gospel as Crist biddiþ hem, Crist is amyddis hem
and þe peple þat þei techen. And, al if prelatis schulden examyne prestis
þat prechen þus, neþeles it were more nede to examyne þese freris þat
feynen hem to be prestis, for þei comen yn of worse ground and ben
more suspect of heresie. Lord! what resoun schulde dryue herto to lette
trewe prestis to preche þe gospel freli wiþoute cuylet or ony fablis or
flatryng, and ȝyue leue to þese freris to preche fablis and heresies and
aftirward to spuyle þe peple and sille hem þeir fals sermouns? Certis þe
peple schulde not suffre such falshed of anticrist. Also Poul, Cristis
apostle, techiþ in bookis of oure bileeue hou God wolde þat he prechide
to þe peple wiþouten such axyng, for, fro þe tyme þat he was conuertid,
þre ȝeer aftir he prechide fast and axide no leue herto of Petir for he
hadde leue of Iesu Crist. Suche nouelries of pseudefreris schulde prelatis
and alle me[n] aȝenstonde, lest þeir falshed growide more and large[r]li
enuenymede þe chirche. Þus schulden prestis preche þe peple freli
Cristis gospel, and leue freris fablis and þeir begging, for þanne þei
prechen wiþ Cristis leue; and herof schulden prelatis be fayn, siþ þei
synnen moche on oþir sidis, but if þei ben anticristis prestis and schapen
to quenche Cristis lawe.

But þe peple comunli trowide in Crist and louede him, and
þus þei obeischen to þis tyme boþe to Crist and his lawe. And Crist
schewide þe cause and þe nede of þis preching *for he seide ripe corn is*
moche and fewe werkemen aboute it. But, for þis werk is meedful and Crist
souereinly perfoormyde it, þerfore [he] techiþ hise disciplis to *preie þe*
lord of þis ripe corn to sende hise werkmen þerto. And here Crist techiþ opunli
þat men schulden not bie þis office, ne take no meede of þe peple to
traueile þus in Cristis name, for þanne þei puttiden vpon Crist þat he
sillide preching of Goddis word, and ȝaf leue to do symonye and boþe
þese ben blasfemyes. But Crist steride hise men to go and telliþ hem þe
peril bifore, but he moueþ hem priuely for greet meede to traueile þus:
'*Go ȝe,*' seiþ Crist, '*for I sende ȝou as lambren among wolues.*' And so we
han maundement of Crist and autorite to go, and forme of þis perelous
goyng þat makiþ it more meedful. But Crist ȝyueþ hise prechours

---

16 or] of   20 and²...lawe (39)] *om.* W   27 Gal. 2. 1–11, Acts 9. 20–31
42 he] Crist   46 and²...blasfemyes] *om.* W

foorme hou þei schal lyue in þis werk. '*Nyle ʒe,*' he seiþ, '*bere sachel, ne scrippe, ne hosis ne schoon, ne grete men bi þe weie,*' ne do þing þat shulde lette þis werk. If ony such helpe to þis werk Crist wolde not þat þei leue it. And þus seiþ Crist þat '*Into what hous ʒe entren ʒe schal seie* 55 *first "pees be to þis hous" and, if þere be child of pees, ʒoure pees schal reste vpon him and ellis it schal turne aʒen to ʒou.* And so ʒoure werk schal not be idil.' But if ypocritis worchen here, al if þei seien suche wordis, þe hous and þe peple ben worse þat þese false men comen among; for Crist doiþ þese vertues in whos name þese prechours speken, and if þei ben þe 60 feendis lemes comunly þei mouen to synne. But Crist wolde not þat hise werkmen wenten aboute wiþouten fruyt, and þerfore he biddiþ hem *dwelle in þe same hous* vpon resoun. But þei schulden not be idil þere ne curiouse in mete ne drynk; but þe peple schulde gladli fede hem, *and þei schulden homeli take þat þei founden.* And þei schulden take no newe 65 rule bi which þe peple were chargid; and neþer part schulde grucche here to do þus as Crist techiþ for it schulde turne wiþoute charge to mede of boþe partis. And good lijf of suche werkmen shulde moue þe peple to do hem good, and deuocioun of þe peple schulde preie hem to take þeir goodis. But gredynesse and auarice letten here þese two partis and, al if 70 boþe þese synnes letten moche fro Cristis werk, neþeles couetise of prestis is moche more perilous in þis caas. For auarice of þe peple may be holpun on many maners, eþer to turne to oþir peple or to trauele as Poul dide, or to suffre wilfulli hungir and þirst if it falle, but coueitise of wickid prestis blemeschiþ hem and þe peple; for comunli þei schapen her wordis 75 aftir þe eende þat þei coueiten. And here þenken many men þat suche prechours schulden be war þat þei comen not wiþ moche peple ne many hors to preche þus, but be paied of comoun diet and þerwiþ redi to traueile, for þei schulden be no cause of synne neþer of hem ne of þe peple. And here it semeþ to many men þat þese newe ordris of freris 80 schulden eþer leue þe[ir] multitude or traueile wiþ her hondis, and if þei diden boþe þese two discreteli it were þe beter; ne take þei not of Cristis lijf to traueile not as Crist dide not, for neþer þei can ne þei may be ocupied ellis as Crist was, but raþer þei schulden take of Poul and oþir apostlis for to traueile, and leue þeir newe tradiciouns, as Petir dide wiþ 85 oþir apostlis and profitide more þan þese men doen. We schulden þenke hou Petir lyuede whanne Cornelius sente aftir him, how symple he was fed and herborid, and hou he answerde. But now freris reuersen Petir and multiplien newe lawis and persoones of þeir ordris, hauynge more þan Petir hadde. And herwiþ þei seien to men þat þei passen bischops 90 and popis – and certis þei seien here þe soþe, if þei menen passynge in

80 and...end] om. Z 87 Acts 10

synne, for vnleeful excesse is passynge to þese freris. And, so as þei
varien in habitis, so þei ben speckid in þeir ordris, for as þe sect of
Sarasyns þei han sum good and sum yuel.

24

The Power of the Pope

Þe tuentiþ article

Cristen men ben not holden for to bileue þat þe bishop of
Rome þat nowe lyueþ in þis peynful lijf is heed of al holy chirche in erþe.
Þis sentence is open by þis, þat Crist alone is heed of holy chirche, as
5   Poule seiþ (in þe firste capitle to *Efesies*, in þe firste capitle to *Colocences*,
and in þe firste pistle to *Corinthis* þe þridde capitle). Þerfore, if þe pope
chalengiþ þis dignite to hym, he is a blasfemer and Lucifer and antecrist.

Oon and tuentyþ article

Cristen men ben not holden for to bileue þat þe bishope of
10   Rome þat lyueþ nowe in synful lijf is a membre of holy chirche, ȝhe þe
leest membre of holy chirche. Þis sentence is open by þis þat no man is
holden to bileue þat þis bishope lyueþ nowe in þis dedly lijf [wel to
God]. Also no man is holden for to bileue þat þis bishope shal be saued
in blis, and ellis he is no membre of holy chirche, as Austyn seiþ (in þe
15   þridde book of *Cristen Doctryne*, in þe secounde reule of Tyconie, þe
prettiþ capitle). Also no man wot of hymself, wiþouten special reuela-
cioun of God, wheþer he is worþy of haterad eiþer of loue (in þe nynþe
capitle of *Ecclesiastes*); and so, wheþer he be of þe noumbre of hem þat
shulen be saued, of þe noumbre of whiche non may perishe, (in þe
20   [foure] and twenti capitle of *Mathew*). Also þe pope may be chosen of

3 þat] þat þat   5–6 Eph. 1. 22, Col. 1. 18, I Cor. 3. 11   **12–13** from Titus D. 1
18 Eccles. 9. 1   **20** Matt. 24. 24; foure] þre

fleijsly cardynals and auerous, by symonie procuride of hymself, eiþer
ratifie, eiþer consent and aproue it. Þanne he is a symonient and an
eretik and acurside antecrist and a sone of perdicion, if he doiþ not
fruytful penaunce. Also siþen Crist, al witty and al holy, chese Iudas þat
was apostle and Sathanas, and a sone of perdicioun, and a deuel incarnat,   25
eiþer in fleishe (in þe sixte capitle of *Ion* and oþer places), muche more þe
vnkunnynge and vicious cumpanie of cardynals, ful of auerice, symonie
and pryde, may chese a Iudas and Sathanas and a deuel incarnat. Wheþer
þe vicious and vnkunnynge colegie of fleishly cardynals shal ȝeue more
grace and holynesse to a wordly prest, chosen of hem by fleisly eiþer   30
wordly affeccioun, þan Crist, God almyȝtti, ȝaf to Iudas, chosen of hym
by souereyn wisdam and goodnesse and loue to al holy chirche, his
spouse? Þe gret Lucifer may not seie þis for shame of open lesynge and
ateyntynge of Ihesu Crist and al holy chirche…

Þe fyue and twentyþ article   35

Cristen men ben not holden for to bileue, wiþouten open
groundyng of holy scripture eiþer of resoun þat may not faile, þat seynt
Petre hadde more power of byndynge and asoilynge þanne oþer apostles
gretly loued of Crist. Þis sentence is open by þis þat, where Petre (in þe
sixtenþe capitle of *Mathew*) seide to Crist, 'Þou art þe sone of þe queke   40
God', Petre seide þis in þe persone of alle þe apostles; and Ihesu Crist
answeride to hym in þe persone of alle þe apostles, whanne he seide 'To
þee I shal ȝeue þe keies of þe rewme of heuenes, and whateuere þing þou
shalt bynde', as seynt Austyn markide pleynly in his book *De Verbis
Domini* in þe þrettenþ sermoun. And þe same sentence is open pleynly   45
(in þe eiȝtenþ capitle of *Mathew*), wher Crist seide comunely to þe
apostlis 'Whateuere þingis ȝe shulen bynde in erþe shulen be bounden
in heuenes.' And in þe twentiþ capitel of *Ion* Crist seide generally to þe
apostles 'Take ȝe þe Holy Goost; whois synnes ȝe forȝeuene ben forȝouen
to hem', where it is open þat þe same eiþer euene power of byndynge   50
and assoilinge was ȝouene of Crist generally to þe apostles. And þis is
seide pleinly in þe foure and twentiþ cause þe firste questioun þe
capitel *si autem* in þe myddis. Þerfore what autorite is to þe bishope of
Rome, successoure of Petre as he feyneþ, to appropre, eiþer reserue to
hymself, pryncipal power eiþer synguler of byndinge and assoilinge   55
ouere alle bishops, successours of apostles of Ihesu Crist? Forwhy Crist
seiþ (in þe eiȝtenþ capitle of *Mathew*), 'Whoeuere mekiþ hymself as þis
litel chijld, he is þe gretter in þe rewme of heuenes', þat is, he is gretter

26 John 6. 70, cf. John 13. 27   **40** Matt. 16. 16   **42** Matt. 16. 19   **46** Matt. 18. 18
49 John 20. 22-3   **57** Matt. 18. 4

by grace in holy chirche in erþe, and is gretter by glorie in þe chirche
60   regnynge in blis. Where it is open by feiþ of Crist þat þe mekist man, and
moste redy in þe chirche to serue God and his breþeren by clene charite
wiþoute takinge of persones, is þe gretter in holy chirche by þe doom of
Crist and of al þe Trynyte? Lord, wher þe bishope of Rome is more
contrarie to Crist in wordis, deedis and lawes, and in seculer lordshipe
65   forboden of Crist specially to clerkis, more þanne oþer bishopis ben
contrarie to Crist? Þerfore he is gretter in power þanne oþer bishopis
þat ben not so depide in erroure and ben more liȝtned of God in kunnynge and holynesse. Truly, if þis resoun sufficeþ to preue þat þe bishope
of Rome haþ more power þanne oþer cristen bishops, successours of
70   apostles, I fynde not ȝit any euydence in holy scripture neiþer in resoun
þat may not faile to shewe suche synguler power of þe bishope of Rome
aboue oþer cristen bishops.

I corilarie

It semeþ resonable to feiþful men þat seint Poul þe gloriouse
75   apostle and feiþful techer of heþen men hadde more power as to many
þingis to edifie holy chirche þanne seint Petre hadde. Þis sentence is
open by þis þat Poule hadde of God mo goostly ȝiftes and gretter,
ȝouen of God to edifie þe chirche, þanne Petre hadde; for Poule trauelide more þanne alle apostles, as holy wrytt seiþ (in þe firste pistle to þe
80   *Corinthis* þe fiftenþ capitle); Poule trauelide more in prechinge and
writynge þe gospel and in rennynge aboute as þorouȝ al þe wor[l]d in
werke of þe gospel, and in suffryng wilfully mo peynes and harder in his
bodi for þe truþe and fredom of þe gospel þanne any oþer apostle dide,
as it is open by processe of his pistles and of deedis of apostles. Þerfore
85   he hadde more power ȝouen of God to edifie þe chirche by more
wrytinge and prechinge and suffrynge of peynes þanne Petre hadde.
Ellis if Petre hadde as muche power as Poule to edifie þe chirche, and
trauelide not so muche þerwiþ as Poule dide, Petir toke þis power and
grace of God in veyn and pryued hymself of his power for mysvsynge
90   þerof. Þerfore, as Poule hadde gretter ȝiftis þanne Petre, boþe in kunnynge, writinge and preching and suffryng for þe gospel to edifie
cristen men, so he hadde more power þanne Petre to edifie þe chirche.
Wherfor Crisostum in his book of preisingis of Poule not onely clepiþ
Poul ful of charite, but also charite itself for excellence of charite to
95   Crist and his spouses holy chirche. And not onely he comparisowneþ
Poule to an aunge[l] and arcaungel, but he enhaunsiþ hym aboue aungels
and archaungels; for þe office of an aungel is to kepe o persone, þe

63 is] for he is   74 resonable] resonablely   80 I Cor. 15. 10

office of arcaungel is to kepe o prouynce eiþer rewme, but Poule kepte
al holy chirche in erþe in liȝtnynge it wiþ feiþful writinge and trew
prechinge and wilful suffringe of deeþ whiche an archaungel may not do.   100
Also Petre, Ion and Iames þat semeden to be pilers of cristen men ȝauen
not þing to Poule, but Poule ȝaf to Petre charitable and wijs repreuynge
and nedful to þe chirche wherby heþen men conuertide to cristen feiþ
weren confermed in þe truþe of þe gospel (in þe secounde capitel to
Galaþies). Þerfore it semeþ to feiþful men þat Poule after Crist passeþ   105
alle apostles in glorie, as he passed in werk and techinge aboute þe
edifijnge of holy chirche, Cristis spousesse.

II corilarie

As seint Poule hadde more power þanne Petre as to many
þingis to edifie holy chirche, so anoþer cristen bishope may haue more   110
power grauntide of þe Lord þanne haþ þe bishop of Rome to edifie holy
chirche in feiþ and vertues by excellence of holy conuersacioun and of
more spedful techinge. Þis sentence sueþ openly of þingis bifore seide
wiþ þe open werkes of a certein pope to be asigned and of anoþer
bishop wiþ whom Crist worchiþ more spedily by grace to edifie holy   115
chirche. For þe pope to be asigned may be Lucifer and Sathanas trans-
figuride into an aungel of liȝt and an heretike by symonie and general
dissencioun made for hym in þe chirche and be an open antecrist; and
anoþer bishope may be most meke and most spedful among dedly men
to edifie þe chirche in feiþ and vertues boþe by werke and word, as it is   120
open of þe worshipful clerk Robert Grosthed bishope of Lyncoln and
and of þe curside bishope of Rome in his tyme.

Sixe and twentiþ article

Cristen men ben not holden for to bileue þat eche determynacioun of þe chirche of Rome is trewe on eche side eiþer to be taken of   125
holy chirche for an article of bileue. Þis sentence is open by þis þat þe
chirche of Rome may faile in feiþ and charite and most al þe cumpanie
of fleisly cardynals, whois office eiþer ordre is not founden expresly in
holy writte may faile in feiþ and charite. Forwhy, if alle apostles chosen
of Crist, ȝhe wiþoute mene persones, failiden in feiþ for drede of deeþ   130
in tyme of Cristis passioun and þanne feiþ of holy chirche duellide in þe
blessud virgyne as doctours heulden comunely, how muche more may
al þe chirche of Rome, as to þe fleiȝsly cumpany of cardynals and of
wordly prestis wiþ proude and auerous religious ful of envie and malice,
faile in feiþ and charite, and ȝit þe feiþ of holy chirche may rest in symple   135

105 Gal. 2. 11–21   116 II Cor. 11. 14   130 Matt. 26. 56

lewide men, and meke prestis and deuoute, þat louen and trauelen
feruently to magnifie holy scripture, and þe truþe and fredom of þe
gospel of Ihesu Crist. It semiþ a wondirful wodnesse and open blasfemie
to sett more stidfastnesse of cristen feiþ in wordly prestis and feyned
religious of þe chirche of Rome þanne in alle þe apostlis chosen of
Ihesu Crist – and ȝit alle þei faileden in feiþ at a tyme, – but þese wordly
prestis and religious moun not faile in feiþ as þei feynen. What wodnesse
is þis to graunte þat þe chirche of Rome may faile openly in charite but
not [in] cristen feiþ ? – siþen feiþ wiþ charite is propirly þe feiþ of
cristen men, and feiþ wiþoute charite is þe feiþ of fendis, as Austyn
preueþ in many placis, and feiþ wiþoute werkis is deed, as Iames seiþ.
A, what wodnesse is þis to graunte þat þe wordly clerkis of Rome moun
liȝtly faile and also failen openly in feiþ formed wiþ charite, whiche is
proprely cristen mennus feiþ, and þat þei moun not faile in deed feiþ
and feiþ of fendis, siþen Crist seiþ in þe foure and twenti capitle of
Mathew and in oþer placis, 'False Cristis and false profetis shulen ryse
and disseyue many men and [ȝeue] grete signes and wondres so þat, if
it may be don, ȝhe chosen men [shulen] be disseyuede'. And in þe
twentiþ capitle of Apocalips, after a þousand ȝeer Sathanas shal be
vnbounden of his prysoun and shal go out and disseyue many folkis.
And in þe secounde pistle to Tesolonicenses þe secounde capitle, 'God
shal sende a worchinge of erroure, þat alle men bileue to leesinge
and to be dampned whiche bileueden not to treuþ but consentiden
to wickidnesse', and antecrist shal come to hem þat perishiden, for
þei reseyuyden not þe charite of truþe. Þerfore, siþen þese profecies
shulen nedis be filled and þe tyme sett in Apocalips is nowe passed, and
þe werkis of þe bishope of Rome in many þingis ben openly contrarie to
þe werkis of Ihesu Crist, whi perseyuen not cristen men þat þe comynge
of antecrist neiȝeþ nowe, and þat þe determinacioun of þe chirche of
Rome boweþ awey fro holy scripture and resoun for her owne pryde
and temperal wynnynge and fleiȝsly lustis'. For þe chirche of Rome
determyneþ oft aȝen holy scrypture, and o conseil aȝen anoþer, and o
pope aȝenseiþ þe sentence of anoþer as it plesiþ hym wiþout nedful
resoun, as it is open in þe fiftyþ distinccioun, in many chapiters and in
many mo places of Decrees and of Decretals, and of Sixte and of
Clementyns. Why perseyuen not cristen men þis contradiccioun and
neiȝinge of antecrist, siþen Crist seiþ in þe foure and twentyþ capitle of
Mathew, 'Whanne ȝe shulen se abhomynacioun of discounfort, whiche
was seide of Daniel þe profete, stondinge in þe holy places, he þat rediþ

---

146 James 2. 20   151 Matt. 24. 24, cf. *vv.* 5, 11   154 Rev. 20. 7   156 II Thess.
2. 11–12   161 Rev. 20. 7   173 Matt. 24. 15

vndirstonde.' And in þe tenþ capitle of Ion [Crist seiþ, 'Bileue ȝe to þer 175
werkis.' And in þe [seuenþ] capitle of Ion], 'Nyl ȝe deme by þe face, but
deme ȝe iuste doom.' And in þe seuenþ capitle of Mathew, 'By her
fruytes ȝe shulen knowe hem.' Þerfore it is to stonde, wiþoute any
drede, to holy scripture and to þe werkis of Crist for a foundement þat
may not faile, and to þe determynacioun of þe chirche of Rome eiþer of 180
any oþer onely in as muche as it is groundide expresly in holy scripture
eiþer in open resoun.

25

The Function of the Secular Ruler

Tractatus de Regibus

Capitulum Primum

Sythen witte stondis not in langage but in groundynge of treuthe,
for þo same witte is in Laten þat is in Grew or Ebrew, and trouthe
schuld be openly knowen to alle manere of folke, trowthe moueþ mony
men to speke sentencis in Yngelysche þat þai han gedirid in Latyne, and
herfore bene men holden heretikis. For wele I wote þat trouthe is an 5
vnspecte, and no man schulde schame of trouthe as no man schulde
schame of God. And herfore tellus þo gospel, þat nyȝt þat Crist was
taken, þo byschop askid Crist of his disciplis and his lore, ande Criste
onswerid scharply to hym on þis manere: 'I tauȝt openly to þo worlde
and no þinge in hid place, for I tauȝt in temple and in synagog to 10
wheche þo Iewes coomen comynly; and aske of hem what I haue saide,
and aske hit not nowe of me'. Ande by þis skille, as men sayne, seynt
Poule wrote in mony langagys, as to Romaynys he wrot in Latyne, ande

175 John 10. 38   175–6 from Titus D.1   176 John 7. 24; sevenþ] fift
177 Matt. 7. 16

8 John 18. 20–1

to Ebrewys in Ebrew, for þo sentence schulde be more knowen and
15 lyȝter to þo peple. And men han writen to þo clerkis, boþe hyȝer and
lowȝere, sentence of Gods lawe, but hit is dyspysid: summe seyne hit is
heresie, summe seyne hit is foly, and somme dedeynen to loke wheþer
hit be sothe or false. And herfore in Ynglysche tunge writen summe
men her sentence, if God wolde moue summe Yngelysche men to holde
20 wiþ treuthe.

Hit ys saide in Laten what office popis schuld haue, and what
schuld be þo office of kyngus by þo lawe of God; and, for to make þis
þinge more knowen, is sumwhat tolde on Ynglysche. Þre þingis mouen
men to speke of kyngis office: furst, for kyngus may herby se þat þai
25 schulden nout be ydel but rewle by Gods lawe to wynne þo blys of
heuen; þo secunde is for kyngus schulden not be tirauntus of her pepul,
but rewle hem by reson þat falles to þer state; þo thrid cause is most of
alle, for þus schuld Goddis law be better knowen and defendid, for
þerinne is mannys helþe bothe of body and soule þat euermore schal
30 laste.

Capitulum Secundum

God seis þat holy chirche is a gode howswife, and made cloþis
of ray to clothe wiþ hir meynye. Cloþus of coloure schuld be prestis, þat
euermore schulde be stable and grounde of oþer parties of holy chirche
by techynge of Goddis lawe. Þo secunde part, rude and grete, schulde
35 be þo comyns. But þo thrid part, as þo chaumpe sotile of sylk or oþer
mater, schulde be noble men þat schuld be bytwixe þese two. Þo chirche
is a nobul man, as mannes spirit, but hit [is] cloþid wiþ body and þre
cloþis of office. Þo [þridde] part of þo chirche is muche praysid in
Goddis lawe, as kyngis and dukis and nobulmen and knyȝttis; but, for
40 hit is no nede to schewe þis by þo olde lawe, se we how Crist dide þat
is lorde of alle. Crist chese to be borne when þo empirer florischid
moste; Criste chese to be worschipid and susteyned by thre kyngus;
Crist payed taliage to þo emperour; Crist tauȝt to pay to þo emperoure
þat was his; Crist ches to be biried solemply of knyȝttis, and he com-
45 myttid his chirch to gouernaile of knyȝttes. And herfore techis Petur
þat cristen men schulden be suget in mekenes to alle maner of men, as to
kyngus as passynge bifore oþer men, and to dukus as next vnder kyngis;
and þese bene in statis to perfoureme þese offices, to take vengeaunce on
yuell men and to prayse gode men. And herfore biddus Petur to wor-
50 schipe alle men, but he biddes to do worschipe to kyngus. And Poule,

38 þridde] secunde   41 Luke 2. 1   42 Matt. 2. 1–11   43 Matt. 17. 24,
Matt. 22. 21   44 Matt. 27. 57–60   45 I Pet. 2. 13–14   49 I Pet. 2. 13–14

þat lerned his witte in heuen, byfore oþer biddis euery meke man in soule be sogett to knyȝttus; but, siþen þer is none powere but ordeyned of God, he þat aȝeynestondus powere, aȝeynestondus God, for he aȝeynestondus þo ordinaunce of God. Noþoles God ordeyned þis power for his chirche, for, if þou be a gode man, þou schuldest be praysed of hem, and if þou be a schrewe, drede þou of God and hem. And þerfore he þat aȝeynestondus iuste powere of knyȝttus, aȝeynestondis God to his owne dampnacion.

Mony syche wordis spekis Goddus lawe of kyngus, but hit spekis not of popis nouþer gode ne yuel. But when venym of dowynge was entrid into þo chirch was þo nome of 'pope' founden: þat sowneþ wonderfull, for hit were a grete wonder þat Criste schulde make his vicare þo man þat moste contraries hym in manere of lyuyng. Wele I wote þat þo pope is noþinge sibbe to Petur but if he lif a pore lyfe ande a meke, as Petur dide, and passe in fedynge of Cristus schepe, wiþ techynge of þo gospel. And, ryȝt as Petur was loued and made hede of apostilis for kepynge of þis office next Criste his mayster, so if þo pope by false name seis he is Cristis vicar, and reseruyt hym in þese þre, he is anticrist...

Capitulum Quintum

Hit were for to witt how þo kyngus iurisdictione schulde be spred in his rewme, and aboute what þinge. But hit is no drede þat by þo law of God, whereeuer þis kynge haþ lordschipe, schulde be þo powere of his lawe, sithen þo kyng schulde mayntene his lordschipe by powere of his lawe. And hit were al one to lete þis iurisdiccioun of kyngus, and to let þo regaly to passe in his fredome, for by þis rewlynge of lawe is mayntend kyngus lordschipe. And, ȝif þou aske by what lawe schulden kyngus lede her rewmus, certis by Gods lawe þat schulde be iche mannus lawe. For he is no cristen man þat is not rewlid by Gods law, and by propur lawe of þo kynge schuld be rewlid his rewme so þat hit be purgid by þo lawe of God. And hit fallis to kyngus to do in her rewmus what dede þat is to done by vertue of þo kynge, for þus doþ God in his rewme alle þo dedis of kynde. And he is ouerlewde þat trowes of þis sentence þat þo kynge doþ alle þo foule dedis þat ben done in his rewme: certis God makis men to trauaile in his werkys, ande God doþ þese werkis more þen men done, and ȝit God ne etiþ ne drynkyth, al ȝif he make þese dedus.

And, if þou say þat mony men by priuelege bene exempt, and ȝit þai dwellen in kyngus rewmes and taken of her godis, certys by

90
þis way is broken þo regaly of kyngus, and hor rewmes bene feblid by anticristis cautel, for he is no legeman ne soget to his kynge (þat is, full sugett to hym by his kyngus lawe). And lordis of kyngedomys boþe more and les seruen to þer kynges eche in his degre; byschopis and clerkys seruen to rewmys þat þai ben inne in seruyce þat fallis to her office, or ellys þai bene no legemen. And þus clerkis in rewmys ben ful

95
necessary if þai done þer office wele – ȝe, if þai ben freris. Ande hit were al one to say þat þes men bene exempt ande not sugett to þeire kynge in dedis of þer office, ande to say þat kyngus bene not fulle lordus of her kyngedome; and on þis wyse myȝt anticriste distroye mony rewmes. Kynges schulden mayntene in þer rewmes suche maner of folk þat han

100
office for to wyrche dedis nedeful to rewmes, as summe men ben ful nedful to preche and teche, as clerkis, ande summe ben ful nedeful to gouerne, as worldely lordys. And make hem [departe] þat haue not office profitable to þo rewme, ne bene sogett to þo kynge, and þai bene not his legemen. Ande by suche traytouris may rewmys sone be loste.

105
Þus kynges maken to syng masse and to do Goddis seruyce.

Capitulum Sextum

But here men douten wher kynges schulden punysche here mennys synnus; ande hit semes þat nay, by resone of iurisdicciouns, for worldely and gostely ben algatys departud. Þo furste fallys to kyngys and þat oþer to prelatis. But here we schal vnderstond þat, as kyngus

110
han byschopis vnder hem her legemen, so done þai by hem werkis of Goddis seruyce to susteyne here rewmes; ande so on two maners may synnes of rewmus be punyschid, ouþer in þat þat þai ben contrarie to Gods lawe and so contrarie to Gods rewme, þat ys holy chirche. On þo furste maner schulden kyngus punysche al manere of synne þat is done

115
in her rewmes for to mayntene hem; on þo secunde maner schulde verrey apostilis punysche synne in rewmes by auctorite of Criste. But þese apostilys schulden not haue in þese rewmes ne propur howse ne dwellynge, but lyue clenly of almes, as Crist lyued wiþ his apostilis to pes of mony rewmes. And þes þat lyuen apostilys lyfe schulden be

120
sugett to lordis and obedient to iche man, as techis Criste[s] lawe; ne þai schuld not be chargyouse to folke þat þai dwellen omonge, nouþer in noumbre ne in place, but trauaile if nede were.

Amonge oþer þinges þat distroyen rewmys, þis is a special þat anticriste haþ brouȝt inne: þat sectis bene in rewmes by auctorite of þo

125
pope and bene nouȝt kyngis legemen, al ȝif þai take here lordschipe more largely þen oþer men and by lesse seruyce, for þus myȝt rewmys

93 þat[1]] 'seruys' þat.

be distroyed by cautels of anticrist. As, if alle þo freris of Yngelonde
hadden howses and godes in þo rewme of Yngelonde, and maden þo
pope lord of hem, þo popis lordschipe were to myche ande regale were
lessid; and þus, by processe of tyme, myȝt þo londe be conquerid al into   130
þo popis honde as oþer rewmys bene. Lord! siþen Criste had no þinge
propur, as a house to rest in, what schulde moue his hyȝest vicar þus
to gete hym lordeschipe? Ande if frerus for þer state may not haue þis
lordeschipe, how schuld þo pope ner Criste reioyse hit on worldely
manere? If þou say þat þo pope haþ myche of þo empyre of Rome, certis   135
sithen haþ þo empire vnthryuen ande oþer worldely lordschipe. And
herfore bad Criste in his lawe þat his prestys schulde haue no parte
amonge hor breþerin of þo heritage, for he wolde be her heritage; and
þus was lordschip holden hole and clene by þo law of God. Summe men
sayne þat, if þo pope were lorde of al þinge in þis londe þat is in þo dede   140
honde of prestys, he were more lorde þan oure kynge: þus forsakynge
of Gods lawe, and floryschyd wordys of anticriste dystroyed rewmes in
cristendame and pes and gode religioun.

26

Church and State

'Lo', said þe Kniȝt...'þou saist þat holi chirche schuld be
distroyed bot if þe clergi miȝt vse her power after Goddes lawe to
help and helþ of mennes soules. Parde, þou woste wele þat I ne said
neuer þe contrarie. Bot I said þat no preste mai haue no maner worldli
power bot all spirituele powere, as I haue openli schewid tofore bi mani   5
diuers places in holi writ and in þe popes lawe. And þer as þou saist þat
a borell clerk schuld noȝt mell him of þe popes lawes ne of men of holi
chirch, I wote wele þat ȝe bene wroþe þerwiþ, for moni of ȝow con
litel of Goddes lawe ne of þe popes lawe neiþer. And þerfor ȝe wold

132 Matt. 8. 20   **137** Josh. 13. 33

10 þat borell clerkes couþ no more þan ȝe, for þan miȝt blynde Baiard be þe
boldest hors in þe cart. And ser, me wondreþ mich of þe, þat þou
schuldest sai so. For all be it þat þou ne can, or elles fewe of þi degre
conne, bot litel of þe gospel wherbi all holi chirch schuld be skill be
reulid and gouernid, ȝit þou art a doctore of decrees and of þe popes
15 lawes; and I ne haue bot litile said þat I ne haue schewid als wele be
þe popes lawe as be Goddes lawe. It semeþ þan þat ȝe be suspect of all
euil doynge þat es reknid and spoken tofor, siþen þat ȝe will noȝt þat
ȝoure awne lawe be aleggid aȝayne ȝowe. And parde, as þou woste wele,
I ne haue noþinge said in abreggynge of ȝoure gostli powere, bot
20 vndernymmynge of þat þat ȝe mell ȝow wiþ worldliche doynges and
wiþ worliche powere, in lessinge and forto abrege þe kinges power,
which I will wiþstonde wiþ all mi hert and all mi connynge. For als me
þink, ȝeue ȝe miȝt haue ȝour will wiþouten wiþstondinge, in a schorte
tyme ȝe schuld haue supplauntid michel of þe kinges power aȝeines
25 Goddes forbot.'

'Parde!, ser', said þe Clerk þan, 'I am þe kinges legeman als
wele as þiself, and als loþe me were þat his powere were abreggid of þat
him aȝt to haue. Bot wele I wote þat be all lawes, riȝt as þe kinge es
lord and souerayne of all temperaltes and temperal gode, riȝt so es þe
30 pope lord and souerayne of spiritualte and spirituale gode, and godes of
holi chirch. For what gode euer þat es ȝeuen to holi chirche it es holi,
and longeþ riȝtfulliche to prestes, as þe popes lawe bereþ wittnes in þe
decrees. And þerfor it es wonder þat ȝe will mell ȝow wiþ ony þinge þat
es ȝeuen to holi chirche, for all maner sich godes es holi and mai neuer
35 after be torned into worldlich mannes power, as þe lawe of holi chirch
bereþ wittnes.'

'Leue sir, I wote wele þat þou art þe kinges lege man, and
aȝtest to maintene him and his reale powere als wele as oni man of his
reume, boþ þou and all oþer prestes, bihsschopes and oþer. Bot it semeþ
40 þat ȝe sai one wiþ ȝour mouþ and anoþer wiþ ȝour hert, and for ȝe
wolde be sotilte encroche to ȝou lordschipe of temperale godes, (and
þat es forboden to all clerkes, as I haue schewid openli tofore), and þat me
þinkeþ þou scheweþ openliche in þat, þat þou saist þat þe kinge ne haþ
no power of no worldlich gode after þat it es ȝeuen to holi chirch, for, als
45 þou saist, all is holi and mai noȝt be put in no temperal mannes posses-
sioun. Lo, how openliche men mow se þat ȝe mene noȝt oneliche to
abrege þe kinges powere bot to distroye holli his regalte. For ȝe haue þe
þridd parte of þis land in ȝour handes, and ȝit ȝe beþe about to purchase
and amortaise euer more and more, so þat, ȝeue ȝe had ȝour will, in

45 is] his

processe of tyme 3e schuld haue all þe possessiouns of þis land in 50
3our handes; and þan, als 3e sayne, þe kinge had no more to done þerwiþ,
and þan had he lost all his souerainte and gouernaile of his land. For,
3eue he wold þan hold oni land, him most hold it of þe clergie, and so
be vnder þe soueraynte and þe gouernaile of þe clergie, and þan were he
no kinge, bot as kinge in a somer game, or elles as a kinge paintid on a 55
wall. God 3eue him grace to be war, and wiþstonde sich tresoune of þe
clergie, or it be wers þan it es! Also, 3eue þat no þinge þat es ones in þe
clergie hondes, 3euen to holi chirch, als þou saist, mi3t neuer be affter
in temperall mannes power, ne no temperall man haue power ne lordschip
þerof, how schuld þan oni clerk bi him mete or drink, or ony oþer þinge 60
þat him nedede, or sell to oni temperall oni maner gode þat þai had?
For no man wold sell hem his gode, ne bigge no3t of hem for mone, bot
he mi3t be maister after of þat mone þat was erst a prestes mone þat he
had solde his gode fore, and also bot he mi3t be maister of oni gode þat
he bo3t of a preste and putt it in worldlich doynge ri3t als him likid. 65
And also in processe of tyme all þe mone of þis land schuld be holi and
no man mell him þerof, bot all be in prestes handes. Lo! sir, sich
abusiounes foloweþ of þat þat 3e ask oþerwise þan Goddes will es, and
a3aynes Goddes lawe, and 3it, for feynid pite and coloure of holi chirch
and semynge holines, nouþer þe kinge ne pepil wollen ne dar no3t wiþ- 70
stonde 3our priue dissaites till þat þor3e Goddes grace þai haue gode
knowynge of 3oure corsid malice. Þat God graunt be tyme, amen!'

'Wele, ser Kni3t', said þe Clerk, 'I se wele þat 3e will haue 3our
will, what be maistrie and elles. Wherfor it semeþ þat holi chirch schall
be born doune; and so þai þat schuld be soueraynes schull be suggetes, 75
and þai þat schuld be suggetes schull be soueraines. And þerfor I can no
forþer, bot God leue and 3eue grace þat it wele be to Goddes worschip;
for, als me þinkeþ, holi chirche es in poynte to be lost and distroyed.'

'Ow! ser Clerk, now I se wele þat þou art at þi wittes ende, for
be þin own wordes it semeþ þat þou ne canst no resoune ne skill for to 80
defend þi cause. Bot ri3t als Iak Roker or a lewd preste answereþ, ri3t
so dostow. For it es þe maner of all sich lewde iauels, when þai ne conne
no forþer, þan þai concluden all þair mater wiþ 'God leue it wele be',
and 'God 3eue grace to make a gode ende'; and all sich wordes semen
holinesse when 3e mene moste venyme in 3oure hert. For who so can 85
oni resoune, he mai wele wit þat I ne haue no3t said in distruccione of
holi chirch, ne in abreggynge of þe lawes ne þe power þerof, bot, als
ferforþ als I mai or can, I haue forþerd and mayntened all þe clergie as
mich as Goddes lawe will. In so mich þat me þinkeþ, and so it es, þat
men of holi chirch a3t to be soueraynes ouer all kinges and oþer men in 90

spritualte, which soueraynte es a seruis þat þai aȝt to do to þe pepil, als
I haue oft said be Goddes lawe; þat es to saie, to minister þe sacramentes,
to schriue and assoile þe pepil, to prech and teche þe pepil, and ȝeuen
hem ensaumpil of gode lif. But in all þinge þat longeþ to temperalte þai
95 schuld be suggetes to þe kinge and to oþer lordes temperales, and, ȝeue
þai wiþstonde þe temperale power, þe kinge and þe lordes temperals
schuld chastise hem and constreyne hem, for þerto þai bereþ þe swerd,
as it es said tofore be autorite of saynte Poule.'

'Sir Kniȝt, þou ne takes none hede how Peter said to Crist,
100 when he bad his disciples to sell her cote and bige hem swordes, 'Lord',
said Peter, 'here bene two swerdes', and Criste answerd and said 'þat'
es ynoȝe' in tokene þat Peter schuld haue boþ þe swerde of temperalte
and þe swerde of spritualte, þat es to mene boþe spirituale powere and
temperal powere; so þat þerbi ȝe mow se þat þe kinge ne haþe no power
105 ouer þe pope ne of þe clergie, bot all schuld be suggetes to him bi þe
gospell.'

'Saynte Mari!' said þe Kniȝt, 'it es litel wonder þof ȝe ouerlede
þe comone lewde pepil wiþ sich fals exsposiciones of holi writt! Parde,
þou wost wele þat, when þat Crist schuld be take, Peter drowe his swerde
110 for to fiȝt and smote of Malkus here, and onone Crist repreued him and
bad him putt vp his swerd, in token þat þe temperale swerde langid noȝt
to him, ne to none oþer preste for to fiȝt ne smyte wiþ no temperall
swerd. But þe swerde þat he schuld smyte wiþ schuld be þe swerde of þe
goste, þat es Goddes worde, as saynte Poule saiþ. And temperall men
115 schulde chastise men bodelich wiþ temperall power, and þat bitokneþ
þat þai bere þe swerde, as saint Poule saiþ. So þat þe pope and þe clergi mai
noȝt do, bot wiþ þe swerde of gode techinge and prechinge, and þe
kinge and oþer lordes schuld constreyne wiþ þe swerde of temperall
powere, as þe pope saiþ in his lawe, and es acordinge to þe gospell and
120 to saint Poule boþ. And þerfor, ser Clerk, ȝeu[e] it vp, and late þe kinge
and oþer lordes vse her powere in temperalte, and þe pope and þe
clergie vse her power in sprituelte; for þan schall holi chirch stonde
wele boþe in temperalte and in spritualte, and þan schall þou haue þat
þou askist of God when all resoune fayleþ þe, þat es when þou biddist
125 God leue it wele be. And God send grace þat þer be a gode ende.
Amen.'

98 Rom. 13. 1   **100** Luke 22. 36–8   **110** Matt. 26. 52, John 18. 11
114 Eph. 6. 17

27

The Lollard Disendowment Bill

And in the same yere at a parlement holden at Westminster the comens putte a bille vnto the kyng of the tempereltees beyng in religious handes, of the which the tenour sewith:

    To the moste excellent redoubte lorde the Kyng, and to alle the noble lordes of this present parlement, shewen mekely alle the trewe comvnes seyynge this sothely: oure liege lorde the Kyng may have of the temperaltees by bisshopes, abbotes and priours, yoccupyed and wasted provdely withinne the rewme xv erles and m^{1}vc knyhtes, vi m^{1}cc squyers and c houses of almesse mo thanne he hath now at this tyme, well mayntened and trevly by londes and tenementz susteyned. And euermore whanne alle this is perfourmed, oure lorde the Kyng may have euery yeer in clere to his tresour for defence of his rewme xx m^1 *libri* and more, as hit may be trevly prevyd. And caste that euery erle may spende by yere iij m^1 markis of londes and rentz, and euery knyht c marcz of rent and iiij plowlonde in his owne demeyns; and euery squyer xl marcz with ij plowlande in his demeyns; and euery house of almesse c marcz, by oueresiht of goode and trewe sekulers, because of preestes and clerkes that now haue full nyh distroyed alle the houses of almesse withinne the rewme; and also for to ordeyne that euery tovne thurhoute the rewme shulde kepe alle pore me[n]ne and beggers which mowe nat travaylle for her sustenaunce, after the statut made at Cambrigge, and, in caas at the forseyde comens myht nat extende for to susteyne hem, thanne the forseyd houses of almesse myht helpe hem.

    And how all this myht be done, wille ye witte that the temperaltes of bisshopes, abbotes and priours extende to the somme of ccc m^1 marke and xxij m^1 markes by yeer. That is for to say of the temperaltes of the erchebisshop of Caunterbury with the twoo abbeys there, Shrevysbury, Coggesale and Seint Osyes ben worth by yeer xx m^1 marcis. Of the bisshop of Deram and the abbey there xx m^1 marcis. The erchebisshop of Yorke and two abbeys there xx m^1 marcis. The bisshop of Wynchestre and two abbeys there xx m^1 marcis. Clerkenwell with the membres xx m^1 marcis. And so amonteth the first c m^1 marcis.

    18 nyh] nyh haue   **20** menne] meyne

The bisshop of Lincoln with the abbeys of Ramsey and Peter-
burh xx m^l marcis. The abbeys of Bury and of Gloucestre xx m^l marcis.
35 Of the bisshop of Ely with the twoo abbeys there, and Spaldyng and
Lenton xx m^l marcis. Of the bisshop of Bathe and the abbeys of
Westminster, Seint Albons and Okeburn xx m^l marcis. Of the bisshop
of Worcetre with the abbeys there and Gloucestre, Enesham, Abyngdon,
Evysham and Redyng xx m^l marcis. And so amonteth the secunde
40 somme, c m^l marcis.

Of the bisshop of Chestre with the abbey there and Bannastre,
and of the bisshop of London, Seint Dauid, Salysbury and Excetre
xx m^l marcis. Of the abbeys of Revous, Fonteyns, Gervous, the abbey of
Grace, Wardon, [V]ay[l]ryell, Waley and [S]aley xx m^l marcis. Of the
45 abbeys of Leycetre, Waltham, Gysburn, Merton, Osney and [C]ircetre
xx m^l marcis. Of Dover, Batayll and Lewes, Coventre, Daventre and
Turney xx m^l marcis. Of Bristow, Northampton, Thornton, Kyllyng-
worth, Haylles, Wynchecombe, Perche3ore, Fressewyde, Notteley and
Gremysby xx m^l marcis. Of Carlehill, Chichestre, Herdeford, Rouches-
50 tre, Seint Marie Ouerey, Bertholomevs, Savtrey, Huntyngdon and
Swynesheede xx m^l marcis. And so amonteth the thridde somme, c m^l
marcis.

Of the bisshop of Norwich with the abbey there and Crovland
x m^l marcis. Of Malvysbury, Bruton, Tewkesbury, Dunstaple, Shir-
55 burn, Taunton, Byland and Burton xij m^l marcis. And so amonteth the
ferthe somme xxij m^l marcis.

And in caas that eny bisshopery[c] or abbeye or priorye [haue
more, it may be addid] for to helpe home that [that] forseyde somme of
ccc m^l marcis and xxij m^l marcis be holich kepte, that eu[er]y persone
60 above seyde mowe clerly be served as ys above wretyn. And thanne shall
duelle clerely xx m^l *libri* and more euery yeer to the kyngis tresorye.

And yitt ferthermore may be getyn c m^l *libri* of moo temperaltes wasted and occupyed amonge worldly clerkes, and fynde therwith
x m^l v c preestes and clerkes. And euery clerke by yeer xl s. And
65 vj m^l cc squyers in the manere byfore seyde.

And thus in alle the rewme may men have xv erles, xv m^l
knyhtes and squyers moo thenne be now sufficyauntly rentyd, and yitt
therto xv vnyuersitees and therto xv m^l preestes and clerkes sufficiantly
fondon be temperell almesse, yif yt lyke the Kyng and lordes to spenden
70 hem in that vse, and the Kyng to his tresour xx m^l *libri* by yeer. And yitt
c houses of almesse and euery houvs c marcis with londe to feden with

44 Vaylryell] Ayryell, Saley] Galey   **45** Circetre] Gircetre   **57** bisshoperyc]
bisshoperve   **59** euery] eny

alle the nedefull pore men and no coste to the tovne but only of the temperaltes morteysed and wasted amonge provde worldely clerkes, the which provde clerkes for alle that is takyn away of here temperaltes mow yitt expenden by yeer in her spiritualtes as hit is extent in the cheker   75
clerelich c m¹ xliij m¹ vijc xxxiiij *libri*, x s. iiijd.ob.

And yitt have we nat touched of colages, of chauntres, of White Chanons, of cathederall chirches with her temperaltes, and chirches with here temperaltes, and chirches appropred into houses of monkes, of Charterhouses, and ne of Frenche monkes, ne of gle[b]es,   80
ne of Bonehommes, ne of spytell[s], ne ermytages, ne of Crouched Freres.

And therfore alle the trewe comeners desireth to the worship of God and profyte of the rewme that thes worldely clerkes, bisshopes, abbotes and priours that arun so worldly lordes, that they be putte to   85
leven by here spiritualtes, for they lyven nat now ne done the office of trewe curates other [as] prelates shulden ne they helpe nat the pore comens with here lordeshippes as that trewe sekulers lordes shulden, ne they lyve nat in penaunce ne in bodely travaylle as trewe religious shulden by here p[rof]ession. But of euery estate they take luste and ese   90
and putte fro hem the travaylle and takyth profytes that shulden kome to trewe men, the which lyf and evyll ensample of hem hath be so longe vicious that alle the comen peple, bothe lordes and symple comvnes, beth now so vicious and enfecte thurh boldeship of here synne that vnneth eny man dredith God ne the devyll.   95

To the which bille as that tyme was noon answere yoven.

80 glebes] gleves   88 lordeshippes] lorldeshippes   90 profession] possession

NOTES

Exigencies of space have imposed certain restrictions on the material and form of reference included. For each text a brief introduction is given, with the addition before no. 6 of a summary account of the Wycliffite Bible. Notes follow on points of obscurity in the text (though largely ignoring questions that arise in the collation of other manuscripts), with some indication of the background to the material and the reappearance of it in other medieval texts. Reference is given to Wyclif's Latin works since, directly or indirectly, the vernacular writers must have had access to them. Some, but not exhaustive, parallels are presented from other English Lollard writings. Few references to contemporary orthodox material have, for reasons of space, been included. In unprinted material and in some quotations from older editions the punctuation and capitalisation is mine; abbreviations are expanded in the same manner as in the texts here edited. Save where the point of comparison would be lost, Latin quotations have been translated.

PART I. THE NATURE OF WYCLIFFITE BELIEF

1. Wyclif's Confessions on the Eucharist

Both confessions are recorded in the two manuscripts of Henry Knighton's *Chronicle*; the edition here is from the earlier, BL Cotton Tiberius C. vii, ff. 179v and 180v–1 (T) which appears (see V. H. Galbraith, 'The Chronical of Henry Knighton', *Fritz Saxl ...A Volume of Memorial Essays*, ed. D. J. Gordon (London, 1957), pp. 136–48) to be a direct copy of Knighton's draft, made in his own abbey of St Mary of the Meadows, Leicester. The second manuscript, BL Cotton Claudius E. iii, ff. 271, 271v–272 (C) has no independent value as it is a direct copy of T. The second confession alone is found in Bodley 647, ff. 63v–64v (B), a miscellany of Lollard texts dating from the fifteenth century. Both confessions were printed from T in the edition of Knighton, ii. 157–8, 161–2; the first was reprinted from Knighton by Arnold iii. 500 and the second from B by Arnold iii. 502–3.

Knighton, writing probably about 1390, inserts these two vernacular confessions into his Latin narrative for 1382, the first reported as delivered before William Courtenay, archbishop of Canterbury, in London, the second as presented in Oxford before the archbishop and his council. Whether the English texts can be regarded as Wyclif's own words seems uncertain, despite Knighton's testimony. Certainly neither of them is a direct translation of any single Latin text by Wyclif, though the statements are an anthology of phrases that can be paralleled many times (the nearest is the *De Fide Sacramentorum* only known in MS Trinity College Cambridge B. 14. 50, ff. 56–8, printed by S. H. Thomson, *Journal of Theological Studies* xxxiii (1932), 361–5, but this is longer and includes patristic citations). Equally it would appear that, since the language of T is more northerly in character than would be expected in Leicester

around 1390, the confessions must have been accurately copied
from a document that had come into Knighton's possession. But
both these points could be explained on the assumption of authorship by followers of Wyclif, whilst the second confession, couched
in the plural, seems especially likely to be a communal expression
of belief. Since Leicester was from at least 1381 a centre of
Lollardy, and since one of Knighton's fellow canons at Leicester
was Philip Repingdon, one of Wyclif's closest Oxford associates
(see below no. 4/60n), the chronicler might well have had access
to Wycliffite *schedulæ* of the sort in which this type of text circulated. It would appear that Knighton's understanding of the
theological niceties of the Eucharistic controversy was poor, since
he introduces both confessions as if they were orthodox, constituting a renunciation of the heresies that Wyclif had advanced;
both, in fact, reaffirm Wyclif's position as that is set out in the *De
Eucharistia* and in all his later writings.

The first three heresies of which Wyclif was condemned in 1382
(see Intro. p. 5) concerned the Eucharist: 'that the substance of
material bread and wine remains after the consecration in the
sacrament of the altar', 'that accidents do not remain without a
subject after the consecration in the same sacrament', and 'that
Christ is not in the sacrament of the altar identically, truly and
really in his own bodily person' (*Fasc. Ziz.* 277–8, Knighton ii.
158). The three statements isolate three interlocking elements in
contemporary Eucharistic theology: the first that, after the words
of consecration, by the miracle of transubstantiation the place of
the bread or wine is taken by the body and blood of Christ; the
second that, to explain this miracle, whilst the colour, texture,
taste and dimensions of bread (its 'accidents') remain, the
reality of bread (its 'substance' or 'subject') was replaced by the
body of Christ; thirdly, that this body of Christ is precisely
identifiable with Christ's corporeal body, born of Mary and now
in heaven. This contemporary position had been reached after
many centuries of debate, a debate which reached its culmination
following the discussion of Berengar of Tours (whose views, as
contemporaries realised, Wyclif to some extent revived) in the
explanations of Aquinas and of Duns Scotus and Ockham. Wyclif
came to his final position as a result of three factors: first, the
evidence of the biblical texts (primarily Matt. 26. 26–9, Mark
14. 22–5, Luke 22. 19–20 and I Cor. 11. 23–7) from which the
fathers elaborated their views and to which, therefore, they and

later scholars must be subordinated; secondly, his realist philosophical outlook which held that the essence of matter was indestructible and that the alteration proposed in the miracle of transubstantiation was therefore impossible; thirdly, an attitude of materialistic scepticism (the bread and wine undergo no change that is apparent to man's senses) coupled with a desire to shift the whole argument onto a more spiritual plane, to a devotion towards Christ, represented by, but not contained in, the sacrament. Wyclif's view, maintained with consistency through the last years of his life (in the *De Eucharistia, De Apostasia, Trialogus* and numerous shorter texts), is fairly expounded in these two confessions. After the words of consecration Christ is present in the bread and wine but not in the same way as he was physically present on earth during his life or is now present in heaven (lines 4–6, 20–4); this dual nature of the bread and wine is comparable to the dual nature of Christ on earth, God and man (lines 24–6), and now spirit and body (lines 32–4). The presence of Christ in the sacrament does not come about by the elimination of the former substance of the bread or wine (lines 35–7). The important aspect of the sacrament is not, however, the precise nature of the substance on the altar but what that substance represents, just as a man looking at a statue considers whom it represents and not whether it is made out of oak or ash (lines 7–9). Though the validity of the words of consecration is not regarded as dependent upon the faith of the celebrant or of the participant (i.e. the Real Presence is not denied), the benefit to be derived from the sacrament is related to the state of mind of the recipient (lines 13–15). This complex view was followed, though with more crudity of expression, by the majority of Lollards.

For more detailed material on Wyclif's Eucharistic teaching see Leff (1967) ii. 549–57 and M. Wilks, 'The Early Oxford Wyclif: Papalist or Nominalist?', *Studies in Church History* v (1969), 69–98.

6 *seuen fote*: the traditional length of a man's body in the grave, cf Gower *Vox Clamantis* vii. 796.

7 Cf Arnold i. 133/19–21 'But oure bileve is sette upon þis point: what is þis sacrid hoost, and not what þing is þere' and MS Titus D.v, f. 17v. This concentration upon the significance of the object, rather than on its physical components, is linked with Wyclif's discussion of language and the metaphorical content of speech; see below no. 21B/33n.

23 See *Missale Sarum* coll. 622; following the consecration the host was broken into three parts.

24–8 Cf *Apology* 47/21ff.

26 Wyclif constantly maintained that his view of the Eucharist did not represent an innovation, but was a return to the beliefs of the church for many centuries

after the death of Christ (see *De Eucharistia* 47ff, *Opus Evangelicum* ii. 143ff). In fact the question of the Eucharist had not been a matter of frequent discussion or hence of close definition, until the twelfth century; the statements of Augustine, Ambrose and others quoted by Wyclif and his disciples were often of ambiguous wording (see below no. 21A/23n). For the twelfth-century discussion see J. de Montclos, 'Lanfranc et Bérenger', *Spicilegium Sacrum Lovaniense* xxxvii (1971).

30 The peculiar authority here attributed to Paul's doctrinal teaching derives from the supposed revelation of such questions when he was 'caught up to the third heaven' (II Cor. 12. 2–4), and is found in many medieval texts (e.g. Dante *Inferno* ii. 28ff).

31, 32, 36 The emendations derive from B, which is clearly independent of the tradition in Knighton. Knighton's text in 32–3 is obviously corrupt, since nothing is mentioned as the necessary comparison; in 36 the phrase translates the common *accidens sine subiecto*.

35 The doctrine of the Eucharist which Wyclif was most concerned to refute was that propounded by Duns Scotus and Ockham (the view of Aquinas, which later became the basis for the Tridentine formulation, seems to have been less widely held in late fourteenth-century England); according to this view, the substance of bread and wine, following the words of consecration, was annihilated and its place taken by the body and blood of Christ, though no complete natural explanation could be given for this miracle. Since Duns Scotus and Ockham were both Franciscan friars, it is not surprising that Wyclif often identified the opponents of his views specifically with the friars; friars, such as the Carmelite Kynyngham, the Franciscan Tissington, and the Augustinian Winterton, seem to have taken the early initiative in the refutation of Wyclif's views (see *Fasc. Ziz.* 43ff, 133ff, 181ff).

52–6 The Council organized by archbishop Courtenay in London was held during May 1382 within the house of the Blackfriars (Dominicans); on 21 May, following the reading of heresies and errors extracted from Wyclif's books, between 2 and 3 p.m. an earthquake was felt in England, damage being particularly severe in Kent and London. The Council thus gained the name of *Concilium Terremotus*; the events were interpreted by each side as a portent confirming its own position (see *Fasc. Ziz.* 272–3, and the Latin poem with English 'O-and-I' refrain written by a sympathiser of Wyclif (printed T. Wright, *Political Poems and Songs* (Rolls Series, 1859–61), i. 253–63 and also found in a Hussite manuscript, Vienna 3939, ff. 223v–225)). For an account of the Council see Workman ii. 246–93.

58–9 The appeal to the king *and his rewme* (here particularly the secular powers of the kingdom) is typical of Wyclif (see Wilks (1972), 109–30), and was sometimes used by the early Lollards (see nos. 3, 26 and 27); only after the Oldcastle rising did the Lollards realise that the secular as well as the ecclesiastical authorities were implacably opposed to them.

59–65 The three parts of the church are here the *possessioneres*, that is the monks, so-called because corporately they, unlike the friars, were allowed to hold property, the friars and the *thridde partye*, that is the secular clergy. From the beginning of his career Wyclif had antagonized the monastic clergy by his criticism of the abuses of their landed wealth (alluded to here line 60); later the friars, despite some early sympathy, incurred his wrath for their disagreement with his Eucharistic doctrine (see Gwynn (1940), 211–69). There is still here an expectation of support from the secular clergy, an expectation largely disappointed though a small number of minor clergy maintained Lollard ideas through the fifteenth century to the early Reformation period (see Thomson (1965) *passim*, and Dickens 16ff).

61, 63 The demand for adequate *growndyng* for beliefs and practices in the church is found throughout Wyclif and his followers; the usual meaning of the phrase is that the belief or practice can be established by reference to the Bible as taught by Christ himself, or as held by the primitive church (cf Intro. p. 6).

2. Sixteen Points on which the Bishops accuse Lollards

The single copy of this text, in MS Trinity College Cambridge B. 14.50, ff. 30v-34, dates from the early fifteenth century. The manuscript consists of two parts, the first 25 folios and the rest, but both are of Lollard origins: the first part contains Wyclif's *Descriptio Fratris* (Loserth 90, f. 20) along with some sermon notes which refer to the *Rosarium* (Intro. p. 7), the second Wyclif's *De Eucharistia Confessio* (Loserth 21, ff. 56-8), quotations from the *Rosarium* and various English texts. The *Sixteen Points* were printed by Deanesly 462-7, with an ascription to Purvey. This ascription is without foundation. Deanesly's chief piece of evidence, that the text occurs after the tract *Aȝens hem þat seyn þat hooli wriȝt schulde not or may not be drawun into Engliche* (ff. 26-30v) which she likewise ascribed to Purvey, is worthless since it can now be shown that this latter text is based on a Latin *posicio* written by the orthodox Richard Ullerston and has nothing whatever to do with Purvey (see 'The Debate on Bible Translation, Oxford 1401', *EHR* xc (1975), 1-18). Contrary to Deanesly's assertions, the text is not particularly moderate in its opinions, despite a tone less polemical than is often the case with Lollard defences, and the slight evidence on its date (see note to lines 96-104 below) points to composition late in the fourteenth century.

Lists of errors and accusations concerning the Wycliffites are found frequently after the 1382 condemnation. Some were intended as the basis of enquiries concerning Lollard suspects: examples of these are the list recorded in the register of bishop Polton of Worcester, in BL Harley 2179 probably from Lichfield, and in use in the later register of bishop Bekynton of Bath and Wells in 1449 (see *BIHR* xlvi (1973), 145-59), and the list that can be deduced from the long series of inquisitions in the Norwich diocese between 1428 and 1431 recorded in Westminster Cathedral B.2.8. The function of these model answers (for which there is a parallel in the text printed in Arnold iii. 455-96) can only be guessed: they may have been intended for use in the Lollard schools (for which see below no. 5/13n). The coverage of the *Sixteen Points* is largely ecclesiastical, save for *Point* 15, and, even within that range, the question of 'private religion', that is the validity of the monastic or fraternal life, is not mentioned.

1-43 The implications of each accusation will be considered in conjunction with the reply, to save unnecessary repetition.

44–9 The writer's point is that each of these accusations contains an element of truth about Lollard belief and an element of error; none of them is simply acceptable or to be rejected. Since a *coupulatif* simply links two clauses or sentences together, denial or acceptance of the whole must go together. The problem of the simple Lollard faced with an opponent better trained in theological argument exercised many writers: see, for instance, Arnold i. 207/31ff 'But algatis be we war þat we confesse not falsehede, and denye not Cristis lawe, for no cais þat mai falle. If we undirstonden not þe witt, graunte we þe forme of þe wordis, and confesse we þe truþe of hem, al if we witen not which it is.'

50 *trewe cristen men*: the words, like the commoner *true men*, refer specifically to the Lollards; Wyclif often refers to himself as *quidam fidelis* (e.g. *Sermones* i Præfatio 3) and to himself and his sympathisers as *fideles* (e.g. *Opera Minora* 245/18). The appellation is in agreement with the claim in no. 1/26 that Wyclif and his followers were alone in the true line of descent from Christ and the primitive church.

55ff The accusation concerning the Eucharist is that of remanence alone, that is the belief that material bread remained after the words of consecration (see no. 1 introductory note, the first heresy of the 1382 list). The reply given is in line with Wyclif's first confession above.

59 Jerome *Epistola ad Hedibiam* PL 22. 986; the same passage is quoted many times by Wyclif (e.g. *De Eucharistia* 200/5–9, *Sermones* ii. 453/19–22, *Sermones* iii. 278/22–5, *Trialogus* 250/21–4).

65 The manuscript includes marginal references to two chapters in canon law, *De Consecratione* dist. II caps. 48 and 79 (Fried. i. 1331–2 and 1346), the chapters being drawn from Augustine and Hillary respectively.

69–80 For the early stages of confessional theory see A. Teetaert, *La confession aux laïques* (Wetteren, 1926). Following the terms of the 1215 Lateran Council, the duty of annual oral confession, followed by participation at the Eucharist, was laid on all confirmed Christians (the decree was incorporated into canon law, *Decretals* lib. V. tit. 38 c. 12, Fried. ii. 887–8). The aim of the decree was to ensure that all received some elementary moral and doctrinal instruction; to this end many handbooks were written in the succeeding period (see E. J. Arnould, *Le Manuel des Péchés* (Paris, 1940), pp. 1–59). But the abuses resulting from this decree, laudable though its intention was, were numerous: those particularly abhorrent to the Lollards were, first, the idea that no contrition was of validity unless oral confession and priestly absolution followed and, secondly, that, conversely, oral confession and priestly absolution automatically brought remission of sins, regardless of the sinner's state of mind. The second, as the handbooks make clear, was a misconception, albeit a popular one; the first was more generally regarded as correct. Wyclif, characteristically, went back to first principles: God alone can forgive sin, since all sin is basically an offence against God; equally God alone can see into man's heart and hence know whether he is truly contrite; it follows that only God can properly pronounce absolution. At best, therefore, confession to a priest and the latter's absolution can only be a confirmatory act, the priest functioning as God's deputy; at worst, when the man confessing is not penitent, the action of the priest is irrelevant and blasphemous. Wyclif outlines this theory repeatedly (e.g. *Sermones* ii. 62/26ff, 138/24ff); Netter refutes it at length *Doctrinale* v. 135–62. In Lollard writings objections to oral confession recur (e.g. Arnold i. 196/3ff, iii. 253/11ff), and are repeated in trials (e.g. in the Salisbury registers of Waltham (1389), f. 222, Aiscough (1440), ii. 52v, Langton (1490), ii. 39, 40, Blythe (1498), ff. 70v, 72v, 78, 79).

73 The margin refers to canon law, *Decretum* II, c. 33 q. 3 c. 83 (Fried. i. 1182).

81–7 The duty of the laity to pay the tenth part of their winnings, whether in cash or kind, to the church, originating in the Mosaic law (Gen. 28. 22, Lev. 27. 30–3, Num. 18. 21–4), existed throughout the medieval period. For a general survey see G. Constable, *Monastic Tithes* (Cambridge, 1964), pp. 1–56, with references given. The theory of tithes was disputed before Wyclif: were they a legal obligation to be paid without question to the clergy, or were they alms to be given to the deserving poor? Wyclif maintained the latter view, for instance in *De Civili Dominio* i. 317ff and later in *Sermones* iii. 471/26ff, and the 1382 condemnation included 'that tithes are free gifts of alms, and that parishioners may withhold them from their parish clergy if these are sinful, and may give them to whom they please' (*Fasc. Ziz.* 280–1). The wording of the *Sixteen Points* seems innocuous, but there are various tendentious implications: that tithes are advance payments for offices to be performed (*for þat ende þat curatis do þer office* 'for the purpose that curates should do their job') rather than formal rights that involve no reciprocal obligation; that the clergy to whom tithes are paid should themselves be otherwise without means for support (thus presupposing the views expressed in answer to *Point* 9). For the view here cf *De Civili Dominio* i. 323/24ff 'there are four ways...to gain tithes, namely, holiness of life, liveliness in the preaching of God's word, perfect administration of the sacraments and holy things, and wise brotherly correction', Thorpe pp. 142–9, the unprinted Lollard texts in BL Additional 24202, ff. 34v, 40v, and later in the present manuscript (f. 45v) where is stated that the church 'myȝt be helid wiþ a schort medicyne: to chese good curatis, and ȝeef hem no goodes but þei performe þe seruice þat falliþ to þer office'. Compare also *Piers Plowman* B. vi. 94, xi. 270ff, and *Mum and the Sothsegger* 653ff.

88–95 Wycliffite objections to the papacy followed a long tradition of anti-papal writings; they are expressed more fully in no. 24 below. Two arguments were fundamental to Wyclif's position: first, that the institution had no foundation in the Bible, the commission to Peter (Matt. 16. 18–19) being a representative assignment; second, that in so far as it was right to recognize any individual as supreme in the church, this should be the man of greatest virtue alive, demonstrably at the time of the papal Schism neither of the warring popes and, more basically, only recognisable by God himself. Wyclif set out his ideas fully in *De Potestate Pape* and reiterated them more briefly elsewhere. As in the *Point* above concerning tithes, the writer here lays stress on the merit of the individual claimant rather than on any entitlement automatically carried by the office.

89 Probably referring to I Pet. 2. 25, where Christ is called *episcopus animarum vestrarum*, combined with I Pet. 5. 4, where he is named *princeps pastorum*.

92 Clement I was probably the third successor of Peter at Rome, flourishing c. 96 (see ODCC); Cletus, identifiable with Anacletus (see ODCC), was reputed to have been the second successor of Peter; both are mentioned in the canon of the mass in the commemoration prayer. See no. 17/61ff for the Lollard view of the source of the papacy in the Donation of Constantine.

95 The concept of antichrist, mentioned in I John 2. 18, 22; 4. 3 and II John 7 specifically, but early associated with the men prophesied in Matt. 24. 5ff and with the events forecast in the Apocalypse, varies in Wycliffite writings (MS Titus D. v, f. 4v comments that the figure 'schal not be a singular person bi himself but an aggregat persone of many riȝt wikkid'). Here the term is understood literally, as in *Apology* 54/16 'Ilk one contrary to Crist is anticrist', but more typical is the expanded version of MS Douce 53, f. 11 'I calle antecrist al þe confederacie of hem þat aȝens Crist and aboue his gospel magnyfien mennys tradiciouns and lawis for wynnyng and delicat lijf, and bisily doen execucioun of her owne wille and comaunding, not reckinge of þe heestis of God and his lawe'; cf *Plowman's Tale* 493ff.

96–104 The power of excommunication was the church's final jurisdictional weapon against those disobeying its instructions; it could be a temporary or a permanent act. Its force was fundamentally moral, but it had severe practical consequences, the denial of all rights to participation in the church's sacraments and hence of the right of baptism, marriage or burial within consecrated ground. In the pursuit of heretics, including after 1401 Lollards, final excommunication preceded the assignment of the convicted person to the secular authorities for execution. Wycliffite objections to this power are the

same as those to priestly powers of absolution, since excommunication is
merely the final withholding of absolution. See Wyclif *De Civili Dominio*
i. 274/9ff, *Sermones* i. 237/17ff, iii. 159/5ff, and the 1382 condemnation 'quod
nullus prælatus debet aliquem excommunicare, nisi prius sciat ipsum excom-
municatum a Deo' (*Fasc. Ziz.* 279); cf *Apology* 13/14ff, 40/4ff. The attitude
here, reminiscent of Matt. 5. 39, may suggest that the persecution of Lollards
has not yet extended to execution and hence point to a date before the enactment of *De Hæretico Comburendo* in 1401.

101   A marginal note gives the reference *Decretum* II, c. 11 q. 3 c. 87 (Fried. i. 667),
a quotation from Augustine.

105–18 For the medieval theory of indulgence see N. Paulus, *Geschichte des Ablasses im
Mittelalter* (Paderborn, 1922–3), i. 212ff, and H. Delahaye, 'Les lettres d'indulgence collectives', *Analecta Bollandiana* xliv (1926), 342–79, xlv (1927), 97–123,
323–44, xlvi (1928), 149–57, 287–343. In addition to objections to the abuses of
indulgences, Wyclif opposed their theory as part of his views on absolution
(see *De Ecclesia* 549/1ff, *Opus Evangelicum* i. 37/36ff, *Trialogus* 357/4ff). The
writer here plays on the wide meanings of *pardoun* and *indulgence* to admit
their legality in certain situations, whilst denying the legitimacy of the 'pardon'
bought for money (cf *Piers Plowman* B. vii. 168ff, xx. 322ff).

108   Cf Ps. Lam. f. 186/1 'And euery seynte þat is in heuene, and eche man lyuyng
in erþe weren and ben but pronounceris of Cristis forȝifnes.' This is the
Lollard interpretation of the promise to Peter (Matt. 16. 19, 18. 18, John
20. 23).

109–12 For this release see more fully nos. 15/77ff and 16/100ff.

117   *sale-pardouns*: that is, pardons sold for money; cf Ps. Bod. f. 136/1 'men of
lustis tellen...how her couetouse schrift fadris assoilen hem as þei sey of synne
by a litil leed not weiynge a pound, hengid wiþ an hempyn þrid at a litil gobet
of a calfskyn, peyntid wiþ a fewe blake drauȝtis of enke, alle þe synnes doon in
manye ȝeeris.'

119–29 The objection is a multiple one, and the answers moderate. The two keys of
Peter (Matt. 16. 19), those of authority and of knowledge, are common to all
priests, but the powers are possessed in varying degrees. The restrictions
already made on the rights of the clergy should be remembered in assessing
the present answer: power of consecration remains, though in the modified
form of Eucharistic doctrine propounded, but that of absolution has been
strictly limited; tithes are payments for service; later clauses further specify
priestly duties. The priesthood of all believers is here allowed only in a limited
sense (cf no. 5/59ff) but, although laymen are held not to be obliged to
preach, the author leaves some ambiguity concerning their ability to do so.
For the view cf *De Eucharistia* 98/29ff 'Indeed according to the witness of
Augustine, Chrysostom and other saints, each predestined layman is a priest';
but the same idea appears also in Gower's *Vox Clamantis* iii. 1023ff.

128   For St John Chrysostom see ODCC; the homilies on Matthew which went
under his name in the medieval period (see A. Wilmart, *JTS* xix (1918),
305–27) are repeatedly used by Wyclif, especially in the *Opus Evangelicum*, and
his followers. The passage alluded to here is PG 56. 762; for further use see
below nos. 9 and 12.

128   *Lyncolne*: that is Robert Grosseteste, bishop of Lincoln from 1235 to 1253, one
of the few recent churchmen admired by Wyclif and his followers (see further
quotations nos. 12, 14). See ODCC and S. H. Thomson, *The Writings of Robert
Grosseteste* (Cambridge, 1940), and *Robert Grosseteste, Scholar and Bishop*, ed.
D. A. Callus (Oxford, 1955), especially pp. 95–6. The allusion here is to Dict 3
(printed E. Brown, *Fasciculus Rerum Expetendarum* (London, 1690), ii. 301).

130–8 Wyclif's views on law are found throughout his theological and political
writings, but principally in the *De Dominio Divino*, concerned with the absolute
law of God, *De Mandatis* dealing with the law of God revealed to men, and
the *De Civili Dominio* outlining the laws binding man to man; this last is
extended in the ecclesiastical field by *De Potestate Pape*. The controversial
element in his views was that dominion is dependent upon virtue, an idea

elaborated from Marsilius of Padua and archbishop FitzRalph (see Leff (1967) ii. 546–9 and M. Wilks, 'Predestination, Property, and Power: Wyclif's Theory of Dominion and Grace', *Studies in Church History* ii (1965), 220–36). This idea is implicit in the present defence that laws, whether of priests or kings, were not binding unless they furthered observance of God's laws; a more extended exposition of the idea is found in no. 25 below. As the theory is here formulated, it is easy to see the dangers of it to church and state, in that each man is apparently to be his own judge of the legality of laws and constitutions (see Aston (1960), 1–17).

139–45 Lollard views on the temporalities of the clergy are more fully expressed in no. 17 below. Wyclif's objections rest, as usual, on two foundations: that priestly possession of wealth or land is against the precepts of Christ (e.g. Luke 9. 3, 12. 33) and of Paul (I Tim. 6. 8), and that disobedience to these commands has led to gross abuses in the church. The ideal of clerical poverty put forward has some resemblance to that of St Francis, but the later sophistication of the Franciscan rule called forth some of the Lollards' most virulent polemic (e.g. Matthew 40–51). Influence from some of the Spiritual Franciscan writers (see D. L. Douie, *The Nature and the Effect of the Heresy of the Fraticelli* (Manchester, 1932) and M. D. Lambert, *Franciscan Poverty* (London, 1961)), who attempted to follow the original letter of Francis's rule, can be traced on the movement (e.g. that of Peter John Olivi in the *Opus Arduum*). The sting in the present mildly-worded passage is *acordyngly wiþ Goddis lawe*, as illustrated by the quoted passages.

145 For the concession cf *Piers Plowman* B. xv. 214–15.

146–54 The argument is over the prime duty of the priesthood rather than over the bishops' claim to control the licensing of preachers (cf Arnold i. 209/9ff, ii. 172/27ff). The comments here appear mild (cf the more extreme Lollard view, Arnold ii. 420/18, *Apology* 44/31ff, and Netter's comments *Doctrinale* vi. 20–27), but the use of hours, for which *matynes* here stands as an example, and masses is considered provisional on their affording the priest opportunity for biblical study, study which can be utilised in sermons.

152–4 The translation is only accurate in its first half, the second being in the nature of a résumé of the whole chapter (cf WB LV *And Y wole that alle ʒe speke in tungis, but more that ʒe prophecie*), a fair one in that Paul's objection to 'speaking in tongues' is that of unintelligibility to others. The interpretation of this gift as *orisouns and lessouns in Latyn* is obviously a distortion of the original sense, but one that had some currency in the debate about biblical translation in 1401 (cf Ullerston's tract, Vienna MS 4133, ff. 198, 201v, 203v–204).

155–63 The objection to prayers to saints is allied to the following doubts about images: that objects of worship other than God are being set up (see Wyclif *De Mandatis* 155/26ff, *Trialogus* 234/8ff and Netter's analysis *Doctrinale* vi. 108–16). In accordance with these reservations (on which see further no. 3/93ff below), the standard Lollard sermon-cycle has a very limited section of homilies for specific saints' days, of which all save two are for biblical saints. The last sentence here objects to over-ingenious singing (cf Arnold iii. 203/18, 481/13, Matthew 169/17) which, as fuller texts explain, obscures the words and attracts more admiration for the skill of the singer than fitting, and to recitation of prayers for money (see no. 16/124ff).

164–72 For the detailed arguments against the worship of images see below nos. nos. 3/93ff and 16/1ff; the issue was not a new one when Wyclif took it up but it became the view most frequently expressed in trials of Lollard suspects (cf Thomson (1965), 248–50). Apart from the command of Exod. 20. 4–5, the danger felt was that men would identify too closely the image with the object it represented.

169 *þat worschipe*: i.e. lawful honour (168).

173–9 The author is more outspoken against pilgrimages: following the previous two *Points*, saints are only to be invoked as supplicants to God, whilst images are only reminders of actuality; pilgrimage therefore serves no useful function. See further no. 16/100ff.

180–7 The tolerance here and respect for material churches may be contrasted with the opinion of an East Anglian heretic in 1429 'þat material churches be but of litel availe and owyn to be but of litell reputacion, for euery mannys prayer said in þe feld is as good as þe prayer said in þe churche' (see *English Historical Documents 1327–1485*, ed. A. R. Myers (London, 1969), p. 865).

183 PseudoChrysostom on Matthew, PG 56.886.

188–92 Cf no. 5/65ff. The pacifist view of the Lollards, a view only rarely found in Wyclif (see *Polemical Works* i. 137/23ff, *Minor Works* 123/20ff and compare Netter *Doctrinale* vi. 169), derives from Matt. 5. 21. The related objection to crusades, intensified by the crusade of bishop Despenser in 1383 in the Low Countries against the forces of pope Clement VII, is more frequently expressed; the Lollard *Opus Arduum* constantly returns to this topic. Cf Pecock *Repressor* II. 564/32ff, Gower *Confessio Amantis* Prol. 212ff.

193–201 For the ceremonies involved see Legg pp. 10–12 (water), 455 (bread), 124 (salt) and 50 (ashes). A similar tolerance for the distribution of blessed bread is found in the practice of Ramsbury, a Lollard 'priest', between 1385 and 1389 (see *JTS* NS xxiii (1972), 414, 418), but the later East Anglian group in 1428–31 rejected the ceremony (Westminster Cathedral MS B. 2.8, pp. 235, 246 etc.).

3. Twelve Conclusions of the Lollards

The *Twelve Conclusions of the Lollards* survive only as the result of the activities of their opponents: a Latin version is found in the *Fasc. Ziz.* 360–69, and both English and Latin forms are found in the text written to refute the *Conclusions*, Roger Dymmok's *Liber contra duodecim errores et hereses Lollardorum*. According to Dymmok and *Fasc. Ziz.* the *Conclusions* were affixed to the doors of Westminster Hall during the session of Parliament in 1395 (i.e. between 27 January and 15 February); Walsingham agrees with this account and adds that they were also nailed to the doors of St Paul's (*Hist. Angl.* ii. 216). Whether they were formally presented to Parliament is less certain. It seems likely, despite the rather ambiguous wording of lines 173–6, that the original version was in English; certainly an English version must have existed early enough for its inclusion in Dymmok's refutation which was presented to Richard II on his return from Ireland in 1396. Dymmok (see Emden, *Oxford* i. 617) was a Dominican friar, by 1396 regent at the London house; his refutation makes much use of the arguments of Aquinas, a fellow Dominican. Netter in his *Doctrinale* frequently alludes to the *Conclusions* (vi. 64, 107, 151, 154–5, 168). Four manuscripts of Dymmok's work survive; in all of them the English of the *Conclusions* has some northern features. The most important, from which the edition here is taken, is Trinity Hall Cambridge 17, which, to judge by the arms and miniature on f. 1, was the manuscript presented to Richard II. The other three are Cambridge University Library Ii. 4. 3, Oxford

Bodleian Lat. th. e. 30 and Paris Bibliothèque Nationale *fonds lat.* 3381; a further copy existed in BL Cotton Otho C. xvi but this section was destroyed in the 1731 fire. The *Conclusions* are spread through the work, separated by Dymmok's replies.

It is immediately obvious that the *Conclusions* are much more intemperate in tone than the *Points*, despite the overlap of subjects. Reference should be made to the elucidations given in no. 2. Dymmok's replies are too complex for summary here, and will only be referred to when they provide elucidation of the meaning of the *Conclusions*.

1 *pore men* is a frequent term used in their writings for Lollard sympathisers (cf Arnold iii. 309/4, 332/1, 455/2, 473/5); *tresoreris of Cryst* constitutes a substantial claim since, as Dymmok observes (p. 28) 'Dei principales thesaurarii prelati sunt ecclesiastici'.

5 *prelacye*: the writer means not only the bishops but the whole system of ecclesiastical government based upon provincial and episcopal jurisdiction; this word, and the related *prelate* are strongly derogatory terms in Wycliffite writings, though Dymmok affects not to understand the meaning (p. 29). *priuat religion* is another Wycliffite term of condemnation, used to signify the religious life adopted by any who have taken formal vows involving separation from the life of the community, and thus covering the life of monks, nuns, hermits, anchorites, friars or secular canons (cf Wyclif *De Religione Privata* I–II in *Polemical Works* ii. 483–536).

7–12 (*Point* 9) The writer obviously feels that the endowment of the church has brought such manifest and multiple harms that proof is not required; cf no. 17 below where the subject is discussed more fully.

8–9 *apropriacion*: the writer is here restricting the sense of the word to the assumption by a religious house of the revenues of a benefice. The original intention of this process was that the house, rather than a more unpredictable lay patron, should ensure a succession of suitable clerks for the living; the abuse, by the end of the fourteenth century a considerable one, lay in the retention by the house of the bulk of the income and the consequent impossibility of obtaining a permanent or well-educated incumbent. For some examples see K. L. Wood-Legh, *Studies in Church Life in England under Edward III* (Cambridge, 1934), pp. 127–53, and Thompson (1947), 109–15; the abuse was recognized by orthodox members of the church, cf Ullerston's *Petitiones* sent by the English church to the Council of Pisa in 1408 (see *Magni et Universalis Constantiensis Concilii* I. xxvii, ed. H. von der Hardt (Helmstedt, 1697), cols 1140–3 'Contra anormalam Ecclesiarum Appropriationem'). Cf *37 Conc.* nos. 6 and 28.

13–24 (*Point* 7 modified) The argument here seems initially to concern only the validity of episcopal ordination: that this is not founded in scripture, and that the outward sign of the tonsure is all that ordination provides; in this sense Netter, *Doctrinale* vi. 64, refutes the clause. But more is probably implied: the basic point is that the only foundation for the exercise of authority lies in virtue and not in the institution. Priesthood is conferred by God on the virtuous man. That this is correct is confirmed by Dymmok's refutation of lines 18–20 (pp. 65–6), which he took to mean that sinful bishops could not confer orders (i.e. the Donatist heresy); compare the 1382 condemnation (*Fasc. Ziz.* 278) 'that if a bishop or priest be in mortal sin, he neither ordains, consecrates (the Eucharist) nor baptises'.

20–4 Dymmok justifies the clerical tonsure (p. 69) by reference to Acts 18. 18. The pun in this sentence, using *crownis* to mean 'tonsure' and 'coin' (from the king's head on the reverse of certain coins), and *whyte hartys* to signify moral purity and the badges worn by the close associates of Richard II, was a common one in contemporary literature (though Netter had to explain the last point in *Doctrinale* vi. 64). It is found in *Mum and the Sothsegger* II. 41–5 and, with slight modification, in *Piers Plowman* B. xv. 504–7. At the foot of f. 1 in MS Trinity Hall 17 are two white harts with gold crowns around their necks in place of collars.

25–35   Neither this nor the related eleventh *Conclusion* is found in the *Points*. The objection to private religion here voiced is mentioned by Wyclif, but never as the primary argument (e.g. *Opus Evangelicum* ii. 42/8ff); compare Arnold iii. 399/28ff, *Apology* 103/29ff, *Upland's Rejoinder* 263, and in anticlerical satire Mann, *Estates Satire* p. 222 n. 32. For the possibility that this issue may be referred to in the Prologue to WB see below p. 174.

28   *þe suspecte decre*: for the so-called 'False Decretals' see S. Williams, 'The Pseudo-Isidorian Problem Today', *Speculum* xxix (1954), 702–7; the reference here is found in PL 130.265.

36–50   (*Point* 1) The statement here is much more outspoken and unambiguous than above no. 2/55ff; the claim of lines 42–4 equally goes further towards the idea of the priesthood of all believers than no. 2/125ff.

41   *Doctour Euangelicus*, that is Wyclif (Intro. p. 6); *Trialogus* 266–77, the sentence here being a brief summary of a long argument.

46   For the origins of the Corpus Christi feast, held on the Thursday after Trinity Sunday, see ODCC and H. Craig, *English Religious Drama of the Middle Ages* (Oxford, 1955), pp. 127–9 and the following account of the connection of the cyclic plays in England with that feast. The observance of the day was formally established in 1264, but tradition from the medieval period onwards associated the liturgy for the feast with Aquinas, who wrote it at the request of the pope.

48   Dymmok's refutation explains this allusion, which turns on the definition of a miracle: Aquinas, he observes (p. 111), would not have regarded the emergence of a chick from an egg as a miracle since the first requisite of a miracle was that 'it should be outside the operation of ordinary nature, which is not the case with the emergence of a hen from an egg'.

49–50   *turnith...defaute*: 'turns to the disgrace of him (i.e. Christ) who was always faithful and without sin'.

51–61   (*Point* 16) Dymmok took this as an attack on the sacraments of confirmation and extreme unction; Netter, *Doctrinale* vi. 168, was more probably correct in regarding it as a rejection of all such blessings. For the ceremonies see Legg pp. 10–12 (water), 105 (oil), 455 (bread), 124 (salt), 137 (wax, and cf further W. H. Frere, *The Use of Sarum* (Cambridge, 1898–1901), i. 147 and see i. 113–17 for incense). Cf *Opus Arduum* f. 190 for similar objections.

62–72   For more fundamental consideration of the relationship between secular and ecclesiastical authorities see below nos. 25–6. Wyclif presents the same objection in *De Civili Dominio* iv. 435/36ff and *De Officio Regis* 142/17ff. The origin of this position lies in the clerical domination of education, and the consequent dependence of the king upon the clergy for his administrative officers; see Pantin pp. 30–46. The danger is expressed forcefully in a sermon in MS Christ's College Cambridge 7, f. 70r–v 'But more comyne perel here þat worldly lordis schulden wisely fle is þat þey han many clerkis in worldly offices seruynge hem...and by þis cautel þe fend of helle haþ take lordschipis fro worldly lordis, and amortisiþ hem and ȝeueþ hem to bischopis and many oþere clerkis'. Dymmok took the point (p. 154) as also an attack on non-residence, as is implied though not stated in lines 71–2; this abuse was particularly prevalent (see Thompson (1947), 102ff, Mann pp. 57–8, and Gower *Vox Clamantis* iii. 137ff), and was one against which the church authorities tried to take action (see *Chichele Reg.* i. lxxx, Lyndwood, *Provinciale* iii. tit. 4).

66–7   Dymmok's reply to this (p. 157) is that the two functions, temporal and spiritual, of the clergy is service of one Master in two capacities 'ad honorem Dei et ecclesie utilitatem'; compare *Piers Plowman* B. Prol. 90, *Apology* 77/8ff, and BL Additional 24202, f. 2 quoting the same biblical passage 'for as þe

lordschipe of God and of þe fend ben contrarious, so þe seculer lordschip of
þe pope is contrarious to þe lordschip of þe kyng, for lordschip of kyngis is
of þe ordenaunse of God, and the toþer aȝenus it.'

73-92 (Cf *Point* 10 and the answer to *Point* 11) The objection is a multiple one: to
prayers for specific dead persons, as contrary to the law of charity which
should not be exclusive; to prayers for those who may be damned, since this
appears to question God's judgment; to the payment of money for prayers and
consequently to the religious foundations established for the purpose of prayer
for the dead. For Wyclif's own views see *De Oratione* in *Polemical Works*
i. 346/28ff, *Sermones* iii. 380/1ff and cf the 1382 condemnation, *Fasc. Ziz.* 281
and Netter *Doctrinale* vi. 105-7. The sources of these objections are, characteristically, that current practice is not supported by the Bible, and that money
and resources are thus diverted from the Church's true need to frivolous
private whim. Though *alle almes houses* are mentioned, the writer is clearly
thinking primarily of colleges of chantry priests, founded to pray for the souls
of the founder and his kin (see K. L. Wood-Legh, *Perpetual Chantries in Britain*
(Cambridge, 1965) and Thompson (1947), 247-91).

85 *þe brode way*, i.e. to hell (Matt. 7. 13).

89 *soulis prestis*: priests paid to pray for the repose of the souls of the departed.

90-2 It is not clear to which book the writer refers. That such a computation did
exist is, however, implied by the Lollard disendowment bill (no. 27 below),
and it seems likely that it circulated before the bill was actually presented. The
bill shows the concern of the Lollards for the public organization and
financing of poor relief. It is noteworthy that Dymmok regarded this clause as
a threat of disendowment: he replied (pp. 175-6) that, even if the inhabitants
of colleges need punishment for their laxity, the endowment was made to
God in perpetuity and hence cannot be alienated.

93-113 (*Points* 12-13) The paragraph is a neat anthology of the arguments and
phraseology concerning images and pilgrimages, for which see in more detail
no. 16.

97 The representation of the Trinity as an old man, God the Father, with a
young man, Christ (sometimes represented as on, or just descended from, the
cross), and a dove, symbol of the Holy Ghost, is a common one; see *Lexicon
der Christlichen Ikonographie*, ed. E. Kirschbaum (Rome, 1968-), i. 526-37 and
plates 6-10, and G. Schiller, trans. J. Seligman, *Iconography of Christian Art*
(London, 1971-2), ii. plates 770-93. It was a representation to which Wyclif
and his followers took particular exception: see Wyclif *De Mandatis* 156/21-8,
Arnold iii. 456/17, 491/3ff, no. 16/6ff below, and cf Netter *Doctrinale* vi. 155.

102-3 The scholastic distinction correctly explained here points to the accessibility of
learned ideas to the Wycliffites; the handbooks, the *Floretum* and *Rosarium*,
include this in their discussion of *adoracio*.

104-5 The two feasts are the Invention of the Cross on 3 May and the Exaltation of
the Cross on 14 September.

105-8 The ironic mention of *Iudas lippis*, as Dymmok's reply makes clear (pp. 190-1),
alludes to the kiss given at the arrest of Christ in the garden of Gethsemane
(Matt. 26. 49); Dymmok's answer is 'honour is the reward of virtue, and so
nothing should be honoured unless it has the character of virtue...but by this
criterion Judas's lips are in no way to be honoured', though it is not self-
evident how this justifies the honour accorded to the instruments of the
Passion.

110-13 Lollard doubts about the sanctity of those canonised by the church (cf Netter
Doctrinale vi. 122-32), deriving from their condemnation of the popes since the
time of Constantine, led to the exclusion of almost all post-biblical saints from
the standard sermon-cycle; for this view cf *Opus Arduum* f. 147v 'Popes of
Rome have canonised many who turn out afterwards amongst the number of
the damned or damnable'. Instead there was an attempt to exalt Grosseteste and
FitzRalph as saints (Arnold iii. 459/1, 281/13, 412/22, 416/20, Matthew 128/26,
Opus Arduum f. 147v, BL Harley 1203, ff. 76, 77v, 79v). The focus of these
objections to saints was most frequently Thomas a Beket (see *Fasc. Ziz.* 409-

10, Westminster Cathedral B. 2.8, p. 274, though cf Wyclif *Sermones* ii. 33/18–35/24), partly, no doubt, as the saint most honoured by pilgrimage in England, but partly as a man regarded as having died in defence of the powers and endowment of the church in opposition to the secular ruler (see Arnold i. 330/28–30 'As sum men trowen þat seint Thomas, erchebishop of Cantirbirie, diede for dowyng of þe chirche, and to defende goodis þerof'). See J. F. Davis, 'Lollards, Reformers and St. Thomas of Canterbury', *University of Birmingham Historical Journal* ix (1963), 1–15.

114–34 (Points 2, 5–6) See no. 2/69n for the objections here. The abuse of the confessional is a commonplace of medieval anti-clerical writing, see Mann pp. 37ff and references. *Piers Plowman* B. xx. 341ff, *Piers Plowman's Creed* 767ff, Gower *Vox Clamantis* iv. 863ff, *Jack Upland* 79.

125 *clause of warantise*: see OED *warranty*; a convenant annexed to a conveyance of real estate, by which the vendor warrants the security of the title conveyed; the vendor under feudal law was obliged, if the receiver were evicted, to yield to the receiver other lands of equal value. The irony lies not only in the right and certainty of the gift of heaven's joys, but also in the promise to provide compensation if the recipient fails of this gift. The reference is to letters of fraternity by which the donor, for a gift to a religious house or order, was promised a share in the prayers and spiritual merit acquired by the house or order; the excessive claims made in the sale of these letters are mocked by further exaggeration (for a general review of these letters see W. G. Clark-Maxwell, 'Some Letters of Confraternity', *Archæologia* lxxv (1926), 19–60 and lxxix (1929), 179–216).

129–30 *þe feynid pardoun a pena et a culpa*: cf. *Piers Plowman* B. Prol. 68 and vii. 3 and Bennett's notes thereon. Indulgences (see Paulus, above no. 2/105n, iii. 376) could not remit guilt, *culpa*, but only the punishment of guilt, *pena*, but the phrase was regularly used in indulgences; see E. Kantorowicz, *The King's Two Bodies* (Princeton, 1957), pp. 239–9 for the confusion in terms which extends into canon law.

130–2 I.e. if the pope's claim were true, then Christian charity would require that he should exercise his power to redeem all men from purgatory. Cf Wyclif *De Ecclesia* 570/28–572/20, and *Jack Upland* 201–3 on friars' trentals 'If þis be sooþ, what schal bifalle of ʒou þat may saue so liʒtli al soulis and suffren hem to be dampned or peyned in ʒoure defaute?'

135–53 (Point 15) See notes to no. 2/188–92. The writer here acknowledges the possibility in theory of 'just war', but points out that the practice of war is such that justice cannot remain after it has begun.

146–9 The objection here is to crusades against fellow-Christians; the reference may be general (cf *Piers Plowman* B. xix. 439ff) but the writer probably has in mind the 1383 crusade of bishop Despenser against the supporters of pope Clement VII.

154–62. Cf lines 25–35 above. Dymmok retorts to this *Conclusion* with the charge that the Lollards impute their own immorality to others (pp. 273ff); the charge must have had early currency as the author of the *Opus Arduum* rebuffs a similar accusation (f. 153); it recurs in Netter *Doctrinale* v. 130–4. It would appear that the practices of the continental Brethren of the Free Spirit were familiar to late fourteenth-century English clerics, and were by some opponents of the Lollards associated with this sect (see *JTS* NS xxiii (1972), 409–10). For continuing concern with unnatural practices see B. D. H. Miller, 'She who hath drunk any potion...', *Medium Ævum* xxxi (1962), 188–93.

161. *þe mantil and þe ryng*: the habit of a nun.

163–71 Two objections are here confused: to unnecessary adornment of churches and religious persons, and to crafts that serve no useful function in secular society. The dislike of the first is explained further in no. 22 below. For the second compare Wyclif *De Statu Innocencie* 498/20ff and Salisbury register Aiscough (1443), ii. f. 53v where the suspect is against vain crafts such as those of goldsmiths and armourers; also *Jack Upland* 40–3 and *Daw's Reply* 575n. For a possible connection between the two points compare the orthodox answer to

Lollard views on images in BL Harley 31 f. 182 'if it were true that the making of images or carvings is against the first commandment, then it would follow that all artists, painters, illuminators of books, moneyers, carpenters, gold-workers, sculptors, and in short all craftsmen who make the likenesses or images of things by carving, weaving or painting would be sinning and illegal.'

174 As in line 90, it is not clear to what book the writer refers. Deanesly p. 282 reiterates the earlier view that this is the *37 Conclusions* (see below no. 24), but there is no reason for the identification.

174–5 The claim is justifiable even as early as 1395; the *Opus Arduum* has a similar statement (see *Notes and Queries* NS xx (1973), 448) and episcopal and secular edicts against Wycliffites bear out the early multiplication of Lollard tracts.

4. Thorpe's evidence about Wyclif's university followers, 1407

The Examination of William Thorpe has been known for some time from the edition by A. W. Pollard, *Fifteenth Century Prose and Verse* (London, 1903), pp, 97–174, a partially modernised version of the early print (STC 24045) probably made in Antwerp in 1530. The text was known to Sir Thomas More; for details about the possible editors of the 1530 print see A. Hume in *The Complete Works of St. Thomas More* viii. 2, ed. L. A. Schuster and others (New Haven and London, 1973), 1077–8. Bale added a Latin version, now incomplete, to the manuscript of *Fasc. Ziz.*, MS Bodleian e Mus. 86, f. 105v and following five inserted leaves, a version he had translated from English in 1543. Foxe included the English in iii. 250–85; he also mentions manuscripts of the work in the possession of early sixteenth-century Lollards in the Chilterns and Burford (iv. 235, 238). Recently two Latin manuscripts have been discovered, Vienna Nationalbibliothek 3936, ff. 1–22v, and Prague Metropolitan Chapter o.29, ff. 188–209 (for the latter see M. Aston, *Thomas Arundel* (Oxford, 1967), p. 326 n. 1), showing that the Examination was an early work that reached Hussite Bohemia in the fifteenth century. Better evidence for the English text is the fifteenth-century copy in Bodleian MS Rawlinson c. 208, ff. 1–91v, taken as the basis of the extract here.

Improbable though this autobiographical account may seem, it is not unparalleled in the Lollard movement (see the letter of Wyche preserved in Prague University Library MS III. G. 11, ff. 89v–99v, printed by F. D. Matthew, *EHR* v (1890), 530–44). In some respects the account can be confirmed from other sources. It should be noted that the date of 1460 given by the print (Pollard p. 174) is not found in either English or Bohemian manuscripts, nor is it in Bale's translation or Foxe's transcription; it must be the date of the manuscript from which the Antwerp print

was made, and have no bearing on the original account. An entry
in John Lydford's notebook (ed. D. M. Owen, Devon and Corn-
wall Record Society xx (1975), nos. 206 and 209) confirms the
assertion Thorpe made in his examination (Pollard p. 165) that he
had been committed to the prison of bishop Braybrook of London
for preaching Wyclif's doctrines. Thorpe is described in the notebook as 'capellano Ebor' dioc.', thus confirming Aston's suggestion that he should be identified with a man of the same name
instituted to the vicarage of Marske, Cleveland, in March 1395
(*Thomas Arundel*, p. 326 n. 2). At the end of the material in the
notebook is the opening of a mandate of excommunication,
written in a different hand; but it seems likely (see note to lines
46–50 below) that the mandate was never put into effect, and that
Thorpe's record (Pollard p. 165) that his release without con-
viction had in some way been connected with Arundel's exile in
1397 should be believed. The second examination by Arundel,
recorded in the present text, was on 7 August 1407 and followed
Thorpe's arrest in April 1407 by the secular authorities at Shrews-
bury where he had been preaching (Pollard p. 121). No record is
preserved of the outcome of the trial. A list of beliefs, drawn
largely from Wyclif's *De Eucharistia*, ascribed to 'Wylhelmi Torp,
cuius librum ego habeo' appears in Prague Metropolitan Chapter
Library MS D. 49, ff. 179v–181v (*Torp(e* is the spelling found in
the Bohemian copies above for *Thorpe*). Taken together with the
two copies of Thorpe's Examination preserved in Bohemia, it is
tempting to speculate that Thorpe, like Payne, fled from persecution in England to Prague. It is possible that the *dominus Wilhelmus
Corpp* mentioned in the letter of Richard Wyche (above p. 155) is
the same man.

The extract here comes from the opening of the Examination,
ff. 19–26v (Pollard pp. 115–20), following Thorpe's recitation of a
neutral but somewhat equivocal creed, and his refusal to take an
oath (for which see below no. 5/64–5n). The early career of
Arundel is described in Aston's biography; his later activities
against the Lollards are referred to below p. 163–4, activities that
led the author of MS Titus D. v in 1413–14 to assert (f. 13v) 'þe
grettist enmy þat Crist haþ in Ynglond...is þe archebischop of
Cauntirberi Arundel'.

23ff From the wording Wyclif's renown was already established by the time
Thorpe met him; this would suggest a date after 1375 for Thorpe's arrival in
Oxford.
46–50 As noted above, Thorpe had been arrested and examined for Lollardy before in

1397; by some method he had managed to be released without making any submission or recantation, and hence this second trial could be regarded as a continuation of the first. Had Thorpe recanted in 1397, his second arrest for Lollardy would have been regarded as a relapse and he would have been subject to the penalities of this, namely perpetual imprisonment if he again recanted, and execution if he did not (see H. G. Richardson, 'Heresy and the Lay Power under Richard II', *EHR* li (1936), 1–28, and *Chichele Register* i. cxxix–cxxxvii). Thorpe's supposition for the future is precisely accurate.

5 off Arundel had reproached Thorpe with having preached for twenty years or more around the countryside, especially in the north (Pollard p. 107); his life as an itinerant preacher was similar to the better documented cases of William Taylor (see Emden, *Oxford* iii. 1852) or Thomas Drayton (see Thomson (1965), 54, 173, 175). The defection of Wyclif's early followers (on which see lines 6 off, 133 ff below) was a grievous blow to the movement, and one that was bitterly resented by the more educated of the disciples outside the university: see, for instance, the defence written by Thomas Palmer of Nicholas Hereford against a letter of reproach of a Lollard, both preserved in the register of bishop Trefnant of Hereford (ed. W. W. Capes, Canterbury and York Society (1916), pp. 394–401).

6 off In all Thorpe mentions six men as Wyclif's special followers: Nicholas Hereford, Philip Repingdon, John Purvey, John Aston (line 129), Robert Bowland and Geoffrey of Pickering (line 133). The first four are well attested from numerous sources; the last two are peculiar to this account. The details of the careers of Hereford and Repingdon are set out by Emden, *Oxford* ii. 913–15 and iii. 1565–7. Briefly, Hereford came to The Queen's College Oxford before 1369; he took orders as a secular priest but was still resident in Oxford in 1382 when the actions of Courtenay against Wyclif began in earnest. He was appointed to preach the public sermon at St Frideswide's Priory on Ascension Day 1382, and took the opportunity to defend Wyclif's views, an action that was clearly popular with a large part of his congregation. A month later he was suspended by Courtenay from all preaching and lecturing, tried but failed to obtain the support of John of Gaunt, was summoned to the Council at Blackfriars in London, but in July fled to the continent, apparently hoping to win support from pope Urban VI. He was unsuccessful and was imprisoned, but managed to escape during a popular rising in 1385. On his return to England he appears to have continued preaching, despite the sentence of excommunication he was under, until his arrest in Nottingham in 1387. By 1391 he had recanted, and in 1393 acted as an assessor for the bishop of Hereford in the trial of Walter Brut, a notorious Lollard. In 1417 he entered the Coventry charterhouse. Because of the note in Bodleian MS Douce 369 of WB EV in the middle of *v.* 20 of Baruch 3 'Explicit trans-lacionem Nicholay de herford' (reinforced by the ending of MS Bodley 959 at that point, and a related note in CUL Ee. 1. 10), he has been thought responsible for much of the work of translation in the EV up to that point. If this is correct, it must apparently assume that the work was done before Hereford left the country in 1382, since his life as a fugitive between 1385 and 1387 would hardly have allowed for the detailed and lengthy work involved.

Philip Repingdon came to Oxford as an Augustinian canon from St Mary's in the Meadows Leicester, though the date of his arrival is uncertain; with Hereford he became the best known of Wyclif's supporters and was asked to deliver the Corpus Christi day public sermon at St Frideswide's in 1382 in which he supported Wyclif's views on the Eucharist. He was summoned with Hereford to appear before Courtenay, and shared Hereford's fate up to the latter's departure abroad. Repingdon remained in England, and in October 1382 recanted and was restored to his position. He became abbot of the Leicester house in 1394, and later bishop of Lincoln in 1404; he resigned the bishopric in 1420 and died in 1424.

John Purvey is a more shadowy figure than either of these, though a Lollard of longer duration. It is not certain that he became a graduate of

Oxford (see Emden, *Oxford* iii. 1526–7), though he is described by Netter (*Doctrinale* ii. 70, vi. 117 etc.) as a learned doctor, glossator of Wyclif's works and the Lollards' librarian. He appears to have been with Wyclif in his retirement at Lutterworth, and certainly became active as a Lollard preacher in the west country after his master's death. He was arrested in 1401, after trial publicly recanted and abjured at St Paul's Cross; later the same year he became rector of West Hythe, a living given him to keep him closely under Arundel's eye. His later career is unclear (see lines 108–9n). Because of Netter's description many Lollard texts have been ascribed to Purvey; none is attributed in a manuscript to him, and the quotations in Netter from a *Libellus de Oratione* and *Liber de Compendiis Scripturarum* have not been identified from any surviving text. Likewise unproven is the frequent assertion that Purvey was responsible for the modifications in the Later Version of WB. See below nos. 24 and 27 for other texts associated with Purvey on the ground of Lavenham's evidence (*Fasc. Ziz.* 383–99).

Robert Bowland is a name not elsewhere mentioned as a heretic and his identity remains uncertain. A clerk of the name appears in Arundel's Canterbury register (Lambeth reg. ii. f. 185v–186), immediately after the trials of Sawtre and Purvey in 1401, accused of immorality with a nun of Nuneaton. He is said to have been rector of the church of St Antoninus in London. That this may be the man meant by Thorpe is perhaps suggested by his choice as judge for his first trial of Philip Repingdon, then abbot of St Mary's Leicester (see Wilkins, *Concilia* iii. 262–3).

For Aston see below line 129 and for Geoffrey of Pickering line 133.

67 St Paul's Cross was the site of a number of famous sermons (e.g. that of Thomas of Wimbledon see, most accessibly, the edition by N. H. Owen, *Medieval Studies* xxviii (1966), 176–97), and as late as 1511 a Lollard suspect claimed that she could hear better sermons at home than at St Paul's Cross (Reg. FitzJames (London) f. 27). Recantation there ensured the maximum publicity for the act. Evidence does not otherwise exist to show that Hereford's public recantation took place there, but Purvey's is recorded in *Fasc. Ziz.* 407.

67 Despite the allegation here, and more strongly at lines 165–6, the evidence for Repingdon's harsh persecution of Lollards is not strong. His register at Lincoln (no. 15; part has been edited by M. Archer, *Lincoln Record Society* lvii–lviii (1963)) preserves material concerning some inquiries (f. 132 of Thomas Nouerey of Ilston near Leicester, ff. 152v and 157v of the vicar of Wilsford, ff. 160v–1 of Leicester suspects and ff. 176v–177 of heretics in Northampton, and cf *Chichele Register* iii. 105–12); the document Vj/o at Lincoln Archives Office preserves the investigations during the visitation of Leicester in 1413. But, considering that Repingdon's vast diocese covered some of the most persistent Lollard centres, Leicester and Northampton, and the area between the two and west towards Coventry, it is remarkable that no execution is recorded for the period. That Repingdon may have retained some sympathy for the views and friends of his youth is suggested by the extent and tenor of his sermons (see Emden, *Oxford* iii. 1567 for manuscripts), by his failure to fulfil the papal command to exhume and dishonour the bones of Wyclif (see Workman ii, 319–20), and by the self-abasement of his will (see McFarlane (1972), 217–18 and *Chichele Register* ii. 285–7).

99 *wolden schaue ʒoure beerdis ful nyʒ*: would go to any lengths; cf Whiting B119 though the phrase seems to have had no fixed meaning.

101–2 The trial took place at the bishop's residence at Saltwood Castle (Pollard p. 107); Purvey's benefice at West Hythe was little more than a mile away, though Purvey himself no longer held it.

108 The benefice of West Hythe was vacated by Purvey by October 1403, and Purvey's career after that is uncertain. If the present account is correct, he was still alive in 1407. A John Purvey *capellanus* appears as a supporter of Oldcastle in the Derbyshire area in the enquiry following the revolt in March 1414 (PRO KB 9.204/1, 60–3). Netter, *Doctrinale* ii. 73, says that he has a book of Purvey's surrendered when he was imprisoned.

113–14 The threat was a serious one, since if Purvey were again arrested for heresy he would have been treated as a relapse (above line 46n).

117ff Wyclif's learning and his moral probity were admitted even by his enemies (as here by Arundel lines 158–9); see the early testimony of Kynyngham 'a wise clerk', 'a doctor eminent in his learning and in his teaching' (*Fasc. Ziz.* 12, 67), or the latter Knighton (ii. 151) 'the most outstanding doctor of theology in those days, considered second to none in philosophy and unmatched in skill in the schools'. For the views of sympathisers cf *Upland's Rejoinder* 85ff and *Piers Plowman's Creed* 528–32.

121ff Only about a third of Wyclif's writings survive in manuscripts in England, and many of this third only in a single exemplar; for the rest, and for further copies, we are dependent upon the manuscripts made by Bohemian scribes during the Hussite period (see *Notes and Queries* NS xx (1973), 444–6). But it is clear that Thorpe's claim was justified, and even as late as 1410 sufficient copies survived in Oxford to make a public bonfire at Carfax (Gascoigne, *Loci e Libro Veritatum*, ed. J. E. Thorold Rogers (Oxford, 1881), p. 116).

129 John Aston (see Emden, *Oxford* i. 67) was in Oxford by 1365, and became an ardent follower of Wyclif. He was noted as a preacher in Leicester, Bristol and Hampshire. Contrary to Thorpe's assertion, it appears that Aston did recant in 1382 (*Fasc. Ziz.* 331–3), though a year later he denounced the crusade of bishop Despenser and by 1387 was again preaching heresy in the Worcester diocese. He was again in Oxford in 1391–2, but his later history is unknown; from Thorpe's testimony here he was dead by 1407.

133 Apart from Thorpe's statements here, Geoffrey of Pickering is nowhere implicated in support for Wyclif. Thorpe's information, apart from this, is confirmed elsewhere: he was a Cistercian monk from Byland in Yorkshire. The Vienna and Prague manuscripts substitute *abbas* for *monke* (line 133), correctly, since he became abbot of Byland by 1397.

146–7 *Moysees chaire...þe chaire of Crist*: cf Matt. 23. 2. A Lollard text in CUL Ff. 6.31 (3), ff. 39v–40v, quoting Jerome, explains *Moysees chaire* as (f. 40) 'þe doctryne of lawe'; the contrast is between the pharisees who taught well but did not practise what they preached, and those truly acting out Christ's teaching, a contrast more fully developed in MS Titus D. v, f. 5v.

163–4 Cf Whiting D43.

5. Confession of Hawisia Moone of Loddon, 1430

The confession is one of a set of about fifty surviving in a manuscript now preserved at Westminster Cathedral Diocesan Archives as MS B.2, a composite volume of which part 8, pp. 205–362, is relevant here. Some account of it is given by E. Welch, 'Some Suffolk Lollards', *Suffolk Institute of Archæology* xxix (1963), 154–65; a full edition by N. Tanner is to be published soon by the Camden Society. The pages, now out of order, represent considerable portions from a court book of heresy cases kept by the officials of William Alnwick, bishop of Norwich, between 1428 and 1431. Foxe used it for iii. 587–600, at which time it contained a little more than it now does, and Usher transcribed parts of it (see Trinity College Dublin MS 775, ff. 119–122v) in the seventeenth century when it was in the archives at Lambeth Palace. The courtbook is the only record of these trials, no mention of them being found in Alnwick's episcopal register at Norwich. The majority of the cases come from the area between Norwich and the coast, on the borders of Norfolk and Suffolk, with a particularly high number from the villages of Loddon, Martham and Earsham. The household of Hawisia Moone at Loddon had obviously been one of the main centres of Lollardy in the village: her husband, Thomas Moone, was convicted of heresy and abjured a few days later (pp. 243b–7), and their servant, John Burell, gave evidence of meetings of like-minded friends at the house (pp. 234, 285–6); a suspect from Martham stated that Hawisia Moone 'is the woman most advanced and learned in the teachings of William White' (p. 275). The confession here (pp. 353–6) follows a Latin statement about the investigation; the paper is somewhat damaged at the outer edge, and the words missing are here supplied in square brackets.

1 William Alnwick, bishop of Norwich 1426–36, after which he became bishop of Lincoln until his death in 1449 (see Emden, *Cambridge* 11), was an active diocesan (see Thompson (1947), pp. 43, 55, 206–46).

8–13 White, Caleys, Pye and Waddon were all burnt for heresy during the years covered by these investigations: White, Pye and Waddon, the last not a priest, in Norwich in 1428, Caleys in Colchester in 1430 (Thomson (1965), 122). White was a particularly celebrated preacher of heresies, brought before archbishop Chichele in 1422 on a charge of unlicensed preaching and heresy from Tenterden (*Chichele Register* iii. 85, iv. 297), where he was again preaching in 1428; many of this East Anglian group claimed to have learnt their doctrines from him, so that it would seem that he must have travelled between Kent and East Anglia before his final arrest and death in Norwich. His final trial is described in *Fasc. Ziz.* 417–32. He is cited many times by Netter as 'quidam magnus...satelles' of Wyclif (*Doctrinale* vi. 66–7, 99, 112, 128–9, 140, 156, 164), proclaiming extreme views. The fourth priest, Thomas Pert, seems to have been the parson at Loddon, and was presumably of the same family as John Pert, a servant of Moone's. The connection between the Loddon group and Tenterden is reinforced by Fowlyn, Euerden and Cornmonger, all of whom, together with Waddon, are mentioned amongst the suspects from the Kentish area in *Chichele Register* iii. 199 and iv. 297–8; Tenterden Lollardy survived the fifteenth-century persecutions and was still flourishing when it was again investigated in 1511–12 (Lambeth register Warham ff. 159–75v), the practices and beliefs then revealed being remarkably like those here. Of the rest, Archer and Bate were convicted of heresy in the present series of investigations (pp. 323–7, 229–33); Thomas Burell, brother of Moone's servant John, was mentioned as a teacher by several heretics though, whether because of damage to the manuscript or because he had fled the district, his trial does not appear; William Wardon was probably of the same family as John Wardon of Loddon condemned for heresy (pp. 205–6). Richard Belward seems to have been the nephew of Hawisia Moone, and another suspect described him as 'bonus doctor' (p. 275); Nicholas was probably his brother, and their father, Hawisia's brother, was probably the John Belward senior of Earsham accused of heresy earlier in 1430 (p. 256). The group thus makes a good example of the close 'cell-system' of the Lollards, and of the way in which geographically scattered groups might be linked either by family or by common teachers, and of the knowledge of other groups that must have existed to explain the rapidity of the journeys between them.

13–16   The holding of *scolae* and *couenticulae* is often mentioned in the episcopal
records (e.g. BL Additional 35205 m. xiv^d and material in Crompton 19ff).
It would appear from the statement of one Lollard in 1485 (Lichfield register
Hales f. 166v), 'it is essential to attend the schools for a whole year before you
will know the right faith', that these schools were serious affairs in which
extensive instruction might be given. Many of the East Anglian heretics
admitted attending them, or organizing them, and some mention the use of
books for the instruction in them. It seems possible that the many Lollard
texts which consist of a series of authorities to support an unorthodox tenet
(see in the present selection nos. 21A, 22 and 24) may have been intended for
this purpose. Cf *Daw's Reply* 100ff where the Lollards are taunted that they
draw away men's wives 'and maken hem scolers of þe newe scole'.

18–25   Objections to clerical baptism and confirmation, though in line with Wyclif's
dislike of unnecessary ritual (*Sermones* i. 217/30ff, *Trialogus* 281/12–288/21,
292/9–295/5), did not form a major part of his thought; amongst fifteenth-
century Lollards they were common (e.g. Salisbury reg. Aiscough ii. f. 53,
Langton ii. ff. 35, 41; Bath and Wells reg. Stafford op. 180b–181b); cf Netter
Doctrinale v. 96–115 and vi. 45–57 and note vi. 53 where East Anglian cases
are specifically mentioned.

34–9   The views on the pope repeat those explained in the preceding texts, but the
final sentence is a particularly clear expression of Wycliffite doctrine; cf *De
Potestate Pape* 360/31ff 'the pope must be the holiest of men, and gets the name
of pope only from that qualification'.

40–6   *singemesses* is not recorded in OED, but its meaning is clear from the context
here and at line 82: it covers chantry priests paid to sing masses for the souls
of the departed (for Lollard objections to this see no. 3/73–92n).

46–9   Cf no. 3/154–62n. As with several of the objections in these East Anglian
confessions, resistance to the fees involved probably played a part (cf *Opus
Arduum* f. 190 for arguments against payments to priests 'pro administracione
quorumcumque sacramentorum').

53–7   For a fuller statement of this view see nos. 25 and 26 below.

64–5   The rejection of oaths followed the instructions of Exod. 20. 7 and Matt. 5.
33–7, and is discussed in Wyclif's *De Mandatis* 201/29–206/20, and in many
Lollard texts (e.g. Arnold iii. 483/3ff, Matthew 278/1ff); *Lanterne* 88/1ff sets
out the conditions under which oaths are allowable.

65–9   Rejection of legal proceedings follows I Cor. 6.5–8, and is found with
frequent criticism of contemporary malpractices in Arnold iii. 215/16ff, 328/
32ff, Matthew 122/27ff, 182/16ff. White likewise rejected execution of criminals
(*Fasc. Ziz.* 431).

69–73   Objections to, and non-observance of, the fasting laws of the medieval church
were not limited to the Lollards (cf G. R. Owst, *Literature and Pulpit in
Medieval England* (revd ed. Oxford, 1961), pp. 435–41), though the eating of
meat on fast days was sometimes the cause of the detection of Lollardy (e.g.
here p. 286 Thomas Moone was seen to have a large joint of cold pork, partly
eaten in his house over the Good Friday and Easter Saturday fast). One
suspect reasonably asserted (p. 275) that it was more meritorious to finish up
remaining scraps of meat on Fridays than to get into debt by buying fish at the
market. Cf *Apology* 44/9ff 'Fastingis are not necesary, wil man absteniþ him
fro oþer synne' and White's position, *Fasc. Ziz.* 427–8.

84–123   For another contemporary form of the standard terms of abjuration see *BIHR*
xlvi (1973), 155–7.

118–21   The records in the Westminster Cathedral manuscript are only copies of the
original notarial documents, written continuously; they therefore show no sign
of the indented edge here described.

PART II. THE LOLLARDS AND THE BIBLE

Introductory Note

Wyclif's name has traditionally been associated with the first complete translation of the Bible into English. The earliest evidence for this appears to be the statement of Henry Knighton, writing in 1390 of the year 1382, who says that Wyclif translated the gospel (*Evangelium*) into English 'so that by him that, which formerly belonged to those clergy who were sufficiently learned and intelligent, was made available to any lay person, even women, who knew how to read' (ii. 151–2). But Wyclif's name does not appear in early manuscripts of the Bible translation, nor does he ever claim responsibility for such a work in his own writings. He did, however, maintain the desirability of having the gospel and the law of the Old Testament in English (see *Opera Minora* 74/1ff, *Polemical Works* i. 116/6ff, ii. 700/29ff). Even if the translation that we have cannot be connected with Wyclif himself, nor can it be shown that Wyclif in any way supervised or participated in the preliminary study, the value of the scriptural text implied by the immense labour that went into the translation accords with the sentiments often expressed by him (e.g. *De Civili Dominio* i. 422/3ff, *De Veritate Sacre Scripture passim*).

The origins and development of the translations have been the subject of long-standing and often tendentious arguments not relevant to the present purpose (see H. Hargreaves in *The Cambridge History of the Bible* ii, ed. G. W. H. Lampe (Cambridge, 1969), 387–415 for a summary and further references). The facts are few. Ignoring the possibility of a lost version (cf M. Wilks, *Studies in Church History* xi (1975), 155ff), an intriguing but chronologically difficult speculation, four stages are discernible from the statements of the General Prologue (below no. 14/ 24–35):

1. an attempt to establish an authoritative Latin text from the welter of variants in contemporary manuscripts of the Vulgate (cf Bacon, *Opus Maius*, ed. J. H. Bridges (London, 1900), i. 77–81).

2. study of the Latin text with commentaries and the *Glossa Ordinaria*, the collection of patristic comments assembled into the margins and between the lines of the biblical text (see ODCC), and the commentary of Lyra.

3. elucidation of the difficulties of the text, and especially of those
   syntactical and vocabulary problems that arise in translation.
4. the translation and then the correction of the translation.

Only the last two stages are peculiar to the work of translation,
and speculation on the origins of the Bible translation has con-
centrated on the last. The name of Nicholas Hereford has come
to be associated with the first translation, a literal one, virtually
unintelligible without recourse to the Latin source; for the
evidence see above no. 4/60n. For some time it has been thought
that MS Bodley 959, ending at Baruch 3. 20, best preserves this
Early Version (EV), but recently it has been pointed out that
Christ Church Oxford MS 145 contains some literalisms not found
in the Bodley MS; since the Christ Church manuscript contains
the whole Bible, this has been used for the text of EV here. At
the other extreme from these literal versions is the idiomatic
translation found in a large number of manuscripts and generally
known as the Later Version (LV). This has been associated, but
without substantive justification, with the name of John Purvey
who has also been held to be the author of the General Prologue
(see no. 4/60n and no. 14 below). For a list of 230 manuscripts of
the translations, a list which can be extended, see C. Lindberg,
Studia Neophilologica xlii (1970), 333–47; this also differentiates
between EV and LV texts.

The relation between these two versions has been much
debated, but until more study is made of all the manuscripts
speculation is fruitless. It seems likely that further investigation
will reveal a spectrum from the extreme literalism of a manuscript
such as Christ Church 145 to the natural idiom of a text such as
is found in the two manuscripts used for LV below. The state of
MS Bodley 959, much corrected and annotated in such a way that
the quires must have been loose sheets when it was done, is a
salutory reminder of the multiple and often textually local effort
that went into the modifications.

Though in 1401 the legitimacy of biblical translation could be
debated in Oxford without any charge of heresy being levelled
against its proponents (*EHR* xc (1975), 1–18), the translation
came soon after to be linked with the Lollard movement. In 1407
archbishop Arundel included in his Constitutions directed against
the Lollard heresy an edict forbidding the possession of vernacular
scripture unless the owner had received prior permission from his
bishop, and unless the translation were one dating from before

the time of Wyclif (Wilkins, *Concilia* iii. 317). After this, possession
of English texts of the Bible was used as evidence against Lollard
suspects (e.g. *Chichele Register* iii. 190, 198 in 1428, and, at the
other end of the period, the material in J. Fines, 'Heresy Trials
in the Diocese of Coventry and Lichfield, 1511–12', *Journal of
Ecclesiastical History* xiv (1963), 160–74). The author of the tract
in MS Titus D. v. written 1413–14 states that (f. 57) 'antecrist
brenneþ þe bokis of Goddis lawe', and laments (f. 25) 'nouȝ
Cristis lawe is raþur matir of persecucion þan of promocion to þo
þat studien it and labouren it to make it knowen. Fewe or welny
none of þe clergie þat ben myȝti men and frendid besien hem in
þe studie þerof.' But the surviving 240-odd manuscripts of WB
suggest that investigation of ownership was neither thorough nor
easy (without the General Prologue (see no. 14) or the glosses
found in a very few manuscripts, heterodoxy is not clear);
orthodox owners of manuscripts are also known (e.g. Henry VI
owned MS Bodley 277).

Lollard writings and the observations of opponents alike testify
to the importance the movement attached to the Bible; for the
first see no. 20 below, for the second see Gower *Confessio Amantis*
Prol. 349ff, Pecock *Repressor* i. 36/23ff, 55/10ff, and the assertion of
the hostile writer of BL MS Harley 31, f. 184v that Lollards held
'that the whole of sacred scripture, understood grammatically, is
literally true'. The first extract, no. 6, has been chosen to show
EV at its most literal; the second reveals how the more idiomatic
style can cope with varying subject matter, from straightforward
narrative to rhetorical invocation. The Glossed Gospels (nos. 9
and 12) could well have been a side-product of the study
described above as stage 2; they use the EV text of the Bible. The
translations in the sermons (nos. 10, 13, 15, 21B and 23) are
completely independent of either version of WB.

6. Wycliffite Bible: Isaiah 53

The EV text is taken from Christ Church Oxford MS 145 (*X*),
ff. 232r–v, a large and handsome manuscript, carefully corrected
in minor scribal errors but, unlike MS Bodley 959, not a working
copy altered in its translation. The LV text is from Corpus Christi
College Oxford MS C. 20 (H), ff. 138r–v, an ample manuscript of
the early fifteenth century containing the LV from I Esdras to

II Maccabees; it was probably one member of a multi-volume Bible.

The greater literalism of EV is evident almost throughout, though occasionally LV appears the more unidiomatic (e.g. 3 *wherfor and we arrettiden not him*). Examples of the modifications made in LV in accordance with the methods outlined in the General Prologue will be noted below in the apparatus to no. 14; notes here are limited to individual difficulties.

2 EV *it shall steȝen vp*: the use of *it* derives from a literal acceptance of the neuter gender of *virgultum* (rendered *quik heg* EV, *ȝerde* LV).

2 EV *he was not of siȝte*, LV *no biholding was*: V *et non erat aspectus*. Lindberg EV v. 305 glosses *siȝte* here as 'beauty', but it seems doubtful whether the English word or Lat. *aspectus* could have such a sense. It seems likely that the EV translator was unclear about the meaning of the clause and took *aspectus* as a genitive.

5 EV *woundid is...defoulid is*: the auxiliary renders literally V *vulneratus est... attritus est*, replaced in LV by the more idiomatic *was*.

5 EV *discipline of oure pes*: V *disciplina pacis nostrae*; LV substitutes the native *lernyng*.

10 EV *þe sed of long age*, LV *seed long duringe*; V *semen longaevum*. Here both versions have equally literal, though varying, renderings of the Latin.

12 LV *ȝelde (eþer dele)*: EV translates *dispertiam* as *delen* which survives as an alternative gloss in LV.

12 EV *of stronge men he shal deuiden spoilis*, a slavish retention of the word order of V *fortium dividet spolia*, though it should be noted that the prop-word *men* has been added to the adjective (cf Fristedt WB ii. xxviif).

7. Wycliffite Bible: the book of Jonah

EV is here printed as the only text, with LV variants in footnotes since they are so few. *X* is again used for EV, f. 283r–v; LV readings are from BL Royal I.C. viii (A), f. 277r–v. The chapter division is here as V (not the variant division of AV), since this is the division followed by the manuscripts; the verse division of V is therefore also followed.

1.5 *þe ynnere thingus*: V *interiora*; again all EV manuscripts supply the prop-word in amplification of the Latin adjective.

1.6 *what*, LV *whi*: EV is a literal rendering of V *quid*; also 1.10.

1.6 *inclep*: the verb is almost limited to WB as a literal rendering of Lat. *invocare*; LV usually alters, as here, to *clepe*.

1.7 *sende we lott*: the EV verb from Lat. *mittamus*, LV having more idiomatically *caste*.

1.7 *to vs*: a literalism from V *nobis*.

1.11–12 *cesen* is influenced by V *cessare*, just as 11, 13 *wente* renders literally V *ibat*.

1.14 *ȝiue not on vs*, the verb translates literally V *ne des super nos*.

2.4 *abouteȝaf*: V *circumdedit*. MED does not record a verb *abouteȝeuen*, but records use of *aboute-* as a prefix on other formations to imitate Lat. *circum-*.

2.7 *into wiþouten ende*: this curious phrase is the normal WB rendering of V *in aeternum*.

2.10 *I shal ȝelde to þe Lord for helpe*: the lack of an object for the verb derives from

V *reddam pro salute Domino* where the object is understood from *quaecumque* in the previous clause.

3.3 *in iourne of þre daȝis*, 3.4 *in iorne of o day*: literal translations of V *itinere trium dierum...itinere diei unius*, the meaning of the first of which is that the city would take three days to cross.

3.4 *vndirturned*: OED records this verb from WB only (apart from one seventeenth-century instance in a different sense), as a translation of *subvertere*.

3.8 Forshall and Madden take *werc bestis* as the subject of *crie*. The modern Vulgate supplies an extra *et* (*et iumenta, et clament*), making *iumenta* parallel to EV *men* as the composite subject of *be...hilid*; given the literalness of WB, however, it is probable that the source Vulgate manuscript had no second *et* and that the ensuing misinterpretation of the sense is correctly represented by Forshall and Madden's punctuation.

3.8 The change of number from *a man* to *þe hondis of hem* follows V *vir...in manibus eorum*.

4.2 *beforn ocupiede*, LV *purposide*; LV has given a better contextual rendering than the slavish EV following of V *praeoccupavi*.

4.6 V *hederam* is correctly translated by WB as *yuy*.

4.11 The unidiomatic EV *spare to* derives from a literal rendering of the Latin dative case in V *parcam Ninive, civitati magnae*.

8. Wycliffite Bible: Luke 15. 11–32

EV is again printed from *X*, f. 331r–v, whilst LV is from Lincoln College Oxford MS Latin 119(G), f. 301r–v, another large Bible manuscript dating from the early fifteenth century and containing a part of the General Prologue (but not the section below) between the Old and New Testaments.

12 *to hem*: V *illis*.

13 The use of *pilgrimage* by both versions arises from the V Latin *peregre*; the normal sense of the word in ME (see OED) was, as now, specifically associated with a journey to a religious place or with a pious intent.

15 EV *burgeisis*, LV *citeseyns*, V *uni civium*; the majority of EV manuscripts have the reading of *X* here, but Forshall and Madden's base text, Bodleian MS Douce 369, second part, has the LV word.

18 *into heuene*: cf MED *into* 19 'against'; the usage derives from V *in caelum*, the motion implied by the Lat. accusative being rendered as *into*.

22 *firste stole*: *stole* in ME meant a long robe; this group was commonly used in ME to render V *stolam primam* in this parable.

22–3 EV *cloþiþ...bringeþ*: *X* is unusual amongst WB manuscripts in its retention here of the old plural imperative.

25 The use of *sinfon* and *symfonye* derives from V *symphoniam*. The translators obviously found difficulty with the second word, V *chorum*. As MED points out (see *croud*), Lat. *chorus* means a circular dance to song or instrumental music, a sense correctly rendered by the first word *carol* in EV. But WB and other medieval translators often used *croude*, a word which strictly means the stringed instrument of Celtic provenance.

29 EV *passede ouer*, a literal rendering of V *praeterivi*.

9. Glossed Gospel commentary on Luke 15. 22–4

These extracts from the Glossed Gospels are good examples of the uncontroversial parts of the texts; no. 12 provides a case where

the Lollard commentators took advantage of the critical position
of the scriptural material. The Glossed Gospels exist in three
forms: a long commentary on gospel passages (see 9B), a short
commentary derived from the first usually by compression and by
omission of some tendentious quotations, both of these proceeding
straight through the biblical book, and a third, known only in
York Minster Library MS XVI. D. 2, where the long commentary
is used only for the texts that serve as the gospels for each
Sunday, arranged in the litergical order, but is supplemented by
the addition of long and often controversial further quotations.
The long commentaries on Mark and John are only known
through the extracts from them found in the York version. The
starting point for the commentaries is correctly described at the
end of the manuscript from which 9A is taken 'Opus fratris Thome
de Alquino extractum a doctoribus diuersis et translatum in
linguam maternam'; that is, the work known as the *Catena Aurea*,
a collection made by Aquinas, following a long-standing exegetical
tradition, from patristic sources, expounding each verse of the
gospel in turn. References to the *Catena Aurea* below are from the
edition by A. Guarienti (Turin and Rome, 1953, 2 vols.). But it is
clear that Lollard commentators had recourse to many of the
sources from which Aquinas drew his extracts, since there are
longer quotations here than are found in the *Catena Aurea*
(investigation of some English copies of the work reveals no
variants that would explain this). Like the *Floretum/Rosarium*
compilations, the original study for the Glossed Gospels must
have been done in a centre with access to an ample library. It has
been usual to associate the Glossed Gospels with the story in a
vernacular defence of biblical translation (see edition by C. F.
Bühler, *Medium Ævum* vii (1938), 167–83) of archbishop Arundel's
commendation of Anne, first queen of Richard II, at her funeral
in 1394 for her possession of 'al þe foure Gospeleris wiþ þe
doctoris vpon hem' (lines 297–8), which the prelate had scrutinised
and found to be 'goode and trewe'. If this were correct, then the
origin of the Glossed Gospels must antedate 1394. But if the
Glossed Gospels are in question, Arundel's perusal must have
been perfunctory indeed, since even the shorter version contains
material (such as that in 12 below) that by 1394 would have been
unpalatable to a member of the established clergy. The reference
should, however, be treated with caution: quite apart from the
lack of explicit identification of the commentary in question, the

section of the vernacular defence in which this occurs does not exist in the Latin debate on which the earlier part was modelled (see *EHR* xc (1975), 4) and may be a later attempt to justify a Lollard text by an adherent of the sect. The attribution of the Glossed Gospels to Purvey (see Deanesly 275ff, 376ff), as likewise of the English tract in which this story of Arundel appears, is without foundation. For further details on the Glossed Gospels see Hargreaves (1969) and the same author's article in *Studia Neophilologica* xxxiii (1961), 285–300.

The extract from the shorter commentary, 9A, is taken from MS Bodley 143, ff. 145v–6v, collated with MS Bodley 243, f. 76r–v; that from the longer commentary, 9B, is from the only surviving manuscript, CUL Kk.2.9, ff. 182v–3. All manuscripts date from the early fifteenth century. The passage in 9B overlaps with 9A at lines 18–20 of the latter text.

The sources of the comments are as follows (the line references are, for brevity, those of the attribution in each case; the bracket following indicates whether or not the quotation is found in *Catena Aurea*, CA): 9A/9 pseudoChrysostom *Homilia de patre et duobus filiis*, PG 61. 782 variant version (CA); 9A/11 and 9A/57 Theophylactus (an eleventh-century Byzantine exegete, see ODCC), PG 123. 955 and 958 (CA); all passages from Bede from his commentary on Luke, PL 92. 525–6 (only 9A/21 and 9B/5 in CA); all passages from Augustine from his *De Quæstionibus Evangeliorum*, PL 35. 1346 (all in CA); all passages from Ambrose from his commentary on Luke, PL 15. 1761–2 (not in CA except 9A/18 and epitome of passage cited in full 9A/52); passages ascribed to Chrysostom in 9A/28, 30 and 9B/32, 37, are printed as epistle 35 in the dubious works of Jerome in PL 30. 253 (for the medieval ascription to Chrysostom see A. Wilmart, *JTS* xix (1918), 322; CA except 9B/32).

9B/16–20 For the sense of this rather obscure passage compare Ambrose PL 15. 1761
'Est enim et aliud mysterium quod nescit, nisi qui accepit dictorum suorum, factorumque signaculum, et quoddam munimentum bonæ intentionis et cursus; necubi offendat ad lapidem pedem suum, et supplantatus a diabolo Dominicæ prædicationis officium derelinquat.'

10. Sermon on Luke 15. 11–32

The sermon derives from the standard sermon-cycle (above p. 11), in the ferial set on the weekday gospels; following the Sarum usage, the gospel is assigned to Saturday in the second week of

Lent. The text here is printed from BL Royal 18. B. ix (G),
ff. 45–6v; copies are also found in fifteen other manuscripts and
emendations to G are introduced on the basis of a full collation
of all these. A set of ferial sermons by Wyclif himself does not
survive, even if it ever existed; the source of this vernacular text
cannot therefore be traced to the master himself. The exegesis of
the gospel text reveals many points of divergence from the
Glossed Gospels, showing that, unless the implications of the text
involved an obvious issue of Lollard belief, no standard tradition
of exegesis was followed. The sermon introduces a few distinctively
Wycliffite ideas, those of predestination and the priesthood of all
believers (lines 99ff) and the Eucharist (line 117), none of them
found in the Glossed Gospels. But the major divergences are in
uncontroversial allegorical interpretations.

1–32 The sermon begins, as in about a quarter of this sermon-cycle, with a straight
translation of the gospel text, a translation which is independent of WB and in
some ways more idiomatic than even LV (e.g. 19 *sle him*, WB *sle ʒe*). In this
example there is no amplification of the text, nor any incidental glossing.

33ff The basic interpretation of the parable, with God as the father, the two sons
as the children of Israel and the gentiles, the return of the younger son as the
conversion of the latter after Christ's resurrection, is a commonplace one; it is
found in the *Glossa Ordinaria*, as in the patristic writers (e.g. Augustine, PL
35.1344–8).

39–40 The endowment of men with *goodes of kynde and goodis of grace* is a common
element in discussion of the fall and the redemption, and enters debate on the
salvation of the righteous heathen; see Peter Lombard on Romans 4. 18, PL
191.1376; Aquinas *Summa Theologica* Ia. q. 95a.1; H. Oberman, *The Harvest of
Medieval Theology* (revd ed. Grand Rapids, 1967), pp. 139–41; compare Ps.
Lamb. 34, f. 181v/1 'in þe bygynnynge of þe world no lawe was ʒouen to þe
puple but þe lawe of kynde and resoun, by goode kepynge of whiche many
men weren made ful holy seyntis'.

44 Job dwelt in the land of Uz, an area south and west of Edom, whilst Jethro,
father-in-law of Moses, came from the land of Midian. The point made here is
that tribes other than that descended from Jacob honoured God for a while,
having *goodis of grace of God*.

50 Cf Rev. 21. 2 and the medieval tradition drawing on the *Song of Songs* (see
R. Woolf, *The English Religious Lyric in the Middle Ages* (Oxford, 1968), pp. 58ff
for a review of its development).

57–8 *to his felowis*: to the devil's associates.

60–71 Objections to worldly knowledge are found sporadically throughout the
sermons, overtly condemnatory in the case of legal learning, less outspoken in
the case of other secular knowledge. The basis of the criticism is that expressed
in Matthew 145/18ff 'þei chargen more statutis of synful men þan þe moste
resonable lawe of God almyʒtty...and herefore þei han many grete bokis and
costy of mannus lawe and studien hem faste; but fewe curatis han þe Bible and
exposiciouns of þe gospelis.'

70–1 The cost of gaining education is mentioned most frequently as a reason for the
clerks' undesirable greed for benefices as a source of money, and their
ensuing non-residence (e.g. Matthew 454/33ff).

91ff The view of the predestined and the *praesciti* (those foreknown to damnation)
here implied was developed by Wyclif from the tradition of Augustine and
Bradwardine; see Leff (1967), ii. 516ff, also *Bradwardine and the Pelagians*

(Cambridge, 1957), and H. Oberman, *Archbishop Thomas Bradwardine, a Four-teenth Century Augustinian* (Utrecht, 1958). Netter, *Doctrinale* i. 22ff plainly regarded Wyclif's determinism as, in many ways, the root cause of his other heresies.

99–101 The interpretation of the *first stole* here is found more elaborately in Wyclif's *De Veritate Sacre Scripture* ii. 148/6ff.

121 The scorn of literal interpretation is unusual in Lollard writings; more frequently found is an exaltation of literal over allegorical methods of inter-pretation (e.g. Arnold ii. 343/20ff, Matthew 343/10ff). It should be remem-bered, however, that Lollard use of the term 'literal sense' is usually the developed meaning of Lyra, quoted in the *Opus Arduum* f. 168 'the literal sense of scripture...is not that which is denoted by the words in the mind, but that which is understood by the things meant'.

134–5 Cf Wyclif *De Perfectione Statuum* (*Polemical Works* ii) 461/10–29.

139 Elder according to the exegesis of lines 34–5, younger because, if their reconcilement is to occur (lines 132–3), they must partake in the nature of this other son according to the sense of lines 76–7.

142–3 I.e. during the life of Christ and in the ensuing period (lines 129ff).

11. Wycliffite Bible: John 10. 11–18

The EV text is again from *X*, ff. 339v–40; the LV text from Lincoln College Oxford MS Latin 119 (G), f. 308.

12 EV *whos þe shep ben not his owne*: this awkward expression and its LV equivalent arises from close translation of V *cuius non sunt oves propriae*; for *own* without a preceding possessive pronoun see OED 2, but even in the ME period this construction was not the usual one.

13 EV *marchaunt*, LV *hiryd hyne*. In all EV manuscripts used by Forshall and Madden except *X* the gloss *or hyred hyne* is added after *marchaunt*; this latter word is a misunderstanding of V *mercenarius*, presumably by association with Lat. *mercor* v. 'to trade'.

15 *X* has the form *kneʒ* which can only be a preterite tense; V has a present verb, *agnosco*, and other EV and LV manuscripts correctly render this is *knowe*.

16 EV *leden hem to*, LV *brynge hem togidere*: the LV translation is a more idiomatic rendering of V *adducere*.

12. Glossed Gospel commentary on John 10. 11–16

For the nature of the Glossed Gospels see introduction to no. 99 above. The text here is printed from MS Bodley 243, ff. 143–4, collated with Trinity College Cambridge MS B. 1. 38, ff. 137–8. The first of these two manuscripts contains the shorter com-mentaries on Luke and John; BL Additional 41175 was originally the first half of the manuscript and contains the equivalent material on Matthew and Mark. The section of the *grettir gloos on Joon* (MS Bodley 243 f. 115v) relevant to the present text survives in York Minster MS XVI. D. 2, ff. 111–118v, under the second Sunday after Easter. The passage printed here, following the opening provided by the biblical text, contains a lot more con-troversial material than either commentary in 9 and departs much more radically from the *Catena Aurea*; not surprisingly there is considerable overlap of criticism between this and no. 13, the sermon on the same text. The criticism of the clergy here found is not peculiar to the Lollards; for a catalogue of faults very similar to that here cf Gower's *Vox Clamantis* iii. 9ff.

The sources of the comments are as follows: the passages from Augustine are mostly from his commentary on John, tracts 46–7, in lines 4, 11 (both in CA), 8, 38, 138, 145, 153–5, 158 (none in CA; CCSL 36. 398–407), and from his sermons *De Verbis Domini* 49–50 in lines 22–3, 39 (in CA), and 45 (not in CA; PL 38. 759–64); from Gregory's *Homilia in Evangelia* xiv in lines 16, 35, 44, 161 (all in CA), and 49, 123, 127, 139, 144, 150, 152 (not in CA; PL 76. 1127–9), and from his *Cura Pastoralis* I. 2 in line 59, III. 4. in line 63 (not CA; PL 77. 15–16, 54); the passages ascribed to Chrysostom are genuine in lines 148, 152 (PG 59. 329, both in CA) and spurious in line 61 (PG 56. 839, not CA); Theophylactus on John is quoted from CA in line 140 (PG 124. 71). The quotations from Grosseteste and Bernard have no counterpart in CA, and are shortened versions of passages in the York manuscript. The passages from Grosseteste in lines 73–80 are from sermon 31 (MS Bodley 801, ff. 193v–5), those in lines 81–91 from sermon 19 (MS Bodley 830, ff. 178–9), and that in line 122 from sermon 14 (printed E. Brown, *Fasciculus Rerum Expetendarum* (London, 1690), ii. 251–2); where Gregory is linked with Grosseteste the latter is quoting the former by name. The passages ascribed to Bernard are in fact by Geoffrey of Auxerre, *Declamationes ex S. Bernardi Sermonibus* (PL 184. 443–9).

8–9 Cf lines 156–8. The metaphorical language used by Christ of himself, and by the prophets concerning him, was of considerable interest to Wyclif in connection with his ideas about the Eucharist. This passage was quoted by Wyclif many times, see especially *De Veritate Sacre Scripture* i. 5; see further below no. 21B.

23 *conuyct loueþ*, a literal rendering of Lat. *convictus...amat*, with a lack of resolution of the past participle similar to that found in EV.

52–127 This long section on the faults of prelates and curates has no counterpart in CA, and can hardly have been to the taste of Arundel if indeed he scrutinised the Glossed Gospels (above no. 9 introduction).

63 The passage here, and those in lines 87 and 89, are quoted also in the sermon attributed to Taylor, Bodleian MS Douce 53, f. 16. With the first cf Ps. Bod. f. 26/2 'as manye þanne as antecrist haþ slayn by his lawe falsly, or lettid to folowe truli þe lawe of Crist, as oftsiþe, in þat þat in hym was, he slouȝ Crist'.

71 Gregory, quoted in canon law, *Decretum* II, c. 1 q. 1 cc. 2–3 (Fried. i. 358).

73–4 Cf *Apology* p. 56/9ff, quoting Odo, 'Prelats not preching are raþer Pilats þan prelatis, spoilars not biholdars, Herodians of Heroud, not heyris of Crist.' Cf Gower *Confessio Amantis* v. 1848ff.

82–3 Cf *Apology* 55/7ff 'Wen þe lesynd of þe herd is a bok of þe schepe, and þei are

opunly maistris of alle iuelis, how are þey not heretyks? namely sin þe word
of dede is more effectuos in werkyng þen þe word of þe mouþ.'

106–22 Parts of this quotation from Grosseteste are found also in Arnold iii. 278/17ff,
469/32ff, Matthew 145/9ff, Trinity College Dublin MS 245 f. 154v, Trinity
College Cambridge MS o.1.29 f. 73 and Bodley 647 f. 68v.

153–4 *lede to...seruauntis*: rendering *illas adducere*: 'ergo et per suos non alter adducit';
the point at issue in Christ's own action of salvation, himself taking the
initiative and not delegating it to others.

13. Sermon on John 10. 11–18

The sermon is on the Sunday gospel for the second Sunday after
Easter in the standard sermon-cycle. The text is printed from BL
Royal 18 B. ix, ff. 72r–v; copies are also found in twenty-one
other manuscripts, and emendations here derive from collation of
these. Wyclif's own sermon on the same text is no. 26 in
Sermones i, and the vernacular sermon shares a number of ideas
with it. This overlap is partly explicable by the common biblical
text, with its invitation to discuss the function of the priesthood,
but must partly result from the Lollard use of Wyclif's sermon
(as, for example, in lines 93–4). There are some interesting
parallels between the vernacular homily and a sermon by
Repingdon written after his recantation of Lollardy.

18–20 The particular allusion is probably to the crusade of bishop Despenser of
Norwich, proclaimed at the instigation of Urban VI in February 1383, against
the supporters of the anti-pope Clement VII; see above nos. 2/188–92n and
3/146–9n.

20–4 Cf no. 12/11ff. Repingdon in his sermon on the same text (found in many
manuscripts, used here is Bodleian MS Laud misc. 635, f. 205v) endorses this
view.

27–9 The objection to elaborate church buildings, here briefly mentioned, arose
on many grounds: that the money would be better spent on poor men (as
primarily here, and *Rosarium* sub *ornatus*), that the splendour of conventual
churches drew men away from their parish churches (Matthew 14/31ff,
322/31ff, 448/28ff), that worthless indulgences were given to extract money for
such adornment (Arnold ii. 382/36ff) and, most basically, that the teaching of
the Bible is against such richness (*Lanterne* 38/23ff, 42/19ff; see below no. 22).
Netter reviews the objections, *Doctrinale* vi. 143–8.

30–1 *bi colour to helpe þe former heerdis*: the exemptions and exceptional rights of the
friars, as compared with the normal beneficed clergy, were justified by suc-
cessive popes as a means of helping the incumbents in the parishes (see
Pantin 124–6, Knowles (1948), 182ff and (1955), 90ff). The rights included the
power to hear confession in any parish provided they had the permission of
the diocesan bishop, and the right to preach. The privileges of the friars were
bitterly resented by many of the beneficed clergy as well as by the Lollards
(see A. G. Little, *Studies in English Franciscan History* (Manchester, 1917),
pp. 100–22, esp. pp. 114–15).

37 *þis sory widewe*: i.e. the true church; cf Matt. 23. 14, Luke 20. 47.

38–40 The *princis of prestis and pharisees* are the ecclesiastical hierarchy (see below
no. 15), especially the orders of friars, and the abuse in question is the appro-
priation of livings, by which a benefice was filled by an ecclesiastical body
rather than by the gift of a secular patron (see above no. 3/8n).

46–8 Cf Ps. Bod. 288 f. 149v/1–2 'Þis flateringe wiþ þe mouþ and lijnge wiþ þe tunge is used among false briþeren þat flateren þe peple in tyme of gaderinge of her godis, and ceessen to preche in tyme whanne þei hope no good to haue.'

48–50 Cf Ps. Bod. 288 f. 174/1 'and þe princis þat as cruel tirauntis regnen in þe chirche in hiȝ dignyte of prelacie, killynge her scheep, rasynge of her wolle.' Repingdon makes a similar comment (f. 205v) on evil priests.

64ff Compare *Jack Upland* 20ff 'Anticrist...ȝeueþ leue to preestis of parischis boþe hiȝe and lowe to leue prechinge and to do lewid mennes office; and ȝit þei takun hire of her parischis neuer þe lasse – as offringis and tiþis and oþere possessiouns dowid for almes'; *Plowman's Tale* 719ff.

64–70 In the case of a living appropriated to a monastic or fraternal house the tithes would be collected annually by one of its members, whilst the services and everyday running of the parish would be delegated to a vicar, often ill-educated and poorly paid for his services by the house. See K. L. Wood-Legh, *Studies in Church Life in England under Edward III* (Cambridge, 1934), pp. 142ff.

14. Prologue to Wycliffite Bible, Chapter 15

The General Prologue to the Bible translation consists of fifteen chapters, of which the last alone directly concerns the translation and is here printed. The first fourteen chapters contain a brief introduction to the various books of the Bible, some material on the fourfold interpretation of scripture and comments in praise of the Bible from the fathers; some comments interspersed make clear the Lollard background of the whole. Nine copies of the General Prologue, many of them incomplete, survive; for the chapter here CUL Mm. 2. 15 (M), ff. 289–290v, has been used for the base text, collated with the other available manuscripts, CUL Kk. 1.8 (K), ff. 27–9, Corpus Christi College Cambridge 147 (C), ff. 17–18, Trinity College Dublin 75 (D), ff. 249–51, University College Oxford 96 (U), ff. 88–94, and BL Harley 1666 (H), ff. 111–111v (for lines 1–21 *synnes and* only, the rest lost). None of the nine manuscripts is attached to the EV translation; two are found with a revision of this (D and MS Bodley 277 which contains only the first chapter), five with LV texts, one on its own (H) and one attached to bits of a LV translation (U). The important point to note is that the Prologue is not the regular concomitant of the LV translation, but an exceptional addition to it. The Prologue was printed in 1540 (STC 25587. 5), and a new edition appeared in 1550 (STC 25588).

The General Prologue has usually been ascribed to John Purvey, though for reasons that are less than decisive. Deanesly discusses the matter (esp. pp. 376–81), but, with the removal of many of the texts Deanesly ascribed without doubt to Purvey (see introductory notes to no. 2 above and no. 24 below and no. 4/60n), the case becomes very weak. Nothing that Netter says of Purvey in his

Doctrinale can be identified with the present work; the material in *Fasc. Ziz.* (383–407) does not mention it. The date of the Prologue is connected with the arguments concerning authorship. In chapter thirteen (WB i. 51) is a reference to complaints of immorality at Oxford 'as it is knowen to many persones of þe reume, and at þe laste parlement'. This has been taken as an allusion to the third conclusion of the *Twelve Conclusions of the Lollards* (no. 3/25–35), and the Prologue therefore dated between the 1395 Parliament at which this latter was presented and the next Parliament in 1397. But, though such a date would fit well the general tenor of the Prologue, the identification with the conclusion is not entirely certain since the terms of the latter are less specific than the reference in the Prologue would lead one to expect. The chief importance of the Prologue is, however, not affected by uncertainties of authorship or exact date: it lies in the evidence provided by it about the work and organisation that lay behind the literal translation and the subsequent modification of this.

5 Jerome on Ps. 87. 6, PL 26.1084.

16 For the identification of the stones allegorically as the gentiles, see Bede's comment on Luke 19. 40, PL. 92.570.

16–17 See Jerome *Liber de Nominibus Hebraicis*, PL 23.817.

20–3 Cf Arnold iii. 186/1ff and *Lanterne* 100/1ff. The phraseology here should not be taken to imply that vernacular scriptures are already forbidden (cf lines 98ff), though it may suggest that persecution already extends as far as execution (i.e. that the act of *De Heretico Comburendo* passed in 1401 already existed). But it would appear from the *Opus Arduum*, firmly dated in 1389–90, that the Lollards often used expressions such as that of line 23 in anticipation of this final penalty.

29 Compare lines 72ff below. The corrupt nature of many Bible texts was deplored before Wyclif, notably by Roger Bacon who commented on the thirteenth-century Paris corrections to the Bible 'their alleged correction is the worst corruption and ruination of God's word; it is far safer and better to use an uncorrected text from Paris than their "correction" or that of any other improver' (*Opus Tertium*, ed. J. S. Brewer (Rolls Series, London, 1859), p. 94). See H. Denifle, 'Die Handschriften der Bibel-Correctorien des 13. Jahrhunderts', *Archiv für Literatur- und Kirchengeschichte des Mittelalters* iv (1888), 263–311, 471–601.

30 Nicholas of Lyra was a Franciscan living c. 1270–1340 (see ODCC), whose commentary on the literal sense of scripture, and especially of the Old Testament, was widely influential. To a translator his comments would be especially helpful, since he knew Hebrew and incorporated explanations of many words from that language into his *Postilla*.

37 The writer is alluding to the tag concerning translation *verbum ex verbo, sensum ex sensu* found, following Jerome's use of it in his preface to the Vulgate, in all medieval works on translation. It appears from what follows, however, that *aftir þe wordis* has here a specialised sense: the invariable translation of one Latin word by one English word, neither more nor less, and the adherence in the English version to the exact word order of the Latin original. The debate is not, as a modern critic might suppose, between a close and a free rendering,

but between a transposition of Latin into English and a close translation into English word order and vocabulary.

41–51 Latin makes use of a greater number of absolute participial constructions than English, and these, if translated straight into English, are misleading. The most natural rendering into English is by a conjunction, usually a temporal one, and a finite verb. For an example see no. 8/13 V *congregatis omnibus*, EV *alle thingus gadered togidere*, LV *whanne alle þingis weren gaderid togidere*; quite apart from the unidiomatic nature of the EV passage, the absence by this time of a fully inflected past participle showing case and number, together with the identity in many verbs of the forms of preterite and past participle, could lead to ambiguity. The difficulty of *resolucion* is that a conjunction and finite verb have to express a definite relation, here temporal, between the subordinate and main verbs in a sentence, a relation which may be undefined in the Latin. As an instance of this may be cited Mark 16. 20 V *illi...praedicaverunt ubique, Domino cooperante*, EV *thei...prechiden euerywhere, the Lord worchinge with*, LV *thei...prechiden euerywhere, for the Lord wrouȝte with hem*. In LV the Latin present participial construction is interpreted as implying a causal connection between the two clauses; but the relation could merely be one of attendant circumstances, not correctly translated as *for* plus a finite verb.

51–6 The problem here is simpler, though it arises from the same cause, the greater frequency of the participle in Latin than in English; the difference from the the last category is that the participle is here in apposition to a word in the main clause rather than forming an absolute construction. For an example may be cited no. 8/20 V *et surgens venit ad patrem suum*, EV *and he risende cam to his fader*, LV *and he roos vp and cam to his fadir*; see also nos. 7/1/1, 7/3/1, 7/3/7, 8/20 (second half), and two in 8/29.

56–8 The writer here refers to the frequent use of the Latin relative as a resumptive subject, for instance Matt. 14. 18 V *qui ait eis*, EV *the whiche seith*, LV *and he seide*. In fact more modifications towards the idiomatic use of the relative are made in LV than are here mentioned, notably the expansion of the relative into a pronoun plus relative, for instance Matt. 11. 3 V *tu es, qui venturus es*, some manuscripts EV *art thou that art to cummynge*, LV *art thou he that schal come*.

58–60 Many variants of this are found. The commonest are the repetition of the verb, as for instance no. 7/1/8 V *quod est opus tuum? quae terra tua?* EV *what is þi werc? whiche þi lond?*, where LV has in the second *whiche is þi lond?*, and of the pronoun, as John 11. 44 V *solvite eum et sinite abire*, EV *vnbynde ȝe him and suffre ȝe go awey*, LV *vnbynde ȝe hym and suffre ȝe hym to go forth*.

60–2 The point here is associated with that dealt with in more detail in lines 188–91, that there cannot be a regular translation of one Latin word by one English word since the semantic ranges of words in two languages are rarely symmetrical. There are various instances in the passages here printed, for instance no. 8/25 V *erat autem filius*, EV *forsoþe his eldere sone*, LV *but his...*, or no. 8/17 V *in se autem reversus*, EV *soþli he turned aȝeen*, LV *and he...* (cf nos. 6/5, 8/11, 20, 28, 32, 11/12, 13).

62–6 The writer has somewhat confused the point here by his example. He is observing the necessity of a more fixed word order in English, a relatively uninflected language, as compared with Latin. In the Latin instance the accusative *dominum* is placed first for emphasis; but this, *englisshid bi þe lettre* in exact form would read *þe Lord shulen drede aduersaries hise*, a rendering which reverses the normal English word order. Obviously this is an extreme example of the danger of a precisely literal rendering, but alteration following from this principle accounts for a large number of the variants between EV and LV. As a simple instance may be cited no. 6/1 V *et brachium Domini cui revelatum est?*, EV *and þe arm of þe Lord to whom is it shewid?*, LV *and to whom is þe arm of þe Lord schewid?*

75–8 Knowledge of Hebrew in the medieval period was uncommon, and in many cases apparent acquaintance derives from copying the comments of a few authors such as Jerome and Lyra; the expression of the writer here makes it

clear that his knowledge is similarly derivative. For medieval contact with
Hebrew scholars see B. Smalley, *The Study of the Bible in the Middle Ages*
(Oxford, 1952), esp. pp. 149ff, 173ff, 329ff.

78–82   The manuscripts of the Vulgate, as of the printed versions of this, contained
the so-called Gallican Psalter translated by Jerome about 392 from a Greek
text associated with Origen. Jerome's Hebrew Psalter, made as its name
implies from the original language, was not completed until c. 400 and never
ousted its rival from liturgical use. The writer's mention of *opere men þat hadden
myche lasse kunnyng* may imply that he thought the Gallican Psalter was not the
work of Jerome; alternatively, he may have been aware of an intermediate
version between the Hebrew and Latin. For the glosses to WB see Forshall
and Madden i. xxxf, and H. Hargreaves in *Studia Neophilologica* xxxiii (1961),
285–300.

82–4   The writer is referring to the discrepancy between the wording of scriptural
passages quoted in Jerome's extensive biblical commentaries (PL 23–6), and
that of extant medieval bibles, a discrepancy which would reveal the hazards
of textual transmission. As the writer acutely observes, the commentaries,
which sometimes involve grammatical analysis, will often provide a check on
the accuracy of the Vulgate itself.

90–4   The comment on recent expositors, more barbed than that on the older
doctors, is in line with the frequent disparagement of *glosing*, a process which
the Wycliffites regarded as departing from the true sense of scripture whether
that was, in the modern terms, literal or figural; cf Arnold iii. 258/15ff,
Matthew 37/25ff, 376/9ff.

98ff   Compared with the material from the 1401 debate on biblical translation (see
EHR xc (1975), 1–18), the arguments against biblical translation here refuted
are vague; this would suggest a date for the present text in the 1390s when
opposition was still unorganised.

104   The Septuagint translators; see ODCC. The Septuagint was the most
influential, and to medieval western scholars the best known, Greek translation
of the Hebrew Old Testament, made, according to legend, by 72 translators
inspired to work without error within a very short time.

113–14 See Jerome's first prologue on Job, translated in WB ii. 670–1, and that on
Daniel, not in WB, PL 28.1291–4.

122–8   Cf Mann pp. 23–4, 221 n. 28; the point here made is that the use of cloth and
horse, not specifically forbidden in scripture, is lawful if done for due cause.

132   *þe foure greete doctouris*: in the Latin church Ambrose, Jerome, Augustine and
Gregory.

144   Cf Chaucer Man of Law's Tale B. 519 where Constance's speech is described
as *a maner Latyn corrupt*, and CUL Ii. 6.26 f. iv, concerning the provision of
vernacular texts 'to Ytaliens bokis of Latyne corrupte'. If *trewe men* has here its
usual technical sense of 'Lollard sympathisers', the reference perhaps includes
Nicholas Hereford (above no. 4/610).

146–7   *De Doctrina Christiana* II. xi–xii (CCSL 32.42).

155–7   Cf Grosseteste Dict 19, MS Bodley 830, ff. 18–20v.

161–5   The examples of Bede and Alfred became standard ones for supporters of
English biblical translation: see Vienna tract f. 198r–v and the English deri-
vative, *Tract Trans.* 131–40, 146–51. The story was usually derived from
Higden's *Polychronicon* vi (ed. J. P. Lumby (Rolls Series, 1876), 354–6) and
William of Malmesbury's *Gesta Regum* (ed. W. Stubbs (Rolls Series 1887–9),
i. 132–3).

165–7   For French scriptural translation see C. A. Robson in *The Cambridge History of
the Bible* ii, ed. G. W. H. Lampe (Cambridge, 1969), 436–52. It is rather more
difficult to be certain of the texts to which the writer refers as belonging to
Beemers and Britons. Czech versions did exist before the Hussite period: see
J. Kadlec, 'Die Bibel im Mittelalterlichen Böhmen', *Archives d'histoire doctrinale
et littéraire du moyen âge* xxxi (1964), 89–101 esp. 92–6. A similar list is given in
the tract advocating biblical translation in CUL Ii. 6.26, f. 13v (for the manuscript see below no. 20).

173-83 The writer is referring first to words that have two divergent meanings (e.g. NE *fast*, 'quick' and 'firm'), but extends this to words whose translation into another language must vary because the range of meaning of words in the two tongues is not the same. That this problem remained a matter of dispute can be seen from the fact that one of the aims in the production of the Revised Version was the elimination of variant translations of the same Hebrew or Greek technical terms in the Authorised Version.

175 *De Doctrina Christiana* II xii (CCSL 32.44).

188 The reference is too vague for certain identification; cf no. 7/1/10 V *enim*, EV *forsoþe*, LV *for*.

194-6 Compare Ps. Bod. f. 29/1 'Here moun trewe men seen and knowe couetouse prechours and false glosers, for noon schulde be so hardi to translate or expowne holy writt in prechinge or in writinge but if he feelide þe Holy Goost wiþynne him, for he is speker and enditer of al holy writt, and of alle þe truþis þat springen out þerof.'

PART III. LOLLARD POLEMIC

15. The Ecclesiastical Hierarchy

The sermon, for such it is despite the absence of any liturgical occasion specified for its use, is here printed from BL MS Royal 18. B. ix (G), ff. 191v–194v, and is collated with the other thirteen manuscripts in which it survives. Twelve of these fourteen manuscripts contain the standard sermon-cycle, to which this and the tract on Matthew 24 (*Of Mynystris in þe Chirche*, Arnold ii. 393–423) seem to form an appendix. The other two manuscripts are St John's College Cambridge G. 25, ff. 97–101v and Trinity College Dublin 245, ff. 96–101. The text was printed from MS Bodley 788 in Arnold ii. 379–89. Wyclif himself wrote on this text, Matt, 23. 13–33, in the course of the *Opus Evangelicum* ii. 28/21ff, but the closer parallel is the *Exposicio textus Matthei xxiii* (*Opera Minora* 313–53), called in some manuscripts, as is the English text, *De Vae Octuplici*. The English tract does not draw all of its material from this source but, even granted the limitations imposed upon like-minded writers by the biblical text, it is plain from some details that the Wyclif tract was before the writer. The date of Wyclif's tract is uncertain, but from the unbridled criticism of the friars must derive from the last five years of his life.

15-17 The errors of popular preaching in the church, particularly that of the friars, are frequently criticised: see Arnold i. 176/22ff, 367/4ff, iii. 274/27ff, Matthew 8/24ff, 105/28ff and *Jack Upland* 233–6 and note.

23-6 The wording here suggests that the friars are specifically identified with the pharisees and this fits the criticisms below in most places; cf Arnold i. 15/11–12 'so þat scribis ben clepid seculer prelatis, and phariseis ben clepid þese newe religious'.

32–4 Cf *Exposicio* 337/31ff; a similar complaint is found in Gower *Confessio Amantis* Prol. 464ff.

36–7 Cf *Exposicio* 337/34f and compare Arnold i. 137/6ff, iii. 441/4ff, Matthew 16/25ff and 320/5ff.

46ff The charge of child-stealing was one of the most frequent and most bitter of those made against the friars; it is found outside the works of the Wycliffites in, for instance, Gower's *Vox Clamantis* iv. 981ff (note esp. lines 1001ff where the same biblical quotation is used). Cf *Exposicio* 339/3ff, Arnold i. 298/34ff, ii. 314/24ff, iii. 190/12ff, 384/25ff and *Jack Upland* 209–13 and note.

58–60 Cf Harley 1203, f. 72v 'oþir ȝyuen smaller ȝiftis þat geten smaller wynnyngis: applis, peris and spicery and panyeris ful of erbis, cuppis, knyues and poudir boxis, gloues and wriþun candelis, orisouns of pardoun and peyntid tablis and siche oþir ȝiftis.'

77ff See more explicitly no. 16/100ff; the author alludes to the practice whereby a vow of pilgrimage could be annulled by the payment of a sum of money, the payment in theory being an equivalent act of charity, but in effect a means of enriching the ecclesiastical hierarchy. The author ridicules this by asking whether the annulment is right before or after the payment: if before, then no payment to a prelate is necessary though almsgiving may be reasonable; if only after, then the 'justice' is purchased by a bribe. The English here follows Wyclif's Latin, note especially 342/10–15. Again the abuse of vows was a frequent topic of medieval satire: see *Apology* 11/22ff, Gower *Vox Clamantis* iii. 235ff.

89 For the personification of simony cf *Piers Plowman* B. ii. 62ff and the Rutebuf passage quoted by J. A. Yunck, *The Lineage of Lady Meed* (Notre Dame, 1963), p. 203, and see that book *passim* for a discussion of medieval venality satire.

95ff Following the play on *dispende/dispense, dispending/ dispensing*, the writer exploits the breadth of meaning of *chaungiþ*, in lines 96 and 100 'exchange', but in line 97 'alter, change'.

113–17 The *pharisees* here as before are apparently the friars. Wyclif similarly objects to the reservation of certain causes, but directs his comments against papal use of this device, *Exposicio* 343/18ff. The aim of reservation was to ensure that major offences against the church were not summarily dismissed by lower officials, with the consequent danger of inconsistency of penalty exacted; the abuse of it was the bribery and expenses to which it gave rise.

117–18 Cf *Piers Plowman* B. iii. 59ff, xi. 53ff.

136–8 For the contrast between God's law on the one hand, and man's law, new laws or antichrist's law on the other, cf Matthew 12/9ff, 145/18ff etc.

180 The objection is to the friars' claims concerning their habits of dress, of Arnold iii. 372/31ff, 382/28ff, 431/6ff, Matthew 315/18ff.

198 Only G has *kyndlyngis*, all other manuscripts having *gendruris*. This latter word is the more uncommon, but MED only gives a single example of the necessary sense here 'offspring'. *Kyndlyngis* is used in this same phrase in WB LV Luke 3. 7 (EV *kyndlis*, var. *fruitis* or *kyndelyngis*), though in Matt. 23. 33 neither word is found; in the citation of this verse in the Lollard texts Ps. Lamb. f. 196/2 and Harley 1203 f. 90v *kyndelyngis* is the word used.

214 Apparently an allusion to Matt. 7. 25–7, the contrast between the house built on rock and that built on sand (WB *on grauel*).

215ff For the persecution of Lollard preachers cf Arnold ii. 69/3ff, iii. 495/24ff, Matthew 11/35ff, 104/11ff etc.

228ff From this point on there is very little parallel between the English text and Wyclif's *Exposicio*; in particular the latter does not deal with the Eucharist.

238 Jerome Epistola 120, PL 22.986, also quoted Arnold iii. 484/24, 522/18.

241 Augustine sermon 272, PL 38.1247, also quoted Arnold iii. 522/7, 379/5, 484/21.

244 Ambrose *De Sacramentis* iv. 5, CSEL 73.56, also quoted Arnold iii. 379/7.

255–62 There is an exact parallel to this ironic transposition of virtues and vices in *Jack Upland* 46–53; Heyworth in his edition pp. 35–6 argues that *Upland* represents the source of this passage in the sermon. But the existence of a

similar, though less extended, list in a sermon attributed to William Taylor
(MS Douce 53, f. 17) makes it likely that all three are drawing on a common
source (the Taylor passage reads 'þus is now pride callid honestee, veniaunce
manhood, glotenye good felouship, leccherie kyndely solace, couetise wijsdom,
symonye oon good turne for anoþir, and vsurie cheuyshaunce'). Cf *Historical
Poems of the xivth and xvth Centuries* ed. R. H. Robbins (New York, 1959),
no. 57.

276 In the light of the comments of lines 303ff, the reference is here to the
Apostles' Creed. A brief Lollard commentary on this is found in Arnold iii.
114–16; the comment in this (116/26f) 'and so, as sum men þynke, þese popys
ne þese prelatys ar nat part of holy chirche' should be compared with the
present text lines 281–2.

288 The text was certainly written at the time of the Schism, between 1378 and
1415, when the western church was split between adherence to two rival popes.

303 The Athanasian creed, used on certain occasions in the liturgical year, and the
Nicene creed used regularly in the mass; cf *Piers Plowman* B. v. 598 and
Bennett's note.

304–5 *but it is...taken it*: 'but it is a reasonable guide to men who receive it of the
will of God'.

305ff Disparagement of the tendency for unsophisticated men to concern themselves
with theological doctrine is found commonly in the late fourteenth century:
Gower *Vox Clamantis* ii. 461ff, *Piers Plowman's Creed* 824ff, and *Piers Plowman*
B. xv. 378ff and xv. 69–72
  '3e moeuen materes inmesurables to tellen of the Trinite,
  That ofte tymes the lewed peple of hir bileue douten.
  Bettere byleue were mony doctoures such techyng,
  And tellen men of the ten comaundementz and touchen the seuene
    synnes.'
The Lollard manuscript Trinity College Dublin 245, f. 160v, divides truth into
four types of varying importance for salvation.

16. Images and Pilgrimages

The text comes from BL MS Additional 24202, ff. 26–28v, an
anthology of works critical of the contemporary church though
not all overtly heretical. The manuscript is of the early fifteenth
century; most of its contents are not found elsewhere, and few of
them have been printed. Though the refusal of honour to images
of saints, and the associated disrespect for pilgrimages, came to be
perhaps the commonest Lollard beliefs, these two questions were
apparently under discussion before Wyclif. Woodford, later an
ardent opponent of Wyclif, discussed the matters in his *Postilla
super Mattheum* dating from 1372–3 (CUL MS Additional 3571,
ff. 117, 119v–122), and it is clear from this that many of the
arguments were already well-worn (see J. I. Catto, *William
Woodford, O.F.M. (c. 1330–c. 1397)* (unpub. Oxford D.Phil.
thesis, 1969), pp. 150–55). Although a number of points go right
back to the eighth century iconoclastic controversy of the eastern
church (see E. R. Harvey, *The Inward Wits...* (unpub. London
Ph.D. thesis, 1970), pp. 179ff), the use of scholastic terminology
and of contemporary examples shows that the matters must have

been debated in the late fourteenth-century schools. Wyclif
himself does not appear to have been very interested in the
questions: in the *De Mandatis* 153ff he inevitably reviews the issue,
but the ideas expressed there are conservative; he mentions the
dangers of idolatry in *Sermones* i. 91/15ff, but admits the usefulness
of images to the illiterate laity; no charge concerning images or
pilgrimages appeared in the 1382 condemnation. The matters were,
however, assiduously discussed in Oxford and elsewhere at the end
of the fourteenth and beginning of the fifteenth centuries. A text
variously ascribed in the manuscripts to Walter Hilton and Thomas
Palmer, *De Adoracione Ymaginum*, has been shown to reflect Hilton's
concern with the topic of images in his other writings (see
J. Russell-Smith, *Dominican Studies* vii (1954), 180–214); John
Deveros wrote various tracts defending the use of images and
pilgrimages (see Emden, *Cambridge* 186); John Sharpe (Emden,
Oxford iii. 1680) wrote a text found in MSS Merton College 68,
ff. 29–31v and Merton College 175, ff. 279–81v; Robert Alyngton,
an associate of Wyclif in 1381 but later writing against him (see
Emden, *Oxford* i. 30–1), composed a *Determinacio de adoratione
ymaginum* found in MS Merton College 68, ff. 32–40; further
tracts are found in MSS Merton College 175, ff. 277–279v (the
first part of which occurs in All Souls College Oxford 42,
ff. 268–269v), BL Harley 31, Royal 6 E. iii and Royal 11 B. x.
The identity of argument and overlapping citation in most of
these suggest that all derive from a continuing debate; an
anonymous tract in Merton College 175 identifies the opponents
of images as specifically 'aliqui execrabiles ypocrite vel lollardi'
(f. 277v). That the debate reached beyond the university in
orthodox circles is shown by the review of the question in
Gower's *Vox Clamantis* ii. 495ff. On the Lollard side, the physical
destruction of images had begun by 1382, as the charges against
William Smith in Leicester recorded by Knighton make clear
(ii. 182, 313); Miss Russell-Smith points to an allusion in a sermon
of Brinton, bishop of Rochester, from c. 1383 suggesting that
this was not an isolated incident (art. cit. p. 200 n. 78). Texts to
support the practical action are also common: as well as that here,
tracts are found in MS Bodley Eng. th. f. 39, ff. 1–8 and 37–8,
the second reappearing in Trinity College Cambridge B. 14.50,
ff. 34–5, and a Latin text by an English Wycliffite is preserved in
Prague University X.E. 9, ff. 210v–214. The attitude seems,
however, to have varied somewhat: in the sermon-cycle the subject

is not much discussed, and moderate texts such as the *Lanterne*
(84/28–85/28) reiterate Wyclif's own reservation that images could
serve as useful instruction, provided they were recognised as
signs alone. On the other hand, the biblical prohibition of Exod.
20. 4, coupled with the abuses in waste of time and money, are
forcibly urged in more extreme texts such as the following (cf
Arnold iii. 462/22ff, Matthew 210/27ff, 279/14ff, *Apology* 85/4–
90/24). Both supporters and opponents of images make use of a
stock series of examples and quotations, many of which are listed in
the Lollard *Floretum* and *Rosarium* under the headings of *adoracio*,
ydolatria and *ymago*, and reappear in the orthodox *Dives and Pauper*
in caps. i–xvi of the First Commandment; Pecock *Repressor* i.
136–255 reiterates many.

5–8 See no. 3/97n.

12–15 Cf Harvey op. cit. p. 178; Leo III in the iconclastic controversy set up the
cross in place of an icon of Christ (see A. Grabar, *L'Iconoclasme byzantin* (Paris,
1957), p. 130).

17 For the idea of poor men as the true images of Christ see above no. 3/99–101
and cf *Apology* 88/28, Thorpe ff. 45–6, *Plowman's Tale* 909ff, *Dives and Pauper*
I lii. 1–75, *Piers Plowman* B. xi. 180 and the trial of John of Bath in Salisbury
register Chaundler ii. f. 17v 'only quicke men ben Goddes ymagis and liknesse
of the Trinite'. It derives from pseudoChrysostom, PG 56.867–8.

21 *þes ymagis ben bokis of lewid men*: perhaps the most frequently cited phrase on
both sides of the argument, cf *Lanterne* 85/21, Douce 53, f. 31v, *Dives and
Pauper* I vi. 1–3, BL Royal 6 D. x, f. 275.

24–33 For this objection to the excessive richness of images, misleading those to
whom they were meant to serve as instruction, compare *Dives and Pauper*
I vii. 25–34, where Dives's objection 'þey weryn nought so gay in clothyng as
þey been peyntyd' is upheld by Pauper.

56–8 The writer is referring to the habit of placing the image of the saint in a
decorated archway or shrine (see the series of figures over the tomb of William,
Lord Graunson in Hereford cathedral (d. 1335) or those in New College
Oxford reredos (1383), illustrated J. Evans, *English Art 1307–1461* (Oxford,
1949), pls. 75, 89).

82–3 Pardons were attached to many shrines, see N. Paulus, *Geschichte des Ablasses
im Mittelalter* (Paderborn, 1922–3), iii. 150–94.

100–8 See above no. 15/77n; *penetaunceris* were officials used by the ecclesiastical
authorities to deal with confessional matters of a serious nature which could not
be handled by the ordinary parish priest (see Thompson (1947), 55–6 and *Chichele
Register* i. 83–4).

124 For the *long cursid preyeris* see no. 15/36–7n.

124 Objections to singing in church are frequent, and usually mention *cnakkyng*:
Arnold iii. 203/18ff, 479/27ff, Matthew 76/8ff, 91/29ff, 169/16ff, 191/4ff,
Lanterne 57/15ff and revision of Rolle's Psalter Ps. Bod. ff. 96v and 133v. The
rejection, apart from the lack of foundation for such practices in the Bible, is
that such singing obscures the words that are being sung (cf *Dives and Pauper*
I lix. 28–33, where criticism is made of those who 'hackyn þe wordis and þe
silablis'), and that time is so taken from the more important matter of
preaching. The objection persisted: compare the curate of Loughborough in
1518 who complained of *pricksong* because 'huiusmodi cantus fuit ordinatus

tantumodo ex superbia' (cited M. Bowker, *The Secular Clergy in the Diocese of Lincoln 1495–1520* (Cambridge, 1968), p. 106).

126 Gregory, *Cura Pastoralis* III. 20, PL 77.85.

127–8 E.g. Augustine sermon 115, PL 38.656.

130–1 Cf *Piers Plowman* B. Prol. 48, v. 522ff, xiv. 195ff.

144–6 For the distances which a middle-class pilgrim, albeit an eccentrically arduous one, might cover, compare the journeys of Margery Kempe to Jerusalem and to Compostella, Rome and many other places in Europe (ed. S. B. Meech and H. E. Allen, EETS 212 (1940), 66, 105, 229ff).

157 *Bromholme*: a priory in Norfolk having a fragment of the cross; cf *Canterbury Tales* A. 4286 and *Piers Plowman* B. v. 231 where Avarice journeys there.

157 *Grace*: at Boxley Abbey near Maidstone (see J. Cave-Browne, *The History of Boxley Parish* (Maidstone, 1892), pp. 46–51).

157–8 *þe...rode at þe norþe dore*: the rood in St Paul's London, also a place of pilgrimage; this and *Grace* are mentioned in MS Bodley Eng. th. f. 39 f. 12v (see notes in E. P. Wilson's edition (unpub. Oxford B.Litt. thesis, 1968), pp. 104–6).

158 *Walsyngham*: a village in Norfolk which had a famous image of the Virgin; cf Thorpe f. 50, *Piers Plowman* B. Prol. 54 and Bennett's note, and v. 230 where it was another of the resorts of Avarice.

163ff Cf Thorpe f. 56 'Whanne dyuerse men and wymmen wolen goen þus...out on pilgrimageyngis, þei wolen ordeyne biforehonde to haue wiþ hem boþe men and wymmen þat kunnen wel synge rowtinge songis, and also summe of þese pilgrimes wolen haue wiþ hem bagge pipis so þat in eche toun þat þei comen þoruȝ, what wiþ noyse of her syngynge and wiþ þe soun of her pipinge and wiþ þe gingelynge of her Cantirbirie bellis, and wiþ þe berkynge out of dogges aftir hem, þese maken more noyse þan if þe king came þere awey wiþ his clarioneris and manye oþer mynystrals.'

178 For the legend of Bartholomew in Middle English see *Manual* 570–1.

184 *Seynt Sithe*: St Osyth; for her legend see *Acta Sanctorum* October iii (Antwerp, 1770), 942–4. Her shrine was at the abbey of her name in Essex.

17. Epistola Sathanae ad Cleros

The text is preserved in a single manuscript, CUL Ff. 6. 2, ff. 81–84v, dating from the early sixteenth century; it has not been printed before. The other contents of the manuscript, written in the same hand, are a copy of the complete text from which no. 18 is taken, and a copy of *Jack Upland*. The composition date of the first of these will be discussed below; Heyworth, the most recent editor of *Jack Upland*, argues for a date for this text 'later rather than earlier in the period 1390 to 1420' (p. 17). In the present letter the few indications of date suggest composition before or about 1400: the allusions to *Lollers*, lines 150, 152, and to their persecution, lines 142–5, coupled with the reference to fighting bishops, line 138, point to a date early in the movement.

The letter is an example of a form of anti-clerical satire common in the later Middle Ages, the *Epistola Sathanae* (or *Luciferi*) *ad Cleros*. The satire appears to have been known in the twelfth century, though the earliest complete example surviving is rather

later; many of the texts are, from similarity of wording, clearly
related to each other. Details of the tradition are given by
G. Zippel, 'La lettera del Diavolo al clero, dal secolo xii alle
Riforma', *Bulletino dell'Istituto Storico Italiano per il Medio Ævo*
lxx (1958), 125–79. Another fourteenth-century English version is
found in Huntington HM 114, ff. 319–25v (edited by R. R. Raymo
in *Medieval Literature and Civilisation*, ed. D. A. Pearsall and R. A.
Waldron (London, 1969), 233–48); Satan here especially praises
the four beggyng ordres (lines 232–3), and may describe Lollards when
he says 'many now in these dayes agens us aryse, the lawes of
that Ihesu Crist prechyng and with all her myghtes and strengthes
enhauncyng' (lines 252–4). A second instance, certainly of Lollard
composition, is found in Latin preserved in the register of John
Trefnant, bishop of Hereford, under 1393 (ed. W. W. Capes,
Canterbury and York Society (1916), 401–5) with the title 'littera
per Lollardos contra viros ecclesiasticos'; an English translation of
this was printed by Foxe, with some comments on its background, in iii. 189–93. A reference, turning the tables on these
Lollard authors, is found in *Daw's Reply* lines 898–9:

'But good Iak, ʒour grace, where be ʒe foundid?
Not in Goddis gospel but in Sathanas pistile.'

The present version is not directly related to either of the
contemporary letters mentioned above, nor to any of the material
mentioned by Zippel though some traditional elements remain
(e.g. with the present lines 41–3 compare the other English
version, lines 34–7 'and the brode light wey *que ducit ad mortem*,
"that ledith to the dethe", without eny prees or steppys of
wrecches of our subiect peple, lay forletyngly undefoulyd,
unhauntyd and unusyd'). But it does appear to be the source of
a later letter, printed with the date 1586 and also surviving, in
slightly different form, in an eighteenth-century transcript of a
sixteenth-century manuscript. This later text is printed by
J. Fines, under the title 'An Unnoticed Tract of the Tyndale-
More Dispute?' in *BIHR* xlii (1969), 220–30. The opening section
derives very closely from the version here, though the material
added in the printed edition is entirely independent. Whether
Tyndale was the *reviser* or not, it seems clear that its *author* lived
much earlier and was a Lollard; it is striking that none of Fines's
evidence for date is incompatible with earlier origin, and that he
mentions Lollard parallels for some phraseology. For other
reformation interest in reworking Lollard texts, see nos. 4 and 18

here, and also Aston (1964), 149–70, J. Crompton, 'John Wyclif, a Study in Mythology', *Transactions of the Leicestershire Archaeological Society* xlii (1968), 6–34.

1–2   The *sectis of perdicion* are, as appears from lines 94ff, primarily the orders of friars, but, as is usual in Lollard polemic, *sectis* can also cover other forms of the religious life. The Latin abbreviation usual on the outer side of a letter is used for the final word of the directive.

6   *coventis*: again the word can be used for any sort of religious establishment; cf Arnold iii. 59/24ff, 60/26ff.

9ff   The writer is using the familiar medieval explanation of the atonement, that of the 'devil's rights' and the deception of the devil, an explanation that can be traced back to Origen (see ODCC *atonement* and cf J. Rivière, *Le dogme de la rédemption au début du moyen âge* (Paris, 1934), pp. 7–29). The devil at the fall of man acquired rights over man, who had to suffer death and hell as the requital of sin; Christ, however, was without sin, and the devil, by falsely laying claim to him at the crucifixion, forfeited thereby his rights over all mankind.

19ff   Cf BL Additional 24202, f. 3 'For riȝt as þe scribis and þe pharisees in þe tyme of Crist hadden counseylis into þe destruccioun of þe chirche and of þe state þat God by Moyses sett hem inne, as shewiþ Crist ofte in þe gospell, so now popis wiþ her cardenalis and here bischoppis han counseylis to þe destruccioun of Cristis chirche.'

62–9   For the legend of Constantine (c. 274–337) see ODCC; the Donation of Constantine made to pope Sylvester I (314–35) purported to give the bishop of Rome primacy over other ecclesiastical authorities within the Empire and to give him considerable temporal wealth and jurisdiction, both in perpetuity. The text was regarded as genuine even by opponents of the papacy such as the Lollards during the Middle Ages, but is now accepted as a forgery, probably of the eighth or ninth century (see ODCC). Wyclif and the Lollards regarded the Donation as the turning point in church history, frequently citing the legend that on the day of Constantine's act an angel appeared to proclaim 'This opyn ȝyfte maad bi Constantyn today is venym sched in þe chirche of God' (*Lollard Chron.* lines 15–16); cf Wyclif *Supplementum Trialogi* 408/32ff, *Polemical Works* ii. 669/23ff, *Opera Minora* 226/2ff; Arnold i. 314/1ff, iii. 340/34ff, Matthew 378/5ff, 475/22ff etc. A similar doubt about the endowment that followed is found in orthodox writers, for instance *Piers Plowman* B. xv. 519–29, Gower *Vox Clamantis* iii. 283.

70–2   For fears of total possession of temporalities by the church see nos. 25–6.

75ff   Despite Wyclif's eventual hostility to the friars, he recognised the similarity of the founding ideals of Francis to his own idea of clerical poverty: see *Trialogus* 361/15–364/16, *Polemical Works* i. 91/16ff. In Wyclif's view the flaw in the fraternal way of life arose from the sophistication of their original views of poverty to allow for effectual possession of property, and hence their involvement in temporal power (see especially *Polemical Works* i. 88ff and the Lollard *Rule and Testament of St Francis*, Matthew 39–51). See above no. 2/139n, and compare amongst orthodox writings *Piers Plowman* B. xv. 409–20, Gower *Vox Clamantis* iv. 711ff.

80   The vital point here is *wiþowt beggery*, cf lines 103ff. The *Regula Prima* of the Franciscan order (ed. H. Boehmer, *Analekten zur Geschichte des Franciscus von Assisi* (Tübingen and Leipzig, 1904), p. 10) provided 'cum necesse fuerit, vadant pro elemosinis', but makes it clear that this was to be regarded as a last resort.

85   The reference appears to be to the Austin and Carmelite orders and some minor groups such as the Crutched Friars and Friars of the Sack; for these latter see Knowles (1948), i. 194–204.

94ff   For the lengthy debate within the Franciscan order see Douie and Lambert (above no. 2/139n) and Leff (1967), i. 51–255.

97 For a satirical description of the richness of Dominican houses see *Piers Plowman's Creed* 153ff.

103ff The argument about the legitimacy of begging by the friars was by no means limited to heretical circles. Before Wyclif the issue had been examined by FitzRalph in *De Pauperie Salvatoris* (ed. R. L. Poole in his edition of Wyclif's *De Dominio Divino*) and in later sermons (see A. Gwynn, *Studies* (1937), pp. 50–67 and *Proceedings of the Royal Irish Academy* xliv (1937–8), 45–7). The question was closely related to the whole problem of the maintenance of the clergy, a problem about which the Lollards themselves were ambiguous (see below no. 23/61ff and note).

106 The writer's chronology is here defective, since the Dominican order was established with the aim of converting men by intellectual argument. The anti-intellectualism of the Lollards is here evident (see Matthew 428/14ff, *Lanterne* 5/16ff and compare *Piers Plowman* B. xx. 271).

113 The damage done to the genuine poor by the able-bodied begging of the friars is often stressed: e.g. Arnold iii. 415/26ff, Matthew 233/12ff, 278/28ff, Trinity College Dublin 244, f. 216v 'we seyen þat, siþ biggynge wiþouten nede, as is stronge bigginge, is ensaumple and mayntenynge of þeues, as it is open wrongful coueytynge of oþere mennes þingis, and so it is þe brekynge of þe tenþe heste of God, so stronge biggynge may for no seruice of God be excusid'; compare *Piers Plowman* B. vi. 117ff, C. vi. 26ff, and x. 98ff; *Plowman's Tale* 165ff.

117 *to preache for mony*: cf *Piers Plowman* B. Prol. 58–9, and BL Harley 1203, f. 70 'þey forȝeten vertues to selle wordis to þe riche, and gretyngis to grete wymmen'.

117–19 Cf no. 3/125n above, also *Jack Upland* 335–41, Arnold iii. 377/19ff.

127 *þe iiij orders*: the Carmelites, Austin, Dominicans (or Jacobites) and Franciscans (or Minorites), whose initials gave the proverbial *Caim* (see Wyclif, *Sermones* ii. 84/37–85/4, *Trialogus* 362/15–22; Arnold iii. 368/27, 398/30 etc). For friars as servants of antichrist cf. *Plowman's Tale* 189ff.

146–8 A reference to Lollard teaching and the translation of the Bible; see introduction to the notes to Part II.

152–3 Compare CUL Ii. 6.26, ff. 60–61v (for the manuscript see no. 20) where different kinds of *Lollers* are described, culminating in Christ as a *Loller* on the cross.

158–9 The reference is too vague to define the date of composition. The identification of the unbinding of Satan (Apoc. 20.7) with the foundation of the friars in the first two decades of the thirteenth century is normal in Wycliffite writings (see *Trialogus* 361/10ff, Arnold iii. 449/10ff); if this is followed here, *þe C yere and more* must be interpreted very generously.

18. Mendicancy

The text is printed from British Library Egerton 2820 (E), ff. 105v–117, collated with Huntington Library HM 503 (H), ff. 109v–122v, CUL Dd. 14.30(2) (D), ff. 94–98v, and CUL Ff. 6.2 (F), ff. 60–67v. E and D are written in the same early fifteenth-century hand; these two and H, of a similar date, are very similar in format and probably derive from the same scriptorium. F is of the early sixteenth century (see above no. 17), but its text is closely related to that of H. Despite its later date, F is now the only complete version of the text from which this extract is taken; E has been used for the base text here since it

contains the whole of the passage, but it is defective at the end
of the complete text; D is defective at beginning and end, and
lacks lines 1–15, 39–62, 91–9 and 110–end of the present extract;
H has lost a small number of isolated folios.

The complete sermon is related to a text printed under the title
of *The Clergy may not hold Property* by Matthew pp. 362–404; this
latter consists of ten chapters, followed by a collection of biblical,
patristic and canonistic authorities in English and Latin supporting
the thesis of the work. It is found in one manuscript, Lambeth
Palace Library 551, again of similar size and format to E, D and
H. Parts of this version were printed abroad in *A proper dyaloge...*
(1530), STC 6813, and in the probably earlier print ([1529?]) (see
Nijhoff and Kronenberg, *Nederlandsche Bibliographie van 1500 tot 1540*
(The Hague, 1919–), no. 4215). In default of a full critical edition,
it is unclear how the two versions are related; the parts of the
text here printed come after the last parallel between the versions.
From the address to the congregation in lines 8–10, 99, 100ff, it
seems that the present version was delivered by an itinerant
Lollard preacher; the type of group that might have heard it, and
discussed it subsequently, can be seen in no. 5 above. Another
tract by the same preacher is extant in BL MS Cotton Titus D. v,
where the present sermon is alluded to on f. 8v; the subjects of
this tract are antichrist and the Eucharist, though topics mentioned here are also briefly covered. The tract can be dated on
internal references between the death of Henry IV in March 1413
and that of archbishop Arundel in February 1414; from the
phraseology of the allusion it would appear that the present
sermon had been written some time previously, and certainly the
tract is a good deal more intemperate. The writer clearly had
access to books and his scholarly pretensions are evident from the
tract (f. 69v) where he excuses himself 'for I haue not nou3 þe
copie of his boke [that of pseudoDionysius] I write not his
wordis here'; he also refers in the tract (ff. 15, 72v) to debates on
the Eucharist in Oxford, and uses grammatical and logical
analyses to support his view (ff. 23v–4, 76v, 91v, 98v).

4–8 The two extremes are those of temporal wealth and feigned poverty; cf. no. 17.
23–41 As an example of the interpretation here rejected see Bonaventura *Apologia
Pauperum* (*Opera Omnia* viii (Quaracchi, 1898), 324).
40–1 The same explanation, but related to the ensuing story of Christ and the woman
of Samaria, is made in Douce 53, f. 25.
41–4 Cf *Jack Upland* 272–4, *Upland's Rejoinder* 330–41.
47–9 For the friars' argument see, for instance, Bonaventura *Expositio super*

Regulam Fratrum Minorum (ed. cit. 423–4), a point reiterated by Netter
Doctrinale iv. 10. The Lollard denunciation was anticipated by William of
St Amour, *De Periculis Novissimorum Temporum* (*Opera Omnia* (Constance, 1632),
pp. 51–2).

67 The omitted passage provides more biblical support for the argument.

70ff E and D have *quilagis*, H *colletis* and F *colegis* or *collagis* throughout this passage;
WB in I Cor. 16. 1 has *collectis* or *gaderingis* EV, *gaderyngis* LV. The word in E
and D is recorded in MED under *coilage* only from *Mum and the Sothsegger* 149.
H's reading is an acceptable alternative, but F's variants are likely to be
misunderstandings of the form in E and D. The same passage is discussed to
similar conclusions in Douce 53, ff. 21–22, Trinity College Dublin 244, f. 218v
and BL Harley 1203, f. 79.

83ff Cf *Apology* 105/21ff concerning the necessity of bodily labour by religious, and
108/3ff concerning able-bodied begging.

89–94 Cf Trinity College Dublin 244, f. 218v 'And þerfore þat biddinge þat Poul
bede collectis to be imaad to þe seyntes in Ierusalem was not biddyng of
beggynge but biddinge of autorite.'

99 The omitted section gives further examples of the friars' false logic.

106ff A similar request for correction is found in MS Titus D. v, f. 100.

124 *my teeme*: the text announced at the start was 'Omnis plantacio quam non
plantauit pater meus celestis eradicabitur' (Matt. 15. 13).

19. Miracle Plays

The text derives from BL Additional 24202, ff. 14–17v, the manuscript that has already been described in the notes to no. 16. The
passage here printed is a little under a half of the complete text:
passages providing elaboration of ideas already set out are omitted
after line 70 and line 195, and the second half of the text, which
reiterates points of the first part, is also left out; this second half
(ff. 17v–21) is separated from the first by a capital, and attempts
to answer the objections of 'an half frynde'. This manuscript is
the only copy of the text; it was printed by J. O. Halliwell in
Reliquiæ Antiquæ (London, 1841–3), ii. 42–57, and by E. Mätzner,
Altenglische Sprachproben (Berlin, 1867–9), I. ii. 224–42.

The subject of miracle plays is not one that seems to have
attracted much attention from the Lollards; the text's inclusion
here is not because of its representative nature in the movement,
but because it has attracted modern discussion as an unusual
contemporary criticism of the plays. For an analysis of the argument see R. Woolf, *The English Mystery Plays* (London, 1972),
pp. 84–101, esp. 85. The *Floretum* has a brief entry for *histrio*,
reduced still further in the *Rosarium*, in which the performing or
watching of plays, not specifically religious plays, is condemned
on the authority of Augustine, Grosseteste, Peraldus and canon
law; the entry, however, has none of the criticism of mimetic
presentation that makes this passage of literary interest. The *Opus*

Arduum mentions last in a list of priestly sins the interest in
'ceteris histrionalibus' (f. 165v); a poem of probably Lollard
authorship may be a satire of the Franciscan encouragement of
plays (see R. H. Robbins, *Historical Poems of the xivth and xvth
Centuries* (New York, 1959), no. 66 but cf note p. 335). Some of
the arguments here recur in other Lollard texts in connection
with the use, especially by the friars, of amusing tales in sermons;
there are also some parallels with the condemnation of *histriones*
and *joculatores* in orthodox medieval texts, e.g. *Piers Plowman*
B. x. 38ff, xiii. 224ff.

5–6 *of ʒildyng...teeres*: 'by giving everlasting joy in exchange for the continual
grief and sorrow which we undergo in this vale of tears'.

6 *myraclis*: the word is used throughout the text in the sense of 'marvellous
event' in the broadest meaning of this term, hence including the whole life of
Christ and not merely those events within it that are now normally described
as the 'miracles'. Side by side with this sense is that of 'miracle plays', of
which this is an abbreviated form (so, for instance, line 47).

47–50 *in takyng...of hem*: 'by taking as plays for the entertainment of our body, of
our pleasure and of our senses, those things which God accepted culminating
in his bitter death, and accepted as a means of instructing us to do penance, of
directing us to flee from the encouragement of our senses and to mortify
them'.

51 Cf Wyclif, *De Mandatis* 433/14–18; Arnold i. 24/23ff, Ps. Bod. f. 85v/2 'we
rede not of Cristis lauʒtir, but of his weping we reden dyuerse tymes'.

70 The omitted passage, opening with quotation of I Pet. 5. 6, reinforces the
lesson of obedience to the will of God.

91–4 The writer's objections are clearly not simply to the introduction of humorous
material into biblical stories (as, for instance, the traditional comic elements in
the plays of Noah or of the shepherds), but also, as the words *for þei lowen at
his passioun* show, to the dramatic reconstruction of the characters and actions
of Christ's opponents in the trial and subsequent events.

126–8 Though known as a Lollard tract against plays, if the text comes from
Wycliffite circles, these were not extreme in their views. Here, and in lines
265–8 the use of painting is admitted in more generous terms than in no. 16;
a passage here omitted (f. 16v) shows more reverence for the Eucharist than
some Lollard texts allow. With the defence view here, cf Pecock, *Repressor*
i. 221/22ff, where images are extolled as arousing devotion above all other
means 'except whanne a quyk man is sett in a pley to be hangid nakid on a
cros, and to be in semyng woundid and scourgid'.

153–5 The writer has in mind the canon law provisions cited in the *Floretum* entry
for *histrio*: *Decretum* II, c. 4 q. 1 c. 1 (Fried. i. 536–7), *Decretum* De Cons. d. 2
c. 95 (Fried. i. 1352), *Decretales* III, tit. 1 c. 15 (Fried. ii. 453). For clerical
involvement with the plays, see G. Wickham, *Early English Stages 1300–1660*
(London, 1959), esp. pp. 140–2, 162–3, 233.

173–4 Cf *Piers Plowman* B. v. 491 and Bennett's note. The distinction is between the
sin itself which is evil, as was the sin of Adam or the rejection of Christ by the
Jews, and the response of God to this evil action through which good results.
The paradox is expressed neatly in the lyric *Adam lay ybounden* (ed. C. Brown,
Religious Lyrics of the 15th Century (Oxford, 1939), no. 83), lines 5–7:

> Ne hadde þe appil take ben, þe appil taken ben,
> ne hadde neuer our lady a ben heuene qwen;
> Blyssid be þe tyme þat appil take was...

179, 183 The section of Ps. 119 in which these two verses occur is used in the office of

Tierce throughout the year (see F. Procter and C. Wordsworth, *Breviarium ad Usam...Sarum* (Cambridge, 1879–86), ii. 57).

180 Ps. 30 was recited at Matins on Mondays throughout the year (*loc. cit.* col. 73).

186 Cf *The Political Songs of England*, ed. T. Wright (Camden Soc. 1839), p. 328.

189–92 The reference here is obscure, but some of the more extreme members of the Brethren of the Free Spirit appear to have denied the existence of hell (see R. E. Lerner, *The Heresy of the Free Spirit in the Later Middle Ages* (Berkeley, 1972), pp. 86, 89, 92).

195 The omitted passage (ff. 16r–v) contrasts the action of Sara in Tobit 3. 17, who abstained from *pleieres* (WB) in the hope of reward from God, with the frivolity of modern priests.

201 Of the surviving English miracle cycles only Chester has a play of Antichrist and one of the Last Judgment (see ed. R. M. Lumiansky and D. Mills, EETS SS 3 (1974), 408–63); though York, Towneley and the *Ludus Coventrie* have material concerning the Judgment, they do not include a character Antichrist. See Woolf, *Mystery Plays* pp. 291–4 and notes.

255–6 *for opere...ful yuel*: 'for others mixed truths (with lies), and make that which is really evil to be considered to be good'.

PART IV. LOLLARD DOCTRINE

20. Biblical Translation

The text is the seventh of a set of twelve tracts in support of the vernacular Bible found in a small manuscript, CUL Ii. 6.26, ff. 41v–46. The manuscript dates from the fifteenth century, is not well written nor consistently spelt; it shows little of the careful supervision that marks most manuscripts of WB or the standard sermon-cycle, though there have been occasional corrections (e.g. f. 62). Apart from the twelve tracts, the only other item is an incomplete text of the Middle English translation of the *Elucidarium* of Honorius of Autun (ff. 79v–101v), a text that has sometimes been associated with the Lollard movement (see Manual ii. 357). Some of the twelve tracts are either found separately elsewhere, often in different and sometimes orthodox contexts, or are extant in a different guise; in the latter case, in default of a critical edition of the whole, it is difficult to be certain which version represents the original. The text here shares most of its material with the commentary usually known as *Pater Noster II*, printed by Arnold iii. 98–110 (I owe this information to Dr Valerie Murray). The texts are not close enough for collation, but reference to the parallels will be made in the notes. Even within this single example, it is difficult to make a judgment about the priority of either version. The statement in *Pater Noster II* 'leve we now þis mater and speke we of þe Pater Noster' (99/23) might suggest the incorporation into this of material not originally

associated with the prayer, a suggestion that is supported by the
complete absence of the translation material from *Pater Noster I*
(for the relations of I and II see A. L. Kellogg and E. W. Talbert,
Bulletin of the John Rylands Library xlii (1960), 345–77). On the
other hand, the parallels between the text printed here and *Pater
Noster II* run in order through the latter text whereas, if this were
not its original position, some ingenuity would be required so to
incorporate it.

The arguments used here are similar to those of no. 14 above,
to those in *Tract Transl.* and in the source of the latter, the Latin
tract in MS Vienna 4133; since the author of the last was Richard
Ullerston (see Emden, *Oxford* iii. 1928–9 for the details of his
life), it is clear that arguments devised by orthodox writers at a
time when biblical translation was not yet a decided issue could
continue to be used by Lollards later.

1–31 Arnold iii. 98/4–99/22.

9–11 Cf the seventh conclusion to Ullerston's text (Vienna MS f. 207v) 'just as the
exercise of preaching God's word...is to be controlled by the wise planning
of bishops, so also should the practice of translation'.

23–4 The alteration of the name of Cain, the first murderer (Gen. 4. 8), is to
associate it with the acrostic on the names of the four orders of friars (see
above no. 17/127n); Dathan and Abiram were two of the conspirators against
Moses and Aaron in the wilderness (Numbers 16. 12ff). For the identification
of the friars as the opponents of translation cf *Opus Arduum* f. 136 'these false
friars also teach that all lay people, however learned, should not study sacred
scripture, nor have it in their own language, nor teach others'. The belief that
ecclesiastical opposition to biblical translation originated in a fear that the
unglossed text would reveal their own faults is frequently found, see Arnold
iii. 258/18ff, Matthew 368/1ff, 376/9ff (cf *Piers Plowman's Creed* 585–6, *Mum and
the Sothsegger* 388ff).

26 For medieval knowledge of Mahomet and Islam see R. A. Southern, *Western
Views of Islam in the Middle Ages* (Cambridge, Mass., 1962). Sergius (see ODCC)
was a seventh-century patriarch in Constantinople, who was one of the main
proponents of the heresy of Monothelitism. For the point here see also the
addition to *Upland's Rejoinder*, Heyworth's edition p. 172/27.

32–5 Arnold iii. 100/5–10, with modifications.

37–49 Arnold iii. 100/21–36.

37–8 Cf Vienna 4133, f. 198 'Christ and his apostles preached in the various
languages of the people.'

42 *Duche* in ME meant German generally and was not limited to its modern sense
(see MED *Ducheman*).

49–52 There is no direct parallel in *Pater Noster II*, though the discussion of the
clause asking for daily bread could have suggested the biblical quotation.

52–65 Arnold iii. 105/33–106/13 on this clause.

65–95 Arnold iii. 109/21–110/23, with modifications.

84–6 Cf *Apology* 74/20ff 'A tokyn of Goddis luf is wan ani stodieþ gladly in holy
writ; holy writ is mikil dispicid for þe sciens of decrees.'

94–5 The expressions here may suggest a date for the piece after 1407, when
biblical translation, and the ownership of copies without licence, was for-
bidden. After this date ownership of Bibles was one of the chief ways in which
Lollards were detected (e.g. the cases investigated by Chedworth (Lincoln reg.

20, ff. 57v, 62) in 1462 in the Chilterns, or by Blythe (Lichfield Record Office B/C/13, ff. 5v.ff) in 1511 in Coventry).

95–110   The only parallel within this passage to *Pater Noster II* is lines 102–104, Arnold iii. 110/27–30.

99–100   The same charge appears in *Lanterne* 11/4ff 'Þus prelatis and freris in þise daies ben traueilid wiþ þis synne [sc. of envy] aȝen þe Holi Goost, and schamfulli sclaundren her symple briþeren þat casten yuel maners from her soule or prechen þe gospel to Cristis entent to turne þe peple to vertuouse lyuyng. Þei seien þis man haþ eten a fliȝe þat ȝyueþ him lore of Goddis lawe. Þis is more foule to eete a flie þan to be a god and chare þise fliȝes. Þus han þey brouȝt her malice aboute to sclaundir for Lollardis þat speken of God.' Since the context is the same as that here, the phrase may have been a common charge (Whiting F349 quotes the *Lanterne* example only).

21A. The Eucharist I

The text comes from Trinity College Dublin 245 (old press mark C. 5.6), ff. 145–146v; the manuscript, like 244 (formerly C. 3.12) in the same library, is an anthology of shorter Lollard pieces from the early fifteenth century, many of which were published by Arnold in vol. iii of his edition or by Matthew. The interest of this piece, not hitherto printed, is as an example of the lists of authorities found in Wycliffite manuscripts on many controversial topics. The purpose of the lists was presumably primarily for instruction in the Lollard *scholae*, but they were also used in trials by suspects (e.g. the trial of Taylor, *Chichele Register* iii. 162–6, or the trial of John Piers in 1440, Salisbury reg. Aiscough ii. f. 52v, where Piers alludes to opinions 'in a quaier in English writen to the whiche Y refferre me'). The plan of these lists is very similar to that of an entry in the *Floretum* or *Rosarium*, though neither of these compilations provided the basis for the present example. A similar and longer list of authorities in English on the Eucharist appears in CUL Ff. 6.31 (3), ff. 27v–37v, and *Apology* 45/30–48/7 and the tract in MS Titus D. v draw on yet others. In all of these lists originality was far from the compiler's intention: the aim was to supply a list of authorities of unimpeachable orthodoxy, and if possible of considerable antiquity, to support a controversial standpoint. The *Apology* states the aim neatly: having quoted St Paul and Augustine on the Eucharist, the writer observes (46/7ff) 'And syn þer wordis are canonized and approuid of holi kirk, oiþer behouiþ to graunt þer wordis, or to denay þe canonizing and aprouing of þe kirk.' MS Titus D. v, f. 69v extends this 'I mynge old sentencis of seinttis wiþ holi scripture...þat men mai se houȝ olde seinttis confermed hem to þe logic of scripture, and to schew þat þe conclusion þat I hold in þis point

is no new doctrine but þe first, and so þe eldest, þat euer was
tauȝt.'

1–7 Cf Aston's confession *Fasc. Ziz.* 330. So far as it goes, this statement was
orthodox, but lines 15ff make clear that this is not the whole belief. The
ambiguity of this first statement makes plain the reason for the phrasing of the
first question in the 1428 list (see *BIHR* xlvi (1973), 153 'First, whether after
the consecration on the altar is the true body of Christ and not the substance
of material bread or wine').

21 The writer has counted I Cor. 11. 23–9 as two instances, reasonably since
the first four verses deal with the institution of the Eucharist, the remainder
with subsequent celebrations.

23 Abbreviated forms of reference to canon law (*þe popis lawe*) are given in the
margins of the manuscript. All quotations are from the *Decretum, De Consecratione* dist. II (Fried. i): they are lines 23–6, cap. 58 (col. 1336; actually from
Bede, but wrongly attributed in manuscripts of canon law); lines 29–36,
a summary of cap. 55 (cols. 1334–5, from Ambrose *De Sacramentis* IV. 4
(CSEL 73.51–4)); lines 36–40, cap. 42 (cols. 1328–9); lines 49–51, cap. 60 (col.
1337); lines 51–4, cap. 79 (col. 1346); lines 54–7, cap. 48 (col. 1331).

26 Jerome Epistola 120, PL 22.986; see also nos. 2/59, 15/238.

36–40 The confession of Berengar after his first recantation in 1059. See *JTS* NS xxii
(1971), 464–5 for Wyclif's knowledge of Berengar; his opponents regarded
Wyclif as reviving the heresy of Berengar (see Woodford, *De Sacramentis
Altaris Questiones lxxii*, MS Bodley 703, ff. 129v–31, Netter *Doctrinale* v doc. 12
'Berengarius magnus magister Wicleffi', and the Dominican author of
Pharetra Sacramenti, MS CUL Ff. 6.44, f. 60), whilst *Opus Arduum* f. 136v and
MS Titus D. v, f. 53 assert that the Lollards alone retain the faith of the
recantation *Ego Berengarius*.

47–9 Augustine sermon 227, PL 38.1100.

57–61 See *Liber de divinis officiis* PL 101.1260; the passage is quoted by Wyclif *De
Apostasia* 106/36–107/5, and discussed by Netter *Doctrinale* v. 47.

67 Augustine's *De Trinitate*, esp. bks. v, vii and ix (PL 42.911ff), from which
quotations supporting this view are taken in the *Floretum* entry for *Eucharistia*.

70 *Ion wiþ þe gilden mouþe*: John Chrysostom; probably a reference to a passage
from pseudoChrysostom on Matthew, PG 56.747–8 (quoted in the list of
Eucharistic proof texts in CUL Ff. 6.31 (3), ff. 34v–35).

79 The main verb is in lines 75–6, from which this section (lines 79–81) follows.

94 *oon singuler persone*: probably Wyclif; the *Opus Arduum* has similar unspecific
references which are designed to be readily understood by the initiated, but
avoid proclaiming affinity to an unsympathetic glance.

96 *capped monkes*: referring to the distinctive hat worn by doctors of divinity; cf
Piers Plowman C. xii. 80 and Skeat's note on the line.

97 Cf no. 1/60–63.

21B. The Eucharist II

The sermon derives from the standard cycle where it appears for
the Sunday within the octave of Epiphany; it is printed here from
G. ff. 17v–18v, and is collated with the twenty other manuscripts
in which it survives. Wyclif's Latin sermon on the same text is
Sermones i. no. 8; this has contributed some material to the
discussion here, and further of the Latin works have been drawn
on for additional points. The English sermon is one of the more
complicated of the cycle in argument, and the commentary may

show both the learning that the sermon writer must have possessed
and the degree to which he could rely upon his congregation's
understanding of theological questions. Though the gospel text
nowhere overtly mentions the Eucharist, the descent of the Holy
Ghost as a dove raises the whole question of signs which was
central to Wyclif's thought on the Eucharist (and indeed to
Lollard thought on images). Parts of the argument here are
quoted without comment in a sermon in MS Bodley 806, ff. 18–19.

1–16 *Sermones* i. 49/29–35.

16–20 Not paralleled in *Sermones* i, but for the sentiment see above no. 2/69–80n.

22–5 The contrast between Christ, abbot of the one religious order, and the sects, ungrounded in the Bible and based on men's traditions, ruled by antichrist's clerks, is a commonplace in these writings, cf Arnold iii. 203/10ff, 276/1ff, 416/19ff.

25–7 Cf *Sermones* i. 51/14–17, and Lyra (GO v. 1033); the point is that John's understanding of Christ at the time of his baptism was a limited one.

33–55 Patristic and medieval exegesis of the dove deals mainly with two questions. The first, alluded to here in lines 35–6, concerned the reason why the Holy Spirit took the form of a dove (and comparison is made with the fire of Acts 2. 3); the traditional explanation (see GO v. 78, Grosseteste Dict 107, MS Bodley 830, ff. 99–100, for instances) relies upon the scriptural properties of the dove and is followed here. The second question may be summarised: was the dove a real bird, and in what sense 'was' the Holy Spirit the bird? The argument of lines 33–55 may be set out in the following way: the dove was actually a bird like other birds (not an optical illusion without physical reality, nor a temporary creation); it could therefore not 'be' the Holy Spirit in the same sense as Christ 'was' man, but temporarily the Spirit inhered in the dove, as a transitory theophany not as an incarnation; it was therefore legitimate to say, notwithstanding the impassibility of the Spirit as part of the Trinity, that the Spirit *was comynge doun in þis dowue*. The argument so far is found in *Sermones* i. 51/34–52/9, and Wyclif's opinion has a long lineage in orthodox exegesis (see Augustine, PL 40.302–3, 1016, 42.851–3, Ambrose, CSEL 73.99, and later Aquinas *Summa Theologica*, IIIq. 39 a6–7). The analogies that follow, lines 42–55, are not found in Wyclif's Latin sermon; they lead to a conclusion that is, of course, heretical. The first analogy concerns Joseph's interpretation of Pharoah's dream, where the seven oxen (and in Gen 41. 26–7 seven ears of corn, not here mentioned) are said to 'be' (V *sunt*) the seven years; here the seven oxen obviously only represent, or 'stand for', the years, and are not themselves in any sense or at any point the years. In the *Trialogus* 266/28–267/4 Wyclif used this analogy in connection with the Eucharist, though he did not there mention the dove; he points out there that Augustine had noted (CCSL 33.216) that the word used of the oxen and ears is not *signant* but *sunt*, and concludes from such linguistic usage (267/14–15) 'sacramentum est corpus Christi, hoc est, ipsum corpus sacramentaliter signat vel figurat'. In the *De Apostasia* 232/37–233/25 Wyclif brings together the question of the dove and the Eucharist. Netter (*Doctrinale* v. 86) refers to the present English discussion, conflating it to some extent with the material in Wyclif's Latin works.

    Involved in this discussion is the nature of language, and particularly that of predication: this is summarised in lines 45–6 and taken up in lines 75–80. Wyclif in *Trialogus* 266/22–4 distinguishes three modes of speech 'Et novisti quod triplex est praedicatio, scilicet formalis, essentialis et habitudinalis'. The English *habitudynel seyng* plainly renders the third, applied by Wyclif to the seven oxen and the Eucharist (267/4–6); the first, *personel seyng*, is less clearly definable here, but is not important to the writer's argument. The vital point is that *bi sum habitude*, that is 'by an established convention of speech', the dove can be said to be the Holy Ghost. The analogy of lines 49–50 derives from Augustine's *De Doctrina Christiana* II. i (CCSL 32.32–3), and the distinction there drawn between *signa naturalia* and *signa data* may through an intermediary have led to the twofold division of speech in lines 45–6.

Finally in lines 48–55 is summarised, in bald and untechnical terms, one of the basic arguments of Wyclif's realist philosophy. The *esse intelligibile* inhered eternally in God, but equally was necessary to the existence of the creature. The view was advanced many times in Wyclif's writings, but a discussion in *De Dominio Divino* uses the same biblical quotation as lines 50–1 and summarises the argument (39/21, 42/25–43/2). For the outcome of this standpoint see S. H. Thomson, 'The Philosophical Basis of Wyclif's Theology', *Journal of Religion* xi (1931), 97–102, and Leff (1967), in ii. 500–10.

56–86 This last section has no counterpart in Wyclif's sermon, and, conversely, the English writer ignores Wyclif's own conclusion. But lines 56–62 echo two ideas found in Wyclif's *De Veritate Sacre Scripture* and elsewhere, first that the methods of speech in the Bible must be correctly understood, and secondly that the doctrine so grasped must be imparted in a form intelligible to the common people (cf no. 20 above).

60 *comoun speche*: it seems likely that the meaning of this phrase, rather than being 'vernacular language', is an anticipation of the argument in lines 62–71. The discussion springs from the unmentioned scriptural passage I Pet. 4. 11 'si quis loquitur, quasi sermones Dei' (AV 'If any man speak, let him speak as the oracles of God'), and attacks the view that this precept should be understood to imply that men should use the same methods of speech as God. Wyclif in *De Veritate Sacre Scripture* writes (i. 6/20–21) 'the form of speech in scripture is the model for all other proper modes of talking', but his understanding of this is in the light of Augustine's argument (*De Doctrina Christiana* IV. vi (CCSL 32. 122)) that men's speech can only imitate poorly that of God (i. 5/10–11 'that eloquence does not pertain to others as of their nature, but only by imitation').

71–3 Aristotle, *Prior Analytics* ii. 15 (see *Aristoteles Latinus* III. 1–4, ed. L. Minio-Paluello (Bruges and Paris, 1962), 121–4, the translation of Boethius).

73–84 Wyclif's *De Veritate* discusses the same examples (i. 5/1–5), to be interpreted *ad sensum misticum*. Two points are here at issue. First, that these are figures of speech, and holy writ cannot rightly be grasped unless they are so interpreted. Secondly, there is a return to the argument of lines 48–55, though with a modification that at first sight seems to produce direct contradiction between lines 75–6 and 54–5. But, whilst the argument of the earlier passage concentrates upon the *esse intelligibile* and, hence, the inherence of all things in God, the later section is concerned to interpret the *modus loquendi* of scripture, by whose *habitude* Christ is described as certain things but not as others. In line 77 *þe toon* and *þe toþir* refer back to *alle þingis* (line 75) and *ech þing* (line 76). The insistence upon the literal understanding of scripture, unless the context provides clear evidence for a figural interpretation (lines 81–3), is in line with Wycliffite views elsewhere (see above no. 10/121n).

84–6 The wording here, taken together with Netter's reference to the vernacular sermon (above lines 33–55n), has been interpreted as evidence for Wyclif's authorship of the sermons (Arnold ii. v). The arguments concerning Wyclif's supposed English writings cannot be settled until modern critical editions of the vernacular texts have been made and questions of date clarified. But the *we* need not be interpreted as an authorial plural (though this was known in the medieval period, see OED *we* pron. 2b), but may refer to the writings of the Wycliffites generally. For the final sally, cf *De Veritate* i. 148/14–15, 151/16ff etc.

22. The Nature of the Church

The text is from *The Lanterne of Liȝt* caps. 6–9, transcribed from
the only complete manuscript, BL Harley 2324, ff. 20v–54v; the
whole was edited by L. M. Swinburn, EETS 151 (1917), where
these extracts are pp. 22–57. From line 59 on the text here
has been collated with a second manuscript, BL Harley 6613,
ff. 11–20; this is now defective through the loss of leaves. Both
manuscripts date from the early fifteenth century and are of small
format. The whole has also been collated with the print by
Redman ([1530?]), STC 15225. Passages of Latin which are
regularly translated into English are omitted silently.

Since *The Lanterne of Liȝt* is mentioned in the trial of John
Claydon, a currier of London, in 1415 and a list of fifteen heretical
tenets from it given (see *Chichele Register* iv. 132–8), this is one of
of the few texts whose Lollard origin is certain. Claydon owned
many English books which were described by the investigator as
the worst and most perverse he had ever seen; he claimed to have
a copy of a sermon preached *apud Horsaldowne*, which may be the
sermon *of þe Horsedoun* of which a mutilated fragment is found in
Bodleian MS Douce 53, ff. 30–32v. In fact, the *Lanterne*, whilst
unorthodox, is not extreme in its expressions. The present
extracts illustrate fully the fifth and seventh heresies found by the
archbishop's investigators, those concerning the church as the
congregation of the faithful and the abolition of rich church
adornment, and allude to the sixth, that private religions are
wrong (lines 79–86).

1–20 Swinburn 22/11–23/7.
   5 Lyra in GO v. 280.
  12 Namely the *congregacio omnium predestinatorum*, lines 22–27; the actual material
      church and its hierarchy, lines 29ff; the church of the fiend, lines 102, 124.
21–7 Swinburn 25/1–7. For Wyclif's view see *De Ecclesia* passim, esp. 2/25ff. Cf
      Leff (1967), ii. 516ff. Netter discusses this in *Doctrinale* ii. 8–83.
28–86 Swinburn 35/35–38/22.
  44 As Swinburn notes, the source is pseudoChrysostom on Matthew, PG 56.876.
      Cf Arnold iii. 487/14f and Ps. Bod. f. 47v/2 'it is litil deynte of a gay chirche
      and a fals curate. And siþin þe stide halowiþ no man, but a good man halowiþ
      þe stide, make we oure hertis clene and honest in loue and herijnge of God,
      for in þat stide is his ioie.'
  53 Ambrose *Liber de Paradiso*, cap. 4 (PL 14.284, quoted in canon law *Decretum* I,
      dist. 40 cap. 9 (Fried. i. 147)).
  57 Cf no. 16/72ff and Douce 53, f. 22v 'sum men anoon caren for susteynynge of
      greet bildyngis of tree and stoon, and recken not of þe susteynynge of þe hooly
      temple of God þat is man.'
  60 Jerome, *De Vita Clericorum* (PL 22.535–6), quoted *Decretum* II c. 12 q. 2 c. 71
      (Fried. i. 710–11).
  71 William of St Amour, *Collectiones Sacræ Scripturæ* (*Opera Omnia* (Constance,

1632)), p. 462, where the comment follows straight on from the Jerome quotation used here. The same pair of passages is found in the *Floretum* under *edificacio*, in *Apology* 48/17ff, and in BL Harley 3913, f. 60v (a notebook written by a Lollard sympathiser); the William of St Amour passage alone is found in BL Harley 1203, f. 83v. William (see *Dict. de. Spir.* vi. 1237–41) was one of the main opponents of the friars in the thirteenth-century controversy. Netter asserted that he had been the source from which Wyclif drew many of his views about the friars (*Doctrinale* ii. 33, iv. 3, 22); certainly, even if Wyclif does not quote him by name often (see *Polemical Works* i. 92/4 for an instance), their views were similar. The author of the *Opus Arduum* lamented the destruction of William's books in Oxford and Salisbury following the condemnation of Wyclif (Brno Mk 28, f. 174v).

74 Bernard, *Apologia ad Guillelmum S. Theoderici Abbatem* (PL 182.915), quoted in *Floretum* under *ecclesia*; the passage is used in BL Harley 1203, ff. 83r–v.

79ff Cf Arnold iii. 380/1ff, Matthew 14/31ff; and *Piers Plowman* B. iii. 48ff where absolution is offered to Lady Meed if she pays for the adornment of a friars' church.

87–134 Swinburn 54/30–57/4.

103 Gregory, *Homilia in Evangelia* 17 (PL 76.1142).

106 Cf Arnold iii. 299/30ff, 376/13ff, Matthew 16/22ff 50/32ff etc.

114 Quoted in the *Floretum* under *leccio* with an incorrect reference.

122 The same complaint is made in *Piers Plowman* B. xi. 300–2; cf also B. xiii. 68, and Ps. Bod. f. 98/2 'siþin syngers chargen not ouerhipping of wordis, but bisien hem faste in spewynge of nootis'.

23. The Duty of the Priesthood

The text derives from the standard sermon-cycle, where it appears, according to the Sarum usage, for the feast of an unspecified evangelist (Arnold i. 175–8). It is here taken from BL Royal 18 B. ix, ff. 128v–129v, collated with the seventeen other manuscripts in which it appears. Two of these, Pepys Library 2616 in Magdalene College Cambridge (W) and Bodleian MS Don. c. 13 (Z), are expurgated; to show the type of material that might be found offensive, the passages so omitted are indicated in the footnotes (from which it can be seen that the expurgation in each was independent of the other). In the case of Z, the scribe was probably himself modifying the text (see *JTS* NS xxii (1971), 451–64), but in the case of W the scribe probably had a manuscript already so altered, since it is only in the Commune Sanctorum, not in the Proprium Sanctorum or the Ferial cycle which the manuscript also contains, that these omissions occur.

Wyclif's own sermon on this text is *Sermones* ii. no. 32; from the beginning of this a little has been taken in the vernacular sermon, but the whole of the end (deriving from the earlier tract *De Sex Iugis*, cap. 5) is ignored by the English writer. The preoccupations of the English homilist are, however, frequently

stated in Wyclif's other writings (see, for instance, *Sermones* iii.
75/20ff and *De Mendaciis Fratrum* (*Polemical Works* ii) 405/1–
406/6). The Commune Sanctorum sermons in the English version
are notable for their concentration upon the duties of the *poor* or
true priest, and on the reactions of the *true man* to persecution.
For the Lollard view of the prime priestly function as preaching
cf *Apology* 30/29ff.

2–7 The ideas here are found in Wyclif's sermon p. 234/10–26, including the
equation of the number of preachers with the number of languages in the
story from Gen. 11. 1–9 (actually seventy but altered by the addition of two by
early exegetes). Wyclif does not name the city. Despite the traditional differenti-
ation of Babel and Babylon, the same place is meant (see ODCC).

9–37 This section has no parallel in Wyclif's Latin sermon here, but cf *Polemical
Works* ii. 405/1ff, 424/23ff, *Opera Minora* 77/17ff. The church insisted that all
priests must obtain episcopal licence to preach, apart from the incumbent in
his own parish (see Wilkins ii. 257, iii. 316, 318, and G. R. Owst, *Preaching in
Medieval England* (Cambridge, 1926), pp. 140–43). Though this rule dated from
before the rise of Lollardy, it obviously affected Lollard preachers badly (see
Arnold ii. 11/13ff, 172/26ff, iii. 333/1ff, Matthew 90/9ff, 135/23ff, *Plowman's Tale*
541ff etc). The writer here admits that the examination of preachers has some
justification (lines 20–21), but maintains that friars, because of their Eucharistic
views, are more heretical than poor priests and, because of their lack of /
scriptural foundation, more in need of amendment.

23–37 The attack here is a double one: that the friars preach useless stories (cf
no. 22/106ff), and that the friars ask money for their sermons.

24 *cuylet*: the word is not recorded as a noun in MED, since Arnold misread MS
Bodley 788 as *ony let* (possible but not correct in the context). All manuscripts,
with one exception, have *cuylet* or variant spellings of the word. The form is
related to the past participle of the verb entered in MED as *coilen*; the verb is
recorded in many instances including Matthew 433/28ff 'þus it is a fendis
boost to a curat to auaunte hym þat he may so myche dispende bi ȝeere, siþ
þei ben cuylid pens of pore men', the meaning being 'collected by alms'.
The root of the word is cognate with *quilagis* above no. 18/70n. The contrast
here (lost by Arnold's error) is between *freli wiþoute cuylet* and *spuyle...and sille*.

27 A side note in the manuscript gives references to Acts 9 and Gal. 2, the story
of Paul's early ministry.

41–7 For the charge that licence to preach is bought by friars and others cf
Matthew 85/8–11.

47–55 Cf Wyclif p. 235/2–24, with the same note that the objects specified are only
to be avoided in so far as they hinder the work of preaching. //

61–94 Netter, not unnaturally, makes considerable play with the contradiction
between the Wycliffites' objections to friars' begging and their assertion that
preachers should be maintained by the faithful (see *Doctrinale* iv. 1–20, esp.
cap. 10). The Lollards defended their position, as here (and cf Arnold i.
63/22ff, 247/14ff, iii. 171/1ff, 312/18ff) by their renunciation of property in any
form as a means of support for preachers, and by their insistence that the bare
necessities (for which I Tim. 6. 8 is repeatedly cited) should be provided for
maintenance of life, in default of which the priest must labour with his hands.
Cf Trinity College Dublin 245, f. 155 (based on Wyclif's *Dialogus*) 'True
prestis þat prechen þo gospel, if þei ben boden of þe peple, may leuefully for
her traueil, for þe tyme þei teche þe puple, take of þem her sustynaunce.'

93 *speckid in þeir ordris*: as well as the usual meaning of *speckid* 'spotted' in the
moral sense, there may be a pun intended on the Pied Friars (Knowles (1971),
249). Cf the Lollard poem on the Blackfriars Council 1382 (*Political Poems and
Songs*, ed. T. Wright (Rolls Series 1859–61), i. 262) 'With an O and an I,

fuerunt pyed freres', and *Piers Plowman's Creed* 64f; also Trinity College
Cambridge B. 14.50, f. 41v–42, 'and so many cloutes ben added to freres reule
þat, ȝif þer bodily abite were varied as þer reule, no harlot in þis londe schulde
were more specked mantyl'.

24. The Power of the Pope

The text forms part of the *Thirty-Seven Conclusions of the Lollards*,
and is printed here from Norwich Castle Museum MS 158.926.4g3,
ff. 21–2, 26v–30v, collated with BL Cotton Titus D. 1 and Bodley
540 (the first two of the fifteenth and the last of the early sixteenth century). A modernised transcript is found in Trinity
College Dublin 246 (formerly C. 1.14), pp. 1–75, and recopied in
pp. 1*–59*. The text was printed by J. Forshall under the title
Remonstrance against Romish Corruptions in the Church (London,
1851); confusingly, it has also been called *Ecclesiæ Regimen*.
See *EHR* xxvi (1911), 738–49, for a Latin text of the main
Conclusions also, without supporting authorities or corrolaries.

   Despite Deanesly's assertions (pp. 266, 282, 374–81) that this
longer text is that referred to in the *Twelve Conclusions* (above
no. 3/90, 174) and that the author of both was John Purvey, there
is no decisive evidence to support either view. Of the *Twelve
Conclusions* nos. 3, 5, 11 and 12 are not represented here, whilst
the implications of 1, 2 and 7 differ from the arguments here
advanced; the absence of any coherent consideration of the
relation between secular and ecclesiastical authorities in *Twelve
Conclusions* marks it out as having different interests from the
present text. Deanesly took over her second conclusion from
Forshall and Madden (WB i. xxv–xxviii) who argued, from
parallel passages between this text, the General Prologue to WB
and the wording of LV, that Purvey was responsible for all three.
But the similarities are susceptible of other explanation, namely a
common heritage of ideas and phraseology between all Wycliffite
works (a heritage that the notes here illustrate). The claim of
Shirley (*Fasc. Ziz.* 383 n. 1), that the book from which Lavenham
extracted heresies and errors of Purvey was the present text, is
also incorrect. Subjects are included in Lavenham's list of eleven
errors which are not represented in the *Thirty-Seven Conclusions*
(e.g. no. VI concerning marriage); conversely there are many
errors in the latter not mentioned by Lavenham; the twenty
references to canon law in Lavenham and the one-hundred-and-
twenty in the *Conclusions* share only three commonplace passages.

From the allusion at the end of the *Conclusions* (p. 156) to persecution 'disciplis of antecrist quenche þe gospel of Crist, and pursue
at here desyr þe verri prechouris þerof and holde hem in prisoun
wiþouten due proces of þe gospel oþir murþere hem priuili' the
date of composition was probably before 1401.

2 This section follows an introductory article on the subject of the papacy, where
it is claimed that the present 'bishop of Rome' has less authority than Peter
and Paul. For this article cf Wyclif *De Potestate Pape* 172/31ff, 261/8ff; *Apology*
1/16ff, and 58/24 'Þer is no pope ne Cristis vicar, but an holy man'. Lines 1–34
are in Forshall's edition pp. 51–4.

9ff Compare the eighth heresy condemned at the 1382 Council (*Fasc. Ziz.* 278)
'that, if the pope is destined to damnation and a bad man, and is consequently a servant of the devil, he has no power over Christ's faithful followers
from any source whatever, except perhaps from Caesar'. The reasons for
Wyclif's belief, fairly summed up by this statement, are set out fully in *De
Potestate Pape*.

14–16 Augustine, *De Doctrina Christiana* iii. 30, 32 (CCSL 32. 102–5); Tyconius was a
Donatist and his second rule concerned the nature of the church. Augustine
replying to this maintained the coexistence of good and evil within the church
on earth, despite their eventual separation in the church in heaven. The
argument on this passage (taken up in Netter's *Doctrinale* lib. ii) depends upon
the definition of *holy chirche*, whether this is the number of those eventually to
be saved, or the actual church on earth. The statements here are ultimately
orthodox since the author makes it clear enough that he is discussing the first
of these.

20 Cf *Piers Plowman* B. Prol. 107–9; also *De Potestate Pape* 196/7–197/20, *Polemical
Works* ii. 674/6–676/15; Arnold i. 209/18ff, ii. 30/20ff, 412/30ff, *Plowmans Tale*
313ff etc.

35 The three articles omitted here deal with the pope's power of absolution and
of excommunication, and with papal indulgences. This present article, though
beginning with another aspect of the papal powers of absolution, in fact
discusses a wider question, the claim that the pope has superior authority to
that of other bishops. Lines 35–182 Forshall, pp. 67–77.

44–5 Augustine sermon 76 (old numeration *De Verbis Domini* 13), PL 38.479.

52–3 *Decretum* II, c. 24 q. 1 c. 4, Gratian's comment using these biblical quotations
(Fried. i. 967–8).

73ff Cf Wyclif *De Potestate Pape* 140/19–31, where the same point is made with the
same biblical quotation.

93 Chrysostom, *Encomium in S. Apostolum Paulum*, PG 63.839–48, esp. 846.

121 For Grosseteste's relation with the papacy see W. A. Pantin in *Robert
Grosseteste Scholar and Bishop*, ed. D. A. Callus (Oxford, 1955), pp. 178–208;
the pope in question was Innocent IV. The writer here gives a misleading
picture of Grosseteste's views of the papacy, but Pantin pp. 191ff points out
how these latter could lead on to the attitude of Wyclif.

124–5 *determynacioun*: the primary sense here is that of 'law made by the pope and
embodied in the canon law', but the word often has a looser meaning of
'official declaration of dogma' (the latter alone recorded by MED).

132 The basis of this is Matt. 26. 56, though the Bible makes no explicit mention
of the faith of the Virgin Mary. The elaboration here is found in exegesis from
the late twelfth century on (see Y. Congar, 'Incidence ecclésiologique d'un
thème de dévotion mariale', *Mélanges de science religieuse* vii (1950), 277–92).

142ff Many of the points mentioned in this section echo arguments in the medieval
debate concerning papal infallibility; see B. Tierney, *Origins of Papal Infallibility 1150–1350* (Leiden, 1972).

145–6 The reference is too unspecific for certainty, but quotations from Augustine making this point are given under *fides* in the *Floretum* (see for instance *De Doctrina Christiana* i. 36 (CCSL 32.29–30)).

166–7   Cf the long analysis of contradictions between biblical commands and recent church law in *Apology* 76/12–80/33.

169–71 All of these references save the first are too vague for identification; but the first is *Decretum* I, dist. 50 and possible contradictions are caps. 9–10 as against cap. 14 concerning the reinstatement of clergy deposed for immoral behaviour; other chapters in the same section have conflicting statements on erring clergy (Fried. i. 178–203).

25. The Function of the Secular Ruler

The text derives from Bodleian MS Douce 273, ff. 37v–44v; the complete text ends in chapter 13 on f. 53. This is the only manuscript known of the text; the other contents of the manuscript are copies of the Lollard works, *On the 25 Articles* (Arnold iii. 455–96) and *On the Seven Deadly Sins* (Arnold iii. 119–67). The present text is based upon Wyclif's discussion of the same question in his *De Officio Regis*, the eighth book of his theological *Summa*. As is usual with Lollard works reliant upon Wyclif's Latin texts, the treatment is very free: the source is revealed by the same sequence of authorities and by the occasional phrase that is literally translated; much discussion is omitted, but some new points are added. The first chapter has no counterpart in the Latin; in the main it reiterates the ideas already exemplified in nos. 14 and 20, but the dangers that a translator faced are vividly expressed by lines 3–5. The text is now printed as the first in *Four English Political Tracts of the Later Middle Ages*, ed. J.-P. Genet (Camden Society, Fourth Series, Vol. 18, 1977).

13–14   For this common medieval belief see also the determination of Richard Ullerston (MS Vienna 4133, f. 203v) citing FitzRalph as his source.

15–18   This is apparently a reference to the rejection of scriptural interpretations advanced by Wyclif and his followers.

21   Probably a reference specifically to Wyclif's *De Ecclesia* and *De Potestate Pape*, the preceding and following parts of the *Summa* respectively.

31ff   The simile depends upon Prov. 31.21–2, in WB (LV) 'Sche schal not drede for hir hous of the cooldis of snow: for alle hir meyneals ben clothid with double clothis. Sche made to hir a ray cloth: bijs and purpur is the cloth of hir.' This whole chapter of Proverbs was regularly interpreted as an encomium of the church. A similar interpretation is given by Wyclif, *De Ecclesia* 484/29–485/10.

35   *chaumpe sotile*: *chaumpe* is the field, or background, of a painted shield or banner, or the background for embroidery; *sotile* has here the sense of 'fine or delicate texture' (OED *subtle* adj. 2). The phrase continues the metaphor of the preceding two sentences, the sense being 'as a finely wrought piece of silk or other material'.

38–50   Drawn from *De Officio Regis* 1/12–26. For the tripartite division of society, and the functions of each see R. Mohl, *The Three Estates in Medieval and Renaissance Literature* (New York, 1933); the division is traditional, cf *Piers Plowman* B. i. 105ff, Gower *Vox Clamantis* iii. 1ff, *Jack Upland* 11ff.

54–8   Cf Ps. Bod. 288, f. 50v/2 'prestis and comouns schulden susteyne trewe lordis þat defenden hem in riȝt aftir þe lawe of Crist; prestis schulden truli enfoormen lordis and comouns in werk and word, and comouns schulden truli traueile to mayntene þese two.'

60–1 Cf above nos. 2/139n and 17/62n.

70 The third and fourth chapters, here omitted, deal with the honour due to kings before all others, and the reciprocal duty of kings to lead virtuous lives to deserve this honour. The fifth chapter opens with a statement drawn from *De Officio Regis* cap. 6 (118/22ff). The answer given in lines 71–86 is a conflated version of p. 118/24–119/7.

87–98 The digression on exemption, though obviously relevant to the subject, is introduced here by the English author; Wyclif deals with the same subject in *Polemical Works* i. 103/4–16. The point at issue was the claim by the clergy, and particularly friars, to be subject to the pope alone and hence exempt from civil jurisdiction. Cf Ullerston's *Petitiones* of 1409 for an orthodox admission of this abuse (ed. H. von der Hardt, *Magni et Universalis Constantiensis Concilii* I. xxvii (Helmstedt, 1697), 1144–51). Cf *Apology* 76/18f 'now new law techiþ þat no prest nor clerk ow to [be] soget to no seculer lord', and Add. 24202, f. 3v 'now popis and bischopis...han here counseylis þat þei ȝyue not tribute to here kyng, and þat þei ben not iseyn his ligge men'.

105 Cf *De Officio Regis* 119/26–7. The argument is that all authority in the kingdom derives from the king, and that therefore ultimately all public action is initiated by the king.

106ff The material here covered follows straight on in chapter 6 of Wyclif's text, though the point concerning ecclesiastical temporalities in the English work (lines 116–22) is somewhat different from that made by Wyclif (that temporalities are the gift of the king to the church in requital for services rendered, and can be removed at the king's pleasure or for default of service; cf no. 2/81n). The English writer follows the tendency of the Lollards to turn from theory to polemic. For the view here compare *Apology* 76/26ff 'And Austeyn, Gregor, Ciprian, Jerom and Isidir kennen, as is put in þe law, þat it perteniþ to seculer princes to punisch þeis þat synnen opunly', and *Lollard Chron.* 103ff 'Therfor seynt Austyn seiþ in his book þat a seculer lord owt to telle to alle his sugettis þe peynes of helle and þe joyes of heuyne, and refreyne hem fro lecherie, couetyse, pride, bakbiting, and oþer synnes, and schall ȝeld reson on domysday for alle sugettis to him'.

123–43 The claim of the clergy to exemption is discussed in the later part of the same chapter of *De Officio Regis* (esp. 129/4ff), but this passage is closer to a later section where the position of the friars is considered (219/12ff).

135 For the reference to the Donation of Constantine see no. 17/62n.

26. Church and State

The text is the last quarter of a dialogue between a Knight and a Clerk found in Durham University Library Cosin V. iii. 6; a description of the manuscript (dated c. 1400) and its connections will be found in *Review of English Studies* NS xxii (1971), 435–42. Since the original parchment is now interleaved with paper containing a seventeenth-century transcript, the passage here occurs on ff. 15v–19v on alternate leaves only. The subject of the dialogue is dominion, and especially the relative authorities of church and state; the Clerk states at the beginning that he is a *doctor of decreeȝe*, has been in Rome and held office in the court of the pope; the Knight is merely described as 'a kniȝt of þe kinges of Yngeland'.

The author's sympathy clearly lay with the Knight, though the discussion proceeds in terms more measured than is often the case. Despite the guise of a dialogue, the core of the text is of the usual type: statement of opinion, backed up by citation of biblical and patristic quotations; the Knight wins the victory by countering the Clerk's biblical authority (lines 107ff). The passage here opens after a dispute on the rights by which the clergy hold property; the Knight's speech points out that the pope and clergy are not essential to the continuance of the church, citing the instance (used above no. 24/130–2) of the survival of faith in Christ at the crucifixion in Mary alone 'and ȝit was scho no preste'.

7 Cf *Piers Plowman* B. x. 286f.

8–9, 14–16 The Knight explicitly sets out the claim that is implicit in many of the texts here: that the Lollard view can be supported from canon law as well as, or better than, the orthodox standpoint. This claim, found in Wyclif's own writings, lies behind the bitter invective against the practitioners of canon law (*Sermones* iii. 487/39–488/9, *Polemical Works* ii. 562/11–18, *Opus Evangelicum* i. 366/37–369/9).

10–11 For this proverb see Whiting B71.

26–7 Cf *Jack Upland* 180 'Frere, whi be ȝe not lege men to kyngis?'

29–30 The argument is complicated by the disparate uses of the words *temperalte* and *spiritualte*. The Knight in lines 89–98 makes it clear that he understands by *spiritualte* the spiritual authority of the church and clergy to minister sacraments and to spread the gospel, and by *temperalte* the secular jurisdiction of the king and his lords to rule all in the kingdom, layman or cleric. The Clerk equivocates: in lines 28–30 he appears to accept this division, but the succeeding two sentences reveal that he has extended the meaning of *spiritualte* to mean not only spiritual authority, but also all possessions of the church. Strictly, as in no. 27/7, 26, 73–5, *spiritualte* in a technical sense meant the revenues of the church deriving from ecclesiastical sources, incomes from benefices, tithes and glebes, whilst *temperalte* meant those revenues which accrued to the church from secular possessions such as manors, lands or tenements left to it. But the Clerk in the final sentence of this speech reveals that he has put both types of revenue together and regards both as inviolable; the Knight proceeds (lines 47ff) to a *reductio ad absurdum* of this position.

47–8 For the assertion cf no. 27 below; cf Add. 24202 f. 13 'þis bischop knowlechiþ and consentiþ þat þe chefe lord of þe possessiouns of his churche is þe pope, and so he bynymmiþ in þat þat in hym is þe kyngis regalie, and his chefe lordschip þat he shuld hafe vpon hym and his godis' and *37 Concs.* 87–8 'Also þe tresour of þe rewme shal be borun out to straungeris...in so moche þat it is opin at þe iȝe to kunnynge men þat, þouȝ oo greet hil of gold were in Ingelond, and no man outake siche Rome-renneris toke of it, ȝea a ferþing, al þe gold shulde be borun out of þe rewme bi hem to straungeris wiþynne a certeyn tyme'. The temporal aspirations of the pope are set even higher in MS Titus D. v., f. 8 'þis antecrist...kan ȝeue a glose aȝenst Moises and Crist also, vndur colour of þe wiche glose þei ben temperal lordis of þe more partiȝe of cristendom, and wol be of alle þe world ȝif þei mai.'

49 *amortaise*: to gain by mortmain, by which lands or incomes were held inalienably by the church. By Edward I's Statute of Mortmain of 1279, it became theoretically illegal for land to pass into the hands of monastic or other religious bodies unless the king issued a licence for this; but in fact large numbers of licences were granted and land continued to be alienated in this

way from secular use and advantage (see K. L. Wood-Legh, *Studies in Church Life in England under Edward III* (Cambridge, 1934), pp. 60–88).

55 *somer game*: cf *Piers Plowman* B. v. 413 and Bennett's note.

57ff The argument is that, if anything once in the hands of the clergy can never be alienated, commerce with the clergy is impossible: the money a clerk gives for goods remains properly his, likewise the goods a clerk sells remain his after the sale. Cf Gower, *Vox Clamantis* iii. 979ff.

74 In fact the secular authorities had, before the date of this debate, challenged the rights that the Clerk asserts, when they seized the temporalities of alien priories on various occasions: see Knowles (1955), 159–65 and A. McHardy, *Studies in Church History* xii (1975), 133–41. In 1414 an act confirmed the gradual suppression of alien priories.

81 Presumably a proverbial phrase; it is not recorded in Whiting, but J6 and J10 provide instances of *Jack* plus a surname as an expression for 'anybody'.

100ff For the clerk's interpretation of the biblical passage cf Netter, *Doctrinale* i. 12, ii. 49, and for a review of the discussion see M. J. Wilks, *The Problem of Sovereignty in the Later Middle Ages* (Cambridge, 1964), pp. 261ff. Cf *Plowman's Tale* 565ff.

119 *Decretum* I dist. 10 cc. 7, 9 (Fried. i. 21).

27. The Lollard Disendowment Bill

The text is printed from BL MS Cotton Julius B. ii, ff. 61–63v, where it forms almost the entire entry for the eighth year of Henry IV's reign (September 1406–7) in a chronicle of London. The whole was printed (somewhat inaccurately) by C. L. Kingsford, *Chronicles of London* (Oxford, 1905), 65–8; an abridgement of this passage in modern English is included in *English Historical Documents 1327–1485*, ed. A. R. Myers (London, 1969), 668–70. A second English copy of the bill is found in BL MS Harley 3775, ff. 120–121v. Here it is introduced by a quite different heading: 'Supplicacio pessima porrecta per Johannem Scharpe domino Humfredo duci Glouernie Regni protectori in subuersionem ecclesie', a heading confirmed by the conclusion 'Explicit supplicacio supradicta non catholice sed heretice porrecta'. Sharp, whose proper name seems to have been William Perkins, was one of the leaders of the abortive Lollard rising in 1431 (see Aston (1960), 24–5, Thomson (1965), 58–60). Though no date is given to the bill in Harley 3775, it was presumably associated by the scribe who added it in a gap at the end of 1431 with the rebellion. The bill also survives in Latin in full in the *St. Alban's Chronicle* (ed. V. H. Galbraith (Oxford, 1937), pp. 52–5) by Thomas Walsingham; the opening is quoted in Walsingham's *Historia Anglicana* (ii. 282–3), and a brief record of the presentation of the bill is given by Otterbourne (ed. T. Hearne (Oxford, 1732), i. 267–8). In these three Latin sources, and in the later, somewhat abbreviated record of Fabyan (*The New Chronicles*, ed. H. Ellis

(London, 1811), pp. 575–6), the bill is entered under 1410. The agreement of the vernacular account in the Julius manuscript with the Latin chronicles in assigning a date within Henry IV's reign suggests that the 1431 association in the Harley manuscript should be rejected. Between 1407 and 1410 it is more difficult to make a decision, though the latter is more likely. The 1407 parliament met at Gloucester, not at Westminster as Julius states; the only possible record of the bill in the *Rotuli Parliamentorum* (iii. 623) is the request in 1410 for the return of a petition presented by the Commons concerning Lollardy, asking that no action should be taken concerning it.

Whatever the date at which the bill was originally presented, its contents seem to have been in circulation within the Lollard movement for a considerable period of time. The core of the proposals appears amongst the heresies and errors of John Purvey *extracti de libello suo hæretico* by Richard Lavenham (*Fasc. Ziz.* 393): there appear the proposals for the seizure of the temporalities of the church and for the establishment with the funds of knights, universities, almshouses and poor priests. Lavenham suggests that a résumé of this scheme was in the book he was engaged in censuring, but that the whole was 'manifeste in quodam alio tractatu speciali'; the wording does not (*pace* Workman ii. 421) necessitate the assumption that Purvey was the author, as opposed to the advocate, of the scheme. The date of Lavenham's examination of Purvey's *libellus* is not given; early critics assumed that it must have been before 1383, believing on the evidence of Bale and Leland that Lavenham died in that year, but Emden (*Oxford* ii. 1109–10) gives evidence that he was still alive in 1399. The position of Lavenham's extracts in the *Fasc. Ziz.* manuscript immediately before Purvey's trial (pp. 400–7) does not necessitate a date for the former in 1401, the date of the latter event; there is no close connection between the contents of the extracts and Purvey's confession.

Walsingham states (*Hist. Angl.* ii. 283) that the calculations of the bill are inexact; Kingsford (pp. 295–6) sets out some possible modifications of the figures to make the computations correct. MS Harley 3775 offers some variants that explain some of the corruptions in the place names of the Julius text. It is noteworthy that, apart from the episcopal temporalities, the religious houses to be deprived are primarily of the Benedictine order, together with those of the Augustinian canons and Cistercians; the

dominance of these three orders makes clear the intention in the
cases where more than one house existed in a town (e.g. Coventry
line 46, where the Benedictine house is meant rather than the
Carthusian, Franciscan or Carmelite houses there). Although the
sums needed to make the provisions proposed are clearly round
figures only, the valuation of the temporalities, as of the
spiritualities in line 76, was probably based on reasoned estimates.
The starting point may well have been the figures of the *Taxatio
Ecclesiastica Angliæ et Walliæ* produced in 1291 under the authority
of pope Nicholas IV (published London, 1802), and modified by
subsequent partial reassessment.

2 *tempereltees*: in this text the word has its technical sense of the income derived
from the secular lands or tenements belonging to the church, *spiritualtes* (line
75) that of income derived from benefices, tithes or similar ecclesiastical
sources (cf no. 26/29n for the looser use of the terms). The *Taxatio Ecclesiastica*
divides the assessment regularly between the two headings.

8-9 The numbers, 15 earls, 1500 knights and 6200 squires, provide an estimate of
the proportions of rank that a medieval thinker might consider proper, even
though the precise numbers are for convenience.

13 Julius has a paraph mark before *and caste*; this has been accepted as indication
that *caste* should be taken as '(you may) reckon'. The *St Alban's Chronicle* alters
the syntax, having understood *caste* as a p.p. 'prout veraciter istud est com-
putatum et probatum'.

14 *markis*: the mark was two-thirds of a pound, or 13s 4d.

15-16 *plowlonde*: the amount of land that could be tilled by eight oxen, a term used in
taxation assessment (see S. K. Mitchell, *Taxation in Medieval England* (New
Haven, 1951), p. 131).

16ff The careful supervision of the income of the almshouses is specified because
of the abuse of these mentioned above no. 3/73–92n. The writer is anxious
that the houses should serve their primary purpose, the relief of genuine
poverty, and not be diverted into their frequent medieval guise of supporting
able-bodied clerks to pray for the souls of benefactors (cf Douce 53, f. 19v
criticising the clergy since they 'confederen to hem for to putte doun vndir
foot þe poore'). For a list of almshouses and hospitals in the medieval period
see Knowles (1971), pp. 310–410.

21 The reference is to the 1388 statute (*Statutes of the Realm* ii (London, 1816),
55–60 esp. 58), confirming previous legislation on this question and providing
that beggars unable to work should remain in their present cities or *villes* but
that, if these were unable to provide for them, they could withdraw to other
places in the same area or to the place where they were born within forty days
of the proclamation of the statute.

22-3 In the present bill no financial provision is made for the towns' support of
their poor, save indirectly through the reform of the almshouses. For the
various medieval attempts to solve the problems of poor law provision see
R. A. R. Hartridge, *A History of Vicarages in the Middle Ages* (Cambridge, 1930),
pp. 155–61, and the studies of W. K. Jordan on later charities (London, 1959–61).

24 For the idea of disendowment cf Douce 53, f. 10 'oure clerkis, and specially þo
þat ben deed to þe world, in so greet a neede of þe rewme shulden be redy to
delyuere up into þe hondis of seculer men alle her poscessiouns and tresours,
...and on þis wise releeue þe chirche of Engelond, and peese it and specialy
þe comyntee'.

27ff The modern forms of the names given (where these differ from the medieval

8   H W W

spellings), and the orders of the foundations, are to be found in the index of proper names; comments here will be limited to problematic names.

41 *Chestre*: at this period there was no see of Chester; the title of 'bishop of Chester' was, however, often applied unofficially to the bishop of Coventry and Lichfield (see *Handbook of British Chronology*, ed. F. M. Powicke and E. B. Fryde (London, 1961), p. 232n). The abbey is the Benedictine house of Chester itself.

41 *Bannastre*: the place meant is uncertain. Harley has *Remest*, whilst *St Alban's Chronicle* has *Rouecestre* (possibly Rocester priory, Staffs., as suggested by Galbraith).

43–4 The easily identified names are all Cistercian houses, which makes certain the emendation of *Galey* to *Saley* (Salley, Yorks.), as supported by Harley and *St Alban's Chronicle*. The last suggests the emendation of *Ayryell* to *Vaylryell* (Vale Royal, Chesh.); Harley in this position has *Answell*, a further Cistercian house, but adds *Valeryall* at the end of the group.

57–60 Kingsford printed Julius as it stands, but the text makes no sense. Harley does not include the sentence, but *St Alban's* supplies the necessary material 'Et in casu quo aliquis episcopatus, abbates et priores plus habeant, summatur residuum ad iuvandum quod predicta summa. . .integre servetur ut quelibet persona antedicta clare possit recipere prout prefertur'. This makes clear that the corruption is an omission after *priorye*, and suggests that *eny* (line 59) should be emended to *euery* (translating *quelibet*).

64 Harley expands the demand for an extra 15,000 priests by specifying 'goode prestes and perfy3t clerkys to preche þe wurd of Godde wythoute flateryng or beggyng or wordly mede to seke þerfore'. Late though this version is, it may here preserve the original form of the text; certainly this keeps the original intention, with priests of the Lollard model, whose function is the preaching of scripture.

68 Harley does not include any mention of universities; the *St Alban's* version speaks of *quinque universitates*. This latter figure seems a much more reasonable one, but Lavenham's summary of Purvey's view confirms the higher number (*Fasc. Ziz.* 393 *quindecim universitates*).

73 *temperaltes morteysed*: see note to no. 26/49.

75–6 The precise total of the value of the spiritualities, £143,734. 10. 4, cannot be confirmed, but addition of the various figures in the *Taxatio Ecclesiastica* suggests that it may be fairly accurate (bearing in mind reassessments in the hundred years after the original reckoning). Although the present bill here seems to allow the retention of benefices by religious officers and houses, other texts make it clear that the Lollard ideal would have removed this means of support (see no. 3/8n); the wording of lines 93–4 suggests that those framing the present bill might have regarded its terms as only one step towards their ideal of evangelical poverty.

77 *colages*: see no. 3/73n; for list of these see Knowles (1971), pp. 411–46.

77–8 In the *St Alban's* text a mistake has been made in the interpretation 'nondum tetigimus de. . .albis canonicis ecclesiarum cathedralium'; none of the Premonstratensian houses (the White Canons) was attached to a cathedral (see Knowles (1971), pp. 184–5 and H. M. Colvin, *The White Canons in England* (Oxford, 1951), pp. 27–193). The *cathederall chirches* are here mentioned since, though in the case of monastic cathedrals (Canterbury, Durham, Winchester, Ely, Worcester, Norwich, Rochester and Carlisle) their revenues were included in the computations above, the calculations for the secular cathedrals (York, Lincoln, London, Salisbury, Exeter, Hereford, Lichfield, Chichester and Wells) concerned the revenues of the bishop alone and not of the cathedral chapter; for the wealth of these latter see K. Edwards, *The English Secular Cathedrals in the Middle Ages* (Manchester, 2nd ed. 1967), pp. 39ff, 228ff.

80 The houses of the Carthusians in England were few: see Knowles (1971), p. 133. By *Frenche monkes* the writer presumably implies the various alien priories, originally dependent upon French houses but, if they survived, taken over eventually by English institutions (see Knowles (1971), pp. 83–6, 181).

80 Kingsford retains the unintelligible *gleves*; Harley does not include this. The *St Alban's* text confirms the obvious emendation ('nec de glebis'). The scribe's difficulty seems to have arisen from the unfamiliarity of the word (see MED), but the objection to this part of a parson's income is found in Matthew 449/5ff '3if persouns hadden no glebe and no propre hous as eritage, þey sueden more Crist and his apostlis'. The mixture of common and proper names is found throughout this list.

81 *Bonehommes*: see Knowles (1971), pp. 203–4; only three houses existed in England.

81 *ermytages*: though hermits were vowed to a life of poverty, gifts were made to churches for the support of a hermit or anchoress (see R. M. Clay, *The Hermits and Anchorites of England* (London, 1914), esp. pp. 204–63), in return for which prayers were offered.

81–2 *Crouched Freres*: again a very small order, see Knowles (1971), pp. 208–11. No mention is made of the other orders of friars in the bill, despite the usual Lollard invective against their wealth. The reason for the omission is presumably the realisation that, since the friars' wealth was vested in the pope, separate and more drastic legislation would be required to dispossess them.

GLOSSARY

The actual forms of the text are entered, not hypothetical infinitives etc. The commonest spelling is treated as the head word; variant spellings not easily referable to a head word are entered in their alphabetical place with a cross reference. Grammatical analysis is only given if ambiguity or difficulty may arise; line references are not included. Phrases likely to cause difficulty are entered under the word within them that departs from its normal sense. Words are only glossed if their meaning departs from that of modern English, or if their form within the texts is likely to cause difficulties of recognition; thus, when one Middle English sense of a word coincides with modern English, but another does not, only the second is here included. Since only forms likely to give rise to difficulty are included, the material given under each head word is not necessarily a full inventory of paradigms found in the texts (e.g. forms of *be* (*v.*) listed do not include those familiar from modern English). Normal Middle English inflections unlikely to cause confusion are not added to the head word.

Except initially *y* is treated alphabetically as *i*; initially *y* is treated as *i* when it has vocalic value, as *ȝ* when it has consonantal value. Initially *i* has been divided between its vocalic and consonantal values. *u* and *v* (and *u* and *w*) are treated according to their values as vowel or consonant, the former being placed first. *ȝ* is entered after *g*, *þ* is treated as *th* in its appropriate position within *t*. The following variants of spelling are not noted: variation of *i/y, u/v, þ/th, sh/sch, c/k, er/ar, ei/ai* (or *ey/ay*), *an/aun, au/aw, ou/ow, o/u* for *OE ŭ, -ion/-ioun/-iun*; variation in syllables not carrying the main stress between *e/i/u*; doubling of vowels or consonants; absence or addition of final -*e*.

abidinge, (*adj.*) *stable.*
abit, *habit, clothing of a religious order.*
able, (*adj.*) *capable.*
abliþ, *makes prone.*
aborcife, *inducing abortion.*
abounden, (*pl. pres. ind.*) *in* ~ wiþ, *have plenty of.*
abouteȝaf, *surrounded.*
abrege, *p.p.* abreggid, *curtail.*
abreggynge, *curtailment.*
accepte, (*inf.*) *favour, show favouritism towards.*
acorde, *agree; in* ~ to, *agree with; it* acordiþ best to, *it agrees best with.*
acordinge, *in* þe moost ~ lore to, *the teaching most in accordance with.*
acordyngly, *in* ~ wiþ, *in accordance with.*
advysement, *consideration.*
afer, (*adv.*) *far off.*
affiaunce, *trust, confidence.*
afore, aforn, (*prep.*) *before.*
aforne, (*adv.*) *formerly.*
after, (*cj.*) *according as.*
aftir, (*adv.*) *afterwards.*
aftir, (*prep.*) *following, according to, following the teaching of.*
agaynus, (*prep.*) *towards.*
age, *in of long* ~ , *long-lasting.*
ageyn (*prep.*) *against.*
agreyd, (*p.p.*) *in* þei were ~ , *they came to an agreement.*
aȝayne, (*prep.*) *against.*
aȝen, (*adv.*) *in return.*
aȝen, aȝens, (*prep.*) *towards, to deal with, against, contrary to.*
aȝenbouȝte, *redeemed.*
aȝenseiþ, *contradicts.*
aȝenstande, aȝenstonde, *oppose, resist;* aȝeynestondus (*3sg. pres. ind.*), *withstands.*
aȝeenthenke, (*sg. pres. sj.*) *think once more.*
aȝenward, *on the contrary.*
aȝt, *2sg. pres. ind.* aȝtest, *ought;* him ~ , *he ought, it was right for him.*
ay, *always.*

al, alle, (*adv.*) *completely, entirely.*
alargid, (*p.p.*) *extended.*
algatis, (*adv.*) *continually, in every way, at any rate.*
al if, (*cj.*) *even if.*
almesse, *in* houses of ~ , *almshouses* (see 3/73n, 27/16n).
alonly, *solely.*
als, *as.*
ambaciat, *diplomatic message.*
ambidexter, *one who improperly holds two offices.*
amyddis, (*prep.*) *in the midst of.*
amonteth, (*3sg. pres. ind.*) *amounts, is reckoned up.*
amortaise, (*inf.*) *hold property in mortmain* (see 26/49n).
and, (*cj. with sj.*) *if.*
anempte, anemptis, anentis, (*prep.*) *concerning, as concerning.*
anett, *dill.*
anguishid, *distressed.*
annexyd, *in* ~ to, *constituting a part of.*
anoie, *impede, injure.*
anon, *immediately.*
anullid, *condemned and privileges removed.*
apayed, *satisfied.*
apertly, *openly.*
apostataas, (*sb.*) *apostates, men who have abandoned the faith.*
apostasies, *violations of religious doctrines.*
appropre, (*inf.*) *appropriate;* appropred, (*p. pl. adj.*) *appropriated to* (see 3/8n.).
apropriacion, *annexation of income to religious house* (see 3/8n.).
arestid, *stopped.*
arette, *pl. pret. ind.* arettiden, *regard, consider;* arettid wiþ, *reputed as one of, counted amongst.*
as, *in* ~ that tyme, *for that time;* ~ to þis world, *in the sight of this world;* ~ to mankynde, *as far as mankind was concerned;* verry ~ , *true that.*
asay, *investigation.*

asailen, *attack.*
aseeþ, *reparation.*
asigned, *appointed.*
asken, askis, *ashes.*
assoile, *absolve.*
assolue, *answer.*
at, *(cj.) that.*
ateyntynge, *condemnation.*
atwynne, *apart.*
auter, *altar.*
avaunsid, *(p.p.) advanced, given benefices.*
aviseliche, *prudently.*
avoide, *put away, remove.*
auoutreris, *adulterers, those who adulterate the word of God, heretics.*
auoutrie, *adultery; of ~ , living in idolatry.*
avow, *vow.*
awmyneris, *almoners.*
awne, *own.*
axidens, *(sb. sg.) accident (see 1/introd. n).*
axiþ, *requires.*

badde. *See beddiþ.*
be, ben, *3sg. pres. ind.* es; *pl. pres. ind.* be, ben, beþe, *to be;* beþe about, *are busy.*
beddiþ, *urges;* badde *(3sg. pret. ind.),* beden *(p.p.) commanded.*
bedrad, *bedridden.*
beemers, *Bohemians.*
beemes, *beams of roof.*
beggerie, *beggery, begging, habit of begging.*
beleue, bileeue, *(sb.) faith, article of faith.*
beleued, bileuyde, *believed;* beleued, *(p.p.) believed to be.*
bere, *p.p. born, in ~ down, overcome, oppress;* beren on hand, *assert;* born up with, *supported by.*
beseme, *appear.*
best, *beast.*
bewperis, *ecclesiastical superiors.*
bi, be, *(prep.) by means of, beside, in;* ~ himself, *for himself;* ~ maner, *in the fashion;* ~ tyme, *in time.*
bycomen, *in ~ in dette, get into debt.*
biddyngis, *commands.*
biddiþ, *asks, commands.*
bie, bige, bigge, bi, *(v.) buy.*
bifalleþ, *belongs to.*
bifore, beforn, biforn, *(adv.) beforehand, formerly.*
bigilid, *deceived.*
biheestis, byhestis, *commandments, promises.*
bihofte, *(3sg. pret. ind.) was necessary.*
biholding, *appearance (see 6B/2n).*
bihoten, *(pl. pres. ind.), sg. pret. ind.* bihi3te, *promise.*
bilye, *slander.*
byndiþ, *(3sg. pres. ind.) condemn;* bounden, *(p.p.) fettered, obliged.*

byneþe, *(prep.) not reaching the standards for.*
biriels, *tombs.*
bisien, *exert.*
bisili, *carefully.*
bisynesse, *solicitude.*
bisshoperyc, *bishopric.*
bitakun, *(pl. pres. ind.) entrusted.*
biþou3t, *(p.p.) considered.*
bitokneþ, *in ~ þat, is indicated by the fact that.*
bytwixe, *(prep.) between.*
blaberyne, *babble, say.*
blyndelyngis, *blindfold.*
bobbiden, *derided, mocked.*
bodelich, *(adv.) bodily, physically.*
boldeship, *arrogance.*
boondis, *(sb.) promises, limits.*
boordis, *tables.*
borell, *(adj.) in ~ clerk, educated layman.*
bot, but, *(adv.) only.*
bot, *(cj.) unless;* but if, *but if, unless.*
bot, but, *(prep.) except;* ~ litile, *only a little.*
botiler, *butler.*
bounde, *(sb.) sentence (sp. of excommunication).*
bourde, *sport, amusement.*
bourdfully, *(adv.) mockingly.*
bourdiþ, *jests.*
boweþ, *pl. pres. ind.* bowen, *turn, convert.*
braken, *(pl. pret. ind.) broke.*
breeche, *loincloth.*
bren, *p.p.* brent, *burn.*
brennende, brynnynge, *(adj.) burning.*
bringe, *in ~ bi, deduce from.*
brothern, *brothers.*
burgeisis, *citizens.*
buxumnesse, *obedience.*

caas, *in in ~ , it may be, perhaps.*
cacchen, *gain.*
capped, *with the hat of a doctor of divinity, i.e. learned.*
caracteris, *symbols;* in ~ , *as signs, badges.*
careynes, *corpses.*
carol, *round dance with musical accompaniment.*
casten, *p.p.* cast(e), *devise, plan, reckon.*
catel, *goods, property, wealth.*
cause, *reason; by* þe ~ , *for this reason.*
cautel, *trick.*
cautelous, *deceitful.*
censuris, *condemnations by ecclesiastical authority.*
certeyn, *in in ~ , certainly;* ben in ~ , *are convinced.*
cesen, *subside.*
chaffare, *(sb.) bargain.*
chafferen, *(pl. pres. ind.) bargain.*
chalengiþ, *arrogates, lays claim to.*
chanouns, *canons regular.*

charge, (*sb.*) *burden, weight, expense, importance, responsibility, precept.*

charge, (*v.*) *consider of importance, hold responsible, value, entrust*; is euene for to~, *is equally to be valued*; chargid to ben of, *invested with*; chargid wiþ, *burdened with.*

chargyouse, *burdensome.*

charmid, *subjected to exorcism or incantation.*

chase. *See* chese.

chaumpe sotile, *finely wrought area (see 25/35n).*

chaungiþ, *alters, exchanges;* ~wiþ, *exchanges for.*

cheer, chere, *welcome, entertainment, face, bearing, manner.*

cheffe, *chief, head.*

cheker, *exchequer.*

chese, (*v.*) 1 *and* 3.*sg. pret. ind.* chase, ches, chese, *pl. pret. ind.* chesen, *choose.*

chesyng, *selection.*

cheueli, *preeminently.*

clene, *simple, clear, pure.*

clenli, *wholly, entirely.*

clennes, *purity, innocence.*

clepen, *call.*

clere, in in~, *financially unencumbered.*

clerid, *cleansed.*

clerk, *priest, scholar.*

cleuen, *remain, cling*; cleuede to, *joined.*

clippiþ, *shears.*

clippere, *shearer.*

closen, *enclose, block.*

clouten, *join, add.*

clouting, *patching, addition.*

cnakkyng, *singing with trills (see 16/124n).*

coddes, *husks.*

coyn, *image or design on coin.*

colages, *colleges of chantry priests (see 3/73n).*

colegie, *college.*

color, colour, (*sb.*) *disguise, pretext*; by ~of, *under the guise of*; vndir~, *as a pretext.*

colour, (*v.*) *conceal;* ~wiþ, *make appear better.*

colourable, *plausible.*

come, 3.*sg. pret. ind.* cam, come, *p.p.* comen, *come*; comen of, *descended from.*

comyn, (*sb.*) *cumin (a herb).*

comyn lawe, *canon law of the church.*

comynte, *community.*

commissariis, *representatives.*

comon, in in~, *with their goods held in common.*

comouns, comunes, *ordinary lay people.*

comowynnge, (*pres. p.*) *talking;* comowned (1.*sg. pret. ind.*) *held acquaintance*; communid (*p.p.*) *disseminated, communicated.*

comparisowneþ, *compares.*

compassion, *sorrow.*

comunely, *generally to all.*

confecioun, *confession.*

conferme, *conform, model.*

conne, con, can, kunne, 2.*sg. pres. ind.* canst, 3.*sg. pres. ind.* can, *pl. pret. ind.* cowd, kouden, *pl. pret. sj.* couþ, *p.p.* koud, *know, know how to;* kunnen not þeron, *have no knowledge about it.*

cunnyng, kunnynge, (*adj.*) *knowledgeable.*

connynge, kunnyng, (*sb.*) *knowledge, learning.*

consecrat, *consecrated.*

conseil, *council.*

constituciouns, *regulations of the church (sp. those set up by the convocation of higher clergy).*

constreyne, *control.*

conteyned, *included.*

continaunse, *behaviour.*

contrarien, *contradict, act against.*

contrarius, *contrary, opposed.*

contryuede, *devised.*

contunuely, *constantly.*

conuersaunt, in weren ~among, *lived amongst, were intimate with.*

conuertid, *turned.*

conuyct, *demonstrably (see 12/23n).*

coorde, *agree.*

copulatif, (*adj.*) *linking.*

coroune, *crown.*

correlary, *corrolary.*

corript, *corrupted, debased.*

corrupting, *alteration, modification.*

cost, *expenditure.*

costage, *expense.*

cote, *coat.*

counfort, (*v.*) *strengthen.*

counseile, (*v.*) *consult.*

counsel, (*sb.*) *instruction.*

coupulatif, (*sb.*) *linking (rather than subordinating) conjunction.*

couetise, coueitise, *avarice.*

couenable, *appropriate.*

coventis, *conventual establishments.*

couertli, *ambiguously.*

cowntenance, *appearance.*

craftily, *skilfully, efficiently.*

cristendam, *baptism.*

crochid, (*p.p.*) *seized, got possession of.*

croude, *stringed instrument, but see 8/25n.*

crownis, *tonsures.*

cuylet, *collection of alms (see 23/24n).*

cuyssyns, *cushions.*

culuer, *dove.*

curatis, *parish priests.*

cure, *ecclesiastical office, benefice, spiritual responsibility.*

curiosite, *idle interest.*

curious, *splendid, costly.*

curs, *sentence of excommunication.*

cursed, *cursed, condemned, excommunicated.*

cursynges, *sentences of excommunication.*

customable, custumable, *habitual.*

customed, *habitual.*

dane, *lord (as a title of a scholar).*

debatis, *disputes.*

decrees, *in* doctore of~, *doctor of canon law.*

ded. *See* do.

dede, *in* bi~, *through observation of action*; in~, *in action.*

dedein, *(sb.) scorn, indignation, anger.*

dedeynen, *(v.) scorn, disdain.*

dedly, deadli, *mortal.*

deed, *(adj.) dead.*

deed, *(sb.) death.*

defame, *denounce, accuse.*

defaute, *lack, defect.*

defende, *protect.*

defensour, *defender.*

defouled, defouliden, *(p.p.) contaminated, spiritually dishonoured.*

degyse, *disguise, strange dress.*

degre, *rank of society, degree.*

deynte, *honour.*

deyth, *dies.*

delen, *assign, give.*

deme, *(v.) judge, consider.*

demeyns, *domains.*

denuncyn, *(pl. pres. ind.) announce, declare.*

departen, *separate, divide.*

departynge, *separation.*

depide, *sunk.*

depraued, *condemned, spoken against.*

derk, *comp.* derkere, *obscure.*

derkid, *sullied.*

derkli, *obscurely.*

determinacion, *doctrine, dogma (see 24/124n).*

determyneþ, *decrees, sets up as a doctrine.*

detʒ, *(sb.) death.*

deue, *deaf.*

dewid, *endowed.*

dewtees, *fees owed.*

diʒt, *arranged, established.*

dyleberacioun, *discussion.*

diocesans, *bishops of the relevant dioceses.*

discipline, dissipline, *moral system of conduct.*

discordiþ, *in* ~from *departs from, disagrees with.*

discrecion, *in* of~, *having moral discernment.*

discreteli, *prudently, privately.*

dysease, *injury, harm.*

disesi, *(adj.) disagreeable.*

disgysing, *newfangled elaboration of fashion.*

disparpliþ, *scatters.*

dispenderis, *stewards.*

dispending, *spending, expense.*

dispensen, *in* ~wiþ, *dispense from.*

dispensing, *dispensation, releasing from vow, mitigation.*

dispensis, *expenses.*

dispreue, *refute.*

dissoloued, *annulled.*

distruyʒe, *destroy.*

dyuers, *different.*

diuersen, *differ.*

dyuersite, *distinction;* for~, *as a means of distinction.*

dyuydiþ, *(3sg. pres. ind.), p.p.* diuidid, *break up.*

dyuynis, *theologians.*

do, done, *2sg. pres. ind.* dostow (*i.e.* dost þow), *pl. pres. ind.* don, done, doun, *sg. pret. ind.* dude, dide, *pl. pret. ind.* diden, ded, *pres. p.* doying, *p.p.* don, do, ydo; *do, perform, act;* do him on þe cros, *put him on the cross;* had no more to done þerwiþ, *would have no more concern with it;* dyd make, *caused to be built;* diden awei, *destroyed;* doying vs to witen, *causing us to know;* don vpon, *put on.*

docken, *shorten, abbreviate.*

doctouris, *the doctors of the church (i.e. Ambrose, Augustine, Jerome and Gregory).*

doctrine, *teaching, instruction.*

dom, dome, doom, *judgment (sp. last judgment);* holy~, *last judgment;* neiþer in ~neiþer ouʒt of~, *neither in the course of legal procedure nor out of it.*

dotaciun, *endowment.*

dote, *become weak and foolish, rot.*

double, *in* ~more þan ʒou, *twice as bad as yourselves.*

douteful, *uncertain.*

doutes, *disputed tenets.*

doutouse, *doubting.*

dowynge, *endowment.*

draf, *chaff, husks, dregs.*

dragth, *measure.*

drawe, *3sg. pret. ind.* drouʒ, drowe, *pl. pret. ind.* drowen; ~to, *go to, attend;* ~him to, *join himself with.*

dred, dreed, *(sb.) fear;* for worldis~, *for fear of the world.*

drede, *(v.), p.p.* dred, *fear, be afraid.*

dresse, *prepare, arrange.*

dryng, *drink.*

dryue, *impel.*

duelle, *remain.*

dur, *(pl. pres. ind.) dare.*

duringe, *lasting.*

durit, *lasted, continued.*

eche on, *each.*

edefien, *promote in virtue.*

eeld, *age.*

eeten. *See* eten.

eft, *again.*
eftsoone, *again.*
eiȝte, *eighth.*
eiþer, *(adj.) each.*
eiþir...eiþir, *either...or.*
eke, *also.*
elde, *(adj.) old.*
ellis, *otherwise.*
encens, *incense.*
encroche, *seize illegally.*
ende, *purpose;* into wiþouten∼, *for ever.*
endentid, indented, *decorated; at* 5/120 *made in the manner of an indenture (two copies made on a single sheet which is then cut in half by an irregular line, each party to the agreement taking one half).*
endiþ, *dies;* endid *(p.p.) used up, completed, accomplished.*
enduwid, *endowed.*
enformed, *instructed.*
enforsiden, *in* ∼hem, *strove.*
englisshe, *translate into English.*
enhaunsiþ, *exalts.*
ensaumple, *(sb.) example.*
ensaumplide, *(3sg. pret. ind.), p.p.* ensampled, *gave an example of, laid down as an example.*
entent, *intention, meaning;* yow gyve your∼ *you devote yourselves.*
entere, *sincere, wholehearted.*
enterly, *fully, wholeheartedly.*
entirlodies, *dramatic entertainments.*
enuenymed, *infected, corrupted.*
enuirounden, *surrounded.*
equite, *righteousness.*
equiuok, *(adj.) ambiguous by reason of homonymy;* wordis∼, *homonyms.*
er, *(cj.) before;* ∼þat, *before.*
ernes, eernis, *pledge, foretaste.*
ernest, *in in* ∼done, *done with such grave purpose;* into most∼, *as a matter of greatest importance.*
ernestful, *earnest, serious.*
ernystfully, *with serious intent.*
erst, *in the first place.*
es. See ben.
essenciali, *(adv.) in essence.*
eten, *(pl. pres. ind.) devour, destroy;* eeten *(pl. pret. ind.) ate.*
eþer, *(cj.) or, either.*
euene, *equal.*
euenecristen, *(sb. pl.) fellow christians.*
euere, euur, *always.*
eueriche, *each.*
euermore, *regularly.*
excusaciouns, *excuses.*
exorsisioun, *exorcism.*
expoune, *expound.*
expresse, *(adj.) manifest.*

expresse, *(adv.) expressly.*
extende, *be able, have sufficient.*
ey, *egg.*

failen, *(pl. pres. ind.),* pres. p. fayland, *lack.*
fayn, *glad.*
faynt, *enfeebled.*
faire, *(adv.) well.*
falle, pret. ind. fel, felde, *fall, pertain, belong by inheritance, come, happen.*
falsehed, *falsehood.*
fame, *reputation.*
farisees, *pharisees.*
faute, *defect, lack (sp. of necessities of life).*
fautour, *supporter, abettor.*
feblid, *enfeebled.*
feele, fele, *many.*
feesten, *(pl. pres. ind.) entertain lavishly.*
feynen, *pretend, prevaricate.*
feynid, *(adj.) pretended.*
feynyng, *(sb.) pretence, assumed behaviour.*
feiþ, *in* to do ∼to, *to keep faith towards.*
fel, felde. See falle.
felaship, *(v.) keep company.*
felawchipe, *(sb.) acquaintance.*
felnesse, *cruelty.*
fend, *enemy, devil.*
fer, *distant, far.*
fere, *fear.*
ferforþ, ferfurth, forfurth, *(adv.) far; so* ∼þat, *to such an extent that;* als ∼als, *as far as.*
ferthe, *fourth.*
figure, *appearance, shape, symbol.*
figuren, *foreshadow, prefigure.*
filled, *fulfilled.*
fynde, 3sg. pret. ind. fond, p.p. fynde, fondon, foundun, *find, devise, provide for.*
fynding, *invention.*
fythte, *fight.*
fleiȝ, *(3sg. pret. ind.) fled.*
fleyinge, *in* to ∼of, *(to teach) to flee from.*
fleiȝes, *(sb. pl.) flies.*
fleyss, fleyssh, *flesh.*
fleijsly, *fleshly, sinful.*
floryschyd, *flowery, ornamented.*
foly, *foolish.*
folily, *foolishly.*
fonned, fonnyd, *foolish.*
for, *(cj.) because.*
for, *(prep.) on account of;* ∼þat þat, *because;* ∼þi þat, *because.*
forbede, p.p. forbedun, forboden, *forbid.*
forbot, *prohibition.*
fordo, pret. fordide, *destroy.*
forȝite, *forget.*
forme, *model of conduct.*
forsaken, *lose, forgo.*
forsoþe, *truly.*

forþerd, *advanced.*
forwhi, (*adv.*) *for indeed.*
forwhi, (*cj.*) *that* (7/1/12 *Vulgate quoniam*).
fouchesaaf, *vouchsafe.*
foul, fowle, (*adv.*) *foully, badly.*
foule, (*sb.*) *bird.*
foulin, *condemn.*
foundement, *foundation.*
foundun, (*p.p.*) *in* ~vpon, *set up by.*
freshe, *freshly.*
frett d, *studded.*
fryndis, *friends.*
fruyt, *food.*
fruytful, *profitable.*
frutuous, *fruitful.*
ful, (*adv.*) *very.*
fulfillun, *fill, feast, perform.*
fulli, *completely.*
furþe, (*adj.*) *fourth.*
furth, (*adv.*) *onwards, in addition.*
furþer, (*v.*) *assist.*

gabbyng, *falsehood, deceit.*
gadiryng, *collection of money.*
gadur, *gather together.*
gatis, *in* manye~, *in many ways.*
gedere, *collect together.*
gedryngis, *gatherings, product.*
gendre, *beget.*
genealogie, *progeny.*
generalte, *in* in~, *in general.*
gessist, *p.p.* gessid, *think, consider.*
get, 3*sg. pret. ind.* gate, *p.p.* getyn, *obtain.*
gileful, *false, misleading.*
gilour, *deceiver.*
gilteris, *sinners.*
gyn, *trap.*
gyven. *See* 3eue.
glade, (*v.*) *rejoice.*
glaueren, *speak deceitfully about.*
glebes, *lands belonging to parsonage.*
glose, *gloss.*
gloson, *gloss, interpret.*
gloterie, *gluttony.*
goyng, (*sb.*) *movement, action.*
good, gode, (*sb.*) *money, wealth;* pl. *goods.*
good, (*adv.*) *well.*
goste, *spirit.*
gostli, (*adj.*) *spiritual.*
gostly, (*adv.*) *spiritually.*
gouernaile, *custody, government.*
gouernaunce, *authority.*
gouernour, *ship's master.*
grace, gras, *grace;* ~of sone, *grace to be a son.*
graunt, (*sb.*) *gift.*
graunte, (*v.*), *pres. pl. ind.* graunteyn; *agree, agree to, allow.*
grauen, *carved.*
greete, (*sb.*) *lamentation.*

grese, (*v.*) *apply salve to sheep.*
greuous, *weighty, important.*
grew, *Greek.*
ground, (*sb.*) *foundation, basis, premise;* in~, *on earth.*
groundiþ, *p.p.* groundid, grunded, *found, base (an argument etc.)*
groundynge, (*sb.*) *foundation, evidence for claim.*
groundliere, (*comp. adv.*) *more thoroughly.*

3ede, 3ide, *went.*
3elde, *give, assign, render.*
3erde, *branch, rod.*
3ere, yere, *year;* by~, *each year;* many~, *for many years.*
3eue, 3iue, yeve, 3*sg. pret. ind.* 3af, 3aue, *p.p.* 3euen, 3oue, yoven, 3ouun, gyven, *give;* for to 3eue to telle, *to give up saying;* 3iue not on vs, *lay not on us;* gyven to, *devoted to.*
3ide. *See* 3ede.
3if, 3eue, (*cj.*) *if.*
3ildyng, *giving.*
3yuyng, (*sb.*) *gift.*
3itt, yit, 3ut, *yet.*
3ou, you, (*refl.*) *yourselves.*

haate, *despise.*
habitude, *convention (of speech).*
habitudynel, *conventional.*
half, *side.*
haliday, *holy day.*
halowe, halowyn, *p.p.* halwed, halewid, halowid; *sanctify, consecrate, honour.*
halowing, halwinge, *blessing.*
halowus, halwen, *saints.*
han, 3*sg. pres. ind.* hat, *have.*
hange, *depend;* hangid, *p.p. in* ~on, *expended on.*
happe, *in* in~, *perchance.*
hardi, *bold.*
haterad, *hatred.*
haunt, (*v.*) *engage in.*
heerd, *shepherd, priest.*
heestis, hestis, *commandments.*
heg, *hedge.*
hele, *salvation.*
helpis, *helpers.*
helples, *useless.*
helþ, *health, salvation.*
hem, *them, themselves;* hemsilf, hemself, *themselves;* her, hore, *their.*
herberwed, herborid, (*p.p.*) *lodged.*
here, *ear.*
hereticous, *heretical.*
herfor, *for this reason.*
heriyng, *praise.*
herin, *hear.*

heering, heryng, *speech.*

heritage, *inheritance.*

hermofodrita, *hermaphrodite, fig. one who improperly occupies two offices.*

herres, *bars.*

herte, *midst.*

herþdene, *earthquake.*

herþoruȝ, *by this means, for this reason.*

herto, *for this purpose.*

hete, *promise.*

hethnesse, *heathendom, heathen countries.*

heuy, *in* ~ towardis, *annoyed with.*

hiden, *dissemble, conceal.*

hiȝe, *(adj.) great, exalted.*

hyinge, *(pres. p.) hastening.*

hillen, 3sg. pret. ind. hilede, *p.p.* hilid, *cover, clothe, conceal.*

hilling, hilyng, *(sb.) covering, clothing.*

hyne, *servant.*

hire, *payment; at* 12/99 *esp. tithes and ecclesiastical payments.*

his, *(v.). See* be.

his, *(pron.) its.*

hold, *pl. pret. ind.* heelden, heulden, *p.p.* holden, holdoun, *hold, contain, consider; in* ~ lowe, *keep down;* ~ wiþ, *keep to, maintain, ally with;* ~ ageyn, *oppose; p.p. obliged, indebted.*

holli, *completely.*

holpen, *(p.p.) assisted, remedied.*

home, *in* helpe~, *help to reach.*

homely, *(adj.) familiar; in* ~ enmyes, *enemies within the fold of the church.*

homely, *(adv.) familiarly.*

honourmentis, *ornaments, adornments.*

hool, *whole, complete, wholesome.*

hopiþ, *hopes for.*

hore. *See* hem.

horsouns, *bastards, wretches.*

humour, *one of the four fluids which form and nourish the body.*

hundruth, *hundred.*

hungir, *famine.*

hurtynge, *(sb.) error.*

iche, *each.*

idil, *in* in~, *in vain.*

if, *if, even if, in the hope that.*

iȝen, *eyes.*

ilke, *same.*

imade, *in* ~ to, *given to, bequeathed to.*

image, *image, likeness, statue.*

ymagerie, *making of images, sculpture.*

ymbren days, *rogation days.*

in, *on, among.*

inclep, *invoke, cry to.*

indented. *See* endentid.

indett, *obliged.*

ynoȝe, ynow, *(adv.) enough, sufficiently.*

intil, *to.*

into, *to, for, until, in the sight of, according to.*

ischer, *doorkeeper.*

ianglen, *chatter, jabber.*

iape, *(v.) trick;* ~ of, *mock at.*

iapis, *playthings.*

iapynge, *(sb.) mockery.*

iauels, *brawlers, rascals.*

ioȝen, *rejoice.*

iornay, iorne, iourne, *enterprise, undertaking, journey; in* ~ of þre daȝis, *that would take three days to travel across.*

iustise, *judge.*

iwis, *Jews.*

kepen, *guard, tend, reserve;* kepynge so couertli in her prechinge, *speaking so ambiguously in their sermons.*

keruyng, *carving.*

kin, *in* ner of~, *closely related.*

kyndam, *kingdom.*

kynde, *nature.*

kyndeli, kyndli, *(adj.) natural.*

kyndli, *(adv.) naturally.*

kyndlyngis, *offspring.*

kynrede, *kindred.*

kirk, *church.*

knit, *(p.p.) put together.*

knowe, *recognize; in it is to*~, *it should be recognized;* knowen, *(p.p.) familiar.*

knowyng, *(sb.) knowledge, information.*

knouleche, *(sb.) information.*

knowleche, knowelich, *(v.) acknowledge, confess.*

knouleching, *(sb.) confession.*

kome, *come.*

kunne, koud. *See* conne.

kunnyng. *See* connyng.

lambren, *lambs.*

langid. *See* longen.

large, *(adv.) freely.*

largely, *comp.* largerli, *extensively, extravagantly.*

largesse, *liberality.*

last, *(cj.) lest.*

lastingli, *continually, with perseverance.*

latanye, *litany, series of intercessions.*

late, *(adv.) recently.*

late, *(v.) let, give.*

lauedy, *lady.*

lawyyng, *laughing.*

lede, *lead, guide.*

leeue, *(v.¹) leave, give up, cease.*

leeuede, *(v.²) believed.*

lefte, *(p.p.) lifted.*

leful, *lawful.*

lefully, *lawfully, legitimately.*

legyauns, *privilege.*

leie, (3*sg. pres. sj.*) *in* ~ *to me* (*Lat. michi* . . . *opponat*) *pledge to me, set before me.*

leiser, *leisure.*

lengere, (*adv.*) *longer.*

leper, *leprosy.*

leprouse, *diseased.*

lerned, (*p.p.*) *instructed.*

lernyng, *source of instruction, correction.*

lesen, *lose.*

leseris, *destroyers.*

lesewis, *pastures.*

lesyng, (*ger.*) *losing.*

lesyng, *lie, falsehood, false report.*

lesse, (*adj.*) *in* þe~, *the things of less importance.*

lessid, *diminished.*

lessinge, *diminution.*

let, letten, *hinder, deprive.*

leten, (*pl. pret. ind.*) *said.*

lettre, *in bi* þe~, *following the original word order* (*see* 14/62*n*).

leue, (*adj.*) *dear.*

leue, (*sb.*) *permission.*

leue, (*v.*[1]) *allow*

leue, (*v.*[2]) *cease.*

leueful, *lawful.*

leuefuliche, *lawfully.*

leuen, *live.*

leueree, *livery, uniform.*

lewed, lewde, *lay, secular, uninformed, foolish.*

licli, *probable.*

licnessis, *in by summe*~, *by similarities in some points.*

lieþ, lyiþ, (3*sg. pres. ind.*)[1] *pertains to.*

lieþ, liþ (3*sg. pres. ind.*)[2] *lies;* lyen upon, *misrepresent.*

lyf, *life, living person;* to lijf and deþ, *in life and death.*

liflode, lyfelode, *livelihood, means of sustenance.*

lift, *left.*

liȝt, lyth, *easy, comprehensible.*

liȝtli, lythli, *easily, likely, readily.*

liȝtned, *enlightened.*

liȝtnynge, *enlightening.*

like, (*adj.*) *similar.*

like, (*adv.*) *likely.*

liking, *pleasure, amusement.*

likiþ, 3*sg. pret. ind.* lykyd, *please.*

lymytid, (*p.p.*) *appointed, assigned.*

lymytours, *friars licensed to beg within certain areas.*

lyth(li). *See* liȝt(li).

lyueres, *those alive.*

lyuyng, *manner of life.*

loke, *examine.*

longen, 3*sg. pret. ind.* langid, *belong to, pertain, befit, be appropriate.*

lore, *knowledge, instruction, teaching, learning.*

losels, *wretches, scoundrels.*

losid, *praised.*

loþe, *in* ~ me were, *it would grieve me.*

lousede, lowside, *loosed.*

lowyn, (*pl. pres. ind.*), pl. pret. ind. lowen, *laugh.*

luste, *pleasure.*

lusty, *energetic, vigorous.*

may. *See* mow.

maynten, *maintain, support.*

mayntenyng, (*sb.*) *means of maintaining.*

mayntenours, *supporters, helpers.*

maister, *master, legal owner.*

maistrie, *authority, superior authority.*

manasit, *threatens.*

maner, *kind, manner, habitual practice.*

mannislaute, *manslaughter.*

manquellere, *manslayer, murderer.*

marchaunt, *mercenary, hired man.*

marken, *in* ~ *to hem, appropriate to themselves.*

marre, *ruin, lead astray, perplex.*

martyrdom, *canonization.*

mateynes, *matins* (*at* 2/25 *probably standing generally for daily hours; see* 2/146*n*).

matrymoyn, *matrimony.*

maugre, *displeasure.*

mawmentis, *idols.*

mawmentrie, maumetrie, *idolatry, idols.*

maundement, mandement, *commandment.*

mede, *reward, financial reward.*

medeful, *praiseworthy, meritorious.*

medefully, *worthily, with merit.*

medlin, (*v.*) *concern, have to do with.*

meyne, meynye, *household, band of men.*

mekiþ, *p.p.* meekyd, *humble, humiliate.*

mell, *interfere, mix.*

membris, menbris, *limbs, parts of body;* 27/32 *outlying estates.*

mendynauns, *mendicants, friars.*

mene, (*adj.*) *ordinary.*

mene, (*sb.*) *method.*

mene, (*v.*) *in* þat es to~, *that is to be understood;* menynge, (*pres. p.*) *implying.*

mengid, *confused, mixed.*

mengyng, (*sb.*) *mixture.*

meritorie, *having merit.*

meschif, *evil condition, trouble, affliction.*

messe, *mass.*

mesure, *moderation.*

meue, *move, urge.*

miche, moche, (*adv.*), comp. mo, moo, *superl.* most, *much; as* moche . . . as moche, *by so much as* . . . *by so much;* most al, *almost all.*

michil, mykul, moche, (*adj.*), comp. more, *much, great, many.*

mynde, mende, *remembrance, intention.*

myndeful, *recollected.*

mynstre, *monastery.*

myraclis, (*pl.*) *marvellous events, miracle plays* (*see* 19/6*n*).

myrþis, *sports, entertainments.*

mysbileue, *disbelief, wrong belief.*

mysese, (*adj.*) *in want.*

mysusing, *abuse.*

mysvsiþ, *abuses.*

mo, moo. *See* miche (*adv.*).

moche. *See* miche (*adv. and adj.*).

mone, mony, *money.*

moraltees, *moral teachings.*

mornyng, *mourning.*

morteysed, *alienated in mortmain* (*see* 26/49*n*).

mossel, *morsel,*

most. *See* miche (*adv.*).

mot, moot, mut, *pl. pres. ind.* moten, *3sg. pret. ind.* most, *must;* him most, *he would have to.*

mouþe, *in* schrift of~, *oral confession.*

mow, *pl. pres. ind.* may, moun, mowen, *may, be able to;* may þer purpose, *are able to carry out their intention.*

mouen, *incite.*

murþirde, *wasted.*

named, *reputed.*

nameli, *especially.*

ne, ny, *nor.*

nede, (*adv.*) *necessarily.*

nedely, *necessarily.*

nediþ, *is needy;* hem nediþ, *is necessary for them; p.p.* nedid, *forced.*

needful, *necessary.*

neyȝen, *3sg. pret. ind.* neiȝide, neȝhede, *approach, draw near.*

neiȝinge, (*sb.*) *approach.*

nemen, nempne, *p.p.* nemlid, *name.*

ner, *nor.*

neþeles. *See* noþeles.

newe, (*adv.*) *newly, afresh.*

nigromancie, *necromancy.*

nyȝ, *near.*

nil, *do not.*

no but, (*cj.*) *unless;* no but (*prep.*) *only.*

nogatis, *in no way.*

noten, *observe, note; p.p.* noted, *well known.*

noþeles, noþoles, naþeles, neþeles, *nevertheless.*

nouȝt, nouth, noȝt, nat, *not, nothing.*

nouþer, *neither.*

nouelries, *novelties.*

obeischen, *submit.*

oboue, *above.*

ocupiede, *p.p.* ocuped, *engaged, occupied, endeavoured.*

of, *of, by, from, out of;* ~office, *by virtue of office.*

office, offis, *duty, function.*

offryngis, *offerings, dues* (*see* 2/81*n*).

oloft, *aloft, up.*

omonge, *amongst.*

on, *in, over.*

one, oo, oon, *one, one thing;* to oon, *into unity.*

oni, *any.*

onys, onus, *once.*

onone, *immediately.*

onprofitable, *unuseful.*

onswerid, *answered.*

oonhed, *unity.*

open, *plain, clear, evident.*

or, *or þat, before.*

ordeyne, *arrange, appoint.*

ordinal, *service book, esp. that containing services for ordination of priests and deacons and consecration of bishops.*

ordinaris, ordinaries, *at* 2/1 *one having jurisdiction in ecclesiastical cases by virtue of his office; at* 5/64 *bishop's deputy.*

ordinaunce, *direction, commandment.*

ordre, *rank, position;* newe ordris, *religious orders (monks, canons, friars) recently founded.*

ordred, (*p.p.*) *ordained, in orders.*

orisouns, *prayers.*

os, *as.*

ost, oost, *wafer or bread used in the Eucharist;* ostis, *sacrifices.*

osteleris, ostelers, *innkeepers, stablemen at inns.*

oþere, oþir, (*adj.*) *other;* ~while, *sometimes, at times;* ~þan, *beyond, different from.*

other, ouþer, (*cj.*) *or;* ouþer...ouþer, *either...or.*

oþerwise, *in another fashion.*

ouȝt, *something.*

oune, *own.*

ourned, *adorned.*

out, *in* ~of, *beyond, outside.*

outmere, *more external, bodily.*

outtakun, (*prep.*) *besides, beyond.*

ouer, (*adv.*) *moreover.*

ouer, (*prep.*) *beyond;* ~mesure, *beyond reason.*

ouercoueren, *cover over.*

ouerehipping, *omission.*

oueresiht, *governance, supervision.*

ouergo, *overcome.*

ouerlede, *mislead.*

ouerlewde, *too ignorant.*

ouerse, *peruse, inspect.*

ow, owe, *oh! alas!*

owen, *ought, should.*

owhere, *anywhere.*

paciencie, *patience.*
paynemes, *pagans, heathens.*
pannes, *pans, vessels.*
panter, *officer of household supplying bread and having charge of pantry.*
parauenture, *perhaps.*
parde, *(exclam.) indeed.*
pardoun, *pardon, at 2/14 esp. indulgence, general pardon.*
part, *extent;* bi sum~, *to some extent;* for manie partis, *to a large extent.*
partener, pertener, *partner, partaker.*
partie, party, *part.*
passe, *pass over, surpass, excel, exceed;* passede ouer, *transgressed.*
passing, *(adv.) preeminently, exceedingly.*
passynge, *(adj.) surpassing.*
pawmentis, *pavements.*
peyne, *torment, punishment;* bi~, *by force, under threat of torture.*
peyntid, *coloured deceptively.*
peyntur, *portrayal.*
penetaunceris, *priests appointed to hear confession and assign penance in difficult cases.*
perceneris, *partakers.*
pere, *equal.*
perfit, *perfect.*
perfoorme, *carry out.*
perile, pereil, *danger, difficulty.*
perry, *precious stones.*
persen, *get inside.*
pershe, *p.p.* perischid, *perish, destroy.*
persone, *in* in þe ~ of, *as the representative of.*
personel, *individual, peculiar.*
persue. *See* pursue.
perteinen, *concern;* it perteneþ not to hym of, *it does not meet to him about.*
peruertiþ, *leads astray.*
pese-holis, *husks of peas.*
pesis, *peas.*
pile, *p.p.* pyld, *rob.*
pilgrimage, *journey.*
pynyng, *exerting.*
pistil, pistle, *epistle.*
piteously, *in a shameful fashion.*
playn, *in* in~, *plainly.*
plenerly, *more openly.*
plesaunce, *pleasure.*
plesinge, *in* þe ~ wille of God, *the will which would please God.*
plesingly, *in a manner to give pleasure;* as~, *as if to give pleasure.*
plete, pletyn, *take up a suit, sue in court of law.*
poar, *power, authority.*
poerte, *poverty.*
poynt, *limit, position;* in ~ to, *about to.*

poyntel, *writing instrument.*
poyses, *poems.*
pondred, *considered, heeded.*
possessioneres, *monks (see 1/59n).*
postillatouris, *writers of commentaries on passages of the Bible.*
postlis, *apostles.*
poten, *put, place.*
pouert, *poverty.*
power, *(adj.) poor.*
power, *(sb.) power, authority.*
practisen, *in* ~ wiþ, *plot against.*
praers, *prayers.*
precious, *spiritually valuable.*
preferryng, *recommending.*
preie, *entreat.*
preiudise, *affliction, injury;* in ~ of, *to the detriment of.*
prelacye, *at 3/5 system of church government by prelates or bishops of lordly rank (in Wycliffite writings regularly derogatory); at 12/33 position of bishop or, more generally, exalted place in government of church.*
prelate, *bishop, exalted dignatory of church (in Wycliffite writings generally derogatory).*
preson, *prison.*
presumeþ, *ventures.*
pretense, *(adj.) pretended.*
preue, *prove.*
prynt, *(sb.) impress on coin.*
priour, *superior, head.*
priss, *money.*
prist, *priest.*
priue, priuey, *private, secret, familiar.*
priueli, *privately, secretly.*
priuen, *deprive, deprive of.*
processe, *argument.*
procuratour, *representative, one duly authorized to act on behalf of another.*
profitiþ, *3.sg. pret. ind.* profitide, *be of use to, advance, be of advantage.*
promitte, *promise.*
propirly, *in his own person.*
propirte, *peculiar nature.*
propre, propur, *individual, peculiar to itseȝ*
proprid, *(p.p.) belonging to.*
pseudefreris, *false friars.*
puple, *people.*
pure, *simple, complete.*
purede, *(p.p.) cleansed.*
purpose, *(v.) intend.*
pursue, persue, *sue for, persecute;* persewed, *continued, persevered.*
puruyaunce, *provision, ordinance.*
put, *in* ~ vpon, *attribute to, allege against;* p.p. putte, *alleged against, forced, obliged.*

quenche, *fail, be extinguished.*
quik, queke, *living.*

quilagis, *collection of taxes* (*see* 18/70n).

quitid, *in* I ~ me to him, *I paid him out,
I made myself even with him.*

quyten, *leave.*

qwete, *wheat.*

qwiche, *which, who;* ~ as, *such as.*

qwoso, *whoever.*

radde. *See* riden.

raþer, *sooner, more;* raþeest, *most quickly.*

raueyne, *robbery;* wolues of ~, *despoiling
wolues.*

rauenour, *despoiler.*

raueschen, *seize.*

raueschinge, (*adj.*) *ravenous, plundering.*

ray, *striped cloth* (*see* 25/31n).

reale, *royal.*

rebaudye, *wanton plays.*

recettour, *harbourer.*

reccheles, *careless.*

recchelesly, *carelessly.*

recken, *care.*

record, (*sb.*) *in* litil of ~, *not recorded.*

recorde, (*v.*) *learn by heart.*

recouncilid, *reconciled.*

recounselyng, *reconciliation.*

redargued, *confuted by argument.*

redi, *quick.*

redili, *quickly.*

refourmed, *refashioned.*

regale, regaly, *royal prerogative.*

regalte, *sovereignty.*

reherse, *repeat.*

reioyse, *in* ~ hit, *have joy from it.*

reknid, (*p.p.*) *alleged, told of.*

relacion, *connection, comparison* (*with Latin*)
(*see* 14/62n).

releuis, *help.*

religion, *in* priuat ~, *the religious life of
monks, friars, nuns etc.* (*see* 3/5n).

religious, (*sb.*) *men of religion, i.e. monks,
friars, canons.*

renegatis, *apostates from the christian religion.*

renne, *run, travel, carry out, disseminate
freely.*

rentyd, (*p.p.*) *provided with revenues.*

repareld, *restored to original condition.*

replicacioun, *reply.*

repreef, *scorn, shame.*

repreuynge, (*sb.*) *reproof.*

reprowable, *reprehensible.*

rerid, *raised up.*

reseruyt, *in* ~ hym, *holds himself back from,
abstains from.*

resolucions, *making participial constructions
into clauses* (*see* 14/41n).

resoluid, (*p.p.*) *changed, broken up into* (*see*
14/41n).

resoun, reson, *explanation, account, statement, sentence, justification, argument, power
of reasoning;* vpon ~, *for a reason.*

resseytis, *places of refuge.*

restingis, *resting places.*

reuli, *disciplined.*

reuersen, *go against, contradict.*

reuokinge, *recantation.*

reward, (*sb.*) *regard.*

rewarded, (*p.p.*) *regarded.*

rewme, reme, *realm, kingdom.*

riden, (*inf.*), *p.p.* radde, *read.*

riȝt, (*adj.*) *proper.*

riȝt, (*adv.*) *properly, completely;* ~ as, ~ so
as, *just as.*

riȝtful, *correct.*

riȝtfulnes, *righteousness.*

riȝtwissenes, ritwesnes, *righteousness.*

rytis, *rites, ceremonies.*

rode, roode, *crucifix.*

rongis, *rungs.*

round, ronde, *complete, entire, round.*

rude, *simple, unsophisticated.*

ryaly, *royally.*

sacrid, *consecrated.*

sacrifice, *offering.*

sad, *constant, firmly established, serious.*

sadly, *surely, firmly, fixedly.*

saȝ, say, saie. *See* se.

sale-pardouns, *pardons sold for money* (*see*
2/117n).

sarsines, sarasyns, *Saracens, followers of
Mahomet.*

saruys, *service.*

sauacioun, *salvation.*

savor, *pl. pret. ind.* sauouriden, *care for,
have pleasure from.*

sawter, *Psalter.*

scabbid, *having scabs.*

schame, (*v.*) *be ashamed.*

schapen, *plot, arrange;* *p.p.* schapun,
prepared.

scharpely, *searchingly, severely.*

schewinge, (*sb.*) *revelation.*

schewiþ, *3sg. pret. ind.* schewid, *reveal, point
to, display;* *p.p.* schewid, *demonstrated,
proved.*

schortli, *briefly, quickly, without delay.*

schrewid, *wicked.*

schrift, *confession.*

schriue, *hear confession and impose penance,
confess.*

science, *knowledge.*

sclaundre, (*sb.*) *disgrace, cause of stumbling.*

sclaundre, (*v.*) *bring shame to, cause to
stumble.*

sclaundres, sclaundrouus, (*adj.*) *shameful,
bringing reproach.*

scrippe, *small bag, esp. that carried by beggars.*

se, *3sg. pret. ind.* sa3, say, saie, si3, *pl. pret. ind.* se3en, sien, *2sg. pret. sj.* se3e, *p.p.* seen, seyn, *see*; seen in use, *commonly visible.*

seching, *seeking.*

sectis, *religious sects (esp. of 'private religions', of monks, friars etc.).*

seeldene, *seldom.*

seid, sayd, *(p.p.) mentioned, called, reputed*; seid of, *spoken of.*

seientis, *saints.*

seyn, *(cj.) since.*

seke, *sick.*

semyde, *in* he ∼ to himsilf, *he considered himself.*

semynge, *(adj.) apparent.*

sende, *pl. pret. ind.* senten, *throw, cast.*

sensible, *pertaining to the senses.*

sentence, sentens, *statement, sense, meaning, opinion.*

ser, *sir.*

serue, *in* and tyme wolde∼, *if there were sufficient time.*

sett, *(v.) in* ∼ remedy, *devise a remedy*; *pl. pret. ind.* setten, *in* ne wee ∼ bi hym, *nor did we take account of him*; ∼ more bi, *took more account of*; *p.p.* set, *established*; ∼forþ, *set down.*

seue, *seven*; seuent, *seventh.*

sewith. *See* sue.

sewrly, *certainly.*

sexte, *sixth.*

sharpliere, *more acutely.*

shend, *(p.p.) ruined.*

shenschipis, *disgrace.*

shiphijre, *fare for passage.*

shrewe, *(sb.) villain.*

shrewyn, *(pl. pres. ind.), pres. p.* shrewynge, *curse.*

hryned, shreynyd, *enshrined, enclosed in a shrine.*

sibbe, *akin.*

siche, *such.*

side, *in* on eche∼, *in every respect.*

sien. *See* se.

signet, *small seal affixed to ring, hence sign.*

significacions, *meanings.*

signyfieþ, *p.p.* signified, *mean, imply.*

si3. *See* se.

si3t, *in* 3yue hymsilf to þe ∼of, *allow himself to see*; he was not of∼, *his appearance was of no beauty* (?) *(see* 6A/2*n).*

siynge, *(pres. p.) straining out.*

siker, *(adj.) sure.*

sikir, *(adv.) surely, safely.*

sille, *sell.*

symbred, *in* ∼askyng, *reading of banns.*

symple, *plainly.*

sinfon, symfonye, symphonye, *number of musical instruments.*

singemesses, *priests engaged for the singing of masses, chantry priests (see* 5/40*n).*

singuler, *special, individual, peculiar to self, exclusive.*

sithe, sithen, *(adv.) afterwards, subsequently.*

siþen, sitthin, siþ, *(cj.) since.*

siþis, *times.*

skile, skylle, skill, *reason, reasoning, argument.*

skilful, *reasonable.*

skilefuly, *justifiably.*

sleeþ, *pl. pret. ind.* slowen, *slay.*

slipir, *slippery.*

slood, *(3sg. pret. ind.) lapsed in sin.*

smacche, *smack of.*

smyten, *(p.p.) struck, driven.*

so, *(adv.) in such a manner*; ∼ many...hou manye, *as many...as.*

so, *(cj.) as*; ∼þei do wel, *provided that they do well*; so þat, *provided that.*

soilyng, *absolution.*

somer, *summer.*

soone, *immediately, quickly.*

sophistris, *sophists, specious reasoners.*

sore, *severely.*

sori, *in* þou art ∼ on, *you are grieved with.*

soþ, *(adj.) true.*

soþ, *(sb.) truth.*

sothely, *truly.*

soþnesse, *truth.*

sotilte, *device, complexity.*

soule, *in* ∼ hele, *salvation of soul.*

soun, *sound.*

sowneþ, *pl. pret. ind.* sowneden, *sound, strike the ear, appear, tend, imply.*

specialte, *in* in∼, *specially.*

speckid, *variegated (see* 23/93*n).*

spedful, *profitable, successful.*

spencis, spensis, *expenses.*

spereth, *shuts, closes.*

spettyngis, *spittings.*

spille, *waste.*

spirituelte, spiritualte, *the ecclesiastical estates of the realm, revenue of church from ecclesiastical sources (see* 26/29*n).*

spytells, *hospitals (esp. for lepers).*

spitleris, *hospitallers, members of an order devoted to heal the sick.*

spoile, spuyle, *rob.*

spousesse, *bride.*

sprongen, sprungen, *(p.p.) risen, arisen, sprung up.*

stablyng, *establishment.*

staring, *glittering, eye-catching.*

stauis, *staffs.*

ste3en, stie, *pres. p.* sti3ynge, *3sg. pret. ind.* ste3ede, steie, *rise, grow.*

ste3ing, sti3yng, *(sb.) ascension*; in ∼ vp, *in the rising*; styynge, *(men) climbing.*

steride, *urged*

steuede, *ascended.*

stidde, *place, position.*

stidfast, *steadfast, well established.*

stidfastnesse, *stability.*

stiflier, *more firmly.*

stille, *silent.*

stilnesse, *silence.*

stiren, *incite.*

stok, *piece of wood.*

stole, *long robe.*

stonde, 3*sg. pret. ind.* stod, *stand, remain, exist, stop;* stonde with, *exist alongside.*

stony, *astonish.*

stoones, *precious stones.*

straunge, (*v.*) *become strange, differ, remove.*

strecche, *extend, reach out;* ~forþ her lyues, *expend their lives.*

strengþe, (*sb.*) *in* in~, *strongly.*

strengþe, (*v.*) *strengthen.*

striueyng, *striving.*

stroying, *destruction.*

studieþ, *endeavours.*

sturdely, *ruthlessly, cruelly.*

sture, *rouse.*

substaunce, *in* beriþ~, *has serious meaning.*

sue, 3*sg. pres. ind.* sueþ, sewith, *follow, imitate, obey.*

suyng, (*ger.*) *in* to~, *for following.*

suerly, *certainly.*

suffice, suffisede, *be sufficient for.*

suffraunce, *suffering, patient endurance.*

suffre, suffur, *allow.*

sumdel, *to some extent.*

sunner, *sooner.*

superflu, *superfluous, unnecessary.*

supplauntid, *taken over.*

suppose, *think, conjecture, expect.*

sure, *secure.*

sustene, *maintain;* susteyned, (*p.p.*) *provided for, financially supported.*

sutiliþ, *plots.*

swelide, *was burnt.*

swerd, *sword.*

swiþe, *quickly.*

swolewis, *abysses of water, gulfs, hence pits of evil.*

tabernaclid, *canopied, enshrined.*

take, *take, deduce, give;* ~to hem, *adopt for themselves; p.p.* take, *arrested;* takin him to, *applied himself to;* tanne, *done.*

takinge, (*ger.*) *in* wiþoute ~of persones, *without making individual exceptions.*

taliage, *tax (strictly a feudal tax levied by kings or lords on their dependants).*

tapsters, *innkeepers.*

tariyng, *delaying, holding back.*

teeme, *text of sermon.*

tellen, *tell, narrate;* ~more bi, *consider more important;* ~nouȝt bi, *consider of no value.*

temperall, *secular, secular man;* lordes temperals, *secular lords.*

temperaltes, *material possessions and rights, secular affairs.*

temperelte, *body of laymen, the temporal estates of the realm, revenue of church from manors, lands etc. (see 26/29n).*

tente, *tenth.*

than, thanne, (*adv.*) *then.*

þat, (*cj.*) *so that.*

þat, (*rel.*) *that which, what.*

þefli, *like a thief.*

þenke, *think.*

þenking, (*sb.*) *consideration.*

þenne, *than.*

þeras, þereas, *where, whereas.*

þerof, *from that source.*

þervnder, *beneath it.*

þilke, *those.*

thingus, *in* þe ynnere~, *the inner parts.*

þink, thinkis, 3*sg. pret. ind.* þouȝte, (*impers. with dat.*) *it seems.*

þise, *these.*

þo, þose, *pl.* those; þo, *in no.* 25 *used throughout, sg. and pl., for* þe.

þorow, *through.*

þouȝ, þou, þouy, þof, *though.*

þred, *third.*

þrestende, *thirsty.*

thret, *threaten.*

thretty, *thirty.*

þrittenete, *thirteenth.*

til, *to (in local sense).*

tirauntrie, *oppressive rule.*

tiþe, *pay tithes, exact tithes on.*

title,[1] *claim, right.*

title,[2] *tittle, least bit.*

to, (*num.*) *two.*

to, (*prep.*) *as, for;* ~þe tyme, *until.*

tofore, (*adv. and prep.*) *before.*

togrowun, *neglected, overgrown.*

tokenyng, *in* in~, *as a sign.*

tollid, *enticed, lured.*

ton...toþir, *in* þe~...þe~, *the one...the other.*

toour, *tower, fortress.*

torendiþ, *tears apart.*

torned, *transferred.*

totreden, *afflict, trample down.*

touchen, *concern.*

toun, *village, estate, farm.*

traystyng, *believing.*

trauel, (*sb.*) *labour, work.*

trauele, (*v.*) *labour, work, exert.*

trauelous, *wearisome, arduous.*

tresoreris, *treasurers.*

tresour, *treasury.*

tretable, *open, intelligible.*

trete, *consider, discuss;* p.p. tretid, *administered.*

treu, trewe, *true, correct.*

trist, (*sb.*) *trust.*

trist, (*v.*) *trust.*

troone, *throne.*

trowe, *believe, believe in.*

trowyng, (*sb.*) *belief.*

trufle, *trifle, matter of no importance.*

truli, *carefully.*

trwþis, *truths.*

turneþ, *in ∼* hem to wynnyng, *contributes towards their material advantage.*

vnable, *incompetent.*

vnbileue, *disbelief.*

vnbunden, *unbound.*

vncouth, *strange, distasteful.*

vndefoulid, *unspotted.*

vnder, *within.*

vndernymmynge, (*sb.*) *reproof, rebuke.*

vndirnommyn, *challenged, rebuked.*

vndirputten, *set underneath.*

vndurstonde, *interpret, imply, understand.*

vndirstonding, (*sb.*) *interpretation, meaning, implication.*

vndirturned, *overthrown.*

vndisposiþ, *disinclines.*

vndoinge, (*pres. p.*) *deciphering, interpreting;* p.p. vndon, *ruined.*

vngroundid, *unfounded (esp. in holy scripture), unjustified.*

vnkynde, *unnatural.*

vnknowyng, (*adj.*) *ignorant.*

vnknowing, (*sb.*) *ignorance.*

vnkonnyngliche, *ignorantly.*

vnkunnynge, (*adj.*) *ignorant.*

vnkunnynge, (*sb.*) *ignorance.*

vnleeful, *unlawful, improper.*

vnmyȝti, *weak, powerless.*

vnneth, *scarcely.*

vnpertynent, *unnecessary, irrelevant.*

vnpytouse, *unrighteous, wicked.*

vnquyetid, *disturbed.*

vnriȝtfulnesse, *unrighteousness.*

vnsacrede, *unconsecrated.*

vnspecte, *unspotted (thing).*

vnthryuen, *failed to prosper.*

vnto, *concerning.*

vntrist, *lack of trust.*

vntruþe, *infidelity.*

vnwarned, *without warning.*

vnwemmed, *undefiled, unspotted,*

vnwise, *ignorant.*

vp, *according to, following, for, on.*

vpon, *over, in.*

usuel, *customary.*

vanytees, *vain things.*

veleynye, *dishonour.*

venge, *avenge.*

uenimous, *pernicious.*

verray, verri, verre, very, *true, real, properly so called.*

verreyly, *truly.*

uertu, *value, use.*

vertues, (*adj.*) *virtuous.*

vesselis, *utensils, goods.*

vylenye, *indignity.*

voide, *idle.*

voydid, (*p.p.*) *annulled, nullified, abolished.*

voluptees, *extravagant pleasures.*

vomed, *vomited.*

waytynge, *watching (Lat. observantes).*

waken, *watch.*

wakynge, (*adj.*) *watchful.*

wane, (*cj.*) *when.*

wannesse, *paleness.*

wante, (*v.*) *lack.*

wanting, (*sb.*) *lack.*

warantise, *act of warranting (see 3/125n).*

ware, *aware.*

warre, wars, *worse.*

wawes, *waves.*

waxen, *See* wexe.

wel, *indeed;* ∼ to God, *to the pleasure of God.*

welderis, *rulers, controllers.*

wele, *prosperity.*

welfare, *prosperity.*

wem, *defilement, spot.*

wende, *go.*

wene, *pret. ind.* wende, *think, suppose.*

werc, *occupation.*

weryinge, *growing weary.*

werkyng, *work.*

werrey, *true.*

werryly, *truly.*

wexe, 3*sg. pret. ind.* wex, *p.p.* waxen, *grow, become;* wex gret, *grew violent.*

whan, *since.*

what, (*cj.*) *in* ∼ be, *what with.*

what, (*inter. and rel.*) *what, who.*

wheþer, wher, (*cj. and inter.*) *whether, which, which of two; also used as interrogatory conjunction translating Lat.* nonne.

who þat euer, *whoever.*

wilful, (*adj.*) *voluntary.*

wilfully, wilful, (*adv.*) *voluntarily.*

wille, (*sb.*) *desire.*

wille, (*v.*), 1 *and* 3 *sg. pres. ind.* wole, 2*sg. pres. ind.* wolt, *pl. pres. ind.* welen, wolen, *pret. ind.* wolde(n), wold, *wish, desire, prefer, will.*

willy, *willing.*

willnynge, *desiring.*

wynnyng, *profit;* biheestis of∼, *commandments about worldly profit.*

wyrche, worche, worschen, 3*sg. pres. ind.*
worchiþ, *pret. ind.* wrouȝte, *p.p.* wrouȝt;
work, perform, act, bring about.
wirkis, *works.*
wyrschipe, *honour, thanks.*
wischen, (*pl. pret. ind.*) *washed.*
wise, *fashion, way.*
wit, witte, (*sb.*) *mind, intelligence, under-*
standing, interpretation; pl. *branches of*
knowledge; bodili~, *physical senses.*
wite, wit, (*v.*) 2*sg. pres. ind.* woste; 3*sg.*
pres. ind. wot, woot, *pres. p.* witende,
pret. wiste, *know, understand.*
wiþ, *against, by means of, in exchange for.*
wipinneforþe, *internally, spiritually.*
wiþoute, *outside, beyond.*
wiþouȝtforþe, wiþoutforþ, *externally,*
corporally.
wiþseyinge, *denying.*
wiþstondinge, (*sb.*) *opposition.*
witing, *knowledge.*
witti, *wise.*
wittyngly, *knowingly.*
wlappiþ, *wraps.*
wode, *mad, maddened.*
wodendrem, *madness.*
wodnesse, woodnes, *ferocity, madness.*
wole, wolt, wolde. *See* wille.
wolle, *wool.*

wombe, *stomach;* wombe-ioye, *gluttony,*
pleasure in eating.
wondir, (*adv.*) *wonderfully.*
wondir, (*sb.*) *expression of surprise.*
wondren, *marvel;* me wondreþ, *it surprises me.*
woodnes, *madness.*
worche, worschen. *See* wyrche.
worching, *action.*
wordely, wordly, worliche, *worldly.*
worschipe, (*sb.*) *honour.*
worse, *of less value.*
worþ, worþe, in wo~, *may evil befall.*
woste, wot. *See* wite (*v.*).
wouke, *week.*
wowing, *courting.*
wowis,[1] *walls.*
wowis,[2] *vows.*
wrd, *word.*
wriȝte, *writ, in* hooly~, *the Bible, scripture.*
wrooþ, *loath, resistant.*
wrouȝt. *See* wyrche.
wrþi, *worthy.*

xuld, *should.*

yeftis, *gifts.*
yere, *See* ȝere.
yeve, yoven. *See* ȝeue.
yitt. *See* ȝit.

INDEX OF PROPER NAMES

Names of persons or places cited from the Bible are not included. Where surnames are usually given, these are entered before the forename. The entries of religious houses here supplement the notes to no. 27; abbreviations used to denote the nature of the foundation are *Aug.* Augustinian canons, *Ben.* Benedictine monks, *Cist.* Cistercian abbeys. Further explanation in the notes to the texts is indicated by *n* following the line number.

SELECT BIBLIOGRAPHY

Only works of major importance, or works which are repeatedly cited, are listed here. In the Introduction and Notes original sources are quoted by title or abbreviated title (shown here italicised in brackets), secondary works by author's name (and date of publication in brackets, where confusion may arise). Occasional exceptions to this, mostly for the sake of brevity, are shown here by brackets following the full reference. References are to page or column numbers, with line references where given following after an oblique stroke; where no editorial line numbers were printed, the ones I have added ignore all headings.

I. WYCLIF

(a) Biography

H. B. Workman, *John Wyclif* (Oxford, 1926), 2 vols. This gives details of earlier biographies.

K. B. McFarlane, *John Wycliffe and the Beginnings of English Nonconformity* (London, 1952).

A. B. Emden, *A Biographical Register of the University of Oxford to A.D. 1500* (Oxford, 1957–9), 3 vols. (Emden, *Oxford*)

(b) Writings

i. Lists of works

J. Loserth, revision of W. W. Shirley's *Catalogue of the Extant Latin Works of John Wyclif* (London, [1925]).

S. H. Thomson, 'Some Latin Works erroneously ascribed to Wyclif', *Speculum* iii (1928), 382–91.

E. W. Talbert and S. H. Thomson, 'Wyclyf and his followers', in *A Manual of the Writings in Middle English 1050–1500* ii, ed. J. Burke Severs (Hamden, Conn., 1970), 518–21. (*Manual*)

Note: the lists of manuscripts in all the above are not complete.

ii. Editions

The majority of Wyclif's Latin writings were edited by various scholars for the Wyclif Society between 1883 and 1921; references and quotations are from these editions except for the following works:

De Officio Pastorali, ed. G. V. Lechler (Leipzig, 1863).
Trialogus, ed. G. V. Lechler (Oxford, 1869).

iii. Criticism
Earlier material is listed in *Manual* (above i).
B. Smalley, 'John Wyclif's *Postilla super totam Bibliam*', *Bodleian Library Record* iv (1953), 186–205.
B. Smalley, 'Wyclif's *Postilla* on the Old Testament and his *Principium*', *Oxford Studies presented to Daniel Callus, O.P.* (Oxford, 1964), 253–96.
G. A. Benrath, *Wyclifs Bibelkommentar* (Berlin, 1966).

II. WYCLIF AND THE EARLY LOLLARD MOVEMENT

(a) Original sources
Fasciculi Zizaniorum, ed. W. W. Shirley (Rolls Series, London, 1858). (*Fasc. Ziz.*)
Henry Knighton, *Chronicon*, ed. J. R. Lumby (Rolls Series, London, 1889–95), 2 vols.
Thomas Walsingham, *Historia Anglicana*, ed. H. T. Riley (Rolls Series, London, 1863–4), 2 vols. (*Hist. Angl.*)
Roger Dymmok, *Liber contra duodecim errores Lollardorum* (Wyclif Society, London, 1922).
Thomas Netter of Walden, *Doctrinale Fidei Catholicæ . . .*, ed. B. Bianciotti (Venice, 1757–9), 3 vols. (Quoted by book and chapter number.)
For other sources see Ia above and IIb below.

(b) Secondary material
H. L. Cannon, 'The Poor Priests; a study in the rise of English Lollardry', *Annual Report of the American Historical Association for 1899* (Washington, 1900), i. 451–82.
A. Gwynn, *The English Austin Friars in the Time of Wyclif* (Oxford, 1940).
M. Aston, 'Lollardy and Sedition, 1381–1431', *Past and Present* xvii (1960), 1–44.
G. Leff, *Heresy in the Later Middle Ages* (Manchester, 1967), ii. 494–605.
J. Crompton, 'Leicestershire Lollards', *Transactions of the Leicestershire Archæological and Historical Society* xliv (1968–9), 11–44.
F. Šmahel, '"Doctor evangelicus super omnes evangelistas": Wyclif's Fortune in Hussite Bohemia', *BIHR* xliii (1970), 16–34.
K. B. McFarlane, *Lancastrian Kings and Lollard Knights* (Oxford, 1972). Note that this is a posthumous collection of lectures, the part on Lollard knights dating mainly from 1966.
M. Wilks, '"Reformatio Regni": Wyclif and Hus as Leaders of Religious Protest Movements', *Studies in Church History* ix (1972), 109–30.
A. Hudson, 'A Lollard Compilation and the Dissemination of Wycliffite Thought', *JTS* NS xxiii (1972), 65–81.

III. LATER LOLLARDY

A. G. Dickens, *Lollards and Protestants in the Diocese of York 1509–1558* (London, 1959).
M. Aston, 'Lollardy and the Reformation: Survival or Revival?', *History* xlix (1964), 149–70.
M. Aston, 'John Wycliffe's Reformation Reputation', *Past and Present* xxx (1965), 23–51.
J. A. F. Thomson, *The Later Lollards 1414–1520* (Oxford, 1965, 2nd ed. 1967).

IV. LOLLARD TEXTS

(a) Original Sources

i. Printed material

An Apology for Lollard Doctrines, ed. J. H. Todd (Camden Society, London, 1842). (*Apology*)

The Holy Bible…made from the Latin Vulgate by John Wycliffe and his Followers, ed. J. Forshall and F. Madden (Oxford, 1850), 4 vols. (*WB*)

Remonstrance against Romish Corruptions, ed. J. Forshall (London, 1851). (*37 Concs.*)

T. Arnold, *Select English Works of John Wyclif* (Oxford, 1869–71), 3 vols. (Arnold)

F. D. Matthew, *The English Works of Wyclif hitherto unprinted* (EETS 74, 1880, 2nd revd. ed. 1902). (Matthew)

The Plowman's Tale, ed. W. W. Skeat in *Chaucerian and Other Pieces* (Oxford, 1897), pp. 147–90.

The Examination of Thorpe, ed. A. W. Pollard in *Fifteenth Century Prose and Verse* (London, 1903), pp. 101–67. (Thorpe)

The Lanterne of Liȝt, ed. L. M. Swinburn (EETS 151, 1917). (*Lanterne*)

E. W. Talbert, 'A Lollard Chronicle of the Papacy', *Journal of English and Germanic Philology* xli (1942), 163–93. (*Lollard Chron.*)

C. F. Bühler, 'A Lollard Tract: on Translating the Bible into English', *Medium Ævum* vii (1938), 167–83. (*Tract Transl.*)

MS Bodley 959 Genesis-Baruch 3. 20 in the Earlier Version of the Wycliffite Bible, ed. C. Lindberg (Stockholm Studies in English vi (1959), viii (1961), x (1963), xiii (1965), xx (1969)).

Jack Upland, Friar Daw's Reply and Upland's Rejoinder, ed. P. L. Heyworth (London, 1968).

The Earlier Version of the Wycliffite Bible (Baruch 3. 20 to end of OT from MS Christ Church 145), ed. C. Lindberg (Stockholm Studies in English xxix (1973)).

ii. Manuscript material

Opus Arduum (see p. 13), Brno University Library Mk 28, ff. 126–216.

Floretum and *Rosarium* (see p. 7); cited by entry.

Ps. Bod. and Ps. Lam.: two manuscripts of Lollard revisions of Rolle's Psalter commentary, Bodley 288 and Lambeth Palace 34.

Douce 53 (Bodleian Library): two Lollard sermons, the first, ff. 1–30, attributed to William Taylor, the second, ff. 30–32v, anonymous and incomplete.

Rawl. c. 208 (Bodleian Library): the Middle English version of Thorpe's trial (see the introduction to the note to no. 4).

Add. 24202, Cotton Titus D. v, Harley 1203 (British Library), Trinity College Cambridge B. 14.50, Trinity College Dublin 244 (C. 3.12) and 245 (C. 5.6): unpublished treatises.

(b) Criticism

M. Deanesly, *The Lollard Bible* (Cambridge, 1920).

S. L. Fristedt, *The Wycliffe Bible* (Stockholm Studies in English iv (1953), xxi (1969), xxviii (1973)). (Fristedt WB)

H. Hargreaves, 'The Wycliffite Versions', in *The Cambridge History of the Bible* ii, ed. G. W. H. Lampe (Cambridge, 1969), 387–415.

E. W. Talbert and S. H. Thomson, as above I(b)i, *Manual* 354–80, 521–33.

A. Hudson, 'A Lollard Sermon-Cycle and its Implications', *Medium Ævum* xl (1971), 142–56.

A. Hudson, 'Contributions to a Bibliography of Wycliffite Writings', *Notes and Queries* NS xx (1973), 443–53.

V. OTHER WORKS FREQUENTLY CITED

(a) Original Sources

Biblia Sacra cum Glossa Ordinaria (Douai, 1617), 6 vols. (GO)

Corpus Iuris Canonici, ed. E. Friedberg (Leipzig, 1879–81), 2 vols. (Fried.)

William Lyndwood, *Provinciale* (Oxford, 1679).

Langland, *Piers Plowman*, ed. W. W. Skeat (London, 1886), 2 vols. (this edition has been used in preference to the more recent edition of G. Kane and E. Talbot Donaldson since it conveniently presents the three versions parallel); Prologue and Passus I–VII of B. Text ed. J. A. W. Bennett (Oxford, 1972).

The Complete Works of John Gower, ed. G. C. Macaulay (Oxford, 1899–1902), 4 vols.

Dives and Pauper, I. 1, ed. P. H. Barnum (EETS 275, 1976).

Mum and the Sothsegger, ed. M. Day and R. Steele (EETS 199, 1936).

Pierce the Ploughman's Crede, ed. W. W. Skeat (EETS 30, 1867).

The Register of Henry Chichele, archbishop of Canterbury 1414–1443, ed. E. F. Jacob (Canterbury and York Society, 1938–47), 4 vols.

Reginald Pecock, *The Repressor of over much blaming of the Clergy*, ed. C. Babington (Rolls Series, London, 1860), 2 vols.

Concilia Magnae Britanniae et Hiberniae, ed. D. Wilkins (London, 1737), 4 vols. (Wilkins)

The Acts and Monuments of John Foxe, ed. S. R. Cattley (London, 1837–41), 8 vols.

(b) Secondary Material

Dictionnaire de Spiritualité (Paris, 1937–). (*Dict. de Spir.*)

Missale ad Usum...Sarum, ed. F. H. Dickinson (Burntisland, 1861–83), 2 vols.

The Sarum Missal, ed. J. W. Legg (Oxford, 1916).

D. Knowles, *The Monastic Order in England* (Cambridge, 1940).

D. Knowles, *The Religious Orders in England* i–ii (Cambridge, 1948–55).

D. Knowles and R. N. Hadcock, *Medieval Religious Houses England and Wales* (London, 1971).

A. H. Thompson, *The English Clergy and their Organization in the later Middle Ages* (Oxford, 1947).

W. A. Pantin, *The English Church in the Fourteenth Century* (Cambridge, 1955).

A. B. Emden, *A Biographical Register of the University of Cambridge to 1500* (Cambridge, 1963). (Emden, *Cambridge*)

B. J. Whiting, *Proverbs, Sentences, and Proverbial Phrases from English Writings mainly before 1500* (Cambridge, Mass., 1968).

J. Mann, *Chaucer and Medieval Estates Satire* (Cambridge, 1973).

Note

When the present book was at the proof-stage, a new account of Wyclif and the Lollard movement appeared in M. D. Lambert, *Medieval Heresy: Popular Movements from Bogomil to Hus* (London, 1977), pp. 217–71.